THE UNSEEN FACE OF JAPAN

The Unseen Face of Japan

David C. Lewis

MONARCH
Tunbridge Wells

ISBN 1 85424 150 8

British Library Cataloguing-in-Publication Data.
A catalogue record for this book is available
from the British Library.

Production and Printing in England for
MONARCH PUBLICATIONS
P.O. Box 163, Tunbridge Wells, Kent TN3 ONZ by
Nuprint Ltd, Station Road, Harpenden, Herts AL5 4SE

CONTENTS

ACKNOWLEDGEMENTS

THIS BOOK HAS developed through several stages, and I am grateful to all those who have contributed towards it in various ways. Initially I intended to write an ethnographic account of the religious practices and beliefs of ordinary Japanese men and women. In conducting this research I am grateful for the help of our many friends in Japan who opened up their lives to my wife and myself, filled in questionnaires for us and were willing to be interviewed in depth. I am also grateful for the help of the local company which in this book I refer to as 'Nissen'.

My appreciation also goes to Professor Yoneyama Toshinao of Kyoto University, Professors Nakamaki Hirochika and Fukui Katsuyoshi of the National Museum of Ethnology in Osaka, and to the Museum staff who processed my questionnaire through one of their computers. For financial support I am grateful to the Economic and Social Science Research Council and to The Japan Foundation. Later the Japan Foundation Endowment Fund and the British Academy provided grants for me to prepare some of my ethnographic material for publication.

More recently, I have been doing further research on Christianity in Japan, and have benefitted from advice and suggestions by a wide variety of people. In particular, I would like to thank Dr. Patrick McElligott for his numerous comments on an earlier draft of this book.

Above all, however, I am grateful to my wife, Ruth, for her help in many different ways, both in the course of my research in Japan and also in my writing this book. To a large extent the basic research was a joint venture, and would not have been possible without her help.

PREFACE

The Anthropologist

'HOW CAN YOU study religion as an anthropologist and at the same time be a committed Christian?' This is a question I have sometimes been asked by my anthropologist friends. An assumption they are making is that having a personal faith somehow makes my findings less 'objective' than those of anthropologists who lack such a faith. By contrast, I believe that having a faith of my own is actually a definite advantage rather than a disadvantage in this kind of work.

Anthropologists strive for objectivity, but can rarely, if ever, break free from the fetters of subjectivity. Increasingly they are recognizing that the anthropologist's own background, theoretical bias, temperament and experiences of fieldwork can channel his or her thinking along certain lines and affect the conclusions reached.[1] However, instead of abandoning anthropology because it has a subjective component, anthropologists try to recognize the limits of these influences and to disentangle them. They also recognize that such an aim might never be achieved completely, but this does not deter them from seeking objectivity.

The dilemma is well summarized by Martin Southwold, who writes:

> 'We do think of ourselves as scientists, objectively observing and analysing the data, and we are right to do so, lest we lapse from standards of honesty and objectivity, rigour and open-mindedness. But the ideal of Science...is not to be embraced too literally and exclusively. We seek to be scientists, but we are also men among men, both in conducting research and in what we make of it. We study by participant observation...and our principal instrument of enquiry is ourselves, as human persons relating to others. In consequence, what we produce is bounded by our personal limitations; it had better be enriched by our per-

vii

sonal assets, which extend far beyond what gifts we may have as scientists in the ordinary sense.'[2]

These comments even apply to apparently 'objective' data such as the size of fields or who owns them, because such material can be viewed through either 'Marxist' or 'Liberal' spectacles—and interpreted accordingly. It is even more difficult to recognise cultural bias when one thinks that one is 'objective' because one is not committed to a particular ideology such as Marxism. In fact, such an anthropologist is still caught up in a system of ideas and values which are not so easily categorized and may or may not be internally consistent. This 'non-ideology' is in effect an ideology in itself. Ideology can become a 'cultural system' in which are caught up many values, attitudes, ideals, motivations and perhaps even emotions which are then expressed in socially conditioned forms.[3] Because they form part of the 'cultural air' which the participants themselves are breathing all the time, these values and attitudes are far less obvious. It is only when one steps outside of this 'non-ideology' into another ideological system that one can more easily recognize the contrasting attitudes, although the similarities can still be overlooked.

Those who do subscribe to a particular, named ideology— whether Marxist, Christian or whatever—are therefore at an advantage in recognizing those areas of their work which are more likely to be subject to bias. The very fact that they subscribe to a relatively coherent system allows them to demarcate more clearly the boundaries between those aspects which are probably influenced by the ideology and those which are less likely to be so. By contrast, someone who is supposedly ideologically neutral might not recognize bias in making certain assumptions which might not actually be warranted by the data or scientific methodology. For instance, when writing about religion there might be an implicit assumption that there is no level of reality beyond what is revealed by ordinary human experience.

In fact, many anthropologists are probably prepared to believe in the reality of various kinds of super-normal phenomena. An anthropologist named Burridge writes that not to 'believe in' phenomena such as trances, stigmata, possession, levitation, walking on hot coals without being burned or skewering the cheeks without leaving a wound is surely equivalent to being a 'flat-earther'.[4] Such phenomena constitute a rather loosely organized morass of 'beliefs' which are probably held at least in part by many anthropologists. Some might 'believe in' these things and others might be prepared to say there is 'something in it', but if they express such beliefs in writing they might be open to the charge of being labelled 'unscientific'. In discussing such phenomena, many are unwilling to deny a belief even if they do not express such views publicly. However, when it comes to a more formalized religious system such as Christianity it remains true that 'the majority of anthropologists are indifferent, if not hostile, to religion—atheists, agnostics or just nothing'.[5]

In dealing with religion, however, it is particularly important to recognise how one's own subjective experience affects one's interpretation of participants' attitudes, moods, motivations or values. Southwold, who is not a Christian, argues that it is an advantage for the anthropologist to include personal feelings and impressions rather than to exclude them. His comments are worth quoting quite fully:

> '...I have freely resorted to value judgements of people and their conduct, have attached weight to my own subjective impressions and feelings, and have drawn upon my own religious experiences...: all of which social scientists as a rule sedulously avoid. So long as I tried to exclude my personal feelings and assessments from my intellectual analysis I was divided against myself and unable to proceed: this book emerged as an integration of what I had striven to keep apart. An anthropologist is a man—and a woman—and if he strives to be less than a man he defeats his anthropology. This, at least, is surely true when the topic is religion: was it not always absurd to expect to understand religion by excluding value judgements, emotions, and personal experience, which are its essence? I am indeed a flawed instrument; but so long as I strove to be a narrow social scientist I was maimed as well.'[6]

Both Southwold and Evans-Pritchard also quote Schmidt, who wrote,

'If religion is essentially of the inner life, it follows that it can be truly grasped only from within. But beyond a doubt, this can be better done by one in whose inward consciousness an expression of religion plays a part. There is but too much danger that the other [the non-believer] will talk of religion as a blind man might of colours, or one totally devoid of ear, of a beautiful musical composition.'[7]

It is therefore an advantage to hold a religious faith when investigating religion, because (a) it helps to demarcate the areas of one's own possible bias, and (b) it affords a deeper insight into the religious experience of others, without which one might be like a blind man trying to describe colours.

However, there is also the issue of how far a knowledge of my own religious beliefs might have coloured people's replies to my questions. The very presence of the investigator is in itself an influence upon the results obtained. In the course of my fieldwork in Japan I noticed this happen twice. One occasion was when a man who initially said that his prayers at the factory had no effect at all said later that perhaps they had 'a little' effect; in the meantime he had asked me whether I think God answers the prayers of Christians. The other occasion was when a Roman Catholic woman said that one of her reasons for a belief in God was because of the evidence for the resurrection of Jesus Christ. Such an answer is a reasonable one for a Christian to give; I had not discussed the issue with her previously, but it might be that through a close friend she had heard of a conversation of mine on such a topic.

However, for the most part I refrained from giving any expression of my own beliefs until the end of an interview, by which time people had already expressed their own views. If I did express an opinion, it was usually in response to a direct question on their part. In any case, they perceived me as a 'Christian' of some kind simply because I was European, so I doubt if my replies were particularly surprising to them. It might even be that my sympathy for religion made them feel more at ease in expressing religious beliefs which they might have been more reluctant to express to one whom they felt was indifferent or antagonistic.

Although these kinds of issues are now more generally understood by specialists on the sociology of religion, it has been necessary to discuss them for the sake of those readers whose interests lie in other areas. Some of them are more interested in the 'applied' side of my research, and it is this aspect of the book which is probably more controversial.

If this book were merely a descriptive ethnography, it would probably cause few problems. It would present some fresh and relatively unknown material on Japanese religion which would be of interest to both specialists and the general reader. My hope is that such readers will still find the ethnography useful even if they miss out the Christian 'applications' at the end of most chapters which are intended for those Christians who wish to communicate the message of Jesus in terms which are relevant to the Japanese culture.

To many anthropologists, this might appear to overstep the conventional boundaries of our discipline. Perhaps they forget that the journal which started out as *Practical Anthropology* dealt so much with missiological issues that it was eventually renamed *Missiology*. Few anthropologists take exception to applied anthropology in other areas, such as race relations or economic development projects. They are also aware that often in the past anthropologists have actively helped colonial authorities, and that nowadays government agencies sometimes continue to seek the advice of certain anthropologists. Little objection is raised if Marxist anthropologists apply their research findings to helping their own ideological cause, so why should a Christian anthropologist be inhibited from doing the same when writing for a Christian publisher?

Many missionaries, however, still feel defensive or suspicious in relation to anthropologists. Certainly there has been considerable antagonism between the two in situations such as those in which some anthropologists have accused missionaries of destroying native cultures and being agents for Westernization. At the same time, however, many anthropologists recognize that far worse effects have come from the exploitative practices of various commercial interests, and also that missionaries have often helped native peoples in their unavoidable encounter with the outside world. In fact, the research findings of many anthropologists owe an immense debt to missionary informants, because missionaries often have a better command of the local language and live longer among the people than do anthropologists.[8]

In the case of Japan, missionaries can hardly be accused of being responsible for corrupting the culture through 'Westernization'. Through many other agencies there has indeed been considerable 'Westernization'—but at a relatively superficial level, in terms of industrialization, styles of dress and so on. At a deeper level, many cultural values and traditions have remained strong. There has been very little 'Christianization' of the people: today the Christian church still represents less than one percent of the population. Although church growth in the past was sometimes hampered by political constraints, in the post-war period the church now enjoys many legal freedoms which allow evangelism and church-planting. Even so, church growth continues to be slow. It seems that the problem is more a cultural than a political one, revolving around the question of how to communicate Christ's gospel in culturally appropriate terms. To solve this question requires a good under-standing of Japanese culture and religious attitudes. It is in this area that I can offer insights based on my own anthropological fieldwork and in-depth interviews with ordinary Japanese people about their religious attitudes, practices and experiences.

Although I include some Christian applications in order to help missionaries and interested lay Christians, I am nevertheless aware that some of my suggestions might be controversial. There are so many denominational and personal viewpoints on various theological issues that one simply cannot please everybody all of the time. However, I hope that by raising such issues I can stimulate mission-aries to think afresh about some of their own assumptions. I do not pretend to have all the answers, but I share those insights which I do have and I also cite other helpful approaches which experienced missionaries have found to be useful.

All missionaries try to make their message relevant to their audience. A lot of this is done by trial and error. What is effective for one audience does not necessarily work for all. Some of my suggestions for communicating the Christian gospel may be more relevant to certain sections of Japanese society than for others. However, I hope that many of the ideas will indeed be relevant, not only to missionaries in Japan but also to Christians in other countries who want to share their faith with Japanese living outside Japan itself.

Many Japanese cultural attitudes and practices continue to be maintained by Japanese living in other countries. This is particularly the case for Japanese workers in Europe, South-east Asia or elsewhere who expect to return to Japan after a few years. In some cities with substantial numbers of Japanese residents there is a tendency for the Japanese to perpetuate their own sub-culture through social networks with other Japanese and the establishment of Japanese schools and other social institutions. Nevertheless, reports from a number of Christian workers indicate that to at least some extent Japanese people living outside their own culture tend to be somewhat more receptive to Christianity.

Japanese cultural values also tend to be held more strongly by first-generation migrants than by second- or third-generation immigrants in, for example, North or South America. In such situations, the younger generations brought up outside Japan may absorb various practices of their 'host' culture while at the same time retaining certain Japanese values. Many of my comments on communicating the Christian gospel to Japanese people are still applicable to Japanese residents in other countries, but some details may not be so relevant for second- and third- generation immigrants.

Spiritual dimensions

At times my interpretation of phenomena, or comments upon certain practices, have been influenced by my own Christian perceptions of the spiritual forces behind them. These entities constitute a hidden and relatively unexplored dimension to the 'unseen face of Japan'. In discussing them, I make use of familiar Christian categories such as 'angels' or 'demons', even though I run the risk of appearing to be ethno-centric or prejudiced in my views. Therefore it is important to note that 'some self-styled Christian groups in historical times have also behaved in ways that could only be described as demonic'.[9] I do not try to pretend that Christianity is perfect, but what I do know is that Jesus came to destroy the works of the evil one, and that through his name Christians today continue to have authority over unclean spirits. The ministry of Jesus was not merely one of teaching a religion but also of demonstrating God's authority and power through exorcisms and healings—which continue today to be signs of the Kingdom of God.

In analysing Japanese religious practices, beliefs and experiences from this spiritual perspective, I am following in a tradition pioneered by George Otis in his concept of *'spiritual mapping'*, which 'involves superimposing our understanding of forces and events in the spiritual domain onto places and circumstances in the material world'.[10] For instance, he suggests that 'the extreme violence associated with so much of Iraq's history in both ancient and modern times may be connected with the malevolent deities worshipped by the ancient Mesopotamians'. This 'important insight...removes from Christians the need to identify other religions as the "enemy"...[because] the victims of the violence are not merely Christian believers but all who have come under the influence of those dark powers in a given cultural or geographic setting'.[11] Similarly, in Japan, unseen demonic forces of different kinds may be at work within and behind certain cultural attitudes and practices—just as they are also in the West. At a deeper level than 'cultural norms' are spiritual realities which seek to influence or control people's behaviour. These forces operate within all the formal religious groupings—Shinto, Buddhist and Christian. By indicating some of the areas in which demonic influence might be operative, my study may help people to recognise and turn away from these practices. Moreover, I believe that through the authority of Jesus Christ and by the power of the Holy Spirit people can be set free from these dark spiritual forces and come into a vibrant relationship with God.

A note on names and Japanese terms

In writing this book, I have made extensive use of my own field-work material and observations, supplemented by those of others whose works have been cited. Because I often refer to real people, I have used fictitious names for them, and have done the same with regard to the firm where they work and the area in which they live.

Most Japanese people refer to those outside the family by their surnames plus the suffix *-san* which in English can be translated as

'Mr.', 'Mrs.' or 'Miss'. I shall retain this Japanese usage when referring to people by their pseudonyms, but I shall usually introduce the person at first by the English form of 'Mr.' or 'Mrs.' Such-and-such. Where full names are used, I am following the Japanese usage of giving the surname first, before the personal name.

There is no universally adopted system of Romanization for Japanese words, but the one adopted here is probably the most common.[12] There is a problem, however, of how to refer to plurals of Japanese words when the Japanese language itself lacks plurals. My own solution is to treat the Japanese words in the same way as words like *kimono* which have already become Anglicized.[13] The *Popular Oxford Dictionary* gives the plural of *kimono* as *kimonos*. Considerations of English style mean that, where appropriate, I have pluralized certain Japanese words by the addition of 's', as in English.

Usually a brief explanation or definition is given when a word is first introduced, but the glossary explains Japanese words which may recur in the text. My brief definitions may not always be sufficient for some specialist terms like *kami* (a word for various kinds of divinities), for which I supply slightly more detailed explanations in the text and give references in footnotes to more comprehensive discussions available elsewhere.

Methodology

My first period of anthropological fieldwork in Japan lasted for about fifteen months, from March 1981 until the end of May 1982.[14] During that time we were living in an ordinary Japanese neighbourhood which I am calling by the fictitious name of 'Aoyama'. As far as possible we participated in the daily life of the community, including occasions for communal ditch cleaning, the local sports day and other such events. After about six months, we distributed a questionnaire to every family on the estate, enough for each adult in every household. In the end, we received forms from 81% of the households on that estate, but, because some houses seemed to be permanently unoccupied at the time, the 'real' response rate was nearer to 85%. By most sociological standards, this is a very high response rate.[15]

At the same time I wanted to do a similar survey on a nearby estate of company housing, which I am calling 'Sakurano'. All the men living there work for a large company which I am calling '*Nissen*', an abbreviation for the fictitious name *Nihon Sen'i Kabushiki Kaisha*, meaning 'Japan Fibres P.L.C.' The '*Nissen*' company is a major producer of synthetic fibres and a variety of other goods. The factory of theirs which I studied is the oldest and largest of the company's thirteen plants located in Japan. Next to this factory, the firm's 'company housing'—known in Japanese as *shataku* accommodation—mainly consists of apartment blocks, five stories high. There are also some detached or semi-detached houses for those higher up in the company. Older wooden houses lacking private bathrooms but sharing a communal bath house are located close to the factory wall and are inhabited by some blue-collar, manual workers.

I needed to obtain permission from the firm to conduct a study in this estate. Through introductions arranged for me by a professor at Kyoto University, and accompanied by a Japanese postgraduate anthropology student, I went to see the personnel manager. He examined my questionnaire, decided there was nothing wrong with it and then offered to have it distributed and collected on my behalf by the local neighbourhood council (*jichikai*).[16] He reckoned that I would have a better response rate if the company did this for me. In the end, I received usable responses from 65% of the households in Sakurano. Some *jichikai* representatives distributed two questionnaires per household, as had been my intention, but owing to a misunderstanding somewhere along the lines of communication most households received only one questionnaire. In these the husband normally filled in the form, apparently regarding it as part of his company duty.

In the end I had 667 usable questionnaires. While these were being processed through a computer at the National Museum of Ethnology in Osaka, we selected seventy people—a little over 10% of the sample—to interview personally. Our questions depended on what they had written in their questionnaires, and provided further understanding of why they performed certain religious practices. More importantly, it showed the attitudes which they held towards such rites.

From May 1983 to May 1984 we had the opportunity to return to Japan for further fieldwork.[17] During this time I was able to investigate in more detail religious rites in the *Nissen* factory itself. I also conducted a further thirty in-depth interviews which ranged more widely than the first seventy. Where answers had become quite standardized in the first seventy interviews, I sometimes omitted such questions in the later interviews. Instead, I was able to ask about other issues which had emerged in the course of my investigations. Overall, one hundred people were interviewed in depth, while a breadth of perspective was given by the 667 questionnaire answers. In this book I shall sometimes give the general statistics from the questionnaires, but the more interesting material comes from the personal interviews which show the attitudes and motivations behind people's religious practices, and which constitute another 'unseen face of Japan'.

CHAPTER

1

Safety First

I N FEBRUARY 1927 Antonio Minelli committed suicide. He had been a chief engineer among the Italian, British and German technical advisors who had helped to install specialist machinery in a Japanese synthetic fibres factory. The reasons for his suicide are not fully known today by staff at that factory, but twice a year one of the senior managers visits Minelli's grave, lights incense and bows as if to an ancestor.

Minelli had left behind a wife in Italy but no children. According to traditional Japanese beliefs, he could become a potentially malevolent 'unattached spirit' (*muenbotoke*) which ought to be appeased.[1] Partly this is because he had no descendants to perform rites for him—though they know he was at least nominally a Roman Catholic. More important, however, was the manner of his death by suicide.

Officials from the factory (who now rationalize Minelli's death by assuming he was mentally disturbed at the time) visit Minelli's grave on the annual anniversary of his death and also during the summer *bon* festival, when the ancestors are said to return to this world. Only a few retired employees still remember Minelli; those who now have responsibility for the rites never knew him at all. They are the Plant Manager, General Affairs departmental manager and Business Affairs manager, who go to Minelli's grave because it is one of the duties of their jobs. The company has

19

assumed responsibility for Minelli's ancestral rites because there was nobody else to do so.

It is a more junior official named Ōishi-san who is given the practical task of cleaning up the grave in preparation for the ritual. He weeds it and tidies it up on the 16th February and on the following day his superiors go to perform their duties.

At 9.00am on the 17th they leave the factory in a company car for the one hour's drive to a public graveyard in Kyoto. In 1984, when I witnessed these rites, both the Plant Manager and the Business Affairs section manager were occupied elsewhere with 'other urgent business', although the latter, Nishihara-san, was represented instead by his deputy, Mr. Nakahashi. Nakahashi-san is responsible for arranging some of the 'non-religious' ceremonies at the company, such as the entrance of new recruits or the awarding of prizes to some 'outstanding' employees on the anniversary of the founding of the firm. His involvement in the more 'religious' side is limited to occasions such as this when he might have to deputize for his boss. Therefore on this day the only senior manager to participate in the rites is the General Affairs Manager, Ōkura-san.

Once they arrive at the graveyard, the driver remains with the car but produces umbrellas from the boot for the others, who have to walk up a pathway to reach the graveyard. There Nakahashi-san fills a bucket provided by the graveyard authorities with water and carries it to Minelli's grave. Ōkura-san carries the flowers which they have brought with them from the factory. Once they reach the grave itself, it is Nakahashi-san's task to put the flowers in the two vase stands, which are already in front of the grave, and also to burn incense.

Meanwhile, Ōkura-san wipes off the freshly fallen snow with his hand to show the inscription on the tombstone. Then, taking the ladle and bucket of water, he pours water over the gravestone to wash it ceremonially. He then stands in front of the grave, facing it, and bows briefly for no more than two or three seconds, with his hands together. Nakahashi-san then does the same—a brief bow with hands together. The two then return to the car and waiting driver, on the way returning the bucket and ladle. Before they leave the graveyard Nakahashi-san presents a gift of ¥1,000 to the custodian of the graveyard; this is the firm's usual contribution on both the occasions when they visit the grave each year. The driver then takes them back to the factory where they resume their normal work.

Attitudes to the grave visit

In the course of his duties at the factory, Ōkura-san has to participate in a variety of religious rites. Although he performs them as part of his work and has no strong objections to them, he also thinks that there are too many such rites, that they take up too much time and that some of them ought to be dropped. Certainly a whole morning of his time was taken up with this trip into Kyoto and back. The same three senior managers who go to Minelli's grave also perform religious rites at the grave of the founder of the firm, whose family participate too. On both occasions Ōkura-san's attitude or feelings are the same—to give thanks for the establishment of the company. As he personally knew neither of the men whose graves he visits, he feels no personal connection with either of them; there are no personal memories evoked in him. In his brief moment of bowing before the grave the thoughts in his mind are of gratitude for what these men had done to establish the factory and company of which he is now a director.

Nakahashi-san's attitude is similar, but he couches his reply much more in terms of *memory*. He says his feelings or thoughts as he bows in front of the grave are those of recollecting or thinking about what he knows of the history of his company and the rôle of Minelli in it. The grave reminds him of those days and causes him to reminisce (*shinobu* or *shinobaseru*). For him or for the firm, the grave rite is a 'duty' (*gimu*), and he has no other feelings about it. One interesting word which he uses, however, in reference to Minelli, is '*daisenpai*'. '*Senpai*' means an 'older colleague', but '*daisenpai*' means a 'big' or 'great' older colleague—that is, a '*senpai*' to Nakahashi-san's own '*senpai*'. As one of the founders of the factory, the Italian is, as it were, an 'ancestor' of the present generation of employees, which includes Nakahashi-san himself.

As a *daisenpai*, Minelli has no family relationship to those who perform the grave rites for him. He is not 'worshipped'. It is not even necessary for those who perform the rites to have any belief in an afterlife. Those who participate can only preserve the *memory* of their *daisenpai*: on behalf of the company they act in the same kind of way as is normally done for ancestral rites—washing the grave, burning incense and bowing before the grave. If Minelli was originally regarded as a kind of unattached spirit (*muenbotoke*), the memorial rites also avert any danger to the company which his spirit might have caused.[2]

'Key themes' in Japanese religion

The grave rites for Antonio Minelli illustrate at least four different themes which often occur in Japanese attitudes to religion:

Firstly, there is the theme of *memorialism*. It is shown in the importance attached to the act of remembering the dead and having somebody take responsibility for performing the rituals.

Secondly, there is a *respect for one's seniors*. In an industrial context this is expressed in overt respect for one's *senpai*, those of the company's 'previous generation' who are more experienced and have gone on ahead. In a family situation, this respect is traditionally supposed to be shown towards older people. Later, these people become ancestors and are honoured by rituals at their graves and at the family's Buddhist altar.

Thirdly, there is a fear of that which is potentially 'out of place' or 'unclean'. Minelli's spirit was in danger of becoming 'unattached' or 'wandering' if nobody performed rites on his behalf. If his spirit were to become a *muenbotoke*, it would be dangerous and potentially vindictive. It is feared because it would be 'out of place' and dangerous. Such concepts are very similar to those used to define 'dirt', which is essentially 'matter out of place'.[3] For instance, grass in an English garden is desirable when it is on the lawn but is 'out of place', plucked up and thrown away if it grows just a few inches from the edge of the lawn, on the flower bed. In the same way, other 'matter out of place'—or, in a religious context, 'spirits out of place'—are treated in the same way as dirt: special precautions are taken to deal with them. For the Japanese, religious rites are very often concerned with aspects of *purity and pollution*, a third 'key theme' in their general culture.

The fourth 'key theme' is that of *safety and security*. If certain disasters might occur through the neglect of particular religious rites, it is 'safer' to observe the rituals than to risk the disaster. Later in this chapter I shall describe how a fear of potential hazards motivates many Japanese to seek security in safety charms and other religious practices.

If certain spirits are feared because they are 'out of place', it is clear that concepts of purity and pollution complement those of safety and security. These two 'key themes' are really the opposite sides of the same coin. In the same way, a respect for one's seniors while they are alive merges into a reverence for ancestors after the older generation has died: therefore these two 'key themes' are also closely related.

However, these 'key themes' are by no means confined only to the sphere of religion. They are manifested in both religious and non-religious forms. It is not necessarily the case that the non-religious expressions of these 'key themes' are secularized versions of religious ones: it seems more likely that certain common cultural values are expressed in a variety of ways. Most or all of these underlying values—what I am calling 'key themes'—can also be found in other cultures outside Japan. However, what gives them their distinctive form in any particular culture is the way in which they interact with each other. Each culture is like a constellation of stars: to the ordinary eye, each star looks fairly similar to other stars (though they do have great differences discerned by specialists), but what gives each constellation its uniqueness is the particular way in which those stars are related to each other. Similarly, the 'key themes' mentioned above can each be found in other cultures, but together they interact in a manner which helps to give a specific character to any particular culture. In Japan, there might be other key cultural values which are also very important, a possible example being the importance attached to community life. The four 'key themes' highlighted above seem to be those which are especially conspicuous in Japanese attitudes towards religion, and for this reason they will be given particular attention in this book.

In discussing attitudes towards Minelli's memorial rites, I quoted some of the key words or expressions which were used. Certain 'key words' seem to occur again and again in many different contexts when discussing attitudes to various religious rites. These words often relate to the 'key themes' highlighted above. Just as Eskimoes have many different words for various kinds of snow, so the Japanese seem to have many different expressions related to safety, memorialism and so on. Language tends to reflect what is important to people in so far as languages tend to develop more detailed vocabularies for those things which are important in the cultures of their speakers.[4] The present chapter will concentrate on looking at further examples of how the 'key theme' of *safety and security* is manifested in Japanese culture.

The Segaki rite

An appeasement of unattached spirits, similar to that for Minelli, takes place every August on behalf of this company, which, as explained in my preface, I am calling by the pseudonym '*Nissen*'. According to traditional belief, the ancestors are said to return to this world (in some versions, coming from hell) for a short time each summer at around the time of the Buddhist *bon* festival. The setting up of a special altar for *muenbotoke* seems to have almost disappeared from urban Japan, as only one person—a woman from a rural background—reported such a practice among those I interviewed in the course of my own research. However, the *Nissen* company has reasons for preserving this rite because the factory was built on the site of an ancient battleground and on the hill behind the factory there are also old tumuli (called *kōfun*).

Every year a Buddhist priest comes to perform the *segaki* rite for these 'unattached' spirits. He is accompanied by Ōishi-san, who alone represents the whole company. Together they go to the summit of the hill behind the factory; there they set up a small altar on a corner of the flat area in front of the company's Shinto shrine. On the altar are arranged grapes, peaches, rice wine (*sake*), rice cakes (*mochi*), apples, flowers, candles and incense. For about half an hour the Buddhist priest chants sutras in front of the altar while Ōishi-san stands quietly nearby.

At the end of the ritual they take the offerings and distribute them around the ground in the area around the edges of the company shrine, leaving the food for the wild animals to eat. The animals are said to be the present day guardians of the graves of the ancient warriors, but it almost seems as if they are considered to be in some sense embodiments of the dead spirits. The traditional *segaki* rite of feeding the hungry spirits has become transformed into a rite of feeding the local animals while praying for the dead spirits in the area. However, it also preserves the 'safety' of the factory in case any ancient spirits in the area still need to be cared for or appeased.

Annual pilgrimage to a Fudō temple

Another Buddhist rite was inaugurated after a fire broke out in January 1955 and destroyed one of the company dormitories for single men. As a result, every year since 1956 a pilgrimage has taken place to a temple of the Fire God, Fudō. It takes place on the day known as *Hatsu-Fudō*, the first day of the year allocated by the almanacs to the worship of Fudō. If that day happens to fall on a company holiday, the pilgrimage takes place instead on the nearest working day.

A new factory for an officially separate company called '*Nissen Products*' was built on the site of the dormitory which had been burnt down. Therefore the Managing Director of '*Nissen Products*' and his General Affairs Manager accompany the *Nissen* contingent in their own company car. Those representing *Nissen* are the Plant Manager (Ueda-san), the General Affairs Manager (Ōkura-san), the section managers of the General Affairs and Personnel Departments and two representatives of the *Nissen* Union. On the way to the Fudō temple they pass close to another *Nissen* factory, whose Managing Director and General Affairs Manager join the *Nissen* convoy at a *rendezvous* outside a large Shinto shrine.

The convoy then travels up into the mountains, stopping on the way for the drivers to put snow chains on the car tyres. They drive up a mountain track until it becomes too narrow for vehicles. Then all get out and the drivers distribute to each person stout bamboo canes (which have been brought in the boots of two of the cars) as aids to keep the people from slipping while trekking the last kilometre on foot through snow a few inches deep. Finally they reach the temple, which is 600 metres above sea level and was formerly used by mountain ascetics for their austerities.

Most of the party climb a short distance further to the summit in order to admire the view. A few of them also look around the outer chamber of the temple. One of them puts ¥200 into the offering box, places his hands together and bows his head just for a moment. Meanwhile, Ōishi-san is at the priest's house announcing their arrival. The older priest sends his two sons, one in his early twenties and the other in his teens, to accompany Ōishi-san to the temple and perform the rites. When they arrive, all proceed into the inner room and sit or kneel in a row with their hands together while the two young men chant for about five minutes.

Then the visitors are invited up to the very front of the temple, to the area behind the offerings and images of the god. There the young men relate the history of the temple and point out a large log in the wall which supposedly brought good fortune to a man 'long ago'.

It is now about 12.45pm. All return to the priest's house, where a table has been set out for lunch. The priest's wife serves them with a delicious cooked lunch of rice, fish, pickles, vegetable soup laced with *sake*, and *sake* to drink with it. The drivers eat separately in an adjacent room where there is a counter for the sale of safety charms. After lunch the *Nissen* personnel manager buys a charm for his own personal use but Ōishi-san buys twenty on behalf of the company. They will be placed in rooms where fire is used for cooking or heating. He pays the temple ¥10,000 for these charms, ¥20,000 for the Hatsu-Fudō ceremony and ¥15,000 as a 'thank offering' which effectively covers the cost of the lunch. While he was making advance arrangements for their visit, the temple had indicated that the 'thank offering' ought to be increased that year in line with general food prices. After lunch, the party returns to their places of work.

Monthly grave rite

After a fire broke out in the *Nissen* factory in April 1973 (in which nobody was killed or injured but there was considerable damage) it was deemed necessary to inaugurate some Buddhist rites every month in order to appease the spirits of those warriors who had died in this area during a battle which took place in 672 AD. Because the area had at that time been a swamp, many people had been swallowed up in the swamp without receiving a proper burial. Although the battle took place on the 22nd of July, the monthly rituals are performed on the 15th of each month (or the nearest working day to it) because the 15th is, in Ōishi-san's words, 'an easy and convenient date in the middle of the month'. Usually Ōishi-san alone represents the company and stands quietly with a rosary in his hands which are put together in prayer. In July, however, the rite takes place on the 22nd, when the Plant Manager and all the departmental managers attend. A Buddhist priest chants sutras and all the managers line up, take a pinch of incense each and put it into a small charcoal brazier. While it burns they stand momentarily in an attitude of prayer. Again, the motivation for the rite is safety, in so far as it was a fire at the factory which was responsible for this rite being initiated.

An example of a Shinto rite

All the rituals described so far have been Buddhist, but the majority of religious rites connected with the company are in fact Shinto ones. Many of them follow fairly similar patterns of prayers, bows and offerings so I shall not describe all of them in detail. The following description of the *Hatsu-uma* ceremony provides a glimpse of the kinds of ceremonies which are performed.

By the lunar calendar which was used in Japan until 1872, the end of winter was marked by a rite called Setsubun, which now falls in early February. On the first 'Day of the Horse' following Setsubun, the 'god of the mountains' was said to descend to the fields to become the 'god of the rice paddy'. On this day was performed the ceremony called *Hatsu-uma*, meaning 'First Horse'.

At 1.30pm the priest from the local Shinto shrine arrives at the factory's personnel office to collect his payment in advance. Ten minutes later he leaves in a company car for the firm's principal shrine on the hill behind the factory. At 1.45pm two minibuses leave from the factory shop, pick up others from the personnel office at 1.50pm, and go on up to the shrine. Those participating are the Plant Manager, all the departmental heads or their deputies, the section managers in the General Affairs Department, Union representatives from both '*Nissen*' and '*Nissen Products*', one male and one female representative from the neighbourhood council (*jichikai*) for Sakurano (the factory's housing estate for married employees), similar representatives from the firm's dormitory accommodation for single employees, and Yoshioka-san. Yoshioka-san is the manager of an independent catering company which ever since the company's establishment has had the *de facto* permanent contract for running the factory's canteens.

The priest and principal officials have already gone into the shrine by the time most participants arrive. They have only a few minutes to warm themselves at a bonfire which had been lit outside the shrine before they have to line up to enter the shrine by passing through the large, red outer portal (called a *torii*). An employee ladles out water over their hands as the symbolic purification before prayer at a Shinto shrine. Another employee hands out paper towels which, once used, are deposited in a bin specially provided for the occasion. The thirty-five participants then proceed up through the row of three smaller red *torii* to the worship area, where they line up in three rows facing the dais.

Nishihara-san, the Business Affairs section manager, gives a brief explanation about the nature of the rite, the character of the fox-god *Inari* and the connections between this shrine and the main *Inari* shrine at Fushimi, a suburb of Kyoto. At 2.00pm the priest goes up to the front and chants, facing the offering table and sacred area containing the symbol of the god. All stand with their heads bowed. The priest bows once, claps twice and bows twice. Then, taking his *haraigushi*, a pole with white paper streamers attached to it, he performs a 'purification' (*harai*) ritual by performing three ritual waves of the wand over the offerings; he then repeats it over the participants.

At Nishihara-san's command of '*Rei*', all bow: '*rei*' can mean 'worship', 'bow' or 'thanks'. The priest then removes the lids from the *sake* vessels and recites a prayer while all listen with heads bowed. Most of them listen solemnly with their eyes shut or lowered but some of them often open their eyes and look round while a few remain standing with their eyes open all the time.

Nishihara-san then announces the next stage in the ritual, which consists of the delegates offering to the deity branches of *sakaki*, the Shinto sacred tree. The priest offers the first branch. Next is Ueda-san, the Plant Manager, and as he bows twice, claps twice and bows once more all the other *Nissen* employees do the same simultaneously. When the other representatives bow and clap, however, they do so by themselves. After Ueda-san, the leader of the company union presents his offering. He is then followed by the male dormitory representative, the *Nissen* 'women's division' representative and then the male and female representatives for Sakurano. Finally Yoshioka-san makes his offerings on behalf of his own company rather than *Nisseh*.

Nishihara-san then announces the '*mikan-maki*', or 'satsuma peeling'. From the offering dais the priest takes two stands heaped with satsumas and hands them to the two men who performed the hand-washing duties. They take the pedestals to each participant in turn. First each one bows, then claps once, takes the satsuma, saying '*Itadakimasu*' ('I humbly receive') and then bows once more. Each keeps his or her own satsuma without peeling it. The two servers hand the remaining satsumas on the pedestals back to the priest, who replaces them on the dais. At Nishihara-san's command of '*Rei*', all bow. This part of the ceremony is then concluded; it is 2.30pm.

Ōishi-san told me that at one time all the participants would peel a satsuma and blow on the peel. This was a symbolic transfer of their sins and pollutions onto the peel, which was then thrown into the fire. Nowadays, however, most participants put their satsumas into their pockets or bags to be eaten later. In the official explanation sheet distributed by Ōishi-san there is no mention of any original meaning connected with the ceremonial purification of sins.

Although this ceremony has become shortened over time, the participants still have other shrines to visit. Just behind the main *Nissen* shrine is another, smaller one which is owned by Yoshioka-san's family. It was built on this spot in order to protect the direction from which evil spirits were thought to be likely to attack the local castle—but the castle was nevertheless destroyed (by human agents) during the Meiji Restoration. Then Yoshioka-san's grandfather, a wealthy fish wholesaler, took over responsibility for the upkeep of the shrine. Now it is part of the Yoshioka family property, and four stones set into the ground near the corners of the shrine demarcate the land owned by the Yoshiokas. In it are enshrined two separate sacred stones, so it is counted as if it were two shrines. In addition, behind the Yoshioka family shrine is a small shrine to the Wakamiya Hachiman deity, a god of silk production, for which *Nissen* have taken over responsibility.

In front of the Yoshiokas' shrine are six closely-spaced *torii*— the entrance portals to Shinto shrines. All the participants stand, two or three abreast, under these *torii* because there is insufficient room for all of them in the shrine precincts. Again the priest chants and claps, again performs a *harai* purification over the precincts and the participants, and chants further prayers. Ueda-san, the Plant Manager, then goes into the shrine precincts and all the *Nissen* men join him in bowing twice, clapping twice and bowing once in unison. Then Yoshioka-san stands up in front, faces the assembled group, and gives a short talk on what he knows of the history of the shrine. He comments that he does not know why the 'Day of the Horse' should be chosen for this ceremony 'but that's the way it's always been for the last 800 years or more'.

Finally the group proceed to the Wakamiya Hachiman shrine at the top of the hill. There the priest bows and claps to the stone symbol of the deity without any *harai* ceremony or special prayers but simply in the same manner as most ordinary people do when visiting a shrine. Having done this, he bows to all the *Nissen* participants, who in return bow to him and then follow him back down the hill to the vehicles. The priest immediately leaves in the company car which is waiting for him. Meanwhile Ōishi-san is waiting at a table set up next to the main *Nissen* Inari shrine, where he distributes small bags of satsumas to all the participants. They all quickly get into the vans and cars to return to their work, because it is cold outside and is beginning to snow again. Ōishi-san and his helpers from the General Affairs department are left to tidy up the offerings (which are later sent to the priest) and to put out the bonfire.

Other Shinto ceremonies

Many other Shinto ceremonies are also performed at the *Nissen* company shrines on the hill behind the factory. For one of these no Shinto priest is actually present, although it is held in the company's main Shinto shrine on the first working day after the New Year. This rite consists of prayers for safety and prosperity, and it is significant that the company's safety committee is especially invited to take part in it.

Other Shinto rites may take place in the factory precincts themselves. For instance, each January there is a ritual re-opening of the factory's martial arts halls. This rite is regarded as having the intention of averting sporting accidents, so the firm's boat team participates in this ceremony too. Throughout the factory there are Shinto charms (*fuda*) in rooms where fire is used. Other portable charms for traffic safety, called *mamori*, are bought by the company and placed in their vehicles.

The theme of 'Safety'

The themes of *safety* and *security* are very prominent in all the religious rites performed in this factory. Some rites are Shinto and others Buddhist, and there are variations in the membership of those who take part, but the alleged purpose of these rites remains the same—to pray for 'safety' in some form or other. Major fires in the factory resulted in the emergence of the *Hatsu-Fudō* and monthly Buddhist rites. Another fire was responsible for the erection of a Shinto god-shelf (*kamidana*) in one of the offices.

However, the religious rituals complement many 'non-religious' attempts to promote a safety consciousness within the firm. In each department there is a 'safety eulogy' (*anzen shō*) which is normally written up on one of the walls. Each morning the employees face it and recite it together. In the General Affairs department it reads:

> '*Today also, not forgetting to smile the whole day long,*
> *Keeping the rules, there is no disaster.*'

In another department the 'safety eulogy' reads:

> *'May today be happy all day through*
> *Just as yesterday was too.*
> *Happiness and safety go hand in hand.*
> *So may safety always pervade our orderly work*
> *In the workplace to which we devote ourselves.*
> *Safety! Safety! Safety!'*

When I asked a section manager in this department what his safety chant said, he was unable to remember it beyond the first line, even though he recited it every morning. Its effectiveness is therefore questionable. Kamata describes how the employees in a Toyota factory all chanted a safety slogan in unison but life on the production line is in fact very dangerous and accidents do often occur.[5]

On the first and sixteenth of each month, or the nearest working days to these dates, the *Nissen* safety committee organize special 'safety days' when everybody wears 'Green Cross' armbands inscribed with the words 'Safety First'. Departments using heavy machinery and which have had no accidents for 5 or 7 consecutive years are awarded a commemorative shield or cup which is kept in the departmental meeting room.

Around the *Nissen* factory there are conspicuous 'Safety First' notices and large notice boards consisting of a graph showing how many months have elapsed since a major accident at the factory. The company's motto is 'Safety First; Quality Second; Production Third'. Before the oil crisis of the early 1970s, the last two items were in reverse order, but always the motto has been 'Safety First'.

Ronald Dore's study of two Japanese and two British factories mentions how similar notice boards and 'Safety First' slogans were more liberally scattered around the Japanese than the British factories. The Hitachi safety roster 'was a feature which had no counterpart in Britain: one man in each work group was made safety officer each week. He was required to do routine checks and record the results in a log book as well as give a verbal report to the foreman'. Dore's observation that 'Hitachi workers wore safety helmets issued by the company in every shop where there were cranes' also contrasts with the situation of the English Electric workers, who 'were urged to buy protective boots and they were offered for sale at a cut rate, but...were not compulsory'.[6] Both at an ideological or 'religious' level, and also at a 'practical' level, Japanese firms appear to emphasize safety far more than their Western counterparts.[7]

Mamori charms

A concern with safety and security permeates many other areas of Japanese religion. It is quite clearly seen in the widespread use of safety charms (*mamori*). Out of 667 people who filled in questionnaires for me, 431 (about 65% of my sample) stated that they had at least one *mamori*—some people having more than one.

The charms are often thought to be 'valid' for only a year: people who believe this buy new ones every year, usually at New Year. They bring back their old ones and leave them at the Shinto shrine in order to be ritually burned in the middle of January. Sometimes, however, people are reluctant to part with a charm on account of its sentimental value if it has been received as a gift from a parent or spouse.

The commonest type of *mamori* consists of a plastic or wooden pendant attached to the inside of a car's front windscreen and inscribed with words such as 'traffic safety'. Most drivers have only one *mamori* but some have several—despite the idea, expressed half as a joke, that one ought not to have more than one *mamori* in a car in case the gods quarrel among themselves. Such ideas nevertheless indicate that the god is thought by some people to be present within the charm in some form, or at least that the charm is a symbol of the deity's protection.

Nowadays some vehicles have as kinds of *mamori* charms red reflector plates inscribed with the name of the Shinto shrine which sold them. Some people pay for their cars to receive a ritual 'purification' (*harai*) performed over them by a Shinto priest. This might be done either when the car is bought or else each year at a regular time, usually shortly after New Year. Many bus or train companies, as well as other businesses, regularly buy *mamori* charms for their company vehicles.[8]

Other *mamori* charms are attached to the satchels of schoolchildren, kept on children's desks, or kept in the briefcases or driving licences of adults. When asked why they have such charms, most people give replies along the lines of 'to be on the safe side', or to have 'peace of mind', 'reassurance' or 'a sense of security'. The words which they commonly use, such as *anshin* ('relief') or *anshinkan* ('sense of security') are those which in many other religious contexts are also used to express motivations or ideas relating to security and 'safety'.

Some people say that having a *mamori* charm in the car reminds them to drive carefully; in that way they feel there is some 'effect' from the *mamori*. Others see the *mamori* as giving them a psychological feeling of confidence while driving. One woman told me how she strokes the *mamori* with her hand after any incident with another vehicle involving a near-miss. None of those I interviewed could give a specific instance in which they could attribute their safety directly to (their) having the charm. On the other hand, many people feel that they are more likely to have an accident if they do not have a *mamori*, so they keep one 'to be on the safe side'.

On one occasion, I was interested to see how a large and conspicuous *mamori* had been removed from a car within half an hour of its going into a ditch near where we were living. The *mamori* was removed well before the pick-up truck arrived to tow it away because it had a broken axle.

Some special concern with safety is to be expected because deep ditches commonly line the sides of Japanese streets and the roads are often narrow and have blind corners (usually with mirrors placed there). A concern for safety is manifested also in 'non-religious' ways, through special 'traffic safety weeks' twice a year, when the town councils might erect reminder flags alongside some roads or try to promote safety consciousness in a variety of other ways. Nevertheless, the special concern with safety seems more than would be expected from road conditions alone, and appears to reflect a deep-rooted concern with safety and security in Japanese culture as a whole.[9]

Christian implications

Christian missionaries generally feel that converts ought to destroy all *mamori* charms. Such a practice is certainly biblical. For example, in Deuteronomy 7:25-26 we read, 'The images of their gods you are to burn in the fire. Do not covet the silver and gold on them, and do not take it for yourselves, or you will be ensnared by it, for it is detestable to the Lord your God. Do not bring a detestable thing into your house or you, like it, will be set apart for destruction. Utterly abhor and detest it, for it is set apart for destruction.' A New Testament example of this took place at Ephesus, where the Christian converts who had practised sorcery publicly burned their scrolls, despite their having been so expensive (Acts 19:19).[10]

A Japanese girl who became a Christian in England after studying John's gospel with my wife Ruth burned her *mamori* charms in the garden. A few months later she returned to Japan. We did not see her again until we ourselves went to Japan about four years later. It was then that we discovered that she and her husband had other *mamori* charms in their home. Certainly there were various social pressures which had made her succumb to having *mamori* charms again, but we also wondered, in retrospect, whether the burning of her original *mamori* charms had actually been a powerful enough break with the past. What brought these questions to mind was our knowledge that the Japanese themselves are used to burning *mamori* charms. Each January many people take back their old *mamori*s and buy new ones, but the old ones are piled up in order to be ritually burned on or around the 15th of January.

Many people also burn in January the New Year decorations which they had put up around their doors. Some also burn the chopsticks they had used for eating the New Year foods. In some cases, these are burned in people's gardens but in many cases they are brought to a Shinto shrine for ritual burning. To throw these things away in the ordinary rubbish is considered sacrilegious: we only came across one Japanese family who did this, but in their case they were following a relatively unusual family custom whereby the New Year decorations were preserved until the Boys' Festival in

May. The more usual custom is for these things to be burned around the middle of January.

We therefore wonder whether a culturally more appropriate way of marking a break with some of these things is for them to be thrown away in the ordinary rubbish. This may be particularly applicable to *mamori* charms, whereas there are further complications involved in the disposal of larger cult objects such as Buddhist altars.[11] I raise this question tentatively, but it is up to missionaries and pastors to decide how to respond to it.

The main point which I have been trying to make in this chapter, however, is that the Japanese have a pervasive concern with 'safety and security'.[12] It is an underlying motivation behind many kinds of behaviour in both religious and so-called 'secular' spheres of activity.[13] How does this relate to the Christian view of life?

The psalms are full of references to God as being our 'Rock', 'fortress', 'shield', 'refuge', 'rampart', 'help', 'salvation' and so on (*e.g.* Psalm 18:1-3; 27:1-3; 31:1-3; 32:7; 46:1; 54:4; 59:9; 91:1-16; 121:1-8; 144:1-2 *etc.*). The concerns of contemporary Japanese people are the same as those of the people who wrote the psalms. God is the one who does protect his people. He also sends his angels to guard us (2 Kings 6:15-17; Psalm 91:11; Matthew 18:10; 26:53).

The following anecdote illustrates how this applied to my wife and myself while we were living in Japan. We were expecting our second child and Ruth was in the early months of her pregnancy when she visited a neighbour's home. There she discovered that the neighbour's children had German measles (Rubella), which could seriously affect our unborn child if Ruth had caught it. Worried, she returned to our home, where we prayed for God's protection. We felt that God was speaking to us at that time through Psalm 91, which promises God's protection from many disasters, including 'pestilence' and 'plague', for those who 'dwell in the shelter of the Most High'. Ruth wrote out this psalm and we used it as the basis for our prayers. When our second son was born he was completely normal.

Japanese people are very concerned for safety and protection in this world. We need to assure them that God does care for them and is able to protect them in this life, here and now. However, he also has a much safer eternal home prepared for those who will heed his invitation. This is the true place of lasting safety which he offers. Concepts of safety and security here and now lead on to a recognition that there is a need for security and salvation in eternity too.

2

Industrial Religion

The End-of-year 'Great Purification' ceremony
(*Nenmatsu Ōharaishiki*)

I T IS 8:20 AM. At the *Nissen* synthetic fibres factory in central Japan the loudspeakers announce that it is time for the morning exercises. Almost all the employees begin to move their arms around, stretch and bend over, although some do it in a rather perfunctory manner.

Work begins at 8:30 am. However, today is the last working day of the year before the factory closes for the New Year holiday. All the firm's chief executives, from departmental managers upwards to the factory director, assemble in a reception room on the second floor of the administrative building. They are joined by representatives of the company's union, making about 50 people in all.

In this room an 'altar' has been erected. On this dais have already been laid a great variety of offerings: *sake* (rice wine), apples, carrots, special celebratory *tai* fish, rice cakes, satsuma oranges and branches of the *sakaki* tree. The assembled participants notice that to the left of the altar a long strip of cloth, over 12 feet long, has been suspended between and over two upright stands, a few feet apart. Surrounding this cloth, called the *tobari*, a Shinto 'sacred rope' has been put up. This makes the area equivalent to the precincts of a Shinto shrine.

'Normally the god is not present in this part of the factory' explains Ōishi-san, the man in the General Affairs department who is responsible for the practical preparations for these ceremonies (and for clearing up afterwards). Similarly, the table on which the offerings are laid also becomes sacralized, although it is used for 'non-religious' purposes only in the course of other formal ceremonies. The wooden offering-stands are used for sacred purposes only.

Ōishi-san further explains the symbolism of the *tobari* cloth. It is to provide a soft landing place for the deity when he comes down to this locality, which is temporarily transformed into a sacred space through the performance of this ceremony.

All the participants take their places in rows facing the dais. The plant manager and other leading executives are in the front row. Then the Shinto priest arrives, dressed in his ceremonial robes. He belongs to a Shinto shrine elsewhere in the city which also has responsibility for the small shrine virtually opposite the main gates of this factory.

The Shinto priest proceeds to the front and takes his seat to the right of the dais. On its left stands Nishihara-san, the section manager in charge of Business Affairs. Having been in the General Affairs department for 30 years, he is more senior than Ōishi-san and acts as 'Master of Ceremonies' for the company rituals. It is he who tells the participants when to bow to the deity.

Nishihara-san then announces the first phase of the rite. This involves the priest going to the front of the dais, bowing before it and reciting a prayer for the god to come. All the employees stand solemnly, most of them with their heads bowed and eyes shut. Then Nishihara-san announces the next phase of the rite. The priest takes the wooden staff to which white paper streamers are attached (which had been placed in readiness on the dais by Ōishi-san, along with the offerings). First the priest waves this stick three times over the offerings. Then, as Nishihara-san commands 'Rei'— meaning both 'worship' and 'bow'—all the participants bow as the priest waves the wand over them in three broad sweeps. This act 'purifies' the offerings and the people.

Replacing the stick with solemn bows to the dais and then returning for a moment to his seat, the priest waits until Nishihara-san announces the next stage of the proceedings. Standing up again, the priest takes a scroll on which a prayer (*norito*) is inscribed and chants it, facing the dais. As it is in classical Japanese, most participants do not know what is said. This first part of the ceremony lasts for about 10 to 15 minutes.

The main part of the rite follows. It involves the priest holding up two strips of cotton cloth (called *nunosaki*), each about 12 to 18 inches long. He had brought these with him and had previously folded them into two lengthways. It appears that at one time only one strip of cloth had been used, but, in order to speed up the ceremony, so that the men can return to work sooner, two cloths are now used instead of one.

Taking a pair of scissors, the priest makes small incisions along the folded edges of the cloths, 25 or more to each cloth, in order that there would be more than enough to represent each participant in the ritual. These strips of cloth are then laid over two wooden offering stands which are picked up by two assistants from the General Affairs department and carried around the participants.

The cloths are offered in turn to each participant, who solemnly blows onto a portion of the cloth and then rips it from the incision to about halfway down its width. This symbolises the transfer onto the cloth of all his sins and pollutions (*tsumi to kegare*) from the previous year. They are transferred through the act of blowing and are then taken away in the cloth.

When the cloths have been passed around the whole group, the priest takes them back, packs them away in his bag and performs some concluding bows to the dais. All the participants again bow as Nishihara-san commands 'Rei'. The priest takes the cloths with him to the Shinto shrine, where on the 15th January they are ritually burnt.

This whole ceremony lasts about half an hour, finishing at 9:00 am, when the factory manager gives a short speech wishing everyone a good holiday and New Year. All the executives and union representatives then disperse to their places of work. The priest is presented with an envelope containing 15,000 yen, his standard fee for such services to the company.[1]

'Sacrifice' in Japanese folk religion

Ōishi-san later explained to me that the symbolism of the ripping cloth is just one variant of common types of ritual prayers which may involve the destruction of the ritual object. He compared it with the burning of *gomagi*, pieces of wood inscribed with prayers which are said to ascend in the smoke to the gods. According to Ōishi-san, the cloth in the ritual described above represents both individual sin (by each person ripping one strip) and also collective sins or impurities by the fact that the cloth is still joined at the edges and is burned as one unit.

I wonder if there is still deeper symbolism in the actual ripping of the cloth. There are remarkable parallels between this ritual and those in other cultures which involve the ritual wounding, killing or destruction of scapegoats or other sacrificial animals in order to carry away the sins of others. A very similar meaning and process of destruction is presented in this Japanese purification ritual. Even if this ceremony is a local one, it is likely that variants will be found in other areas, especially now that Shinto priests are trained at the same Shinto institutions on a national basis.[2]

Missionaries to Japan have often reported difficulties in communicating the concept of sacrifice. Both animal and human sacrifice are referred to in the ancient chronicles, but they are no longer found among the Japanese. The word *ikenie* is an indigenous Japanese word for 'sacrifice', but its meaning is no longer religious.[3] On the other hand, the concept of 'sacrificial' self-giving on behalf of others is widely found in Japanese culture; there are many examples of it in Japanese history and literature. At an ordinary domestic level, it could be said that many parents work 'sacrificially' on behalf of their children, in order to pay for their children's education. In general, the *concept* of sacrifice *is* present, but its *form* is coloured by various aspects of Japanese culture. Although animal sacrifice is not found in Buddhism, within Shinto there are rituals which do involve the symbolism of vicarious sacrifice, even if this is expressed through the use of inanimate objects rather than animal victims. Might it be that an increased awareness of the contents of such rituals and their meanings could help missionaries to present the Christian concepts of sacrifice to the Japanese in a culturally more meaningful way?

The variety of religious rites

Many different rites take place in this factory, of which the *Nenmatsu Ōharaishiki* is but one. The above description indicates only a little of the extent to which Japanese businessmen do participate in religious rituals as part of their work. Other rituals commonly performed in Japanese factories include:

a) New Year safety prayers
b) Prayers for prosperity on the first Day of the Horse in February (*Hatsu-uma sai*)
c) Rites commemorating the founding of the firm
d) Calling in a Shinto priest to perform rites called *jichinsai* intended to pacify the god of the vicinity whenever a new building is erected or a major new piece of machinery is installed
e) The purchase of *mamori* safety charms each year for all the company's vehicles
f) Preservation and maintenance of printed prayer plaques (*fuda*), generally for safety, in office buildings.

Particular factories may also perform rites which are specific to them but might have parallels or variants elsewhere. The following is a list of such rituals at the firm which I studied:

1) Calling in a Shinto priest to open up the *judō* and *kendō* halls for another year, by a purificatory rite each January
2) Prayers to the god of the hillside on which the company housing is built
3) An annual pilgrimage to a temple dedicated to the god Fudō (a god of fire) in order to pray for protection from fire.
4) Visits twice a year to present offerings and prayers at the graves of a former managing director of *Nissen* and of Minelli, the Roman Catholic Italian engineer who helped set up the factory but committed suicide there in 1927.
5) Distribution of foods to the wild animals living on the hillside on which the company housing is built, because the animals are

thought to be embodiments of the gods who protect some ancient graves on the hillside: that is, the Segaki rite.
6) Monthly offerings and prayers within the factory precincts itself.

I have already described some of these rites in chapter one, and further brief descriptions have been published elsewhere.[4] Several other scholars have reported the widespread and possibly increasing practice of religious rites in Japanese companies.[5] Anecdotal evidence from residents in Japan further testify to the widespread occurrence of religious rites in many factories. For instance, an English teacher at a steel works in Toyama told me that every month there are rituals and prayers to promote both safety and prosperity.[6] An experienced missionary also reports, 'Even in modern banks, where there is not the same risk of accident at work, considerable pressure is put on employees to take part in religious observances as representatives of the bank: *e.g.* when an important customer dies the bank is obliged to send a representative to the funeral. This involves the offering of incense *etc*.'[7] On Mount Kōya many firms have established memorials where they hold services for the spirits of former company presidents and employees who died while serving the company.[8]

Further evidence that *Nissen* is by no means exceptional comes from the reports of similar kinds of rites at the work places of non-*Nissen* employees whom I interviewed or who filled in questionnaires for me. For instance, a section manager of a pharmaceuticals firm mentioned how 'twice a year (Spring and autumn) we pray for the spirits of those animals used in vivisection at work, giving thanks for the spirits of the many animals used for such research purposes'.[9] A section manager for a railway company reported, 'prayers for safety: prayers that there should be no fatal accidents as there *are* many such accidents in the electrical and associated industries'. An employee for a major Japanese broadcasting company told me that all their new company cars receive a special 'purification' (*harai*) at a Shinto shrine. Other non-*Nissen* company employees mentioned rites such as the *Hatsu-uma sai*, a 'Great Purification rite', *jichinsai* ceremonies and New Year shrine visits on behalf of the company. In some cases participation was restricted to the senior management, whereas in other cases (such as *jichinsai* rites) there was felt to be social pressure exerted on the workers to participate too. The purpose of most of these rituals was reported to be the promotion of safety or prosperity.

The existence of a religious dimension to company life is an 'unseen face of Japan' about which many company employees are unaware. When asked about company rites of a religious nature, only departmental or section managers mentioned rites such as the end of year 'great purification' or the *hatsu-uma* rite. When filling in my questionnaire, those who were unaware of company rites left blank my question on religious rites in the workplace: therefore the response rate for this item was 40% for departmental managers and 41% for section managers but dropped to no more than 13% among 'chief clerks' (*kakarichō*) and foremen, and only 10% among blue-collar workers. Those lower down the *Nissen* hierarchy were generally aware only of *jichinsai* rites, some general prayers for safety, the firm's Christmas party or the Summer Festival for children—at which offerings are made to an image of Jizō, the god who is supposed to protect children. (Participation in the Christmas party and Jizō *bon* is more of a voluntary nature, and their 'religious' content is minimal.)

The influence of Yoshioka-san

A key figure behind the scenes in the religious aspects of *Nissen* factory life is the 'catering manager', Yoshioka-san, who describes himself as an 'amateur medium'. Technically he is the managing director of his own catering business, which runs all the *Nissen* factory canteens. He has also set up a factory in Thailand for rearing prawns and other sea foods for commercial markets.

Yoshioka-san describes his revelations from the spirit world as 'mental flashes' which can take the form of premonitions or revelations. The following quotations from an interview with him illustrate the kind of influence which he exerts over some people in the *Nissen* company:

'This morning Ōishi-san found that a tree in the park around the *Nissen* shrines had been blown over and was tilted at an angle. He didn't know what to do about it, so asked me to find out from the spirits if it would be better to cut down the tree or straighten it up again. He did not want to risk the wrath of the local gods (*kami*) if he were to take the wrong course of action.'

'One of the men here at *Nissen* had a stomach problem and came to me for advice. I told him to go to pray to [the statue/idol of a particular Buddhist deity] near to the local high school. The man recovered so I presume he acted upon my advice.'

'The *Nissen* factory in Ishikawa prefecture has only 200 employees because it is largely mechanized, but these men clubbed together to buy a Shinto idol (*yashiro*) for the factory. The manager of the Ishikawa factory came to consult me about their proposed installation of this *yashiro* (in its own small shrine precincts) and to ask my opinion about the best kind of *yashiro*, where to find a craftsman to make it and other such details. He then bought the *yashiro* and it was installed at the Ishikawa factory in June 1984.'

'The manager of the *Nissen* factory in Ibaraki prefecture came to consult me because he had been involved in a series of traffic accidents. We prayed together at my family shrine on the 6th and 16th of that month. He then returned to Ibaraki prefecture and ceased to be involved in any traffic accidents after that. Some time later, in 1982, that manager came back here and took back with him a *yashiro* for the factory in Ibaraki.'

The term 'idol' is normally avoided in most anthropological literature because of its derogatory connotations. Normally anthropologists refer to an image or statue instead. However, I use the term 'idol' in this context in order to refer to an image in which a spirit has been invited to dwell. Yoshioka-san explained to me that after the wooden image is made by a specialist in Kyoto there is a special ceremony for the deity to enter the *yashiro*. Whereas previously the statue was merely an image, this ceremony transforms it into the dwelling place for a god. The ceremony is described by Joya as follows:

'When a Buddhist picture or sculpture is completed, a *kaigen-kugyō* or eye-opening service is held. It is a rite to install soul into the statue or picture.

The eyes are already painted in the picture, or carved in the statue, but the eye-opening service is required to make it worthy of worship. At the service, a painting brush is passed over the

Buddha's eyes in the imaginary act of painting them... Eyes are regarded as the 'windows of the soul', and by opening them, the soul is activated to reach others, it is said...'[10]

In this sense, the term 'idol' is more appropriate than 'image' or 'statue' in order to refer to a statue or image which has had its 'eyes opened' or become 'activated' by having a spirit invited to reside within it.[11] It is interesting that the concept of the eyes as 'windows of the soul' has a parallel in the teachings of Jesus: 'Your eye is the lamp of your body. When your eyes are good, your whole body also is full of light. But when they are bad, your body also is full of darkness. See to it, then, that the light within you is not darkness...' (Luke 11:34-35).

Yoshioka-san described various other experiences in which he had become aware of the presence of spirits of the dead. For example, when he went on a holiday to Guam he visited some wartime trenches in which Japanese soldiers had been killed. As was his habit, he began to recite Buddhist sutras. Later the spirits revealed to him that his actions in Guam had enabled the spirits of twelve dead soldiers to return with him to Japan.[12]

The Bible strongly prohibits the consultation of mediums and deliberate attempts to make contact with spirits of the dead (*e.g.* Leviticus 20:27; Deuteronomy 18:9-13). In a study which I conducted among nurses in Leeds, England, I discovered a statistically significant correlation between involvements with spiritualism or Ouija boards and experiences interpreted as 'the presence of the dead'.[13] In probably the majority of cases, such experiences of 'the presence of the dead' are likely to indicate demonic activity or influence in or around the person. Exodus 20:3-6 and Exodus 34:7 have sometimes been interpreted in the light of contemporary experience which indicates that some demonic activity can be transmitted from one generation to the next.[14] It is significant in this regard that Yoshioka-san thinks his mediumistic powers are hereditary and says that one of his sons can bend spoons like Uri Geller. (In his case the probable presence or influence of hereditary demons is relatively conspicuous. However, those with experience of 'exorcism' often find that demonic spirits of various kinds are passed on in many family lines—among both Christians and non-

Christians—but the influence of these demons can be cut off in the authority and name of Jesus Christ.)

'Belief' in the efficacy of religious rites

In contrast to the occult influences from Yoshioka-san, the fact that the *Nissan* company's President in Tokyo is supposed to be a Christian has no apparent effect on the company. It was Ueda-san, the Managing Director of this particular factory, who told me that the President and his wife were Christians, but he did not know their denomination. On the occasion of the anniversary of the founding of the firm, the President and other past or present board members attend the Shinto rites at the main company shrine on the hillside behind this factory. There is no indication that the President's own religious views are different from those of any others.

When the film department began to have a serious accident rate, its departmental manager decided that on the first workday of every month he and his section managers should go to the company's main shrine to pray for safety in their department. However, their accident rate still continued to be high. One day the inconsistency between their prayers and actual experience was highlighted when they returned from their prayers for safety to find that one of their men had accidentally cut off his finger on a machine. Two years later this film departmental manager told me that he thought the firm's religious rites 'have no technical effect'.

Nishihara-san, the Business Affairs Section Manager, says about the rites, 'It is important to preserve old traditions; it is not scientific but spiritual. I've not thought about whether or not they have any effect and I don't know whether or not they do.'

Ueda-san, the Plant Manager responsible for the whole factory complex, told me that he has no faith in the religious rites at all.[15] He takes part in them simply as part of his work because all his seniors (*senpai*) do it. In public, his position is that he believes in it, but in his heart he has no faith in the rites at all.

Ōkura-san, the General Affairs Departmental Manager, also says that he thinks the rites have no effect but he performs them because they are part of his work and he has no strong objections to them. 'If I objected to it,' he says, 'I would have to say what the meaning of the rite is, but as there is no strong custom of specifying exactly what the meaning is, I participate because, as General Affairs manager, it is part of my job.' In general, he feels that there are too many religious rites at *Nissen*, that they take up too much time and that some of them ought to be dropped.

However, the Personnel section manager says that if any of the rites were to be neglected 'something bad might happen to the fortunes of the company'. He considers it 'safer' to continue the rituals. Like those above him, he has to participate because of his work but he is more prepared to say that the *kami* do protect the company in some way from disasters.

One of the men under him, who participates in the rite for the opening of the sports hall, also says that the *kami* protect.[16] He says that he has a 'holy feeling' when he participates and that the rite serves to 'unify the spirits' of the participants.[17] At about the same level in the General Affairs Department is Ōishi-san, whose attitude to the rites, when first asked, was that they do have some kind of effect. However, when pressed about specific ways in which he thinks the safety prayers have an effect he says that there is 'no direct visible effect, just a spiritual one'.

Overall, those at the top of the company, who have to take part in more rites than any others, are also the ones who are most willing to deny any personal faith in the efficacy of these rites. By contrast, those lower down the firm's hierarchy are more likely to profess some such faith—even when asked in private without their replies being overheard by any others. Perhaps they feel reluctant, even in private, to express doubts about the official company ideology, whereas those nearer the top have less to lose by voicing their doubts to an outsider—although such doubts are not expressed in public. Even the union leader adopted the official 'company line' when he gave the opinion that the rites do have some effect 'otherwise the company would not perform them': however, his replies were communicated through a third party because 'unexpected business' meant that he was unavailable for interview at the time originally arranged.

A total of eighteen people were asked about their attitudes to the rites. Of these, sixteen were principal participants and two were helpers who assist with jobs such as pouring water over the hands of participants as they enter the shrine. Both of these helpers are low in the firm's hierarchy and both say they think the *kami* do protect, one of them saying he 'believes 70%'. Correlating the eighteen replies with the informants' positions in the firm's hierarchy, an interesting pattern emerges:

Table 2.1 Attitudes to company rites

	Position in Company		
	High	Middle	Low
'Rites have no effect'	5	1	
'Spiritual but not technological effect'	2		
'Effect only on one's feelings'	2	2	
'God does protect and the rite does have some effect'		4	2

There is therefore a strong indication that those most sceptical about the efficacy of the rites are, ironically, the very people whose jobs require them to participate most often in those rites and who have taken part in them for several years. They are the high ranking company officials of departmental manager level, or higher, whereas those lower in the hierarchy have a more limited range of rites in which they participate or have not been obliged to do so over so many years.

Two possible explanations for this finding are:

1) The top management have less to risk by expressing scepticism than those lower down the hierarchy.

2) Their longer experience of the rites and of not noticing any tangible result from them has in itself encouraged private scepticism. The experience of the film departmental manager who came from the Shinto shrine to find that one of his men had cut off a finger shows how such scepticism can be easily generated.[18]

Compulsion and duty in religious rites

Mr Mita, a middle-ranking employee at *Nissen*, says that when a new building is erected or new piece of heavy machinery installed in his department, he is expected to attend the Shinto *jichinsai* ceremony for appeasing the god of the locality. He told me that it is with reluctance that he has to participate, even against his will, because it is a company ceremony and he feels obliged to take part.[19] Almost all those in the department attend the ceremony, because, even if they are not 'ordered' to take part, those higher up in the firm 'invite' them to do so if they have nothing else to do. Because few of them have specific tasks which have to be done without delay at that time, virtually everyone in the department does attend the *jichinsai*. Mita-san also has to participate in the annual Shinto rite for the (re-)opening of the *Nissen* sports hall, which he attends out of a sense of duty to his firm. Similarly, the Production manager, who is higher up in the firm than Mita-san, says he takes part in religious rites only out of a sense of obligation (*giri*) to his company. Various others, including Ueda-san, the plant manager, also said that they participate as part of their work or because others do so.

The perception of this sense of obligation increases as one rises in the firm's hierarchy. Most *Nissen* employees replied 'No' to an item in my questionnaire about whether or not all employees must participate in religious rites in their place of work. Only one replied 'Yes' and three wrote that 'only those concerned in the rites participate'. Another wrote in more detail that there is 'no strong pressure, but if one goes in to work that day all the company members participate'. However, it was noticeable that four of those who do participate in at least some of the more 'religious' rites at the company shrine left this question conspicuously blank—even though two of them had already listed rites in which they participate.

For those at the top of the hierarchy there is an example to be set to those lower down. They might also be conscious of possible effects on their careers if they did not participate in the firm's anniversary rites when the top management come down from Tokyo. The same holds true of those further down the hierarchy, especially if they have no ideological basis for refusing to participate. The only ones likely to have such an ideology antagonistic to participation in the rites are those belonging to what are viewed as 'extreme' religions like the Sōka Gakkai or evangelical Christianity. It seems, however, that even among some of these people participation in the rituals might be a 'safer' option than risking one's reputation or career chances by refusing to take part. Once they have begun to participate without protest it is more difficult to refuse to take part some years later if they reach the higher rungs of the company ladder.

The same was true in many Japanese businesses when Emperor Hirohito was in a critical condition prior to his death. Watanabe notes,

> 'Employees of the big firms with their headquarters close to Otemachi in Tokyo trooped off to sign their names at...the Imperial Palace. Such acts had nothing whatever to do with their personal feelings toward the Emperor. It was simply that if a colleague or a senior employee went to sign the *kichō* [a book to sign for expressing one's regard for the Emperor], workers were obliged to do likewise for fear of being labelled as someone who would not make enough effort...Similarly, workers engaged in silent prayer or wore black whether they wanted to or not...'[20]

Industrial Mission in Japan?

A recognition of some of these social pressures which can be faced by Japanese Christians in their places of work leads one to consider the place of industrial mission in Japan. In Britain there are Industrial Missions and Industrial Chaplaincies, and in France there are Roman Catholic 'Worker Priests': is it feasible to consider such developments in Japan?

In the *Nissen* case, Mr Yoshioka already has a kind of occult 'industrial mission'. He is allowed to propagate his religious beliefs and to influence company policy on religious matters. Though it was not explicitly stated, he was probably the one who discerned that the fire in 1973 took place because the firm had neglected to perform rites on behalf of those who had died in the area over 1,300 years previously, in 672 AD.

To some extent, Christian industrial missions in the West have benefitted from a certain acceptability among nominal Christians, whereas in the Shinto-Buddhist context of Japan the term 'mission' can be much more threatening. However, there could be certain

advantages if Christian strategy in Japan were to pay more attention to the *company* as a focus of evangelism, while not neglecting
the equally important need for church-planting in local neighbourhoods.

One problem often faced by missionaries in Japan is that they
have far more access to women than to men. In many neighbourhoods this is because the men are at work for most of the day and
come home late: therefore they are not so easily available for
evangelistic events.

Although this is true of many neighbourhoods in which missionaries work, it is not necessarily true of estates of company housing
(*shataku*). In my questionnaire I asked about hours of work and
about time spent commuting to and from work. Replies from men
in the *shataku* estate showed quite a different pattern to those from
men in an adjacent estate of owner-occupied housing:

Table 2.2   Hours of work for men

	Shataku *estate*	*An owner-occupied estate*
Up to 40 hours per week	30%	23%
41-45 hours per week	18%	12%
46-50 hours per week	32%	28%
51-60 hours per week	18%	23%
61-90 hours per week	2%	14%

In addition, those living in the *shataku* live very close to their
place of work, except for a minority who have been transferred to
other factories but are temporarily still living in their original
shataku accommodation. This difference is shown by Table 2.3:

Table 2.3   Commuting times for men

	Shataku *estate*	An owner- occupied *estate*
Up to 1 hour per week	34.5%	6%
1-2 hours per week	38.0%	12%
2-5 hours per week	21.0%	21%
5-10 hours per week	2.0%	29%
11-20 hours per week	3.0%	28%
Over 20 hours per week	0.5%	4%

It is clear that men living in *shataku* accommodation do tend to have more leisure time available than those who own their own homes. This might be because they are relatively younger: the average age of the *shataku* apartment dwellers is in the early thirties but many are in their twenties and some in their early forties. The firm also provides company dormitories for unmarried employees. There is some social pressure for men to have saved up enough money by the time they are in their forties for them to buy homes of their own, often with the help of a company loan. However, this still means that for about ten to twenty years of their lives they have been living in *shataku* accommodation. During this time they have generally more leisure time available to them than is the case for those who live in their own homes but commute further to work. As most religious activities, including Christian ones, tend to be relegated to the sphere of 'leisure', might it be that an increased focus of missionary efforts among *shataku* dwellers would give greater opportunities for sharing the Christian gospel with younger men?

Next to these *shataku* apartments belonging to *Nissen* is a field where fathers often play ball or fly kites with their children. Sometimes it is used as a baseball pitch when the company team play against teams from other firms. On one such occasion I was able to join the spectators and get to know some of them in an informal manner. In advocating evangelism among company employees, one missionary has suggested that the Christians could postpone their services until Sunday afternoon or evening in order to be able to join the men at their sports on a Sunday morning.[21]

Shataku wives also have relatively more time for 'leisure' activities, as there is some covert pressure on them not to obtain employment elsewhere. Because their very address indicates where their husbands work, it would reflect badly on the firm if local people thought the firm were paying their employees so poorly that their wives 'had to' go out to work. One woman in this *shataku* estate had outside employment as an advisor to a publishing firm, but she only worked for two hours per week. Some other women coached high school students or taught specialist crafts but these were for 'pocket money' rather than as 'serious' employment. One woman transcribes books into Braille as voluntary work.

Kinoshita mentions how *shataku* women may fear company 'spies' who report on their activities. If they step 'out of place' it might jeopardize their husbands' promotion chances or else result in their being transferred to a less desirable part of Japan.[22] Perhaps such fears lay behind the attitude of one *shataku* woman who refused to have an English class meet in her home because it was taught by a foreign missionary. This is certainly a problem for missionary access to such neighbourhoods, because women such as this one do not want to be conspicuous. However, when this same woman later invited me to her home she also invited round many of her friends and neighbours to meet me at the same time. In this way she did not stand out as 'unique'. Soon my wife and I began to receive invitations to some of these other homes too. Therefore it is possible to break into these social circles if only one makes the effort.

Often the relatively close-knit social structure of Japanese businesses has been depicted by missionaries as a 'barrier' to the gospel. However, instead of being a 'barrier', it could be turned into a door for *opportunity*. With a little effort, it is possible to develop relationships within a firm. In doing so, foreign Christians may find that they enhance their understanding of the pressures which some of their Japanese fellow Christians might be facing daily.

In fact, one foreigner was already living in this *shataku* estate— an Indian engineer employed by this firm. We also met in Japan an English woman who was employed by another firm to teach English to its employees. She was not a formal 'missionary', but she was a Christian. Once I had begun to develop contacts at *Nissen*, one of the firm's section managers asked me if I would teach English to the men in his section one evening per week. This provided me with further opportunities for getting to know these men, and at times led to my sharing with them about Jesus.

Admittedly, I had a certain advantage in not being a 'missionary', and in having academic connections which facilitated my acceptance by the firm. It may be harder for those who already have the title of missionary and whose visa and tax restrictions may hinder such activities. However, the door is wide open for Christian businessmen—and here I include not only Westerners but also Asian, African and Latin American Christians—who may have access to Japanese company life in a way which is denied to some conventional missionaries. Perhaps my own experience might encourage them to develop social relationships within these companies and pray for opportunities to share the love and power of Jesus with those around them. In this, they might have opportunities which are less accessible to many conventional missionaries. Certainly Japanese Christians employed by such firms do have these kinds of opportunities, but they also face particular kinds of social pressures which need to be understood. In facing these constructively, they need sensitive pastoral guidance and supportive prayer. If at all possible, they also need the support of a Christian group within the company itself.

Few missionaries have had much previous experience of business life in the West. For this reason, they may be poorly equipped to give pastoral advice to Japanese businessmen. However, there may be Japanese pastors or businessmen within their churches who are more aware of the kinds of pressures faced by company employees and who may be better equipped as counsellors. If missionaries are themselves inadequately aware of the pressures faced by businessmen, they need to be able to call on other Christians who do have such experience. In this ministry, there is the need for wider co-operation among those with different gifts and backgrounds who can complement each other. If such people cannot be found within a single church, they may need to draw upon skills available elsewhere in the Christian church, perhaps even within other Christian denominations.

On the whole, with some notable exceptions, there has been a tendency for churches of different denominations in Japan to be relatively insular, even 'clique-ish', and to co-operate relatively poorly with other Christian groups. Industrial mission in large companies provides a concrete instance of an area in which inter-denominational co-operation is essential. Within the *Nissen* company and its *shataku* I came across individuals belonging to several Christian denominations, but there is no inter-denominational Christian meeting of any kind organized on a company basis. Other types of interest groups—particularly the company sports teams—have their place in company life, but there is no Christian organization. An experienced missionary who commented on the first draft of this chapter admitted, 'it is the churches which are at fault here; they do not encourage their members to seek out other Christians for fellowship. The problem is largely an inter-church one.' In the same context, he remarked that my book 'presents an opportunity to challenge the church in Japan to encourage cross-denominational fellowship in large companies. This has been greatly neglected and has hindered the witness of Christians in industry.'[23]

Actually, a similar appeal for greater Christian involvement in Japanese industry was made also in 1932 by the Commission of Appraisal for the Laymen's Foreign Missions Inquiry, chaired by W.E. Hocking. Their report included the following passage:

> 'The first labor union in Japan was organized in a Christian church. But now there is a real danger that missions and the churches which have been nurtured by them will remain out of touch with labor unions and their aspirations. Labor union leaders of the present generally do not work with missions nor indigenous churches. They do not find the people interested in their problems or in sympathy with their aims. Without in any way committing the mission or church to a labor program, we believe that more intelligent effort should be directed toward understanding the questions at issue in the labor organizations.
>
> This commission recommends that missionaries make the acquaintance of labor union leaders, endeavor sympathetically to understand their aims and ideals, and to merit their confidence, and in general cultivate cordial relations with them.'[24]

Nowadays a common stereotype of Japanese company unions

sees them as pawns in the hands of the management who, after a ritualized bargaining process each Spring, generally accept a realistic wage increase and conveniently forget about their more militant demands.[25] Occasionally more 'meaningful' strikes have taken place, especially if job security (at least for the elite 'core' workers) has been threatened by what are perceived as unfair dismissals. However, even if company labour unions may seem to be almost puppets of management, they can nevertheless play an active rôle in many firms and carry an influence which should not be overlooked.

I do not wish to imply that this area has been completely neglected by Christian missionaries. There are several examples of industrial mission (or 'occupational evangelism') of one kind or another, including the Nishijin Labour Centre in Kyoto and the Kansai Labour Evangelism Fellowship (which was formed in 1956 through the efforts of a missionary named Henry Jones, in collaboration with Japanese colleagues such as Takenaka Masao). These kinds of efforts have also led to increased co-operation between different churches: for instance, a joint industrial mission in Hiroshima has involved twenty-two Protestant churches. Takenaka Masao has also been involved in the establishment of Shūgakuin House in Kyoto, where lay people can receive help in discovering what it means to be a Christian presence in a factory, office or trade union. Conferences are organized also for those in various professions to discuss specific issues relevant to them.[26]

Neither do I wish to imply that mission strategy should shift entirely from neighbourhood to company: both are very important. I merely wish to highlight the need for industrial mission to complement other forms of evangelism in order to counteract a continuing weakness in the church as it is at present. Certainly the pressures faced by Christian businessmen at work have tended to contribute significantly to church membership leakage.

The influence of company pressures on those attracted to Christianity is further confirmed by an experienced missionary in Japan who commented,

> Most Japanese in the situations portrayed [at the *Nissen* factory] see participation in religious rites as 'part of the job', but can you

imagine the dilemma a devout Christian would face if promoted to the position of personnel manager at *Nissen*? David's... description clearly portrays one of the greatest stumbling blocks to Japanese men considering becoming Christians or even attending a church. They are aware of the great difficulty that becoming a devout Christian would involve them in. Time and time again I have spoken to men who have been deeply impressed by the Gospel and the Christian life, only to conclude that for them personally it is impossible, the complications would be too great... This fact is illustrated by the small church I pastor here. Half the membership is made up of Christian couples or married men. However, 80% of these couples or married men run their own businesses. It is this that makes it possible for them to live consistent and dedicated Christian lives.[27]

Christians who refuse to participate in Shinto or Buddhist company rites may face ostracism, and for this reason businesses in some rural areas have even refused to employ Christians. One response to this problem has been the setting up of Christian businesses in which Christian prayer and worship at the workplace are substituted for Shinto or Buddhist rites.[28] I am told that one such company is the Omi Brotherhood in Shiga prefecture, a firm which handles mentholatum products for the whole of Japan and which has set up Christian secondary schools and a large hospital in the same town. Apparently the group was started by a missionary who was confronted with the problem of Christians unable to find employment.[29]

Nevertheless, in modern industrial situations in Japan, it seems to me that those very social structures which many missionaries have perceived as 'hindrances' to the gospel might actually be used for the development of Christian fellowships within businesses. I shall conclude this chapter by mentioning the case of a Japanese section manager who became a Christian. Rather than being baptised immediately, he waited until, through his witness, his colleagues also became Christians. Then they were all baptised together. As a result, they could all make a stand for Christ together in their firm and, as a group, exert an influence within the company itself.

CHAPTER
3

Shrine and Temple

'*D* O YOU HAVE a religion? If so, which?'. In response to this item on my questionnaire, Mr Yasuda ticked the box for 'Shinto'. When I later interviewed him in more depth about his religious attitudes, I asked him why he had chosen the option 'Shinto'. He replied, 'I'm a Shintoist because my family have a *butsudan* (a Buddhist household altar)'. After his wife then pointed out that having a *butsudan* would make him a Buddhist, not a Shintoist, Mr Yasuda realized his mistake and declared, 'In that case, I'm a Buddhist and not a Shintoist after all'.

I also asked those I interviewed how many times in the previous year they had visited a Buddhist temple (*tera*). Most people would think about the question and then give a reply such as 'once or twice', or 'two or three times'. However, when I then asked how many times they had visited a Shinto shrine (*jinja*), most people would say, 'Oh, I was counting those in with the Buddhist temples'. It was only when they were forced to distinguish between the two types of institutions that they tried to classify particular places as either Shinto or Buddhist. Sometimes one spouse would ask the other whether a certain place were a Shinto shrine or a Buddhist temple, because they were not sure themselves.

Often these replies referred only to those occasions when the person had a specific intention to pray or 'worship', such as at New Year. They would not count the occasions on which they had visited a temple or shrine for 'sightseeing' purposes.[1] When I asked specifically about such visits, they would then say that they had been several times. While there, they might also have prayed, even if rather perfunctorily. At a Shinto shrine they would ring a bell— said to be either to alert the god to their presence, or else to 'wake the god up'—and then perform the conventional Shinto ritual of two bows, two handclaps and another bow. Their thoughts at such times express prayers for the safekeeping of their own families or for special help with forthcoming events such as university entrance examinations. Some shrines 'specialize' in certain types of requests: for example, in Kyoto at a Shinto shrine called the *Kitanotenmangu*, which is dedicated to a famous scholar of the eighth century AD who was later deified, one can see many prayer plaques (*ema*) inscribed with requests for help in academic examinations. Just as many people do not distinguish in their minds between the Buddhas and the Shinto gods, they are also unaware of theoretical distinctions between the manner of prayer at Buddhist and Shinto institutions.[2]

In English, it has become conventional to use the word 'temple' for Buddhist institutions in Japan and 'shrine' for Shinto ones. However, the distinction between Buddhism and Shinto in Japan is to some extent an arbitrary one. Before 1868, Shinto shrines were often found in the precincts of Buddhist temples; moreover, Buddhist scriptures, images and decorations were used in Shinto shrines, and the same priests often officiated at both kinds of ceremonies.[3] Sometimes today, a Shinto shrine might hold a *bon* dance to 'welcome the ancestors' even though ancestral rites and *bon* ceremonies are normally Buddhist. It was only in 1868 that Shinto and Buddhism were officially separated by a political decree, but nowadays there remains relatively little distinction between them in the minds of many ordinary people.

When I asked people about their feelings at shrines or temples, they gave a variety of replies, such as feelings of 'peace', of 'a washed spirit', 'thanksgiving', 'a solemn or devout mood', 'asking for something', 'closeness to my ancestors' or 'sightseeing'. Hardly anyone distinguished very clearly between feelings at a Shinto shrine as compared with those at a Buddhist temple. For most people, the feelings were the same. It was noticeable that two men who did sense a difference in atmospheres were both professional musicians. Perhaps their musical sensitivity gave them a sensitivity to these spiritual atmospheres too.[4]

Common attitudes which fail to distinguish very much between Shinto and Buddhism partly account for the official statistics on religious affiliation in Japan, which are notoriously ambivalent. Various religious organisations presented 'membership' figures to the Ministry of Education, but when these are totalled up they show that the number of Shintoists, Buddhists, Christians and others account for over one and a half times the national population.[5] Many of these official figures are based on very arbitrary estimates and are quite unreliable.[6]

Nevertheless, there is a general 'division of labour' between Shinto and Buddhism, whereby Shinto rites are concerned with the first half of the life cycle (such as birth and marriage) whereas Buddhist ones concentrate on funerals and memorial rites. Shinto emphasizes ritual purity but Buddhism deals with the pollution of death. In general, it might be said that in Shinto the emphasis is on *beginnings* but in Buddhism it is on *ends*.

The two complement each other. Various scholars have noticed how there seems a parallelism between Shinto rites during a person's lifetime and Buddhist ones after death.[7] Even the year itself, by the traditional calendar, might have been seen as having a Shinto first half and a Buddhist second half: the New Year rites are predominantly Shinto ones, but the Buddhist *bon* festival in the summer used to occur exactly six months later, in the middle of the seventh month.[8] The Gregorian calendar messed up this symmetry, because the bonfires traditionally lit for the *bon* festival could not be so easily lit during the 'rainy season' which still affects many parts of central and southern Japan during July. The *bon* festival now occurs in August instead.

Shinto also involves a greater sense of *community*, especially during Shinto festivals, whereas Buddhist rituals for the dead tend to focus more on *individuals*. On the whole, Shinto festivals tend to be more in the public domain, whereas Buddhist ones tend to be more private affairs.[9]

The duties of Shinto and Buddhist priests

For the most part, the Shinto priesthood tends to be a hereditary occupation and is mostly practised by men, although I have been told that occasionally there can be women priests too.[10] Two Shinto priests whom I interviewed told me that they are 'often' consulted about 'all sorts of things', but they did not go into details. From the cases which I have come across, Shinto and Buddhist priests are mainly consulted only for the purpose of arranging ceremonies such as weddings or funerals. Sometimes Shinto priests are also asked about possible supernatural causes of illness, including infertility, or questions about divination, such as choosing an auspicious name for a child. Examples will be given in later chapters.

Some Shinto priests may become specialists in certain forms of divination, and be consulted about this, but for the most part the duties of Shinto priests are connected with particular festivals. Some of these festivals are community affairs; others are life-cycle rituals affecting particular families, such as weddings or the dedication of children.

Buddhist priests have their time largely taken up with performing memorial rites for those who have died. I interviewed a Buddhist priest of the Jōdo ('Pure Land') sect, who told me about his average day. He gets up between 6.00am and 7.00am, recites sutras in front of the statues in the temple for about ten to fifteen minutes, then cleans the interior of the temple for about ten to twenty minutes. After this, he joins his wife and children for breakfast. His religion does not forbid marriage, drinking alcohol or smoking, all of which he does, and his household furnishings reflect a standard of living which is about the same as for most middle-class families.

At about 9.00am or 10.00am this priest leaves to go to the home of a local family for one of their memorial rites. Sometimes he travels to more distant parts of the city to visit families belonging to his temple who have moved elsewhere. Each rite takes an average of about thirty to forty minutes. He never stays more than an hour at most, even if he stops afterwards to chat with the family over a cup of tea. Such conversations are generally about current events rather than about religious topics.

Each day this priest visits an average of two or three homes, or

seventy to seventy-five a month. For each visit he receives a fee of
¥3,000.[11] His 'bonus' comes in the form of four or five funeral
services per year, for each of which he receives an average fee of
¥100,000. The rest of his time is spent with his family, talking with
friends, watching television or participating in other recreational
activities. He rarely gives a public sermon because the occasions for
these are limited to special festivals at the temple, which are
comparatively rare. This is why relatively few Japanese people
have ever heard a Buddhist sermon.[12] On the whole, religious
teaching in Japan tends to be transmitted more through the family
than through the clergy.[13] In the family it is also more concerned
with practice than with doctrine.

Kami and *Hotoke*

Shinto deities are usually referred to as *kami*. The term can refer to
a wide variety of spirits, ranging from mythological deities with
human form, such as the Sun Goddess and her descendants,
through to the spirits of animals, plants and certain rocks (which
are thought to be the abode of spirits because of their peculiar
shape or huge size). Spirits can reside in natural features such as
waterfalls or the ocean, in places around a home such as the
kitchen or the toilet, and also in man-made objects such as mirrors—which in many Shinto shrines constitute the *shintai* ('god-
body') in which the deity is located.[14] Other objects or phenomena
which have been regarded as *kami* include 'the qualities of growth,
fertility, and production; natural phenomena, such as wind and
thunder; natural objects, such as the sun, mountains, rivers, trees
and rocks; some animals; and ancestral spirits. In the last-named
category are the spirits of the Imperial ancestors, the ancestors of
noble families, and in a sense all ancestral spirits...'[15]

Examples of historical people who have been accorded the
status of *kami* include the Emperor Meiji and Sugawara Michizane,
the scholar enshrined at the *Kitanotenmangu* in Kyoto.[16] However,
'at a more humble level, deceased human beings all attain the
status of a deity sooner or later', largely through the agency of
ancestral rites.[17] There is a structural parallelism between the
ancestors and the Shinto *kami*, in so far as the ancestors 'have the

same protective function as the *kami* of the *kamidana* [household Shinto god-shelf], but are worshipped at a different place and in different ways'. Usually Buddhist memorial rites for individual ancestors are discontinued after the thirty-third or fiftieth anniversary of the person's death, but in some households the memorial tablet for that ancestor is then transferred from the household Buddhist altar to the Shinto god-shelf. In parts of Aichi prefecture, it is said that after the memorial rite on the thirty-third anniversary of the ancestor's death the spirit of the deceased ancestor washes its body and becomes a *kami*.[18]

Although this transfer of the memorial tablet (*ihai*) from a *butsudan* to a *kamidana* is relatively unusual in urban areas, the thirty-third (or sometimes fiftieth) anniversary of the death nevertheless marks a significant stage in the ancestor's status. At this point there has been a development whereby the spirit becomes no longer primarily 'prayed for' but instead becomes one which is 'prayed to'—though largely as one of the collectivity of the ancestors rather than as a particular individual.[19]

The term *hotoke* also needs some further explanation. In ordinary speech it can refer both to spirits of the dead and also to the Buddhas and Boddhisattvas of Buddhism. Ronald Dore distinguishes between these in written English by referring to the latter as *Hotoke* (with a capital 'H'). About half his sample felt there was a difference between the two, either seeing the *hotoke* as much more 'intimate' and more important to the worshipper, or else viewing the *Hotoke* as of higher rank in some supposed hierarchy. At the family *butsudan* one is generally concerned with the *hotoke*, whereas the *Hotoke* are mainly thought of as guides and guardians of the soul after death.[20]

In some parts of Japan (particularly in rural areas and among some of the 'new religions') there is a fear of spirit 'possession' and of curses. It is believed that both living and dead human spirits can affect others, and that humans can also be 'possessed' by the spirits of certain animals, such as foxes, dogs and snakes. These animal spirits are passed on in certain family lines from one generation to another. Ordinary families avoid marriage with these affected families because the spirits can be transmitted through both sexes, and because the local people know of no way in which they can get rid of these spirits.[21] In some of the Japanese 'new religions' such as Mahikari and Agonshū the spirits which interfere with or manifest in people are identified as certain ancestors or as samurai warriors (who may bestow on the 'possessed' person a kind of vicarious prestige).[22]

Many Christians with experience in ministries of 'exorcism' have also found that some kinds of demons do seem to be passed on in family lines, and Christians with gifts of discernment have sometimes seen spirits resembling certain animals. These spirits can affect apparently 'normal' individuals—not only those who are more severely or obviously 'demonized'. (This is a better translation than 'possessed' for the biblical term *daimonizomai*[23].) The good news, however, is that through the authority of Jesus Christ and the power of his Holy Spirit people can be set free from the influence of these ancestral spirits.

Tamashii and Hi no Tama

In Japan, there are local and individual variations in the terminology used to distinguish different kinds of spirits. For instance, Smith reports the following stages in the regular progression of the souls of the dead:

shirei: spirits of the newly dead
nii-botoke: 'new buddhas'
hotoke: buddhas
senzo: ancestors
kami: gods[24]

Some of my own informants would place *senzo* ('ancestors') as equivalent to *hotoke* but nearer to the living than the Buddhas ('*Hotoke*' in Dore's terminology). Many of my informants would not really distinguish between *Hotoke* (Buddhas) and *kami* (gods). Their conceptualization seems to be:

shirei
nii-botoke
senzo or *hotoke*
Hotoke or *kami*

Despite differences of terminology, however, there is a general cognitive and emotional emphasis on those who have died within living memory, as compared with more distant ancestors who are eventually no longer distinguished by separate rites but are merged into the collectivity of the ancestors.[25] In practice, the dividing line is provided not only by the formal rites on the thirty-third or fiftieth anniversary of a person's death but also by 'memory'. This same motivation of memorialism may serve also as a reason for choosing to honour a recently departed person who is not strictly an 'ancestor' but is somebody whom the living wish to remember.[26]

In addition, those influenced by Shinto ideas of the dead might identify the first three categories as *tamashii* (spirits) which eventually become *kami* (gods). Alternatively, they might identify the *shirei* (or *shiryō*) as 'raging spirits'—those who died with a negative frame of mind, such as resentment or jealousy—which are not dissimilar in their effects to *muenbotoke* or *gaki* ('wandering' or 'hungry' ghosts).[27]

In Japanese folk religion 'the human spirit or soul was given a special name—*tama*. Human life was believed to begin with the receiving of a *tama* at the time of birth, and death was due to the departure of the *tama*. The *tama* of people still alive were called living souls (*seirei*) while those of deceased people were called souls of the dead (*shirei*).'[28] However, *tamashii*, *reikon* and *rei* 'are used sometimes as an alternative to *hotoke*, or to mean the 'soul' of a dead person in the intermediate period before it becomes a fully-fledged *hotoke*...*Mitama*, *rei*, *shinrei* are used as equivalents for *kami*, though there is sometimes a suggestion...that *mitama* means something like the 'essence' or the 'soul' of the *kami*. *Shinrei* are generally the inferior type of *kami* such as the *kami* in the earth which are ritually quelled or pacified before building operations, or the *kami* which operate in talismanic *fuda*.'[29]

Seven of those I interviewed said they had seen a 'fireball' (*hi no tama*) and described it as a red, orange, purple or 'blue-green' glow or 'star' which was seen for a short while and then disappeared. Although 34% of my questionnaire sample professed a belief in these 'fireballs', most of those questioned about it said they had 'heard' that 'other people' had seen them. Often these fireballs are interpreted as the spirits or ghosts of dead people, since the word *tama* can mean not only spirit but also a ball or sphere (though written with a different Chinese character). It is not clear whether fireballs influenced the word for spirit or vice-versa, but we do know from written accounts that the fireball phenomenon has been witnessed in the course of many centuries.[30]

A detailed account of a fireball was given by a fifty-one year old woman who before marriage had worked for *Nissen* and had seen the fireball in the factory precincts:

> 'It was just after 7.00pm at night and I was standing by the shop in the factory with a couple of friends when we saw over the personnel office [at least 600 yards away] something red, glowing like a firefly, jumping about very slowly, which then drifted off towards the south and disappeared. It was about a metre or so in diameter.'

This woman was from a rural background, had been educated to high school level but not beyond, and was from a relatively religious family, as indicated by her father's decision to become a Shinto priest after his retirement. When she saw the fireball she wondered if it meant that someone had died.

The other six informants who claimed to have seen one themselves had done so as children at about the age of nine or ten, or 'while in primary school', and always at twilight or at night. Two examples are as follows, the first from a female and the second from a male informant:

> 'I have once seen a fireball, as a child; I don't know what it is. It's a kind of star, or meteorite—a very big blue-green light; I've never seen anything like it. It was when I lived by the coast. I was playing by the places where they tied up the boats and I saw it fall then in the sky.'

> 'I believe in fireballs because I've seen one, in Niigata. I didn't know what it was at the time, but it was outside a house where someone had died. I was 10 years old then and my family saw it too.'

A 'pseudo-scientific' theory which purports to explain this phenomenon claims that the light comes from the potassium emitted by the bones of dead people. In fact, the man just quoted above resorted to this theory when pressed about his interpretation of his experience. However, only two of my informants had seen the fireball in a graveyard, the place where one would expect to see them if the potassium theory had any validity.[31] Others saw the fireballs on the roof of a house, in the sky above Kyoto and in the places described in the above quotations. Only one person mentioned that the potassium explanation for fireballs is unlikely to hold nowadays because cremation rather than burial is the legally prescribed norm.

Originally I was sceptical about these reports of seeing fireballs because most of them occurred during childhood, but I am now much less inclined to rationalize away such accounts. I presume that the woman who saw one as an adult and was with others who also witnessed the same phenomenon must have seen *something*, even if we might argue about how to interpret the observation. Her account is very similar to one reported from West Africa by an anthropologist whom most people would regard as a 'credible witness' and whose ethnography is now regarded as 'one of the most valuable of the works on the Tiv'.[32] Like my Japanese informant, this female anthropologist was probably in her twenties and was with others who also witnessed the phenomenon:

> 'At tree top level down by the market I saw a ball of light moving slowly and steadily through the air. There was a gasp and a sighing from the people about me. It went out, not falling or dimming, just suddenly extinguished...Another ball of light followed. We stared at it in silence. It too went out, all at once, absolutely.'

She further comments that 'no human being could have caused those lights' and that other European observers in that part of Africa had reported such phenomena but had dismissed them with that 'comfortable tag' of 'electrical phenomenon'.[33]

Similar kinds of accounts have been reported by other people too. For example:

'I was conducting investigations...near the Togoland border

and had to stay at a Rest House near the sea. Going early to bed I was awakened by the cries of birds, the barking of dogs, *etc.* and was amazed to see a large bright light ascend from the sea and sway within my vision, and after some time it moved straight over the Rest House, and by getting out of bed and looking upwards from the window I could see it immediately overhead. A similar occurrence was repeated the following night. Exactly one month later I was 180 miles away from these recorded events, and at my house in Accra. I was awakened by a shout from my servant that there was a 'big moon' over the house. Again it was repeated and left me mystified...'[34]

'In northern Nigeria during the 'Gindiri Revival' of 1972 a pastor was knocked up to go to a church some distance away where the congregation had gathered after midnight, unbidden, to hear the word of the Lord. As he walked through the African bush that night he was guided by a globe of light, waist-high, going before him.'[35]

This second example is cited by Gardner as a modern parallel to the globe of fire which was once seen over the head of St. Martin of Tours, a fourth century Christian who became renowned for his healing ministry. The circumstances in which these Christian experiences occurred would seem to indicate that what was perceived as a globe of light or of fire might have been an angel. In Exodus 3:2 we read that 'the angel of the Lord appeared to him in flames of fire from within a bush'.[36]

However, interpretations of these phenomena need to bear in mind St. Paul's warning that 'Satan himself masquerades as an angel of light' (2 Corinthians 11:14). It is possible that some reports of fireballs might have been re-interpreted as UFOs.[37] In this context it may be relevant to cite the experience of a Russian Christian who told me how God showed her in a dream that she should have nothing to do with trying to contact UFOs; shortly afterwards she read an article by an Orthodox priest showing how UFOs were from the devil.[38] In a survey of religious experiences among nurses in Leeds, which I conducted in 1986, the only nurse who mentioned seeing a UFO was one who gave talks on astrology and had been described as 'spiritually sensitive' by a clairvoyant.

In Britain, reports of UFOs and other unexplained lights are commonly associated with the sites of megalithic stone circles such as Stonehenge and other places associated with occult and witch-craft activity such as Pendle hill in Lancashire; often the timing also coincides with occult or 'New Age' festivals.[39] Frequently these sites are found in mountainous areas (reminiscent of the 'high places' at which ancient Canaanite deities were worshipped). Several observers have noted how the lights seem to possess consciousness or intelligence, sometimes following people around.[40] In association with the lights are sometimes seen other spiritual beings, the descriptions of which seem like demons.[41] Further evidence that these kinds of phenomena may often be demonic comes from George Otis, who reports that in Nepal 'mysterious lights perched atop high mountain peaks have come hurtling down' towards the residences of Christian workers 'only to be driven off by urgent rebukes in the name of Christ'.[42]

It appears therefore that often these kinds of lights are indicative of demonic activity, and that they seem to be associated in particular with occultic rites in mountainous areas. In this context it is pertinent to note that many Japanese mountains have been regarded as gods, to which offerings and worship have been offered, or on which ascetics and mediums have sought communion with the *kami*.[43] For example, Mount Fuji 'is devoted to the worship of Kono-hana-sakuyahime-no-mikoto, consort of Ninigi-no-mikoto, great grandfather of the first emperor. On the edge of the crater is a small shrine, while at several places around the base of the mountain are large shrines dedicated to this same kami'.[44]

Therefore I am now inclined not to dismiss accounts of fireballs, but to see them as pointers to a spiritual reality which can have both angelic and demonic dimensions. The context of some appearances might indicate whether they are more likely to be angelic or demonic, although in other cases one might have to withhold judgement. However, one can at least say that those who already have a personal relationship with God can receive his deliverance from the effects of possible demonic influences and can enter into a new life in which God's angels are fighting on their side.

Dimensions of Shinto

'In its general aspects Shinto is more than a religious faith. It is an amalgam of attitudes, ideas, and ways of doing things that through two millenniums and more have become an integral part of the *way* of the Japanese people.'[45]

'Although called by a single term, Shinto is scarcely one orderly system of beliefs; it is, rather, a conglomerate of primitive beliefs and practices surrounding spirits, souls, ghosts, and the like.'[46]

At one level, Shinto might be described as a form of 'animism', in so far as Shinto divinities are believed to be present in many natural objects such as trees, rocks or mountains. However, there are many other dimensions to Shinto. A common classification is to demarcate three main types of Shinto, namely shrine Shinto, sect Shinto and folk Shinto. Shrine Shinto is the most obvious form, as it encompasses public festivals and other rituals associated with shrines. 'Sect Shinto' refers to thirteen different religious groups which the government in the Meiji era (1868-1912) did not wish to incorporate into the officially favoured 'State Shinto'—the form of Shinto which continued to be promoted by the government until the end of the second world war. Nowadays 'sect Shinto' groups like Tenrikyō or Konkōkyō are often regarded as belonging to the 'new religions', or else as being nineteenth-century precursors of them. The category 'sect Shinto' was to some extent created artificially by the Meiji government's policies of promoting a particular brand of Shinto: the same applies to 'folk Shinto' as a 'catchall' term for various popular customs which have a loose connection with shrine Shinto.[47]

The Shinto of the Imperial House is either regarded as a fourth type or else as a sub-category of 'State Shinto'. The most famous aspect of Imperial Shinto was the Emperor cult, which in its most fully-developed form lasted until 1946, when the Shōwa Emperor (known during his life as Emperor Hirohito) officially renounced any claim to divinity. In 1989 there was considerable controversy over his Shinto funeral rites because of perceived associations with the former Imperial cult. In 1990 there were also controversies over the enthronement ceremonies for his son Akihito.[48] At that time 'the National Christian Council in Japan maintained for a full year a hotline to serve pastors and lay persons concerned with this issue'.[49] Christians and others regarded governmental participation in the rite as violating the constitutional separation of religion and the state.[50] A leaflet produced by a mission working in Japan explains the reasons for their concern:

> 'The most important ceremony on 22nd November will be the *daijōsai* (Great Food Offering Ritual). In this Shinto ritual, the new emperor communes at dead of night with gods of heaven and earth, and lies down with the spirit of the sun goddess (Amaterasu Ōmikami). **In this ritual, the sun goddess (maker of the Japanese islands and people) imparts the status of divinity to the new emperor.'**[51]

Reports in leading Japanese newspapers and by certain scholars agreed that the rite was one in which the Emperor 'takes on' or 'acquires' a 'divine character' by receiving the spirit of the sun goddess.[52] What is not so clear is how this actually takes place. Essentially the *daijōsai* is a first fruits ceremony in place of the usual first fruits festival (*niiname matsuri*) held in other years, but at the *daijōsai* communion meal the Emperor 'becomes the repository of the rice-*kami*'.[53] However, the presence of the *shinza* ('god-seat') which resembles a bed, having a well-defined pillow and coverlet, has led to speculations about whether or not the ceremony at one time contained a rite of sexual intercourse between the goddess and the Emperor. Nowadays the Emperor does not even touch the *shinza*, let alone lie on it.[54] Even if its original function has been forgotten during the centuries in which the ritual has been perpetuated, the *daijōsai* nevertheless continues to represent some kind of symbolic communion and re-affirmation of the special relationship between the Emperor and the Sun Goddess.

The spiritual significance of the *daijōsai* is highlighted by George Otis, who cites it as an example of the more general principle that 'evil spirits will generally remain entrenched in an area...until their original invitation is revoked—an action that, unfortunately, is rarely taken...People are almost universally reluctant to renounce events and systems that they perceive to be legitimate— if unflattering—elements of their own heritage...By repackaging ancient rites of spirit welcome and appeasement as popular, and seemingly more benign, festivals and pilgrimages, the tenant rights of demonic powers are thereby reaffirmed by successive generations'.[55]

Despite the continuation of these traditional rites, however, popular interest in the Emperor has apparently waned since the second world war: many of the expressions of sentiment for the Shōwa Emperor around the time of his death were generated by a sense of obligation that one should follow the example of political and industrial leaders.[56] Crump reports that most Japanese were much more interested in the fall of Margaret Thatcher or *sumō* wrestling in Fukuoka than they were in the *daijōsai*.[57] For most ordinary Japanese people at an everyday level, Shinto is concerned with rituals connected with birth, marriage and certain other occasions. Apart from these life-cycle rituals, Shinto affects many people just once or twice a year. One of these occasions is that of the local shrine festival, often in the summer, which generally affects only those living in the immediate vicinity. The other occasion is at New Year, when most people visit a Shinto shrine.

New Year shrine visits (*Hatsumōde*)

The connection between Shinto and concepts of purity and pollution can be seen quite clearly at New Year. In the last week or two of December, all householders have a thorough clean-up of their homes, including scrubbing the entranceway (*genkan*) and garden path, the cleaning of fly-screens, and clearing out some unwanted items from the home. There is also a feeling that outstanding debts should, if possible, be paid off before the New Year.[58]

Spiritual renewal or cleanliness is said to come from the chiming of the Buddhist temple bells 108 times between midnight and about 1.30am (or later) on New Year's Day. This is said to symbolize the removal of the 108 sins recognized by Buddhism. Quite a number of people—I estimated it to be about 10% of those living around us—attend the temples at this time. There they pray for a safe and healthy year and ask for their hearts or spirits to be 'washed' or 'renewed'. Those who do not attend the temples themselves often watch the events on television instead.

Many more people go on New Year's morning to Shinto shrines. In 1981, 78% of my questionnaire sample had done so.[59] Both Buddhist temples and Shinto shrines advertise on posters at local stations and elsewhere, encouraging people to come to 'wash the heart (or soul)' (*kokoro o arau*).[60]

However, this symbolism of washing is applicable only to those who have not been ritually polluted. Such pollution comes especially from the death of a close relative during the previous year. In urban areas Shinto priests in fact have no idea whether or not most of the visitors at New Year have recently experienced the death of a close relative and they therefore allow anyone to visit their shrines. Nevertheless, four of the hundred ordinary people whom I interviewed (not counting priests, Yoshioka-san or others interviewed for special purposes) had abstained from New Year shrine visits on account of ritual pollution. These four were all men, three of whom had experienced the death of a parent or grandparent, while the fourth considered himself polluted by having participated in the memorial rite (*hōji*) for the thirty-third anniversary of his mother's death.

To some extent these men's non-participation in *hatsumōde* (New Year shrine visitation) was on account of either respect for, or fear of, the attitudes of other people. One of them, whose father had died, said he would not normally pay much attention to the ideas of ritual pollution 'but others round here [in the *Nissen* company housing] would think it odd if I went to a shrine, so for the sake of appearances it's better not to go.' However, the taboo was in fact broken by the unmarried sister of a young man who abstained because their grandfather had died. This sister works at a department store in Osaka and after work accompanied a group of other salesgirls on a midnight visit to the Yoshida shrine in Kyoto. The family later joked about her breach of the taboo, saying that if she received any divine punishment (*bachi*) as a result, then it would also affect her companions in what they called a 'domino effect'.[61]

Related to these ideas is the prohibition on sending New Year's cards if there has been a death in one's family or among one's close relatives during the previous year. Families which have been so affected instead send out a card with a black or grey border explaining that they are unable to send New Year's cards to those to whom these would normally be sent. These apology cards are delivered in the normal post, and are therefore kept separate from the New Year cards which are collected together by the post office and delivered all together in a bundle on New Year's Day.

Most people have no antipathy towards *hatsumōde* even if they might not always bother to observe it themselves. Some prefer to have a 'sleeping New Year' when they rest at home, but the same people might visit a shrine in other years. As New Year is the only time when all department stores and shops are shut, Shinto shrines in scenic places are obvious choices for family outings. Those who definitely avoid the practice tend to belong to a more exclusive religious group—particularly Christians and Sōka Gakkai adherents, who go to their own meetings instead.[62]

I asked fifty-five people who visited a shrine at New Year about their motives and attitudes towards the practice. Some mentioned more than one motivation, but Table 3.1 classifies their answers according to their first (and presumably principal) replies:

Table 3.1   Attitudes towards New Year shrine visits

		Number of cases
(a)	To pray for safety or happiness in the coming year:	14
(b)	To pray for the safety of a child:	1
(c)	A 'custom because everyone else does it':	13
(d)	'To celebrate the New Year' or 'To taste the New Year atmosphere':	6
(e)	'To make a distinction (*kejime*) between the years':	8
(f)	'To wash one's soul':	3
(g)	'Something bad might happen if I don't go':	3
(h)	Other reasons:	7

Some of the miscellaneous attitudes grouped together here as 'others' include references to recreation or the use of leisure time. For example, one woman said there was nothing else to do when all the shops and other places are shut at New Year, so 'I'd go crazy if I stayed at home!'.

An intention to pray is implicit in the replies of the three people in category (g) above, who go in order to be 'on the safe side'. They fear possible misfortune should they not go. Counting them in with those in categories (a) and (b), it can be seen that only eighteen out of fifty-five people mentioned a specific intention to pray. One of these is a man who goes to pray for his daughter's safety rather than his own, 'because', he says, 'it's boring for me'.

Another eleven people—in categories (e) and (f) above—refer to concepts associated with purity and pollution. The idea of making a 'distinction' (*kejime*) or marking a 'stage' (*kugiri*) is closely tied in with concepts behind those of purity and pollution—namely, that things should be kept in their proper places, with well-defined boundaries: what transgresses the boundaries is 'out of place' and in this sense is equivalent to 'dirt'. This will be discussed further in chapter six.[63]

The remaining individuals tended to view the shrine visits primarily in terms of leisure and recreation. This is an aspect of Shinto which can also be seen in other events, such as Setsubun and the annual shrine festivals.[64]

Setsubun

In farming villages throughout Japan the beginning of a new agricultural cycle was marked at the end of winter by the celebration of Setsubun. This was immediately followed by the beginning of Spring, when, during the *Hatsu-uma* rites, the 'god of the mountain' descended to become again the 'god of the rice field'. With the relative decline in the importance of agriculture in urban Japan, the significance of Setsubun seems to have decreased too. All those I interviewed who observe Setsubun in a more 'serious' manner, by attending Shinto shrines, were from rural backgrounds.[65]

One of these is the Ikeda family. Mr. Ikeda is a professional bicycle racer. Each year at Setsubun the family take his bicycle with them to Hiyoshi Taisha, a famous shrine on Mount Hiei to the north-east of Kyoto, where the bicycle is ritually 'purified' by a *harai* ceremony. This costs them ¥5,000. They regard Setsubun as 'more important than New Year' for Shinto shrine visits. It is at Setsubun that the Ikedas buy their safety charms for the coming year, one of which Mr. Ikeda always wears round his neck when competing in races. (Most other families buy their charms at New Year.)

Mrs. Yoshida is another lady who visits Shinto shrines at Setsubun. She tries to catch one of the rice-cakes (*mochi*) which the priests throw at that time to the crowd. So far she has been unsuccessful, but she says it would bring her considerable luck if she were to catch one. Another lady who visits a shrine at Setsubun does so in order to buy beans, which she then offers at her household god-shelf (*kamidana*) during the day. In the evening her family use them in the customary Setsubun ritual (described below) which is performed by virtually all the families interviewed, including also Christian and Sōka Gakkai families. They regard it as just a 'game' or merely a 'custom' which they observe because it is 'fun'. Hardly anyone (apart from the few who visit a Shinto shrine) see Setsubun as in any sense 'religious'.

The details of this custom vary a little from family to family but essentially it involves the throwing of beans and shouting 'Out with the devil and in with good fortune!' (*'Oni wa soto, fuku wa uchi'*).[66] In some households, the family members throw the beans separately, in their own rooms—the wife in her kitchen, the husband in his study, the children in their bedrooms and all together in the living room. Other families all together throw the beans out of the windows into the garden (for 'out with the devil') and might also throw some beans into the inner parts of the house (for 'in with good fortune'). Among families with younger children one family member might put on a devil mask made at kindergarten or primary school and try to dodge the beans thrown at him or her by the other family members. Often it is the eldest son who does this, but sometimes it is the father or a member born in a year which is the same as the current one by the animals of the Chinese calendar.

Afterwards, in all households, all the family members eat the number of beans corresponding to his or her age that year—although some older people admit that they no longer eat exactly the number for their age. This has another similarity to New Year, in so far as traditionally people used to reckon their ages by the number of New Years through which they had passed: everyone used to add an extra year to their ages at New Year. Another similarity involves the driving out of evil. This is because shortly after New Year men dressed in demonic-looking lion masks, accompanied by a musician, visit shops and houses in many older residential areas in order to perform a ritual 'exorcism' by dancing in front of the building to 'drive out demons'. The amount of time they spend at each place depends on the amount of money they are given by each householder or shopkeeper. On a ritual level, it nevertheless has the same overt purpose as the Setsubun rites. In this way, there are close parallels between the elements of purification and exorcism at both New Year and Setsubun.

Shinto *matsuri* ('festivals')

Many Shinto shrines have an annual festival (*matsuri*) which involves perhaps thirty or forty men carrying a portable shrine (*mikoshi*) around the borders of the 'parish'. Within the *mikoshi* are carried emblems of the deity (*go-shintai*, the 'body of the god'). That some people do regard the emblems as incarnating the deity is shown by the behaviour of two men standing near to me at a *matsuri*. As the *mikoshi* passed them, they bowed towards it, the older man also removing his hat.

The small shrine almost opposite the main gate of the *Nissen* factory does not have a permanent priest of its own, but is looked after by a priest from a larger shrine a few miles away. Nevertheless, this little shrine holds its own *matsuri* which includes processions by three *mikoshi*. One of these is considerably larger than the other two and is carried by a team of about twenty men. Almost all of them are students who are paid for their work and are provided with refreshments along the way. Before starting out from the shrine they had drunk at least one crate of beer between them and were showing signs of intoxication; several of them also finished off the remaining bottles when they returned to the shrine afterwards.

This larger *mikoshi* was carried around the main shopping streets of the local district and ended up at the main gate of the *Nissen* factory. After bringing the *mikoshi* inside the factory precincts, the young men put it down and went inside one of the company's reception halls for refreshments. I was later told that the company's bill for refreshments had come to between ¥30,000 and

¥40,000. They had also contributed ¥5,000 per person towards the wages of those who had carried the *mikoshi* and had provided a free lunch at the factory for the students. After lunch they helped with carrying the two smaller *mikoshi* on different routes around the perimeter of the factory. One of these *mikoshi* is carried by middle and high school students, helped by the university students, with younger children pulling it on ropes attached to the front. A much smaller *mikoshi* is placed on a wheeled platform and pulled along by children, with a little assistance from one or two adults. Each child is given a bag of sweets and biscuits as a reward. At intervals along the way, the whole procession stops for drinks of fruit juice given out by representatives of the local neighbourhood council, who had set up special booths for this purpose.

The festival goes as far as the older houses of 'Sakurano', the estate of company housing behind the factory, but not as far as the newer, owner-occupied estate which I call 'Aoyama' (located just beyond Sakurano). Only five out of seventy residents of these areas questioned about their attendance at this *matsuri* had ever been to it or seen it. Four of these lived in Sakurano, of whom three had seen it only once and the fourth had watched it about twenty times over a period of thirty years. The only Aoyama resident to have watched it was a man who had been brought up in the older parts of this city, but had only seen it once, ten years previously.

By contrast, twenty-three people had been to watch the more spectacular *matsuri* held in the city centre, and two others had watched it on television rather than going to see it themselves. This *matsuri* consists of thirteen heavy 'floats' on wheels which are dragged through the narrow streets of the city centre. Some of those on the floats occasionally throw out *chimaki* charms and sweets into the crowd, who on the whole see the event as largely a form of entertainment rather than religion.

The procession is preceded by a Shinto rite at 8:30am to pray for the safety of all the participants and for the gods to choose the order in which the floats should proceed; this is decided by drawing lots. Then the floats are led on their way by the priest of the shrine which organises this *matsuri*. He told me that in the first half of the festival he feels in a 'serious mood' because he is offering himself to the deity, but on the way back in the afternoon the rhythm of the music is much faster and he enjoys himself as he sweeps along in his colourful robes at the head of the procession. During the lunchtime break at 1:00pm the participants go home to change out of their formal clothes (with family crests on) into long flowing clothes in which to enjoy themselves. They also take the opportunity to drink some *sake*, which helps to put them in a festive mood.

This *matsuri* resembles the famous Gion *matsuri* in Kyoto in having tall 'floats' with musicians seated on top of them. The beat of the music is also like that of the Gion *matsuri*.[67] However, I cannot remember large drums being played at the Gion *matsuri* but these were part of the repertoire of the musicians in this city which I'm calling 'Ueno'. At the 'Ueno *matsuri*', university students play the large drums, those aged between ten and sixteen play the hand drums and younger children ring bells. Flutes and pipes are played by those skilled in wind instruments, and all the musicians have regular practices together, in neighbourhood groups, during the month before the festival.

Christian parallels?

There are many similarities between the carrying of a *mikoshi* and the Old Testament practice of carrying the Ark of the Covenant. Even the festival atmosphere with musicians resembles that of the Old Testament. One could even see similarities between going around the 'parish' and marching around the walls of Jericho!

A similar custom has been revived by some Anglican churches, which at Rogation time have processions around the parish to 'beat the bounds', to declare that those within the parish are under the blessing of God and also to pray for them to come to faith in Christ. A more modern extension of these traditional practices is the notion of 'praise marches', popularised in Britain by Graham Kendrick. The idea is now spreading across Europe, and there are similar Christian practices in Africa and other parts of the world.

Some Christians see 'praise marches' merely as kinds of Christian witness, but others have begun to view them as one form of attack against the demonic powers in a particular locality. Related to this perception are theological understandings of the way in which localities can become demonized. Through human sin, the ground is cursed (Genesis 3:17), and cries out against murders committed upon it (Genesis 4:10). As sin in an area increases, the land itself can become 'an object of cursing' (Jeremiah 44:22) or 'defiled' so that it vomits out its inhabitants (Leviticus 18:25-28).[68] The angel sent in response to Daniel's prayer was detained by a spiritual power described as 'the king of Persia' (Daniel 10:13). Many Christians think that such territorial spirits are included in St. Paul's references to various kinds of demonic forces as 'rulers of this age', 'authorities', 'powers of this dark world' or 'spiritual forces of evil in the heavenly realms' (1 Corinthians 2:8; Ephesians 6:12; Colossians 2:15).

Some of those experienced in prayer for 'cleansing the land' say that in cases involving occult ritual defilement of a building or area it is often necessary to employ Christian rituals (including the use of consecrated oil) in order to re-consecrate the territory for God.[69] This is a dimension of spiritual warfare which may be particularly relevant in Japan.

The Christian consecration of land involves prayer and the rebuking of evil spirits. It seems to me that any effect which 'praise marches' might also have on territorial spirits is dependent upon the amount of prayer which has gone into the project. I am influenced in this by the account of an evangelist who told me of how he had helped with a mission organized by a church in London. When he was being shown around the streets by one of the church leaders, he sensed a difference in the 'spiritual atmosphere' between one group of streets and another. Later he commented on this, and was then told that the church had been using a map to pray in turn for individual streets. Those which they had already covered in prayer were those where the visiting evangelist felt a greater spiritual freedom, whereas he felt more oppression in those roads which had not yet been prayed over.

Some Christians have also experienced feelings of 'spiritual disquiet' in places which often turn out to have been associated with occult rituals. 'While some individuals elect to shrug off these negative feelings as subjective mood swings, more and more Christians are coming to the realization that what they are experiencing is related directly to the presence and influence of unseen territorial spirits'.[70] In Japan my wife and I have at times experienced these kinds of influences in the course of my research, and we had to 'learn the hard way' about the necessity of praying for the Lord's protection when entering shrines or temples.[71]

In Japan, which has been regarded as a 'difficult' country for Christian missionary work, there is a need to pay attention to the country's 'spiritual geography', the foci of demonic power at certain locations and the manner in which there may be interlinkages between them. The 'resistance' to the gospel is not merely cultural, but also spiritual. This is also a contributing reason why the Japanese appear to be more receptive to the gospel outside Japan than when they are in their own country. However, reports from many other parts of the world testify to the powerful effects of intercessory prayer in releasing geographical areas from the dominance of territorial spirits.[72] Therefore Christians in Japan, and those elsewhere who pray for Japan, need to 'avoid wasting valuable spiritual ammunition on inconsequential or phantom targets'.[73]

There is a need for increased prayer against the spiritual forces of darkness in each area. Moreover, relatively few Christian churches in Japan have begun to organize 'praise marches', or any other Christian substitutes for *matsuri*. On the whole Japanese 'praise marches' have been confined to larger cities like Tokyo or Osaka where there are more Christians to support them. One wonders what would happen if Christians in other Japanese cities, towns and villages were to go out on the streets in praise and worship. Is there a Japanese 'Graham Kendrick' who could compose relevant and vibrant Christian songs for such purposes? Are Christian churches willing to take seriously the possibility of praying against demonic forces which exercise influence over local neighbourhoods?

Both 'praise marches' and also 'prayer walks' need to go hand in hand. There is a need for persistent intercession, and also the need for proclamation of the Kingdom of God accompanied by praise and worship. Often this is made even more effective by the fact that churches from a number of different denominations join together for such events. It remains to be seen what could happen when Christians in Japan regularly join with other churches in united prayer and public proclamation.

CHAPTER

4

Unless the Lord builds the House...

MR. INOUE HAD an itch on his penis. It itched both internally and externally. He also had pain while urinating and during sexual intercourse. Although he had been to the hospital, they had been unable to find any medical cause of the itch. In the end, they had told him it was psychological.

When the symptoms persisted, however, the Inoue family asked the opinion of a Shinto priest. He told them that their house, which dated from the nineteenth century, had a storehouse on its diagonal boundary: this boundary was also its 'devil-door' (*kimon*). The *kimon* is the direction from which evil spirits are thought to be likely to enter a house. However, the Shinto priest said that cement and similar items should not be heaped up in the *kimon*. Neither should bicycles, dogs or various other items be kept there, otherwise misfortune would befall the family.

About three years previously the Inoue family had replaced the doors of this storehouse and this had involved the noise of carpentry and the hammering in of nails. According to the Shinto priest, this breach of taboo regarding the *kimon* had brought on Mr. Inoue's illness, although other aspects of the building's direction-lore were wrong too. He prescribed three courses of action which, he claimed, would together heal Mr. Inoue's illness.

Firstly, Inoue-san had to place offerings of salt and a dish of water every day at the *kimon*. Secondly, he and his wife had to make a journey on a particular auspicious date to a peninsular on the coast 120 kilometres away. This was in a direction which would nullify the inauspicious direction in which the house had been built. They were to remain at that peninsular for four hours before returning to their home town. This they did.

Thirdly, each month the Shinto priest comes to perform a ritual purification of the *kimon*. For this, the family have to prepare an offering consisting of seven different colours—such as red apples, yellow bananas, white radishes, and so on. Normally this ritual is on the fifteenth of each month, but if this is inconvenient, owing to the hours of business of Mr. Inoue's shop, the ritual can be performed instead on the nearest convenient date to the fifteenth. However, the fifteen-minute ritual must be performed between 1:30 pm and 1:45 pm: as these times are decided 'by the gods', no member of the family must be late. All arrive in good time, including Mr. Inoue's younger brother and his wife who help out at his shop and were present when the storehouse doors were replaced. So far, Mr. Inoue's illness has not yet been cured by this treatment.

The *kimon*

A respect for the *kimon* or 'devil door' is very widespread in Japanese tradition. Its location is determined by various rules of geomancy, but for houses built on a square or rectangular plot the 'rear' devil-door (*ura-kimon*) normally lies on the north-east and the 'front' one (*omote-kimon*) on the south-west of the building. For those built on a more triangular plot, the whole diagonal side might form the *kimon*.

In older parts of modern cities, it is not uncommon to see small shrines built on a *kimon*: I know of one house which displays a conspicuous notice asking passers by not to let their dogs foul the *kimon*. Such obvious signs of *kimon* observance are not so conspicuous in modern housing estates, but this does not mean that they do not pay some kind of attention to it. Instead, they might plant special bushes or shrubs in that direction in order to protect the *kimon*.

The most common plant used to protect the *kimon* is called the *nanten* tree. Nowadays *nanten* is usually written in the Japanese *hiragana* syllabic 'alphabet', but by a play on words the sound could also be rendered by the Chinese characters 難 ('nan') and 転 ('ten'), a combination with the meaning of 'disaster-turning'. (Such plays on words quite often form the basis for certain kinds of religious or 'superstitious' practices.)

Mr. Murata, for example, says that one must not let the *nanten* trees grow as tall as the eaves of the house. His attitude is influenced by his stepmother's experience of twenty years previously: 'She was a very healthy and strong woman but took a very long time to recover from a stomach operation. The local Shinto priest said this was because our *nanten* had grown up to the eaves and advised us to cut some of it down. We did so, and shortly afterwards my stepmother fully recovered. It might be a superstition... but I don't know.'

This experience also influenced Mr. Murata to be careful of another taboo which says that the entranceway (*genkan*) of a house should not face north. His chosen house plan did involve the *genkan* on that side, so he asked the architect and builders to construct the house at a slightly oblique angle, so that the *genkan* would not face due north.

In the Niigata area where Mr. Murata grew up, there was an idea that one should not plant fruit trees in the garden, but Mr. Murata disregarded this part of the local folk-lore. To some extent this may be because other variants of this idea actually say the opposite—that it is good to have fruit trees in the garden. This comes from a play on words, involving the homonyms *mi* (実) for 'fruit' and *mi* (身) as a reading for the word 'body'. To say 'the fruit hangs down' (*mi ga narisagaru*: 実がなりさがる) can also mean, written differently, that a person is unhappy (*mi ga narisagaru*: 身がなりさがる). Therefore it is said that one should not have fruit trees in one's garden. However, other local traditions come to the opposite conclusion. They say that 'to bear fruit' (*mi o musubu*: 実を結ぶ) has a good meaning and its homonym written with the character for 'body' (身) also has good implications regarding the union of a man with a woman.

Another family, the Sueharas, also had particular reasons for observing the tradition that one should not have a fruit tree inside the territory of one's home. Theirs is a three-generational family in which Mr. Suehara's parents live together with him and his wife and son. In 1973 Mr.Suehara's elder sister died while she was a student at a university in Kyoto. The family do not normally discuss the circumstances of her death, but it was apparently a suicide through her drinking some chemical fertilizer. Local gossip says that she had fallen in love with a sports instructor but her mother had disapproved of the match as she considered only 'arranged' marriage (*miai*) to be 'proper' or socially acceptable. Whether or not this was really what had provoked her daughter to drink the chemical fertilizer, it is now the case that the mother refuses to eat any kind of food which has been treated with chemical fertilizer. (Her daughter-in-law has to shop at specialist natural food shops.) Moreover, the mother also had a fig tree cut down in their garden shortly after her daughter's death. She was not available for interview about this. However, her son, who told me about this, said that her behaviour might have been related to the superstition against having fruit trees in the territory of one's home. The mother's action was shortly after her daughter's death and seemed to be some kind of reaction to it.

Those living in company housing (*shataku*), which consists mainly of apartment blocks, do not normally worry about *kimon* taboos. A concern about the *kimon* becomes more manifest when people buy their own homes. I asked a total of twenty-five home owners about their attitudes towards the *kimon* and obtained the following replies:

Table 4.1   Attitudes to the *kimon* among some home owners

Planted *nanten* trees	6 people
Planted *asebi* bushes	1 person
Placed salt in *kimon*	1 person
Keeps area clean	2 people
Avoided putting toilet there	1 person
Checked proposed plan of house with a carpenter or priest regarding *kimon* prohibitions	3 people
Concerned about *kimon* but it was too expensive to alter the plan of the house accordingly	1 person
No attention yet paid to *kimon*, but might look into it if any disaster befell the house	1 person
Deny any concern with the *kimon*	9 people

The list in table 4.1 is arranged according to the principal practices reported by each household, but some families observed more than one of these: often those who plant *nanten* trees, for example, also keep the area clean and avoid having the toilet there. One man who bought a pre-fabricated house asked for a few modifications in its design to be made in accordance with direction-lore. Instead of the steps leading to the main entrance going from the south-west corner of the plot (the *omote-kimon*), he had them ascending parallel to the road on the front side of the plot; the visitor then had to turn right in order to face the door. This man also had the garage put on the right of these steps, rather than on the left, in order to avoid the *kimon*. He also keeps *nanten* trees in his *ura-kimon* and had a protective *fuda* charm placed on the roof beams during a special Shinto 'roof-raising ceremony'.

The family who planted *asebi* trees did so because a peddler selling the plants told this woman that *asebi* was 'lucky' in the *kimon*. She had not heard of this tradition previously, but bought some *asebi*, planted it in the *kimon* and found that in her garden the plants soon withered in that location.

On the whole, greater emphasis is placed on protecting the corner as seen from the outside than on protecting the inside of the same corner. In Japanese there are different words for corners as seen from the outside versus the inside: these are *kado* and *sumi* respectively. The main internal rule for the *kimon* is that it should not be polluted by the toilet. One informant said the reason for this is that in traditional houses demons could enter the house through the bamboo water pipe. Some people nowadays simply say that the *kimon* should be kept 'clean', but others extend the prohibition on lavatories to anything involving water, including the bathroom and kitchen.[1]

Jichinsai and *mune-age shiki* rituals

The *kimon* is only one aspect of a variety of practices concerned with keeping a house safe. A more common observance is to have a Shinto *jichinsai* ritual performed in order to pacify the local deity when a new house is erected. It relates to the Shinto idea that spirits or 'gods' (*kami*) of some kind are to be found almost everywhere—in trees, rocks, mountains and so on. These spirits need to be placated if man disturbs their territory by erecting a building. The *jichinsai* is performed after the site has been cleared and prepared for construction but before the first breaking up of the ground.[2]

A week or so before the rite, four bamboo poles are erected at the corners of the site and paper 'streamers' in a Shinto style, attached to ropes, are strung between the poles. In the centre of the area a small mound of sand about one foot high is prepared, often with some *sakaki* leaves (from the Shinto sacred tree) around or next to it. Through consultation with a Shinto priest, a day is chosen which is both convenient and also auspicious by the traditional system of 'lucky' and 'unlucky' days. On that day, the priest arrives at the appointed time and chants prayers for the consolation or pacification of the local *kami*. Often these last for little more than five minutes or so. Offerings of *sake*, *sakaki* and sometimes other items are then presented by the priest, by representatives of the construction company and by the purchasers of the house. Each of them then places a spade in the mound of sand and moves it slightly in order to make an incision in the earth, as a ritual start for the construction process.[3]

Attitudes towards this rite among those I interviewed tended to be relatively pragmatic. Many said the ritual was included in the cost of the building rather than being an optional extra, so they had had the rite performed in order to have the full value for their money. Others said that the builders 'preferred' to have a *jichinsai*, so they complied in order not to offend the workmen. Some households who had bought ready-built new homes from a construction company did not know whether or not a *jichinsai* had been performed, but assumed that it had. I came across only two instances in which no *jichinsai* had been performed. In one of these, the man had decided to save the ¥5,000 *jichinsai* fee but had instead thrown a *mamori* safety charm into the sand which would be mixed with the cement. Another family had their house built at a discount by employing a firm where a relative worked: they decided not to have a *jichinsai* but instead they had a Shinto 'roof-raising ceremony' (*mune-age shiki*).

Several households had a *mune-age shiki* performed in addition to a *jichinsai*. In the course of constructing a standard house, a wooden frame is erected first, and it is followed by the roof before the walls and floors are made. Putting on the roof is a symbol of a house which is erected but half complete. Both the *jichinsai* and *mune-age shiki* are times for celebration and the drinking of *sake* by all concerned. They are also occasions for offering prayers for safety. Often a *fuda* talisman is attached to the main beam of the house, under the roof, while a Shinto priest is paid to recite further prayers for safety. Some interpret these rites as being for the safety of the workmen but the majority view them as prayers for the safety of the house and its future occupants. When asked how effective they think the rites have been, most people replied 'Don't know', or else said, 'They might have had some effect because the house has not yet been damaged by a fire or earthquake'. A few people expressed some scepticism, saying 'probably the rites have little or no effect'; nevertheless, they still had the rites performed as a 'custom' in order to please either the workmen or the informant's parents—who paid for the rites.

When a Japanese Christian has a house built, a pastor is often called in to perform a Christian equivalent to the *jichinsai* or *mune-age* rituals. Often psalm 127 is read, prayer is offered for the safety of the building site workers and for God's blessing on the house, and then a suitable hymn is sung. A Christian missionary reports that the non-Christian workers are usually glad that the ceremony was performed, are intrigued to hear a religious rite in which they understood the words, and are not at all concerned that the ceremony was a Christian one. As far as they are concerned, the ceremony indicates that the builder or owner of the house recognizes the element of danger and is concerned for their welfare. Afterwards, everyone drinks a little *sake* and each worker receives a monetary gift from the owner as a way of saying 'Please give of your best and try to complete the work on time'.[4]

Moving into a new home

Traditionally, the timing of one's move into a new home can also be important. For example, the Kaneda family wanted to move into their new home on an auspicious day, so they asked an expert in geomancy (whom they knew as a friend of Mr. Kaneda's mother) to check over the house. This lady said the position of the house was 'very bad', so the only time they could safely move in was at Setsubun, the traditional date for the end of winter or beginning of Spring. The Kanedas followed her advice.

Another family buying their home from a previous occupant asked a fortune-teller about an auspicious time for their move. According to this expert in 'life-fate divination' (*unseihandan*), who made use of the husband's date of birth in his calculations, the best month that summer for the move would be in May. June would be 'bad'. However, the previous occupants were unable to move out until June. Therefore the buyer handed over the money and acquired legal ownership of the house in May, even though they could not move in until June.

Some people say that one should not build or repair one's house or change its structure too much when one is in a *yakudoshi* year: these are ages in one's life when one is thought to be particularly susceptible to illness or misfortune. There are those who also say that in such years one should not change one's position at work and that one should take special care of one's body especially when in a different environment, such as on a business trip.[5]

New Year decorations and chimaki charms

During some Shinto festivals in which tall wheeled 'floats' or wagons are pulled through the streets, those on top of the 'floats' might throw out to the crowd of spectators lucky charms called *chimaki*. These are made of woven leaves, almost in the shape of a hand, which are hollow when thrown from the festival floats but at other times of the year might be sold commercially and contain a traditional sweet. Some say that any 'luck' from a *chimaki* comes only if one manages to catch it during a festival, not if one buys it. Nevertheless, others who have bought or been given one say that it gives them some feelings of 'security' and they still hang it up as a good luck charm outside their homes. The only exception which I encountered was a woman who supported the Communist party and at first appeared to have very little to do with religion. She seemed embarrassed when I asked if she had a *chimaki* and she then produced one from a high shelf where it had been out of sight.

Some informants consider that the special decorations put up above or beside the front door of a house at New Year and Setsubun are equivalent to safety charms. At New Year the decorations consist of straw tied in various shapes as tassels or 'horns', usually also with leaves and a satsuma orange. Sometimes there are Shinto paper streamers attached to them as well. Normally such decorations are placed over the front door. Often pine branches (*kadomatsu*) are tied to the doorpost or gate. There might also be a more formal decoration, consisting of a cluster of bamboo trunks and leaves, placed at the side of the entrance way.

By the traditional Japanese calendar, Setsubun marked the traditional end of winter and was therefore a kind of New Year too. Nowadays it usually falls between the 3rd and 5th of February, owing to the Japanese adoption of the Gregorian calendar in 1872. However, in the Kansai area (near Kyoto and Osaka), where I did my fieldwork, there still remains a custom whereby at Setsubun many households put the head or skeleton of a sardine either in the *genkan* (entrance-way) or next to the doorpost outside the house. This seems to be a parallel to, or perhaps a variant of, the custom of putting New Year decorations there.

I asked a small sample of twenty people what these symbols meant to them. Approximately one third gave answers in terms of 'custom'. Another third said 'Don't know', or had never thought about the matter. However, the remaining third, after a little reflection, gave answers which saw these emblems as similar to safety charms. They referred to the decorations as 'a kind of *mamori*' or 'a *yakuyoke*'—both terms for protective charms. Others described the decorations as 'something to keep the Devil out' and 'a symbol of the god'.

These people had all put up a New Year decoration in their homes but only a few of them had put up the Setsubun sardine. However, those who put up the sardine tended to be among those who saw the emblems as similar to *mamori* charms. These interpretations of the decorations are the ones which are most important at a 'practical' or 'folk' level, irrespective of whatever might have been the 'original' meanings of the emblems—something which now can never be proved decisively.[6]

Further evidence for a correlation between New Year decorations and safety charms comes from the fact that the decorations tend to be put up by those who already possess a Shinto god-shelf (*kamidana*) or a *mamori* safety charm. At New Year in 1982 I made a note of which houses had put up decorations in a modern estate of owner-occupied houses which I am calling by the fictitious name of 'Aoyama'. Table 4.2 shows that those households which put up New Year decorations and *chimaki* charms are far more likely to have a *kamidana* and/or a *mamori* too, as compared with those households where neither New Year decorations nor *chimaki* charms were put up.

Table 4.2 Correlation between New Year decorations, *kamidana* possession and ownership of *chimaki* or *mamori* charms

Households	With both New Year decorations and *chimaki*	With *chimaki* charm but no New Year decorations	With New Year decorations only	With neither *chimaki* charm nor New Year decorations
% with a *kamidana*	65.2%	42.8%	38.1%	15.6%
% with at least one spouse possessing a *mamori*	82.5%	71.4%	73.2%	55.9%
% with both spouses possessing a *mamori*	69.5%	42.8%	40.2%	28.6%
% with neither spouse possessing a *mamori*	4.3%	7.1%	13.4%	22.0%

Reading across the rows in Table 4.2, it can be seen that households already possessing a *kamidana* and at least one *mamori* charm are much more likely to put up *chimaki* charms or New Year decorations too. All of these are specifically associated with Shinto and are often concerned with safety in some form or other: at a *kamidana* the standard daily prayer is that one would 'pass each day safely'.

By contrast, there is no connection at all between owning a Buddhist ancestral altar (*butsudan*) and putting up *chimaki* charms or New Year decorations. The proportion of households with a *butsudan* who also subscribe to these other practices is virtually constant, as shown by Table 4.3:

Table 4.3 Lack of correlation between *butsudan* ownership and putting up New Year decorations or *chimaki* charms

Households	With both New Year decorations and *chimaki*	With *chimaki* charm but no New Year decorations	With New Year decorations only	With neither *chimaki* charm nor New Year decorations
% with a *butsudan*	30.4%	28.5%	33.0%	33.8%

In my whole sample of 211 households, only sixteen had no *kamidana*, *mamori*, *chimaki* or New Year decorations. Three of these sixteen families contained at least one member who is a Christian of some kind. Two of the remaining families belong to the Sōka Gakkai, a Buddhist 'new religion' which regards Shinto as a 'false religion'. Another two families are publicly known to support the Communist Party, which might indicate some atheistic values, but even among these there are interests in astrology or other kinds of 'supernatural' phenomena. Some of the other families who did not put up New Year decorations in 1982 might do so in other years—as indicated by the comment of one lady who said that she did not put up the decorations because she had no guests that year!

Christian implications

When I asked a group of men at the *Nissen* factory about the meaning of the sardine at Setsubun, most had no idea what it meant but one of them suggested it was 'a symbol of the god'. I then asked, 'Which god?', but none of them had any idea.

In Athens, St. Paul began his evangelistic message by referring to their altar to an unknown god (Acts chapter 17). This altar was apparently linked with the ministry of Epimenides, whose poetry Paul refers to as those of a *prophet* (Titus 1:12,13). Similarly, in many other cultures around the world there are already customs or traditional beliefs which can become 'springboards' for communicating the Christian gospel in terms which are relevant and easily understood by the people.[7]

These New Year decorations and Setsubun sardines might be analogous to the Athenian altars to an unknown god. This group of men at the *Nissen* factory seemed intrigued by the thoughts which I shared with them along these lines. My general approach, here somewhat elaborated, was as follows:

'Why is it that the skeleton of a sardine at Setsubun should be 'a symbol of a god'? Why do some people think it protects them? A skeleton is a *symbol of death*! Why should a symbol of *death* become that which protects those inside the house?

It is interesting that the ancient Jewish people had a very similar custom. They also had a symbol of death on their doors which protected them from evil. When God liberated them from slavery in Egypt, they had to kill an animal—a lamb—and put its blood on the top of their doorframes and on the sides of their doors. These are just the places where nowadays Japanese people place their New Year decorations! It is also on the doors that the Japanese place their own symbol of death at Setsubun, as a 'symbol of the god' or as something to protect them!

When the Jews placed their symbols of death—the blood—on their doors, it was the fourteenth of the first month (Exodus 12:2, 6-7). Traditionally, in farming villages throughout Japan, the most important New Year celebrations were focussed around the fourteenth of the first month. Nowadays we refer to it as *ko-shōgatsu*— 'little New Year'—but in traditional farming villages it was actually the main New Year festival. It was only after the Japanese adopted the Western, Gregorian calendar that these customs got shifted to the first of January and many Japanese began to forget these traditions of their ancestors.

In the same way, both the Japanese and the Jews eat special foods at this special time. For the Japanese, these foods are merely 'a custom', but for the Jews it is a special memorial of the time when God delivered them from slavery.

Setsubun, the end of winter, was also like another New Year festival for the Japanese. So the symbol of death put on doors at Setsubun is also like the symbol of death which the ancient Israelites put on their doors to protect them from death. God saw the blood on their doors and spared them when the firstborn of the Egyptians died.

As you know, the Japanese economy has traditionally been based on agriculture and fishing. So the New Year decorations and the Setsubun sardine are symbols of that which is important in the traditional economy. The ancestors of the ancient Israelites had been mainly pastoralists, herders of animals, and their animal sacrifices represented what was important in their economy too.[8]

Both for the Japanese and for the Jews, there is a special significance attached to the firstborn child and special heir. The Japanese know how important it is to give thanks for blessings received, and they specially give thanks for the first-fruits of their crops, which are offered to God. In the same way, the Jews offered to God their first-fruits, not only of their crops but also of their animals. Even their first-born children were to be dedicated to God, but these were not to be sacrificed. Instead, God provided a substitute so that the first-born sons would not be killed. This was the meaning of the Passover lamb: it died instead of the first-born of the people.

However, the people had to choose to put themselves under the protection of the lamb. They had to allow the substitute to die instead of them, so that they could be spared. This is why they had to put the blood of the lamb—a symbol of death—on their door-frames.

Later generations also had substitutes for their first-born sons in the priests who represented them before God (Numbers 3:40-51). However, God knew that these substitutes and sacrifices were not really sufficient, because all people are imperfect and our hearts are dirty in some way or other. We offer our first-fruits to God because they are special, the best of our labours, but we ourselves are still dirty while God is so pure and holy.

It was for this reason that God himself provided a very special sacrifice to be a substitute for us. Only Jesus Christ was without sin, pure and clean in God's sight. The Jewish leaders put him to death on the fourteenth day of their first month, just at the time when their Passover lambs were being sacrificed. Jesus became the true Passover lamb who died instead of us all. If we choose to put ourselves under his protection, he will become for us an everlasting protector from the evil one.

The customs of the Japanese people at New Year and Setsubun are merely signs which point us to our need for protection. They tell us that a symbol of death actually gives life and protection. But the Japanese do not know which God these symbols represent. The God of heaven and earth knows that the Japanese people recognize these truths, but that these sardine skeletons and other emblems are just *symbols* of a much deeper truth.[9] Now the Japanese people need to recognize their need for a permanent protector from the evil one who will protect them always, not just at certain times of the year, and indeed will be with them for ever.

Jesus is the special priest and the special substitute who was sacrificed on our behalf. All we have to do now is to put ourselves under his protection, that we might dwell in his house in security for ever.'

The sermonette given above interweaves traditional Japanese concepts with the parallel customs of the Jewish Passover. However, I do not wish to imply that the Japanese are descended from the Jews or are a remnant of the 'ten lost tribes'. The high priest of an important Shinto shrine (one called by the term *jingū*) recounted to me in some detail how certain place names in the north of Japan are supposedly derived from the names of some of the northern tribes of Israel.[10] There are certainly interesting parallels between the layout of Shinto shrines and the Hebrew tabernacle or temple.[11] For myself, I take the view that it is possible to build on these similarities without necessarily going as far as this Shinto priest, who claims that there was actual genealogical descent. Rather, it is sufficient to say that parallel customs in different parts of the world might, in at least some cases, point to parallel perceptions of spiritual realities. Moreover, what is preserved in Japan as a 'custom' might also be similar to the altars to the 'unknown god' in ancient Athens. They point beyond themselves to that which is greater, and ultimately find their fulfilment in Jesus Christ.

CHAPTER

5

A Time to be Born...

'AFTER MY FIRST child was a girl, my husband's family wanted so much for me to bear a boy. So when I became pregnant again, with my second child, my husband's relatives urged me to have a test to find out the sex of the baby. If I had a girl, they wanted me to have an abortion. However, I refused to do this, and I did bear another daughter despite the pressures which my in-laws were putting on me.'

Another mother said, 'My first two children—a girl and a boy—were born for the sake of my husband's family, to produce a male heir. We then stopped trying for any more children, but my unplanned third pregnancy presented me with an opportunity to bear this child for myself rather than for my husband and his parents.'

These quotations illustrate the importance attached in many families to the bearing of a male heir. The first quotation also illustrates the use of abortion as a possible means of family planning. Among married women as a whole probably one third have undergone at least one abortion.[1] If these mothers later develop other medical problems, they sometimes attribute them to the aborted foetus, but the cause is seen as 'spiritual' rather than 'physio-medical'.[2] *Mizuko kuyō*—memorial services for aborted children—have become increasingly popular.[3] Prayer plaques (*ema*) at some Shinto shrines sometimes carry apologies and ask for forgiveness from the aborted foetus.[4]

Protective charms during pregnancy

Most mothers, however, do want to have their babies and are very concerned that the child should develop properly and be kept safe in the womb. Pregnancies in Japan are said to last ten months, as calculated by the old lunar calendar; by the traditional Chinese calendar, not only the years but also the days are assigned animal names. It is on the Day of the Dog in the fifth lunar month of pregnancy that expectant mothers first put on a special waist-sash, called a *hara-obi* (literally, 'stomach-sash'). Those expecting for the first time usually have the sash tied on for them by a mother, mother-in-law or doctor. The Day of the Dog is chosen because it is thought that bitches have easy deliveries.

There are several different varieties of these sashes or cummerbunds. Traditional woollen ones are about fifteen feet long and are tied several times around the abdomen, whereas shorter and simpler modern corsets come with velcro attachments. The simpler types are becoming more popular because each expectant mother is expected to continue wearing a sash for the next five lunar months. Women whose later pregnancies coincide with the hot humid summers of central and southern Japan often alternate two or three of the simpler sashes on a daily basis in order to wash them. Nevertheless, the older variety is usually the one which is put on initially, on the Day of the Dog in the fifth month of pregnancy, even if the expectant mother later changes to another type. Older women told me how they had continued to wear the more traditional type of cummerbunds during the summer even though they were very uncomfortable.

People differ a little in which reasons they stress for wearing the sash, but their reasons fall into three basic categories:

1) to protect the child physically
2) to keep the womb warm
3) to keep the child small so that childbirth might be easier.[5]

I asked twenty-five women whether or not they had worn such a sash (*obi*), and all of them had done so.[6] Two of these were Christians. All except one had worn the *obi* for each pregnancy. The one exception was a very thin lady who wore it for her first child and 'only sometimes' for her second and third children, saying that she did not need it then. Her attitude seems to be largely based on the idea that the womb should be kept small to facilitate an easy childbirth and that her own muscles were sufficient for this task. The *obi* is not intended to 'keep the womb small' in order to disguise the fact of pregnancy: on the contrary, most women announce to their neighbours the fact of their child's conception as soon as the pregnancy is confirmed; shortly afterwards they begin to wear pregnancy dresses which tend to emphasize the bump through their plain styles rather than detracting from it by lines or patterns.

The religious aspect of this practice becomes more obvious when the *hara-obi* is bought from a Shinto shrine or, occasionally, from a Buddhist temple. Otherwise, a sash bought in an ordinary department store might be taken to a shrine for the shrine's seal to be stamped upon it or for a safety charm (*mamori*) to be attached to it. Sometimes a paper talisman (*fuda*) is sewn into the cloth of the *hara-obi*. All but one of those I asked about the wearing of a *hara-obi* had also observed one of these religious practices. The exception was a Christian lady who had conformed to the practice of putting on the *obi* on the Day of the Dog but had not taken it to a shrine for its seal or *mamori*.

When an expectant mother goes to a shrine she is often accompanied by her mother. Occasionally, a mother-in-law might accompany the young mother instead, but there are usually specific family circumstances why the mother-in-law goes instead of the woman's own mother. Sometimes, if the expectant mother's own mother lives a long way away, she might buy the *obi* on behalf of her daughter and send it to her by post. In such cases the *hara-obi* is usually bought from a shrine and tends to be of a more traditional design.

The *mamori* attached to a *hara-obi* is for a 'safe birth' (*anzan*). Although normally bought from a Shinto shrine, I came across four cases in which the *mamori* was bought from a local temple, where the whole ritual, including prayers for safe childbirth, cost ¥3,000. It is noteworthy that the temple's seal, stamped onto the *hara-obi*, is in the form of a dog. One woman also bought from this temple a *fuda* plaque for safe childbirth. On the 101st day after her baby was born, she returned to the temple and exchanged this *fuda* for a 'childrearing' (*kosodate*) *mamori*.[7] (It should be noted that this is just after the family gathering on the hundredth day after birth which marks the symbolic (if not actual) weaning of the baby.)

A less common practice associated with the *hara-obi* was reported by Mrs Ikeda, the wife of the professional bicycle racer. She went to Hiyoshi Taisha on Mount Hiei, where her name was inscribed on the *hara-obi* in brush calligraphy, a *mamori* charm was attached to it, and then both she and the *hara-obi* received a *harai* (ritual purification ceremony) from the priest. Later that same day, after returning home, the *hara-obi* was put on her by her mother-in-law.

Sometimes *anzan* (safe birth) *mamori* charms are bought on other occasions during pregnancy. For example, one couple said that they stopped to buy such a charm when they were driving in the countryside and happened to pass a shrine specializing in safe childbirth charms. Another lady visited many places in Kyoto where there were statues or shrines of the Bodhisattva Jizō, the 'tutelary deity'—one might say 'patron saint'—of children; at each of these places she prayed for a safe childbirth. Others make similar requests on the inscribed prayer plaques at Shinto shrines.

When asked whether or not they think these prayers have any 'efficacy' (*kikime*), many mothers reply that they have never really considered the question. They tend to give one or both of the following answers:

a) 'Yes, the prayers probably do have some effect, simply because the child was born safely and healthily.' A number of people qualify this by saying that they cannot tell whether the safe child-birth was a direct result of the safety charm or would have happened in any case.
b) 'For me, the important issue is not so much whether the charms have any direct, observable, physical effect on the safety of the child. Rather, what is important as far as I am concerned is the sense of 'peace of heart' (*anshin*) or 'sense of security' (*anshinkan*) which I feel the charm gives me.'

A third, subsidiary answer sometimes given as an afterthought to either of these two replies is that the *hara-obi* would have some kind of 'effect' by keeping the womb warm and perhaps helping to cushion it from any bumps. However, they are unable to say whether or not the safety charm itself has any effect on the situation.

Only one woman expressed a half-doubt about the effectiveness of the charm. At first she replied, 'Yes—it has an effect because the child was born safely', but then, as an afterthought, she mentioned how for her first child she had experienced considerable lower back pain and had a difficult birth. Nevertheless, the joy of having her child far outweighed the pain and it was not until years later, when I questioned her, that she in any way considered whether or not her experiences in labour reflected at all on the efficacy of her pre-birth rituals.

This post-childbirth rationalization that because the child is healthy the charms might have had 'some effect' needs to be seen also in the context of attitudes towards abortion. After a woman has already borne two or three children any unplanned later pregnancies are often terminated by abortion: this tends to reduce the numbers of children with congenital medical problems being born to women in the latter part of their child-bearing years.[8] Nowadays, the tendency by most families to limit their numbers of children to no more than three is rationalized by saying that there is not enough space for larger families in modern homes. The only families I know of with four or five children are either (in three cases) Christians who disapprove of abortion as a means of birth control or (in one case) a family whose third and fourth children were twins.

Hatsu-miyamairi

The *hatsu-miyamairi* is the first visit to a Shinto shrine by a newborn infant and the child's mother. Normally it is called *o-miyamairi* (the honorific form of the term *miyamairi*), but because *miyamairi* can also refer to shrine visits in general I am here using the more technical term *hatsu-miyamairi*. Essentially the *hatsu-miyamairi* is a kind of dedication of the infant to the deity. It normally lasts for about ten to fifteen minutes, during which the family stand together in front of the priest at a shrine. The mother, who normally wears a kimono for the occasion, holds the infant in her arms while the priest recites a few Shinto prayers and then performs a ritual purification (*harai*) over the child, by three formal waves of the 'sacred staff'. After this the priest inscribes in black charcoal (because it is easily washable) the character for 'big' (大) on the forehead between the eyes of male children and the character for 'small' (小) in the same place on female children. There may also be a colour difference between the sexes, whereby the boys' marks are often done in black and the girls' in red.

Apart from the obvious connotations of males being normally larger than females, most sources which I have consulted are unable to supply any explanation for this symbolism. Normally people say that it is a 'custom' or, in a few cases, that it is 'a sign that the gods see the child's face and look after the child from then on'.[9] Nevertheless, the overall purpose of the rite is clear: the child is presented to the deity and put under the god's special protection.

In rural areas the god of the village shrine is normally the special guardian household deity (*ujigami*) of each family, so newborn babies are dedicated to that god (*kami*).[10] One woman said that after her baby was born her father went out in the middle of the night to the local village shrine in order to tell the *ujigami* about the birth of his grandchild. Usually the shrine chosen for the *hatsumiyamairi*, especially of one's firstborn child, is the *ujigami* shrine of one or other parent. The main reason for this is that an expectant mother usually returns to her own parents about six weeks before the expected date of delivery and stays there for another six weeks or so afterwards. To a large extent this custom is linked with the widespread attitude that if the mother in a household becomes ill there is nobody who can take care of her properly except her own mother.[11] For the birth of her first child an expectant mother might make a journey of perhaps a few hundred miles to her parents' home, and repeat such a journey for the births of subsequent children. Otherwise her mother or parents come to stay with their daughter for a while.[12] These patterns are summarized in Table 5.1:

Table 5.1 Overall percentages of chosen places for giving birth

	First child	Second child	Third child
Mother's natal home (or nearby hospital)	55.6%	46.7%	24.8%
Father's natal home (or nearby hospital)	6.3%	6.8%	9.2%
Couple's own home (or nearby hospital)	31.6%	40.5%	57.8%
Other locations	6.5%	5.9%	8.3%

In general, there is a trend whereby first children are born at the home of their mother's parents whereas subsequent children tend to be born at the couple's own home. At such times the husband or, more often, the wife's mother helps the wife to look after their older child or children, who by then might be in kindergarten or school and are less able to go with their mother for a prolonged stay at their grandparents' home. Sometimes there is a feeling that a couple should try to 'balance' the claims of both in-laws by going to the husband's parents for the birth of a second or third child; in other cases, the couple are already living with the husband's parents or else go there because the wife's parents are ill or dead.

How these practices affect *miyamairi* rites is shown by Table 5.2, which compares *miyamairi* observances with the birthplace of each child.

Table 5.2 Overall percentages of children receiving *miyamairi* rites[13]

	First child	Second child	Third child
Mother's natal home (or nearby hospital)	82.5%	79.2%	81.5%
Father's natal home (or nearby hospital)	86.1%	93.5%	100.0%
Couple's own home (or nearby hospital)	81.0%	64.7%	61.9%
Other locations	75.7%	51.8%	44.4%

In each column of table 5.2, the percentages in the two upper rows are greater than those in the two lower rows. This indicates that the presence of the grandparents, especially when the baby is born at the grandparents' home, has an influence upon whether or not a *miyamairi* is performed for the child. This substantial grand-parental influence corresponds to the reports by many of those interviewed who said that they performed the rite because their parents wanted it done. Often they called the rite a 'custom' which the grandparents felt strongly ought to be continued for their grandchildren, partly because it is the 'proper' and socially expected thing to do. It also happens to be a rite which the proud grandparents can attend near their home and which conveniently takes place when their newborn grandchild is with them.

This has a number of pastoral implications for Christian mission-aries, who need to be aware of these pressures. The problem is illustrated by the experience of a Japanese woman who became a Christian while she was studying in England. After her return to Japan, she later experienced some pressure from her parents, who wanted her to marry. She told them she would only marry a Christian, so her fiancé made some profession of faith and they were married at a YMCA. They were living in Kyushu when eventually their first child was born, at a hospital near their home, and they were at first able to avoid having a *miyamairi* performed for him. However, when they later took their son to visit his grandparents, in Tokyo and in the Mount Fuji area, they felt unable to resist their parents' demands that they should fulfill this 'Japanese custom'. As a result, the child had two *miyamairi* cere-monies, once for each set of grandparents; *mamori* charms for the infant's general protection were bought at the same time.

By contrast, it can be seen from table 5.2 that there is a marked decline in the percentages of second and third children who receive *miyamairi* when they are born at their own home or elsewhere (such as at a nursing home) away from the direct influence of grandparents. On the other hand, those families whose second or third children are born at or near the father's natal home—perhaps to compensate for the first one being born near the mother's parents—show an increase in the percentages receiving *miyamairi*. For the first and second children, the pressures to conform to 'custom' seem about the same irrespective of the sex of the baby. However, for a third child there is much more pressure for a boy to receive *miyamairi* than for a girl. This is particularly the case if he is the first male born after two sisters and therefore regarded as the principal heir. These findings are shown by table 5.3:

Table 5.3 Percentages of children receiving *miyamairi* compared with the sex and birth order of the child

	First child	Second child	Third child
Male children			
Percentage in sample	51.6%	49.4%	51.6%
Percentage receiving *miyamairi*	51.0%	51.8%	60.6%
Female children			
Percentage in sample	48.4%	50.6%	48.4%
Percentage receiving *miyamairi*	49.0%	48.2%	39.4%

In urban areas, children born at or near their own parents' home are often taken to the nearest convenient shrine, rather than to a specific *ujigami* shrine. Most parents prefer to take their children to larger, prestigious shrines which act rather like 'cathedrals' in attracting visitors from a much wider area, who often say they go as 'tourists'. These shrines often charge more for their *hatsu-miyamairi*, so the choice of shrine may rest on a balance between convenience and prestige.

Generally, the *hatsu-miyamairi* takes place about a month after the child is born. Traditionally it was governed by concepts of purity and pollution, because a newborn infant and post-partum mother are both regarded as 'polluted by blood' and unable to attend a Shinto shrine until a certain time has elapsed.[14] Local rules about the timing differ a little from place to place, but those most commonly mentioned by my informants were the 32nd day after birth for a boy and the 33rd day for a girl. In parts of Kyushu the boy's date is the 30th or 31st day after birth, but the girl's date is consistently the 33rd.[15] Perhaps the choice of the 33rd day after birth for a girl is linked with the common idea that women encounter a critical stage in their lives at the age of thirty-three, as will be detailed in chapter seven. This in turn might be related to plays on words such as 'three-three' (*san-san*), which means either 'birth after birth' or else, when pronounced as '*sanzan*', can mean 'misery'.[16] However, such associations do not explain the different dating for a boy. Probably the difference is related to the idea that pollution lasts longer for a girl, which in turn might be connected with the more frequent pollution by blood which occurs throughout the female life cycle because of menstruation and childbirth.

Comments on Christian parallels

These concepts are very similar to those of the Old Testament. In Leviticus chapter twelve there are regulations dealing with purification after childbirth, which Mary complied with after the birth of Jesus (Luke 2:21-24). These regulations also involve a much longer period of ritual uncleanness after a daughter is born than after a son is born. For both sexes, the Mosaic law stipulates longer periods of ritual uncleanness than is the case in Japan. Both in ancient Israel and in modern Japan, the woman has to wait until the days of her purification are over before she is allowed into a sacred place.

Some branches of the Christian church in Europe, including the Church of England, used to hold special services for 'the churching of women' after childbirth, but such services have been abandoned by many modern churches. Many modern Western Christians are inclined to be sceptical of such practices, regarding them as outdated. Western missionaries to Japan are probably unaware that they even hold such assumptions, but they may nevertheless, even unconsciously, carry over such attitudes in a Japanese cultural context. Should they be willing to re-think their own assumptions and ask whether or not there is a place for respecting these kinds of attitudes among the Japanese?

In modern Japan, 'women also abstain from bathing and washing their hair during menstruation: the resumption of bathing after menstruation then marks the return to the 'clean and normal' state, just as in the case of sickness. Even today, there are beauticians who make sure their customers are not menstruating before they will agree to wash their hair.'[17] Although some of these ideas are declining, the overall cultural emphasis on purity and pollution remains strong, as will be detailed in the following chapter. This is something which Christian missionaries can respect, and even acknowledge that in this respect the Japanese attitudes are more 'biblical' than those of many Western churches. Many Christians would argue that these ceremonial observances are no longer necessary, because they have been fulfilled or abrogated through the death and resurrection of Jesus Christ (*e.g.* Romans 3:21-22; Ephesians 2:14-15; Colossians 2:13-14 *etc.*). If so, this is good news they can tell the Japanese. On the other hand, there are Christians who still today assert the relevance and importance of many Old Testament practices, such as having one day a week specially for God, tithing, avoidance of occult involvements or avoiding sexual relations with close kin. Some argue that dietary and agricultural laws also make good sense from a nutritional perspective.[18] Whatever position one might take on this, one needs to approach Japanese attitudes with respect, recognizing that they are similar to those of the Old Testament. It might even be appropriate for Christians to affirm the value of the underlying principles and to develop positive Christian substitutes. Many Christian churches have services for dedicating newborn infants to God: perhaps in Japan these should be made more prominent and try to involve grandparents and other relatives too.[19]

Shichi-go-san: the 7-5-3 ceremony

When girls are aged three and/or seven, and boys are aged five, another Shinto rite takes place in their lives. In that year, on or around the 15th November—depending on convenience and holidays for the families involved—such children are smartly dressed up, the girls in kimono, and taken to a Shinto shrine. There they all sit in a group while the priest reads various Shinto prayers and performs over them the *harai* rite of 'purification'.

In my interviews with parents, it turned out that social pressure was again a strong motivation in their participating in this rite. However, this time the pressure comes less from grandparents and more from other parents and the children's peer group. Sixteen people mentioned a fear of their children feeling left out if they did not perform the rites; similar feelings might lie behind those who said that they as parents felt a 'satisfaction at having done the rite' or that it was a 'problem of the heart' for the parents and their own feelings.

Such social pressure extended also to two Christian families. One family belonging to an independent evangelical church admitted, apparently with some embarrassment, that they 'just dressed up the children and walked in the gardens of the shrines but didn't have the *harai* performed'. Perhaps a more positive approach was reported by a Roman Catholic family whose church had a special service during November for children at these ages, who dressed up and were given a special blessing by the priest. In Los Angeles a Japanese language church named Centenary United Methodist performs a Christianized version of *shichi-go-san* in which children aged three, five and seven are given a ceremonial blessing. 'Even those outside the church have come seeking this service, and through this exposure several have been led to Christ'.[20]

Despite the widely-perceived social pressures to conform to the custom of having a *shichi-go-san* ceremony, I nevertheless came across one 'ordinary'—not particularly religious—family who had resisted such pressures on the grounds of the expense involved and had not put their children through the ceremony. Another family reduced the expense by calculating their children's ages so that they could both have the ceremony at the same time; in this way the contribution to the shrine (of about ¥5,000) was made only once rather than being doubled by taking the children in separate years. For their five-year old son they used the conventional 'Western' way of calculating ages, which is now used for most purposes in Japan, but for their daughter they used the traditional Japanese *kazoe* system. According to this system, a child is reckoned as being 'one' at birth; then at each New Year an extra year is added to his or her age. So their daughter, who would have been two years old by the 'Western' method, was counted as being three years old in the November when the rite was performed.

Seijin no hi: **the Adults' Day Ceremony**

This traditional system of adding on one year to each person's age at each New Year was universally practised up until the mid-nineteenth century. After the adoption of the Gregorian calendar in 1872, and especially after the Second World War, the 'Western' style of calculating ages became the norm. However, a remnant of the practice seems to have been preserved in the choice of January 15th for celebrating Adults' Day. In traditional farming villages this was the date for all major New Year celebrations. January 15th, the 'Little New Year' (*ko-shōgatsu*) remained locally important in many farming villages but in urban areas it now marks the culmination of the New Year celebrations.[21]

On this day, all those aged twenty celebrate their 'coming of age' (which gives the right to vote). Many of them respond to the invitations which they receive from the city council inviting them to attend a special meeting at the town hall. There they listen to what they consider to be boring speeches from the mayor and other local dignitaries, but they do appreciate the special commemorative gifts, such as an engraved pen, which they receive at the same time. In some cities, this ceremony is followed by an optional visit to a Shinto shrine.

For those who entered the *Nissen* company direct from high school, without going to university, there is a brief religious rite to mark their coming of age. This *seijin shiki* at the firm's principal Shinto shrine takes place on or about the 15th of January and consists of prayers relating to the new recruits' ambitions, hopes and expectations in the company.

There are a number of parallels between the 7-5-3 ceremony and the Adults' Day celebrations. Girls receive from their parents their first child's kimono at the age of three and their first adult kimono when they are twenty. Only rarely will they wear the kimono again, and after marriage they will have the long sleeves cut off; therefore Adults' Day, like the 7-5-3 ceremony, is a time for taking many photographs. For many girls, the formal photographs showing them attired in beautiful kimono for Adults' Day are taken by professional photographers and will be used in the matchmaking arrangements if the girls have an arranged marriage.

Not uncommonly these photographs are taken in the scenic gardens of a Shinto shrine, or perhaps at a Buddhist temple. It is usual for those who enter the precincts of such places to pray as well: a common proverb—or superstition—says that it is 'unlucky' to pass through the *torii* entrance portal of a shrine without praying there. The majority of visitors do indeed bow or pray at some point during their visit. Many people, not necessarily celebrating Adults' Day, also visit shrines on the 15th of January in order to return 'used' *mamori* charms and to buy new ones.

The boys dress up in dark suits and ties for Adults' Day, just as they were dressed up for the 7-5-3 ceremony fifteen years' previously. They too will have some commemorative snapshots taken, often in a shrine, temple or park, though these might not necessarily be the ones given to a go-between in an arranged marriage.

Some parents treat their twenty year olds to an expensive meal, but most youngsters go out with their friends. The girls might go shopping or have a meal at a prestigious department store, while the boys might go to a bar or coffee house together. Boys who have girlfriends might spend at least some of the day together with their girlfriends, whereas those without often put five yen into the offering box at a shrine and pray for the gods to give them girlfriends. Girls without boyfriends often do the same. The five yen involves a play on words between the '*go-en*' meaning 'five yen' and another reading of the word '*go-en*', using different Chinese characters, to mean 'honourable relationship', or 'honourable karma',—that is, courtship or marriage.

Another 'religious' element of Adults' Day, for many people, is the consultation of fortune-tellers. Special booths for palmists or astrologers are set up on the restaurant floor at the top of many prestigious department stores, or perhaps in their entrance lobbies. They attract in particular those (mainly girls) who want to know about their future marriages and those (mainly boys) who want to know about their future careers. Afterwards, they often describe such consultations as 'half curiosity' or 'half fun', and are often unwilling to say to what extent they 'believe' in it.

A further parallel to the 7-5-3 rites is that many of those who visit a shrine on Adults' Day also buy a *mamori* charm. Some describe it as a 'souvenir' (*kinen*) to remind them of the day. They might return it the following year and buy a new one, but some might keep it a number of years. This is particularly the case for girls who visit a shrine reputed to specialize in matchmaking and who might keep the charm until they marry.

For the girls, the Adults' Day rites are overshadowed to at least some extent by prospects of marriage in the following few years. Almost 90% of the women I interviewed had married between the ages of 22 and 25, irrespective of whether their marriages had come about through an 'arrangement' (*miai*), 'love' (*ren'ai*) or through an 'introduction' (*shōkai*), which combines elements of both the other two forms. Marriage is not such an immediate prospect for the men, since they tend to marry about five years later than the women: among those I interviewed, 85% had married between the ages of 24 and 31. Many of them will be finding employment at about the age when many girls will be marrying. In this way, Adults' Day is a marker indicating an approaching change in the life-cycle when many young men and women leave home for the first time. The women become wives in another household, while single men may start to live in company dormitories separate from the *shataku* homes for married men. Similarly, the 7-5-3 rites mark a transitional period in the children's lives when to a limited extent they also begin to move out from the home: at the age of four they begin to attend kindergarten (initially for just a few hours once or twice a week) but at the age of six compulsory education begins as they enter primary school for the first time. Often professional photographers are employed to take photographs of the children in their new uniforms for kindergarten or primary school; otherwise the parents take their own snapshots.

Both the Adults' Day and the 7-5-3 rites have become markers of a transitional period in the life-cycle when a 'parting' or leaving of the home in some way is imminent, even if this is only a partial 'parting' through going to kindergarten or primary school. For some, the parting will come the following April, at the beginning of the academic year, and for some adults the final parting might be delayed a year or two until they graduate from college. The modern educational system does not correspond exactly to the ages marked by the Adults' Day and 7-5-3 ceremonies, but in general terms the timing of these rites still tends to correspond to transitional periods in a person's life. There is a 'parting' which needs to be acknowledged; corresponding to this is an 'entering' into a school or company—or another family through marriage—which is also the focus of ritual behaviour.

The importance of 'age' in Japanese society

Some churches publicly acknowledge the fact that children are about to start school or that a person is leaving to go to college, or to start work elsewhere. They might even pray for such people during a service. However, they tend not to mark the occasion with any more special ceremony or formality. An exception is the Roman Catholic blessing on children whose ages correspond to those of the Shinto 7-5-3 rite. Might it be appropriate for Christian churches to consider some more elaborate and 'memorable' ways in which to mark such events—perhaps by having a party?

I raise this question because of the importance attached to 'age' in Japanese society, both in religious and non-religious contexts. Let me cite a few non-religious examples in order to emphasize the cultural significance of age, especially differences in relative age.

Studies of rural Japan have shown how systems of age-grading have been widespread up until the recent past and have often survived in a more attenuated form up to the present time.[22] Although such age grades are less conspicuous, or formally absent, in urban areas, relative age continues to exert a considerable influence on status hierarchies. For example, when the girls play tennis at a local middle school there are clear status differences from ages of just one year apart: the first years can only stand around the edge and watch, whereas the second years are allowed to pick up any ball which leaves the court and, after bowing to one of the players, throw it back to her; the third years are the ones who actually play tennis.

Similarly, in a family, older children are addressed by younger ones using terms for 'older brother' or 'older sister'. To ask a child to play with a younger brother or sister, adults may use a form of request which can be translated as 'do the favour of...'. In this, they 'project onto the older child a verb which is used for action from a superior to an inferior. Younger children learn to ask an older child to play using the converse of this form, used from an inferior to a superior.'[23]

Such behaviour is illustrative of a more general age ranking in Japanese society at large. There is a widespread distinction between seniors (*senpai*) and juniors (*kōhai*), plus a relatively small residual category of 'equals' (*dōryō*).[24] *Senpai-kōhai* terms can be used in a general sense to refer to all those older or younger than oneself in an organization, but usually they refer to people of the same sex with whom one has continuing, frequent interaction.

Large companies absorb age gradations into their hierarchies based on length of service with the firm, and take both these factors into account when assessing wages.[25] At Hitachi, a person's year of entry into the firm is indicated by his or her uniform number.[26] When an 'age' cohort enters a company they receive their training and orientation together as a group. Those who underwent training together continue to relate to each other as a clearly defined group and are seen as such by others.[27]

There is also a sense of propriety or etiquette which inhibits juniors from expressing too directly opinions which are at variance with a senior's, at least while in the latter's presence. Either they remain silent or they voice their opinions in a circuitous manner.[28] Among neighbours, a woman in her twenties or thirties appears to accept graciously the unsolicited advice of a woman in her fifties, thanks the older woman politely even if it is none of the other woman's business, and then decides for herself whether or not to act on the older woman's advice.

These distinctions apply when there is a clearly noticeable difference in age, of at least ten years. In such contexts more formal language is used by juniors towards seniors; similar formal language is employed at first with strangers of a similar age to oneself, but might be dropped as the two become better acquainted.

Various devices might be employed to ascertain relative age. Appearance alone is often a sufficient guide, perhaps accompanied by leading questions about the kinds of popular songs the other can remember or what kind of school they were attending during the war or occupation period. If more detailed information is desired, it is generally impolite to ask the person directly, but an indirect way is by asking which 'animal' year of the Chinese twelve-year cycle the person belongs to: '(*Anata wa*) *nani doshi umare desu ka?*'. From the other's reply, coupled with observation on approximate age, the questioner can work out the other's year of birth. The overt purpose of the question, however, is to find out something about the other person's character: the questioner then makes a polite comment about one of the good traits of that animal, such as the sheep being gentle and good-tempered, the mouse being 'economical' by hoarding things, the cow being patient or the wild boar keeping straight on its path without turning aside.

Particular titles of respect are accorded to older people of a grandparental generation. Even if they have no genealogical relationship to the speaker, they are addressed by terms of respect: *o-jiisan* ('grandfather') for males and *o-baasan* ('grandmother') for females. They are viewed as a distinctive age group for whom generalized kinship terminology is appropriate, rather like young children in England might refer to their parents' close friends as 'Auntie' or 'Uncle' such-and-such.

Special respect is paid to people who are accorded the title '*sensei*'. This is usually translated as 'teacher' but it is often applied to professional people too, such as a doctor or dentist. Teachers of traditional arts such as flower-arranging, the tea ceremony, judo, and so on, are normally called '*sensei*'. As these usually involve an experienced older person teaching a younger person, normally greater age is also implied by the honorific title '*sensei*', even if there may be occasional anomalies in this nowadays.

These kinds of attitudes may be carried over into the formal and honorific ways in which God is addressed in church worship. Even in some of the more modern translations of the Bible 'the translators could not dispense with some special mode of expression different from ordinary conversation. To have Jesus Christ speaking in ordinary conversational language is still considered inconceivable and undesirable'.[29]

Further Christian implications

Christian missionaries and pastors in general acknowledge the importance of age, at least in theory, but perhaps need to apply this recognition more practically in the life of the church. Chinese and African migrants to Britain have told me how shocked they were at the general disrespect paid to old people in the West. This attitude in Western society, which also affects the church, is liable to be carried unconsciously by Western missionaries to Asia and Africa. They are particularly prone to undervalue the honour which in most of these cultures is traditionally accorded to older people.

In this respect, many Asian and African traditional societies are closer to the biblical standards than is the church in the West. The sixth of the ten commandments reads, 'honour your father and your mother, so that you may live long in the land the Lord your God is giving you' (Exodus 20:12). Jesus emphasized the importance of this commandment by quoting it and criticizing the religious leaders of his day for the way in which their traditions allowed people to circumvent God's command (Mark 7:9-13). St. Paul further reinforced the importance of this commandment and its basic principles (Ephesians 6:2-3; Colossians 3:20).

There needs to be balance. Young people are often impatient at what is perceived to be narrow-mindedness in the older generation, while older people can become over-critical of failings in the young. What is needed is *respect*, because when respect breaks down the relationships also suffer. It is necessary to encourage youthful resourcefulness and enthusiasm in the churches but at the same time to recognize the need to respect the feelings and opinions of older people. Often the older generation has a valuable resource of accumulated experience, knowledge and wisdom which needs scope for expression. On the other hand, younger people need freedom to learn for themselves, including the freedom to make mistakes and to learn through such mistakes. The pastoral demands in balancing such tensions are enormous, and I am not offering any easy answers. What I am suggesting, however, is that Western missionaries recognize this to be an area in which they are liable to be blinded by their own cultural presuppositions. It could well be that in this respect traditional Japanese values are closer to the biblical standard. If so, the church can be strengthened by seeking to incorporate into its practice those aspects of the Japanese culture which are in themselves worthy of respect and are consistent with biblical values.

On the other hand, Christian pastors and missionaries are often addressed by church members as '*sensei*'. This is a cultural norm, but the values and attitudes behind the use of honorific titles such as '*sensei*' among Christians might be questioned in the light of Christ's teachings in Matthew 23:8, 10 and 11, which say,

> 'But you are not to be called 'Rabbi', for you have only one Master and you are all brothers...Nor are you to be called 'teacher', for you have one Teacher, the Christ. The greatest among you will be your servant.'

Like '*sensei*' in Japanese, the Hebrew term 'Rabbi' 'became a popular title which applied to many varieties of people... In some cases it referred to people who held official teaching positions but at other times was an honorary title. In either use rabbi designated respect for wisdom, intelligence and experience.'[30]

On the basis of the above scripture, 'missionaries have complained for years' about the use of '*sensei*' in church situations, but 'Japanese Christians often are not sure what to say', so 'they play safe, rather than risk offending' the other person.[31] Whatever one's position on this issue, it seems that often the designation of foreign missionaries as '*sensei*' tends to create an unnecessary social distance between fellow Christians. It may be appropriate to reconsider the ways in which linguistic conventions tend to create barriers between Christians rather than break them down. The widespread use of honorific forms, both inside and outside the church, means that it would be unrealistic to expect any change in this area to be easy, but we may seriously question whether existing practices are necessarily appropriate for the Christian church. All Christians are called to be 'disciples'—learners—with the same divine teacher.[32]

On the other hand, there is certainly a place for *respect*. We are told to 'respect those who work hard among you, who are over you in the Lord and who admonish you' (1 Thessalonians 5:12), and to 'obey your leaders and submit to their authority... so that their work will be a joy, not a burden...' (Hebrews 13:17). In the light of these scriptures, we can compare Christ's words in Matthew 23:9, 'And do not call anyone on earth 'father', for you have one Father, and he is in heaven.' with the commandment 'Honour your father and your mother' (Exodus 20:12), as Jesus himself stressed that we should honour our parents (Mark 7:9-13). It seems that these right and proper obligations of respect and obedience need to be kept in the context of our all belonging to God's family. When titles and human status assume greater importance than they ought, they can produce unnecessary barriers to Christian fellowship. It is this which Jesus was condemning in Matthew chapter 23, and which might also be applicable in the Japanese context.

Whatever position one might take on the use of titles such as '*sensei*' in a Christian context, a more important issue concerns *attitudes towards* pastors and teachers in the church. Boyle writes that what he calls the '*sensei* syndrome' is one of the most important causes of a 'growth barrier' in many churches, whereby further numerical growth tends to be stifled once a congregation has about one hundred or so members. '... The loyalty of laity to the founding pastor or the pastor who particularly influenced their lives is especially strong and can subconsciously cause them to make things difficult for a new pastor, or make them reluctant to transfer membership when moving to a new city... This '*sensei* syndrome' also has the unfortunate effect of producing a weak theology of the laity in Japanese churches'. It is commonly thought that only those with specialized formal training 'can perform... the priestly, the pastoral and other functions in the church... In practical terms, 'the priesthood of all believers' is seldom realized, and lay persons simply help the pastor perform his or her duties. The concept of the gifts of the Spirit given to all for the upbuilding of the church is still relatively unknown, and the professional pastor typically tries to take on everything himself, so that he becomes progressively busy as the church grows, thereby creating a growth barrier'.[33]

To counteract this problem, Boyle preached on the concept of spiritual gifts at the congregation of the United Church of Christ in Japan where he was a missionary pastor. Because the ideas were new they were received with interest but also 'a certain amount of scepticism'. Better results were obtained from his encouragement of greater lay participation in the worship service, Bible studies and other activities, so that 'the feeling of ownership by the participants has risen dramatically when compared to the old 'lecture' method that was used previously'.[34]

There are therefore problems in combining Japanese cultural norms of respect for those in positions of authority with certain Christian principles and practical issues of church growth. These problems are by no means insurmountable, and a sensitive approach to them may be able to incorporate traditional values into structures which are flexible enough to allow greater growth in the whole. One model of Japanese corporate organization—as in factories or business hierarchies—depicts the authority structures as a hierarchical network with strong vertical bonds but weak horizontal ones.[35] These links are portrayed as inverted 'V' shapes in which subordinates have strong attachments to a single leader but weak attachments to one another. In large organizations, such as big business corporations, the section or departmental managers have similar ties of vertical loyalty to their superiors but relatively weak ties with one another. The network of vertical loyalties thereby forms a hierarchy from the Company Director down through various layers of leadership to the workers at the bottom.

This model has a number of weaknesses and should not be adopted uncritically.[36] However, it is a pattern of leadership which seems to be successfully used by many rapidly growing Buddhist 'new religions' and to be culturally acceptable to the Japanese. It also allows flexibility for organizational growth. To what extent it should be used as a model for church organization is debatable. At the moment a kind of caricature of this model seems to be practised in many churches whereby the pastor is at one level and all the laity are at the level below him. In these churches it is necessary to incorporate other levels of leadership who can share the pastoral responsibilities. If the practice of some of the Buddhist 'new religions' might serve as a model, there is also a need to develop other kinds of group attachments which cut across but bring added strength to the vertical structure. This is being done already by a number of churches. Examples are the loyalties to church youth groups, healing teams or other special interest groups. Growing churches need a balance between maintaining a strong respect for their seniors and the training of potential leaders from the younger generations.

CHAPTER

6

Purity and Pollution

I N ONE FORM or another, concepts of 'purity and pollution', or
distinctions between 'clean' and 'dirty', are found throughout
the world. However, cultures differ in which things are considered to be 'clean' or 'dirty'. For example, in the previous chapter it
was noted how menstrual blood and childbirth have been considered sources of pollution in both ancient Israel and modern Japan,
whereas other cultures may hold different attitudes to such matters.

Shinto rites in Japan almost always involve some reference to
the driving out of impurity and the restoration of purity.[1] The
entrance to Shinto shrines (and to some Buddhist temples) contains
a hand-washing place where running water can be scooped up to
rinse out one's mouth, wash one's face or, more commonly, simply
to rinse one's hands. This is concerned with 'outward' purification,
whereas 'inner' or 'spiritual' purification comes from the *harai*
ceremony. During this ritual, the priest takes a pole (called the
haraigushi) which is waved in three broad, stylised strokes over the
place or people to be purified. Shinto prayers (*norito*) often contain
references to, or petitions for, the driving out of pollution, sometimes by asking for both pollution and sins (*tsumi*) to be thrown
into the depths of the sea.[2]

Instead of a simple dichotomy between 'clean' and 'unclean' in
Japanese folk religion, Japanese anthropologists speak of a tricho-

tomy which incorporates within it the contrasts between 'purity' and 'pollution', 'sacred' and 'profane'.[3] Their categories are as follows:

Hare: auspicious or happy formal occasions such as New Year, Shinto *matsuri* festivals, *miyamairi* and other Shinto ceremonies.

Kegare: polluting occasions, such as funerals, memorial rites, childbirth, menstruation, wounds or injuries. The pollution can come either from death or blood.

Ke: usual, common or ordinary occasions involving a neutral state which is neither *hare* nor *kegare*.

These concepts can be applied to space (Shinto shrines *etc.*) as well as to time.

Namihira describes how one or other of these categories might become particularly emphasized in certain localities, as illustrated by a village or hamlet (Tani no ki buraku) which she studied in Kōchi prefecture. There the people fear possession (*tsuki*) or curse (*tatari*) from a wide variety of spirits, both spirits of the dead and also those of other people who are alive. They fear also malevolent effects from a variety of other sources which can be diagnosed by a shaman (*kitōshi*) or medium.[4] Namihira says that the people seem to emphasize *kegare* more than *hare* or *ke*. The same observations could be interpreted by some Christians as showing that these people have a valid fear of demonic powers; their conclusion would be that these people need to be set free through the power and authority of Jesus.

Elsewhere, Namihira comments that in urban areas the concept of *kegare* is virtually absent from attitudes towards pregnancy and childbirth.[5] Her observations tie in with the attitudes of urban Japanese women who told me that during their periods they normally abstain from sexual intercourse for practical reasons such as not staining the sheets. They were not motivated by concepts of pollution or by religious prohibitions.

Nevertheless, other aspects of purity and pollution concepts do remain strong in urban areas. A fear of contamination from one person to another makes the Japanese very reluctant to use second-hand objects. In general, they never use second-hand clothing unless it is from a family member or a close friend. Some people even leave second-hand books out in the sun for a few hours for the sun's rays to kill any germs before they use them.[6] Most Japanese are reluctant to take anything from the pile of goods thrown out on 'big rubbish' (*ōgata gomi*) days, even if these include tables, televisions and other objects still in good or usable condition. A concern with purity and pollution pervades many other aspects of daily life, as can be seen from some of the following examples.

Food and eating utensils

Those eating utensils which are used to convey food to the mouth are often personalized in a family, so that each family member has utensils which are never used by any others. Chopsticks, tea cups and rice bowls have distinguishing patterns or sizes by which they can be easily identified. The rice bowl might be included because sometimes rice remaining in a bowl towards the end of a meal is mixed with tea to make *ochazuke* and the resulting mix is drunk directly from the rice bowl.

Guests are given special chopsticks called *waribashi*, consisting of a single piece of wood split most of the way down from the centre to form two chopsticks joined at one end. They are bought already wrapped in individual paper sheaths and are presented in this form to the guests. The guest removes the *waribashi* from the wrapping, breaks apart the two chopsticks and uses them for eating. By their very nature, *waribashi* can be used in a fresh state only once. Afterwards they are thrown away because it is obvious that they have been already used.

'Many Japanese find it very uncomfortable to eat sandwiches in American cafeterias, since they must eat them not only with 'dirty' hands, but with hands even dirtier than usual; they just handled money to pay for the sandwiches. The Japanese consider money extremely unclean, since, they say, bills and coins are handled by anybody's dirty hands.'[7] Sandwiches in Japan are usually served already cut up into small pieces with a cocktail stick in each piece, whereas more traditional foods are eaten with chopsticks.

After a meal all plates and dishes are washed up scrupulously in strong washing up liquid, rinsed at least twice and are left to drip dry. Then the sides of the sink are wiped round with the particular cloth used for that purpose, and other surfaces are wiped with their own special cloths.[8] Japanese who have visited British homes have sometimes commented that they consider English methods of dish washing to be insufficient and the use of tea towels to be suspect for hygienic purposes.

Food is always wrapped up securely. Partly this is a protection against cockroaches which in summer are found in almost all Japanese houses and many lower-level apartments, but the wrapping also partly reflects a more pervasive cultural concern. Often two or three layers of packaging are used in marketing and selling goods, despite the protests of some groups about the waste involved.[9] Particularly for gifts, great attention is paid to the different layers and types of wrappings, which may conclude with a specially inscribed band indicating the nature of the occasion. There are similarities between such wrappings and forms of traditional costume, which conclude with an elaborate sash, and further parallels in the use of polite speech to 'wrap up' one's 'real intent' and to demarcate boundaries between social 'insider' and 'outsider' groups.[10]

House arrangements

When entering a house, one leaves one's shoes in the entranceway (*genkan*) and steps up into the house, often then putting on slippers provided by the host. On entering a room having traditional straw matting (*tatami*) on the floor, these slippers in turn are left at the doorway and one remains on the *tatami* either barefoot or wearing socks or tights.[11] These restrictions on footwear relate to a more general distinction whereby what is 'above' is pure and what is 'below' is polluted: a result of this dichotomy is that underwear for the lower half of the body must be washed separately.[12]

In the formal Japanese-style room of most houses is an alcove (*tokonoma*) which is usually decorated in a simple but tasteful manner by a hanging scroll (often containing a seasonally appropriate picture), a single vase of flowers and sometimes a prized ornament such as an ornate doll in a glass case. At meals the place of honour is next to the *tokonoma* and the 'lowest place' is generally furthest away from it, by the door. Guests entering a room containing a *tokonoma* tend to cluster around the doorway out of politeness and deference to one another. They can understand very well Christ's comments about taking the lowest place until being invited to take a higher one (Luke 14:7-11); however, what is more challenging to the Japanese is Christ's instructions to invite the poor, crippled, lame or blind who cannot repay one's hospitality (Luke 14:12-14).

The Japanese attitude of deference towards the *tokonoma* suggests that the place has some religious or 'sacred' associations. These can be traced in the history of the *tokonoma*. Wheelwright reports that the *tokonoma* developed as a place to exhibit a secularized form of the hanging scrolls which were originally hung over Buddhist altars or in religious halls.[13] However, this loose connection with religion, or a 'secularized' form of it, does not explain the deferential behaviour accorded to the *tokonoma* today. A clearer connection between the *tokonoma* and religion is given by Yanagita, who writes, 'the meaning of etiquette about the *tokonoma*...is understood when we regard it as the seat of the *kami* (god)'.[14] The process by which this association came about is detailed by Hashimoto, who writes that, in the seventh century A.D.,

> '...the Emperor Temmu...issued a decree in March of the fourteenth year of his reign which ran thus: 'My people shall make a place of honor in every home and make it an altar.' So the people made this 'place of honor' in the main room of their homes,—the '*tokonoma*' of the present day,—and in this place the Shinto believers hung a scroll of the Sun-goddess..., while the Buddhists hung pictures of Buddha, or placed an image of Buddha.... With the passage of time the Sun-goddess was put into a wooden box ('*kamidana*'...), and the pictures and images of Buddha were transferred into gilded boxes, which ultimately became the '*butsudan*'..., while it became customary to hang pictures of scenery instead in the *tokonoma*.'[15]

A link between the *tokonoma* and memorial rites is reported from one village, where memorial plaques (*ihai*) were taken from the *butsudan* and put in the *tokonoma*, along with offerings of fruit and vegetables, on the principal occasions for ancestral rites (*bon*, *higan*, New Year and *hōji* memorial rites) and a scroll with a Buddhist mandala was put there on 'important Buddhist occasions'.[16] In another village, in which the primary occupation was fishing, there was a similar connection between the *tokonoma* and funerary rites, but the *tokonoma* was normally associated with Shinto by having in it a scroll on which was inscribed the name of the Sun-goddess. Apparently this was a permanent scroll which remained in the *tokonoma* even during the Buddhist rites at *bon*. However, it was replaced by a scroll depicting Fudō, the Buddhist god of fire, when a faith-healer came for a healing rite.[17]

This association with the Sun-goddess is similar to a pre-war idea, reported from part of Kyushu, whereby the *tokonoma* was connected with the Emperor (who was considered to be a direct descendant of the Sun-goddess). A Western visitor at that time wrote,

> 'I was privileged to be shown the '*tokonoma*' ... The word means a place to lay a bed ... The room is reserved as a guest-chamber in which to lodge the Emperor. It is the cherished dream of every loyal Japanese that some day the Emperor may extend to him the unspeakable honour of seeking a night's lodging at his humble home. So there is the room waiting for the honoured guest ... '[18]

Such sentiments are relatively rare in modern Japan, and might have disappeared altogether, but Christians might wish to use this concept in presenting Christ as the Emperor of all who desires to live among us, and even within us, through the indwelling presence of his Holy Spirit.

At New Year many households place in the *tokonoma* a rice-cake (*mochi*) shaped like an ancient mirror. This 'mirror rice-cake' (*kagami-mochi*) evokes connotations of the Shinto story about how the Sun-goddess was enticed out of a cave by seeing her reflection in a mirror; the mirror also became one of the three symbols of the Imperial family and has commonly been used in Shinto shrines as the god's dwelling place (*go-shintai*).[19] Originally these *mochi* at New Year were dedicated to the god of the New Year.[20] As the *tokonoma* often contains Shinto talismans too, it might have replaced the former 'toshidana' god-shelf for the god of the New Year.[21]

Safety charms (*fuda* or *mamori*) are often kept in the *tokonoma* instead of in a *kamidana*, in households lacking a formal god-shelf. Sometimes other religious items are kept in the *tokonoma*, such as a hanging scroll on which has been stamped the seals of Buddhist temples visited by the family. In several households the *butsudan* is placed in a special cupboard adjacent to the *tokonoma*. The Suehara family, whose daughter committed suicide, have a kind of ancestral altar (to be described on page 192) which they place inside the *tokonoma* itself.

The *tokonoma* is always kept clean, neat and decorative—a 'physical' counterpart to its 'spiritual' purity. The *tokonoma* is certainly not a 'polluted' place but neither is it ritually 'normal' (*ke*): rather, it exhibits characteristics of a 'pure' or 'sacred' (*hare*) area in contrast to the rest of the house.

Coming into a house is in some respects like entering a Shinto shrine. After the pollution of a funeral, people throw salt over themselves before entering their homes. However, even when returning from work or school it is still customary to wash one's hands in order to wash off the dirt from the outside world.[22] A *tokonoma* containing a safety charm is not regarded as so 'sacred' as a *kamidana*, which in turn is not so 'sacred' as a Shinto shrine, but all of them exhibit the same kind of separation of social or sacred space. In practice, they form a continuum in so far as all are symbols of, or even residences of, Shinto deities.

In this sense the house itself can become a kind of 'sacred' space. Entering the house from the outside can be a transition from *ke* to *hare*, and involves not only the shedding of shoes but also the bringing of a gift if visiting the home of another person. The gift, which normally consists of food, is usually first presented by the recipient as an offering at the household altar and is only later consumed by the family. The same process was observed when my wife and I were visiting in March a household which had a stand of dolls erected for the Girls' Festival. Although this home had a *kamidana*, the housewife presented our gift at the Girls' Festival display and left it on this dais. She did the same with the gift from another visitor who called round while we were there. In this context, it should be noted that such displays of dolls are often erected in the *tokonoma*.[23]

It is possible that the custom of offering gifts to deities may have contributed to the origins of the widespread practice of gift-giving.[24] Nowadays, however, a visiting gift (*o-miyage*) also establishes a relationship with the householder. In a sense, the giving and receiving of a material gift facilitates the transgressing of social boundaries from 'outside' to 'inside'. The material gift can more easily pass where human beings are at first excluded, but once the gift has helped to establish a relationship it becomes easier for the person to enter too. Food is particularly symbolic in this case, because of its implications of commensality and fellowship.

However, in a modern house not all the inside is 'sacred' or even 'clean': the toilet is particularly 'unclean'. In traditional farm houses, the toilet (of a hole-in-the-ground type) was in a separate building, but in modern buildings it has become incorporated into the structure of the house itself. Nevertheless, a symbolic boundary is preserved between the toilet and the rest of the house. Special slippers are kept there for use in the toilet only. They often have the word 'toilet' printed on them, but, even if not, they are conspicuously different in colour or texture from other slippers used in the house, so that there will be no confusion of boundaries. From a very early age children are socialized into regarding the bringing of shoes into the house, or of toilet slippers into other rooms, as a serious and 'dirty' act which must be avoided.[25]

These attitudes are highlighted by the account of an English missionary who used the church toilet but then forgot to change out of the toilet slippers. Her behaviour provoked a very strong reaction and she had to return the slippers immediately. She had not only brought the slippers from a polluted (*kegare*) place but had even brought them into the sacred (*hare*) space of a Christian worship area. Such behaviour was perceived as a kind of defilement even by Japanese Christians who subscribe to general Japanese notions of purity and pollution even if they do not practise the Shinto expressions of these.

A Japanese lady in England who went to the toilet at the home of a British anthropologist started to read an article in a copy of the

Reader's Digest kept in the toilet room. However, despite the anthropologist's assurances that it was perfectly alright for her to borrow the magazine and read it elsewhere, she could not bring herself to take the publication out from that 'dirty' room. Instead, she continued to read the article when she needed the toilet again.[26]

'Western', flush-style toilets are often refilled via a kind of wash basin on top of the cistern so that the user can rinse his or her hands before the water then fills up the cistern itself. In other cases, the area containing the wash basin often provides a transitional space between the toilet and other rooms. The toilet slippers might be used in this area too, but in other cases the boundary in the use of slippers is between the toilet and wash basin areas. An extreme case is the toilet at the headquarters of Ōmotokyō, a Shinto-derived 'new religion', in Kameoka, where the toilet area and wash basin area are both in the same room but are separated by a shallow step. Separate sets of slippers are provided for each area, necessitating two changes of footwear between the toilet area and the outside world.

The other location in or around the house which is subject to special care in terms of purity and pollution beliefs is the *kimon* or 'devil-door'. This was discussed in chapter four so I shall not dwell further on it here, except to stress that the Japanese place particular emphasis on protecting the *outside* of the *kimon* corner rather than the inside.

To a certain degree, the practice of frequent baths might also be related to concepts of purity and pollution. Most people bathe at least every other day, many daily and some twice a day. Very hot baths are the rule, partly because those that induce sweating are thought to be not only relaxing but also therapeutic, in so far as 'dirt' from outside the body can be eliminated. This is a metaphysical kind of dirt which relates to Shinto ideas of purity and pollution rather than bacterial theories of infection.[27] However, there are several other benefits to be enjoyed from taking a bath. These do include physical hygiene as well as physical therapy (in the relaxing of muscles and helping to relieve stiff shoulders and aching backs). Baths at night before sleeping not only serve as social 'boundary markers' between day and night but also warm up the body, especially in winter, when traditional houses have relatively little heating.[28] In traditional public baths, there were also social benefits in the opportunity to talk and hear the latest gossip, whereas in modern urban apartments and other congested housing the bath has become the only place where one can be alone at home and relax for an extended period.

Nevertheless, the attitude towards the bath as a place to be kept scrupulously clean is reflected in the style of bathing by which one washes with soap outside the bath and rinses off the soap with bowls of water before enjoying the main long soak in the bath. The bath has become a locus of physical cleanliness *par excellence*, and is comparable with the position of the *tokonoma* for 'social' or 'spiritual' purity.

On a physical level, the bath is in strong contrast or opposition to the *genkan*, the entranceway where one leaves behind one's shoes and the outside dirt carried on them. A similar contrast between 'clean' and 'unclean' is manifested on a spiritual level in the contrasts between the *tokonoma* and the *kimon*. These oppositions are depicted in figure 6.1:

Figure 6.1

	PHYSICAL	SPIRITUAL
'CLEAN'	BATH	TOKONOMA [or *kamidana* in some houses]
'DIRTY'	GENKAN	KIMON

All houses contain a *tokonoma* even if they do not contain a *kamidana* or *butsudan*. Modern apartments, however, do not have a *tokonoma* and their residents are exempt from concerns about the *kimon* because they do not own the property. Some older houses do not have baths but all have a *genkan*. Formerly, many toilets were in separate sheds outside farm houses, but nowadays they are usually inside the houses. However, like the *genkan*, their boundaries can only be transgressed by the changing of footwear. In this way, toilets have become partially assimilated to the *genkan* in the schematization depicted in figure 6.1. Both of them are 'dirty' places outside the 'house proper' and both require the putting on of footwear not worn in the main parts of the house.

The schematization of figure 6.1 can therefore be given a new dimension of 'outside' and 'inside', whereby the *kimon*, *genkan* and toilet are 'dirty' and are 'outside' the main living space of the house. Contact with these areas involves special care and prohibitions.

Figure 6.2

	PHYSICAL	SPIRITUAL
'INSIDE'	BATH	TOKONOMA
'OUTSIDE'	GENKAN OR TOILET	KIMON

The bath, however, is ambiguous, in so far as traditional public baths are outside the house but 'inside' the 'social space' of the community. Modern baths, by contrast, are inside the house but 'outside' the 'social space' of the family. Its association with water, however, continues to put it in direct opposition to the *kimon*. This is also true of the kitchen, where water is used, but which in many traditional farmhouses was an earthen-floored area adjacent to the main part of the house; it was necessary to remove outside footwear when coming in from the kitchen.[29] Therefore in older-style houses all these areas were separate from the 'house proper' except for the *tokonoma* (and most such houses would have had a *kamidana* too); this tends to confirm the idea that entering the house is like entering a sacred area from which should be excluded both 'physical' and 'spiritual' dirt.

In modern houses, these former 'peripheral' areas have been brought within the confines of the house itself but the social boundaries are kept distinct. Spatial and footwear boundaries automatically keep the *genkan*, toilet, bath and *tokonoma* rooms distinct. Moreover, not only should all rooms using water be kept away from the *kimon*, but ideally the *genkan* should be kept separate too.

These physical boundaries are reinforced at a social level.

Callers at the door might be kept in the *genkan*, where discussions can sometimes last half an hour or more without a neighbour being invited into the house. Reinforcing the social separation of the *genkan* is the fact that in many houses it is impossible to see further into the living areas from the *genkan*. When guests are invited in— often coming by appointment so that the housewife can clean up the house first—they may be entertained around a low table in the formal guest room containing the *tokonoma*. They tend to be kept segregated and in some middle-class homes do not enter the ordinary living areas of the family. In particular, they are strictly excluded from the kitchen, which is allowed to be untidy and perhaps even 'dirty' through the accumulation of grease from frying certain foods. Within a marriage, the kitchen is traditionally the woman's domain. Attitudes are changing nowadays, but in some more conservative circles a husband who helps his wife in the kitchen might be referred to disparagingly as a 'cockroach husband' (*gokiburi teishu*) who is 'out of place' in the kitchen.

Health and hygiene

'Dirt' has been defined as 'matter out of place'.[30] For example, Lock writes that in Japan using a cloth used for cleaning a sink in the place of one used for wiping the stove or kitchen table is 'a cause for great concern' because 'boundaries have become confused'. However, her informants state specifically that 'their concern is not about bacteria but about something else, which they can only describe as "dirt".'[31] Such concepts influence many other attitudes towards health and hygiene.

Certain illnesses can be regarded as both 'shameful' and in some sense 'polluting'. Families known to us who have been affected by tuberculosis, skin cancer or breast cancer tend to be reluctant to specify exactly what kind of illness a family member is suffering from. Even when the neighbours knew that a person was ill but did not know exactly the type of illness involved, they were often reluctant to acknowledge to the sick person's family that they knew about the family member's hospitalization. Such an admission would involve not only an obligation to visit the sick person in hospital but also a reciprocal obligation for the sick person's family to bring a return gift once their relative has returned from the hospital.

There is widespread concern about marriage into families affected by some types of cancers, tuberculosis, mental illness, colour blindness, or contact with atomic bomb radiation. A history of such illness in a family may be sufficient reason for a prospective marriage to be called off, even if the prospective partner is merely a descendant of the affected person and has no personal history of such illness.[32] Marriage into such families is considered to produce pollution of the family 'blood' or 'stock' (*kettō*). Similar pollution can come from marriages into outcast groups like Koreans or people called *burakumin* who in previous centuries had specialized in making leather goods and other trades involving contact with carcasses.[33] Marriage creates bonds where formerly there were boundaries, so the removal of a boundary is cause for great concern, lest pollution should enter.

Attitudes to medicine reveal another sphere in which illness can be linked to concepts of purity and pollution. Mahikari, one of the 'new religions', regards conventional medicine as 'poison' and actively discourages its members from taking medication.[34] There is also a fairly widespread Japanese attitude that East Asian herbal medicine produces fewer side-effects than 'Western' synthetic medicine; there has therefore been an increased use of traditional herbal medicine in recent years.[35]

'Red' pollution: birth and menstruation

In Shinto thought, blood is a source of ritual pollution. Childbirth, which also involves the emission of blood, is sometimes called the 'white' pollution (*shiro fujō*) to distinguish it from the 'red' pollution of menstruation and the 'black' pollution of death. However, the degree to which a mother is regarded as polluted varies considerably from one place to another. Often her transition from 'pollution' (*kegare*) to 'normality' (*ke*) took place on the fifteenth day after childbirth, and was marked by a simple ritual such as the washing of her hands, but in other areas the pollution could last as little as seven days or as long as thirty.[36] Among my urban informants, customs connected with childbirth are regarded as being sensible medical advice rather than being connected with purity and pollution. For at least a week, and normally two weeks, after giving birth most mothers are forbidden from getting out of bed except for vital functions and to feed the infant. They are told not to read, write or watch television because their eyes are said to be adversely affected by such activities in the first few weeks after childbirth. Those who break this rule after a while because of boredom might be criticized for doing so. Even if the mother is allowed out of bed after a week or two, she is not normally allowed out of the house until three or four weeks after the birth.

In former times, many villages had special parturition huts, which were sometimes used also for menstruating women.[37] Perhaps this still affects the way in which modern husbands tend to be excluded from being present at the childbirth, though this attitude is beginning to change. It is recorded that in some traditional villages the husband used to assist his wife during labour by supporting her back, but in other villages men were excluded owing to a folk belief that if a man were present all subsequent labours would require the presence of a man or else the labour would be extremely hard.[38]

Menstruation, as another form of pollution by blood, is not nowadays regarded as specially 'polluting'. Many women do not even know about the former rules forbidding menstruating women from visiting Shinto shrines. Nevertheless, some modern mothers still do not warn their daughters about the onset of menstruation.[39] As the average age of menarche is becoming younger, this role is beginning to be taken over by primary schools and the media. Nevertheless, the event can also be celebrated as a family event by the eating of a special meal which includes festive red bean rice, some of which might be sent to the girl's grandparents, uncles or aunts if they are not able to be present.

Some women feel they are 'dirty' while menstruating and wash underwear worn at these times separately from other clothing worn below the waist. There are some who feel a need to isolate themselves too: by law, all working women are entitled to take up to two days off per month for their menstruation, but few take advantage of this right unless they have particularly painful periods.

'Black' pollution: death and funerary rites

Death is a highly polluting event for a family and necessitates a number of ritual practices, some of which are noted elsewhere in this book. A few other examples include the following:

1) During the household's period of formal mourning and ritual pollution, a white curtain or sheet is often draped over the *kamidana* in order to prevent the gods from becoming polluted too.
2) During this same period the family should abstain from other contacts with Shinto institutions. Sometimes this is not possible, as in the case of a young man whose grandfather died less than a week before the young man's wedding. As all the invitations had been sent out, the wedding took place but the widowed grandmother remained at home.
3) Participation as an official in Shinto festivals (*matsuri*) is also prohibited for those who are polluted by the death of a relative within the previous forty-nine days. However, in one such instance the official's relative died so close to the time of the festival that there was no time to arrange a substitute, so the official, in whose home a float had been kept, did participate even despite the prohibition.

'Lucky' and 'unlucky' days

Many Japanese calendars show a cycle of auspicious and inauspicious days, which tend to follow a six day cycle, but with occasional irregularities. One of these is known as *butsumetsu*, the 'Buddha's death' day, but in most people's minds it is not consciously connected with death and pollution, even if they recognize the meanings of the written characters. It has become simply an 'unlucky' day which should be avoided for weddings or other happy occasions.

Another such day is called *tomobiki*: its name means 'pulling a friend', and is taken to mean that if a deceased person's friends were to attend his wake or funeral on a *tomobiki* day they too would be pulled into death. Death is the only time when most people pay any attention at all to this date on the calendar, but I have heard of families who have preserved a corpse in dry ice for an extra day or two in order to avoid a *tomobiki*.

Most people know the meaning of only one other day in this cycle, the very auspicious day known as *taian* or *daian*. It means 'great safety' and is said to be a lucky day for anything. If possible, weddings are arranged to coincide with a *taian*, although some people are content simply to avoid a *butsumetsu*.

Although 38% of my questionnaire sample said that they 'pay attention' to these dates, they do so only on rare occasions. None of those questioned about their attitudes to these dates expressed a personal 'belief' in the truth of these ideas. Instead, they say that a *tomobiki* should be avoided for funerals 'in case any of the friends invited believed in it'. Socially, it is 'safer' to avoid a *tomobiki* day for a funeral even if none of those present express any 'belief' in the taboo. The taboo continues to have social force because such private scepticisms are unknown.

Few people know the meanings of the other three dates on the 'Buddhist' calendar. Among those I interviewed, one couple could state the meanings of two of these, *sengachi* and *sakimake*, but did not know the meaning of the remaining one, *shakkō*. *Sengachi* ('early victory') is said to be lucky in the morning and unlucky in the afternoon, whereas *sakimake* ('haste loses') is regarded as being unlucky in the morning but neutral in the afternoon.[40] Only one informant, a thirty-year old woman from a rural background, gave the meaning of *shakkō* ('red mouth'), saying it is a day when 'midday is lucky'.[41] Though she has sometimes consulted the calendar to see on which of these days an examination or other important event would take place, usually she could do nothing to change the timing of the event. For her, an auspicious day or time could only supply her with 'relief of heart' (*anshin*) or a 'sense of security' (*anshinkan*).

Divisions and compartments: the bamboo tree

Concepts of purity and pollution lay particular stress on distinctions between categories and the fixing of boundaries. Many of the Japanese people whom I interviewed referred to the bamboo tree as an illustration of such concepts. They spoke of New Year rites, the 7-5-3 rites and other events such as *yakudoshi* years (to be discussed in chapter seven) as like the 'nodes' (*fushi*) or 'internodes' (*fushime*) of a bamboo tree. Other common terms used to refer to such events included 'a distinction' (*kejime*), 'a stage' (*kugiri*) and 'a fold' (*orime*).

The life cycle begins with the 'red pollution' of birth, whereas the 'death cycle' (of memorial rites) begins with the 'black pollution' of death. One might almost say that the rites associated with these are to some extent aimed at overcoming the dangers involved in these polluting events. These remain the events which are most hedged around with ritual sanctions in modern Japan, whereas any former traces of purity and pollution concepts associated with menstruation, marriage or other events in one's life have either disappeared or else become relegated to 'superstitions' like those for lucky and unlucky days. Purity and pollution taboos have remained strongest at the major transition points into this world and out of it into the next one.

However, these transition periods—the markers or boundaries between one stage and another—are essentially ambiguous, neither on one side nor the other. Because they are ambiguous, they can become 'dangerous'.[42] Attitudes towards purity and pollution tend to be closely associated with concepts of 'danger'. On the other hand, to remain within one's preconceived and well-defined boundaries is felt to be 'safe' by comparison. Concepts of 'purity and pollution' and those of 'safety and security' in essence constitute two sides of the same coin.

Christian implications

Concepts of purity and pollution, in some form or other, are probably universal. Some of these Japanese concepts have biblical parallels, especially in the early books of the Old Testament. Although the laws of Moses codify some of these ideas, it is clear that some of the concepts had been already present for a long time previously. These include attitudes towards menstruation (Genesis 31:35) and a distinction between 'clean' and 'unclean' animals (Genesis 7:2-8; 8:20). It is not surprising that concepts and attitudes having such a long history are to be found not only among the Jews but also among many other peoples.

Tithing was also practised in patriarchal times (Genesis 14:20; 28:22). Linked in with this was a recognition that one's best, and especially one's first-fruits, belonged to God. In Genesis 22:1-18, Abraham's willingness to sacrifice to God even the first-fruit of Sarah's womb—their son Isaac—foreshadows the instructions in Exodus 13:11-16 and Numbers 3:40-51 about the first-born belonging to God but needing to be redeemed by a substitute. Probably a similar recognition about the importance of giving God one's best, the first-fruits of one's produce, lies behind the story of Cain and Abel. Whereas Abel brought to God the 'fat portions from some of the firstborn of his flock', Cain merely brought 'some of the fruits of the soil' as an offering to the Lord (Genesis 4:3-4). It is noteworthy that the Hebrew word for 'first-fruits' is not used here. That, I suggest, is why God 'looked with favour on Abel and his offering' but not on Cain and his offering (verses 4 and 5).

This is an important concept to recognize in Japan too. In this chapter I have mentioned how the Japanese usually present gifts received from visitors first at a *kamidana* or other kind of domestic 'shrine'—even at a Girl's Festival display—and do so before the gift is unwrapped. This principle of giving one's 'best' to God is one which Christians can take note of. A further extension of this concept is that what is offered as one's 'first-fruit' needs to be pleasing to God. In particular, it is to be 'clean' and set apart for God, which is the essence of holiness. For us, this dedication to God is also 'in view of God's mercy' because a substitute has been offered in our place. Therefore we are urged to offer our own bodies as 'living sacrifices, holy and pleasing to God'—which is our 'spiritual worship'. (Romans 12:1). This is a New Testament fulfilment of these ideas concerning first-fruits, purity and holiness.

In the New Testament, the most common expression for a 'demon' literally means an 'unclean' (or 'dirty') spirit (*e.g.* Mark 1:23,26,27; 3:11,30; 5:2,8,13; 6:7; 7:25; 9:25; Luke 6:18; Acts 5:16; 8:7). It is interesting that the same vocabulary was used of ritual uncleanness through neglecting to wash one's hands (Mark 7:1-5). Jesus went on to say that what really makes a person 'unclean' is what comes from within, from the heart, including 'evil thoughts, sexual immorality, theft, murder, adultery, greed, malice, deceit, lewdness, envy, slander, arrogance and folly' (Mark 7:14-23). On another occasion, he used the same kind of vocabulary to tell his disciples, 'You are clean, though not every one of you', implying that Judas was 'dirty' (John 13:10-11).

A retired missionary with many years experience in Japan wrote to me that she had found it was more effective to speak of 'clean' and 'dirty' spirits when trying to communicate Christian truths to the Japanese. Her experience confirms my own impressions, that these concepts are much easier to communicate than trying to explain words like 'sin'. This is especially applicable to Japan, where the customary word for 'sin' (*tsumi*) also has the connotations of 'a crime'.[43] At New Year, Japanese people visit shrines and temples in order to 'wash their hearts'. The concept of a 'clean heart' is widely understood. Of course, for Christians to speak of 'clean' and 'dirty' spirits, or hearts, requires an explanation of how God can 'purify their hearts' by faith (Acts 15:9). It also involves receiving the indwelling presence of Christ's Holy Spirit (Luke 3:16; John 14:15-20; 16:7-15; Romans 8:9; 1 Corinthians 6:19-20; 2 Corinthians 5:5; Ephesians 3:16-17; Colossians 1:27; 1 Peter 2:5 *etc.*). To speak of allowing God to 'wash' us clean and to put his 'clean' and Holy Spirit within us seems not only to communicate more effectively but also employs the kind of vocabulary used by Jesus himself.

CHAPTER
7

Illness and 'Calamitous Years'

Consultation of mediums

MYSTERIOUS ITCH ON the penis of Mr. Inoue was described in chapter four. His younger brother, also known as Inoue-san, developed a 'mysterious' fever in his former home which 'Western' medical doctors were unable either to diagnose or cure. Suspecting that his fever might be due to a curse (*tatari*) from his ancestors, this Mr. Inoue asked the opinions of three different people.

First he asked a distant relative (his elder sister's husband's mother), who was a kind of local 'wise woman', what she thought. As she was unable to give an opinion, Inoue-san went to a priest at a large, prestigious Shinto shrine who told him that his illness had come from tiredness and would heal naturally. Finally, Inoue-san went to a medium in his area who told him that his mother's brother had died of cancer and wanted memorial services (*kuyō*) performed on his behalf. These had to be done by both Inoue-san and his mother together, and if the rites were not performed Inoue-san would not recover. Furthermore, each morning and evening for two weeks they were to pray to the mother's brother at the *butsudan* in his house: they had to put their hands together, chant and tell the ancestors (*hotoke*) that they were relying on the deceased uncle for healing. Having done that, they had to take fresh, clear water and pour it out from the house over the entranceway (*gen-*

139

kan) and around the house. This was to remove ritually all contamination or pollution, so that Inoue-san would recover. While
doing this, they had to remain silent and not reply to any passer-by
who greeted them. The family faithfully followed all these instructions but Inoue-san himself was unable to be present for all of it
because of being hospitalized: he therefore had to listen to all the
praying and chanting over the telephone.

At the same time the medium said that the family had neglected
the worship of the Bodhisattva Jizō, statues of whom had stood
both in front of and behind the Inoues' house. The one behind had
been moved several yards when their house was built and the
family did not perform rites (*kuyō*) to it. The medium said they
should begin to pray to, and put offerings before, both of the Jizō
images, so that Inoue-san would recover. This they did, but the
illness still persisted for several weeks before Inoue-san finally
recovered.

The following year Mrs. Inoue, then aged twenty-five, gave
birth to their first child, a son. For three weeks she stayed in bed at
her mother's home, looking after her infant, before returning to
her own home and re-commencing her normal household tasks.
Shortly afterwards she became very weak and found herself unable
to get up or move around for long without becoming exhausted.
This condition persisted until the child was seven months old.
Neither conventional 'Western' medicine nor traditional East
Asian herbal medicine (*kanpō*) seemed to have any effect. After
the illness had continued for five months she asked her husband's
mother to consult the medium on her behalf, to discover whether
or not she might be suffering from a supernatural curse or punishment (*tatari*). This time the medium said there was no problem with
her worship of Jizō, but she had neglected the ancestors (*hotoke*)
and the cult of the Shinto gods (*kami*). [In any case, Mr Inoue, then
aged thirty-two, had no formal responsibility for the ancestral cult
because he was a second son and his elder brother was responsible
for it.] The medium said that the Inoues were to rely on more, and
pray more to, both the *hotoke* and *kami*.

Moreover, the medium told Mrs. Inoue that at 8:00am each
morning she was to take boiling hot green tea to the *genkan* of her
house, chant and pray (for recovery from illness) to all the ances-

tors of her family. However, she was not to utter any word of explanation to any neighbours or passers-by. Then she was to pour the tea outside and let it flow from the *genkan* into the drainage channel in front of the house. Mrs. Inoue continued with this procedure for one month until she recovered. In her view, her recovery was due, at least in part, to her faithful performance of this ritual. She explains the significance of the *genkan* as the place where not only people but also *hotoke* and *kami* enter the house and watch what is happening.

Shortly after this, her son became ill with an unexplained high temperature and lethargy. Thinking that it might have been from the same cause as Mrs. Inoue's illness, the couple consulted a medium, who prescribed the same course of treatment (of boiling tea poured from the *genkan*). The only difference was that this time it had to take place at 7:00am each day. This 'treatment' was continued for two weeks and the child recovered. By this time the family were wondering whether their misfortunes might be due to the house they were living in. The house was also relatively old and they were living rather too close for comfort to Mr. Inoue's parents, so these factors all together influenced their decision to move across the city in 1982.

Two older men whom I interviewed had also consulted mediums regarding some kind of illness. A forty-nine year old man had a teenage son with a pain in his right hip. The cause could not be diagnosed by the hospital even after X-Rays. It was then that the lad's father consulted a medium, who said that there was no spiritual cause for this pain. The medium suggested acupuncture, which relieved the pain for a while but treatment was still continuing at the time when I interviewed this man.

A similar case involves a fifty-two year old man who suffers from gallstones. To treat them, he takes both 'Western' and East Asian herbal medicines. [His wife takes a more sceptical view and says his stomach complaints are due to his eating too much too quickly!] This man also suffers from a conspicuously patchy loss of hair, which he attributes to his gall problem. However, he also consulted a medium to check whether or not it might have been due to some spiritual cause such as neglecting rites for one of the eleven generations of ancestors for whom he is responsible. The medium assured him that his was a purely medical problem and not a spiritual one.

It is noticeable that both of these two older men are relatively scrupulous about performing ancestral rites every day: the first man openly boasts about being 'more religious' than his neighbours, while the other keeps a careful note of the anniversaries of death of his ancestors and performs rites when appropriate for them. It might be that such men are more prone to suspect supernatural causes for unexpected illnesses partly because of their strict observance of ancestral rites: this suggests that at least one element in their motivation for performing those rites is a fear of supernatural vengeance if they are not performed properly. By contrast, the following three cases, in which Shinto priests are consulted, involve younger people with no *butsudan* or formal responsibilities for the ancestral cult.

Consultation of Shinto priests

Mr. Katsumi is one of the few *shataku* dwellers to have a *kamidana*. He bought it five years previously when he began to experience serious blood clotting which necessitated frequent hospitalization. Now every day he prays at the *kamidana* for health, both for himself and his family, and he gives thanks for their continuing health.

Mr. Yamamoto is another *shataku* dweller with a *kamidana*, who also bought his *kamidana* at a time of illness. In his case it is a glandular problem causing excess fluid retention and overweight, a condition which has persisted for twenty years. Every evening his wife gives thanks to the ancestors for the family's health—a relatively unusual case of *ancestors* receiving prayer at a Shinto god-shelf, as will be discussed further in chapter nine.

Mr. and Mrs. Matsui are both from an older neighbourhood of the city and had been friends since childhood. They first met at an abacus class but had known each other for twelve or thirteen years before they had begun to date. Almost three years later they got married, but after being married for five years they had still been unable to conceive a child. It was then that they consulted a Shinto priest, who advised them to install a *kamidana* in their home and to pray daily for fertility to the Shinto gods. Mr. Matsui constructed a home-made *kamidana* and they both prayed daily at it for almost a year before a child was conceived. After their daughter's birth, the Matsuis took her to the Shinto priest for him to choose her name (by divination). Now they visit that shrine every month 'without fail'. Both there and daily at their domestic *kamidana* they give thanks to the Shinto gods (*kami*) for the gift of their child. We noticed how they also keep a *mamori* safety charm continually attached to their daughter's clothes, for her continued protection.

Fertility was the speciality of the 'goddess of the mountain' on which the *Nissen* company housing was built. Hers is one of the four smaller shrines around the hillside, in addition to the company's main one, for which *Nissen* has responsibility. It is said that her speciality was the granting of fertility to childless couples. However, being female, she is said to pay attention only to her male devotees and not to the petitions of women. Therefore all participants in the ritual for her *reisai*—what I call her annual 'feast day' (like those of Catholic saints)—have to be male. [Actually, the firm does allow one of its office girls to have the job of photographing the rites for the company magazine, but she does not take part in the prayers.]

In rare cases in traditional Japanese villages, a special parturition hut for those giving birth might even be located inside the precincts of a Shinto shrine, even though this would normally involve the tabooed contact between the sanctity of the shrine and its pollution by blood.[1] A great variety of other kinds of deities also specialize in healing particular kinds of illnesses.[2]

In traditional Japan illness often prompted the consultation of shamans or 'faith-healers', who still survive in some areas today.[3] This shamanic tradition also influenced the characters of the women who founded some of the 'new religions' which were sometimes started in the nineteenth century but have become especially popular since the Second World War.[4] Many 'new religions' whose shamanic roots are less obvious also emphasize healing, magic and miracles.[5] It is notable that these have developed particularly since about 1970 and that a relatively high percentage of their adherents are younger people, in their twenties or thirties.[6] These seem to be the religions which attract the younger generations, perhaps because they are looking for a faith which really 'works'. During the same period there has been a parallel development in many Christian churches which have attracted younger people through an openness to prophecies, 'speaking in tongues', healing and exorcism.

Some Christian implications

How can shamanic, non-Christian religions produce healings? Is God at work in them? If they are demonic, 'how can Satan drive out Satan?' (Mark 3:23)? Medical anthropologists are usually prepared to admit that some folk therapies do 'work', but that the healings can be 'explained away' in various ways, such as the natural course of the illness, the efficacy of certain active ingredients within folk medicines or the healing of psychosomatic complaints—*i.e.* through one's state of mind affecting one's bodily state.[7]

Elsewhere I have suggested another, spiritual explanation of how healings could be produced by occult powers. We know that in the New Testament there are a number of cases of illnesses being produced by demons (*e.g.* Matthew 9:32-33; 12:22; 17:15-18; Luke 13:10-13). However, illnesses such as asthma or epilepsy—which can at times be caused by demons, though not invariably so—are periodically manifested rather than being constant conditions. In these cases, apparent 'cures' might be produced if the demon, co-operating with an occult 'healer', becomes 'latent' or inactive and ceases to manifest its presence as a sickness. However, it is not actually cast out.[8]

The emphasis on miracles and healing among Japanese new religions is only one of the package of features which has facilitated their rapid growth. During the same period the Christian church in Japan has, on the whole, experienced relatively slow growth. In chapters twelve and thirteen I shall discuss these contrasts in further detail. Here it is sufficient merely to note that as a result of my own detailed research in following up cases of healing and investigating related phenomena, I have become convinced of the need for a greater openness to the power of the Holy Spirit in communicating the Christian gospel.[9]

In my comprehensive follow-up study of John Wimber's conference in Harrogate, I not only investigated cases of divine healing at the conference itself but also asked people to what extent they had put such training into practice in their own local situations. I found that those who had prayed for other Christians reported varying results, but that often 'something happened' when they prayed for non-Christians. In some cases, it led to the person's conversion, and in other cases brought them to re-assess their relationships with God.[10] I am therefore convinced that in Japan also there is a necessity for healings and other gifts of the Holy Spirit to accompany the preaching of the gospel, as divine confirmations of our human testimony (Mark 16:20; Acts 14:3; Hebrews 2:4).

Yakudoshi: Years of Calamity

Healing and illness relate also to another complex of Japanese folk beliefs, known as *yakudoshi*, which are years in one's life when one is thought to be especially susceptible to illness or misfortune.[11] Many Japanese people are only aware of, or pay heed to, what I call the 'principal' *yakudoshi* years. These occur at the ages of thirty-three for women and forty-two for men. They are probably to be explained by reference to plays on words. 'Thirty-three' might be pronounced as '*sanzan*', meaning 'hard', 'difficult' or 'troublesome', whereas 'forty-two' could be pronounced as '*shi ni*', meaning 'to death'.[12]

Many people are also aware that the years preceding and following a major *yakudoshi* are *yakudoshi* years too. These years are called the *maeyaku* and *atoyaku* respectively, while the main *yakudoshi* year is called the *honyaku*. In addition to the ages of thirty-three for women and forty-two for men (which in some versions is given as forty-one), some people are also aware of other 'major' *yakudoshi* years at the ages of twenty-five and sixty-one for men and nineteen and thirty-seven for women. Fewer people are aware of their 'medium' and 'minor' *yakudoshi* ages, which are tabulated in Figure 7.1. This sets out the *yakudoshi* years as listed at an important Shinto shrine in the city where I did my fieldwork, although there are minor regional variations in the years counted as *yakudoshi*. However, in Figure 7.1 I have also taken the liberty of sub-dividing the 'major' *yakudoshi* years into 'principal' versus other 'major' *yakudoshi*s, and of sub-dividing the 'minor' *yakudoshi*s into those differentiated by sex versus those which are not[13]:

Figure 7.1   *Yakudoshi* years for men and women

	Men	Women
Principal *yakudoshi*	42	33
Major *yakudoshi*s	25, 61	19, 37
Medium *yakudoshi*s	24, 26 41, 43 60, 62	18, 20 32, 34 36, 38
Minor *yakudoshi*s differentiated by sex	18, 19, 20 32, 33, 34 36, 37, 38	24, 25, 26 41, 42, 43 60, 61, 62
Minor *yakudoshi*s undifferentiated by sex	1, 4, 7, 10, 13, 16, 22, 28, 40, 46 49, 52, 55, 58	

Common attitudes towards *yakudoshi* years

One *shataku* man suggested that the 7-5-3 rites might somehow mitigate the *yakudoshi* at the age of four; his wife added that four year olds often injure themselves when they fall off their tricycles, so they 'need to be careful' at that time. Because *yakudoshi* ages are reckoned by the traditional *kazoe* system whereby a child is one year old at birth and adds on an extra year each New Year, children aged four by this reckoning are aged three by the 'Western' system which nowadays is normally used for the ages of children participating in the 7-5-3 rites. At one time, however, both sets of ages would have been reckoned by the traditional system without any overlap.

Among my informants, the most common reason for taking special precautions in one's *yakudoshi* is a theory that one's body changes at these critical points, making one particularly susceptible to illness. Some claim that it has been proven 'scientifically' that the body deteriorates or 'becomes tired' at the ages of thirty-three in women and of forty-two in men. A few said more precisely that 'the hormone secretion levels of the body change' or that 'the incidence of cancer rises after these ages'. One man told me, 'past data shows that it is not a superstition but scientific: at these ages parents receive a mental shock as they reach a crossroads in life when their children marry or leave home.' He, like the others, was unable to give me the 'scientific' source of such claims. Rather, it appears to be a 'pseudo-scientific' gloss on a traditional folk belief.[14]

It is noteworthy that those who assert that the belief is 'scientific' are mainly those without a high degree of specialization in medical or scientific fields of study. Two men with such a background—one a dentist and the other a professor of pharmacology at a leading research institution—both dismissed such explanations. In Japan 'biorhythms' are likewise claimed to be 'scientific' and, like *yakudoshi* beliefs, they are invoked as a way of rationalizing accidents after they have happened.[15]

In the same way, misfortunes in a *yakudoshi* year can be explained afterwards as due to one's *yakudoshi*. For example, Mrs Ikeda was twenty-six years old and in a 'minor' *yakudoshi* when we interviewed her. She said,

'You're always told about people getting illnesses to an unbelievable extent in their *yakudoshi*s, and it's been just like that for me this year. I've had nothing but illnesses: my eyes have been aching recently and my child went down with chicken pox. It's been like that all the time this year.'

Sometimes informants themselves question whether an illness is really anything to do with their *yakudoshi*. For instance, Mrs Kimura was very tense for a few days after a major row with her husband. A symptom of her tension was a stomach ache. At that time she speculated whether or not it had anything to do with her *yakudoshi*, but after the ache disappeared she abandoned the *yakudoshi* idea.

Several people mentioned hearsay cases of misfortunes happening in a *yakudoshi*, but only a few could give specific examples of such misfortunes happening to themselves. These few cases are:

'I lost a tooth this year, my main *yakudoshi*, which is the first sign that one's getting old: the second is loss of eyesight and the third is loss of sexual appetite!'   (Man, aged 41)

'Though I agree with my husband that *yakudoshi*s are not scientifically provable, nevertheless when I was nineteen I was ill in hospital for three months and when I was thirty-two I broke a leg and had to use crutches while it was in plaster.'

(Woman, aged 33)

'In my *maeyaku* things did not go smoothly at work for several months.'   (Man, aged 43)

These examples involve people who were relatively close to their own *yakudoshi* ages and could remember them well. By contrast, three men in their forties who had each experienced serious illnesses (meningitis, a heart operation and a stomach illness) while in their later thirties were all convinced that their illnesses had 'no connection' with their own *yakudoshi*s. The fact that more minor illnesses which do occur in a *yakudoshi* year are attributed to the fact of the *yakudoshi* shows the subjective element which is involved in the interpretation of these illnesses.[16]

Some personal illnesses are the kind which would be expected from the widespread 'folk' interpretation of *yakudoshi*s as times when the body is said to deteriorate and degenerative diseases become more prevalent. However, breaking a leg or uneasy relationships at work do not fall into this category. Neither do the majority of other misfortunes which informants attributed to *yakudoshi*s, because these all involved a third party. Six such cases were reported to me, as follows:

Female informants

'My husband's mother died young, when my husband was forty-one and in his *maeyaku*.'
'My father died when I was thirty-three.'
'My younger sister died when my husband was aged forty-two.'
'My older sister's child became ill and died when my sister was thirty-three years old.'
'My mother died when I was thirty-two.'

Male informant

'My wife had an accident when she was nineteen and one of the children also had an accident when my wife was thirty-three.'[17]

This last example does involve an accident to the wife when she was nineteen but the second part of it, about the child's accident, does not conform to the theory of 'bodily change' during a *yakudoshi*. It is noteworthy that all five examples cited by women are those involving a death. These are the kinds of stories which can easily feed into the popular image of such events often taking place during a *yakudoshi*. Many of those who said they had a 'belief' in the occurrence of misfortune during *yakudoshi* years, but were unable to give any definite instances from their own experience, often told us that they had heard of such tales through 'my grandmother', 'acquaintances' or 'other people'. Some simply said it was 'ancient wisdom', 'said from of old'. It appears that such tales can then become amalgamated with the 'pseudo-scientific' explanation in everyday 'folk tradition'.[18]

'Belief' in *yakudoshi* years

It is very hard to measure to what extent people actually do subscribe to *yakudoshi* beliefs. What can happen is that younger people deny any belief but when they actually reach their own principal *yakudoshi* years they do go to a shrine and buy a protective charm to avert any possible disaster that year. Certainly a few men who in 1981 had written on their questionnaires that they did not pay attention to *yakudoshi*s had by 1984, when in their early forties, in fact bought special charms or visited particular shrines on account of entering a *yakudoshi* year. As women have their principal *yakudoshi*s earlier than men, this change in attitudes when one actually enters one's *yakudoshi* probably accounts for the fact that 55.5% of women versus 44% of the men wrote on their questionnaires that they 'pay attention' to *yakudoshi*s. Overall, 48.5% of the 664 people who answered this question said that they do pay attention to *yakudoshi*s, 34% that they do not and the remainder felt unable to give a definite reply one way or the other.[19]

Two women who said they did not pay attention to their

*yakudoshi*s had been pregnant at the time. There is a belief among many women (though not all had heard of it) that the effects of a woman's *yakudoshi* are nullified if she bears a child in that year. Mothers who had borne a son during their *yakudoshi*s claimed that the calamity is averted if the child is male, whereas those who had borne a daughter said that a child of either sex can take the disasters away—though one of them (who had three daughters and no son) did admit that a son 'would have been better'. As the sex of the unborn child is normally unknown when the mother enters her *yakudoshi* at the beginning of the year, it is noticeable that those who did bear sons during their *yakudoshi* years had also gone to pray for safety and protection and to buy protective *mamori* or *fuda*. One woman who claimed that the birth of her daughter had taken away the 'calamity' of the mother's *yakudoshi* nevertheless took extra special precautions because she had already had a previous miscarriage and her husband was in his *yakudoshi* at the same time as she was in her thirty-seven year old one. They both went to a large Shinto shrine for the three consecutive years of their *maeyaku*, *honyaku* and *atoyaku* where they received a special 'exorcism' or 'purification' (*yakubarai*) and bought charms which they each wore around their necks for the whole year.[20]

The use of charms or the performance of special shrine visits to avert the anticipated effects of one's *yakudoshi* introduces an element of circularity into people's logic. If one expects misfortune to occur and it does occur, the beliefs about *yakudoshi*s are reinforced, but if one took precautions and no misfortune occurs then the need for such precautions might be reinforced. However, any 'belief' might still be mingled with scepticism, as shown by the common attitude that 'because nothing disastrous happened to me, I suppose the charm might have had some effect'. Others take a more cautious view and say that the charm's 'effect' is more psychological than technical: it gives 'reassurance' (*anshin*) or a 'sense of security' (*anshinkan*). It is noticeable that the three people cited earlier who attributed some personal misfortune in their own lives to the influence of a *yakudoshi* all hold attitudes of this kind, as they had all taken the ritual precautions. For example, the man who had lost a tooth said that the *mamori* charm which he wears next to his skin each day has some 'effect' only in a 'mysterious' rather than 'visible' manner: 'it is efficacious if it gives relief of heart', so that 'to believe is to be reassured'.[21]

Shrine visits during *yakudoshi* years

Among those who do pay attention to *yakudoshi*s, some do so only for what I call their 'principal' *yakudoshi* whereas others also pay attention to at least some other *yakudoshi* years. How this attention to *yakudoshi*s is manifested in practice is mainly by special shrine visits and the buying of protective charms.

Among the one hundred people whom I interviewed in depth, there were forty-five who said they 'pay attention to' *yakudoshi*s. Of these, thirty-four had visited a Shinto shrine to buy a *yakuyoke*, a 'charm to take away calamity', and had done so especially because of their entering a *yakudoshi* year.[22] The most popular local shrine for this is one I am calling the Iwadani shrine, located about five miles from where I did my fieldwork. It was visited by twenty-five out of these thirty-four people. Nine other shrines were mentioned as venues for *yakudoshi* prayers, but only one mentioned the local 'Nishiyama' shrine, saying that it was the *ujigami* shrine for the area. Other shrines visited were famous large ones elsewhere in the region or in more distant parts of Japan near where people were staying with relatives over the New Year season.

Often Iwadani was visited in addition to these other shrines. Sometimes people would go to Iwadani in their main *yakudoshi* year (the *honyaku*) but go elsewhere in their *maeyaku* or *atoyaku*. Most people go to the Iwadani shrine between the 15th and 17th January. According to the traditional calendar which emphasized the 'little New Year' (*ko-shōgatsu*) on the 15th January, the first few days of the New Year were the 15th to 17th January. This was also the time when everyone in the community added a year to his or her age. It might be that Iwadani became famous for *yakudoshi* charms partly because its *gomeinichi*, the special day for worshipping its *kami*, falls on the 17th January. This is also the time when many people return 'used' *mamori* charms to shrines for ritual burning.

Yakudoshi charms

Many people buy standardized *fuda* or *mamori* charms against the effects of a *yakudoshi*. Some people, however, buy special charms which they might give as gifts to a loved one. Examples include:

a) A pair of chopsticks given by a wife to her husband in his *yakudoshi* year as a 'substitute *mamori*' because the chopsticks are made of *nanten* wood, the significance of which was explained in chapter four.

b) A mother gave her daughter, in the latter's *yakudoshi*, a cord for a kimono sash. The daughter says the cord (*obi-himo*) is a commercial one from a department store and does not know why her mother gave it to her. She says that at first she did not think very much about the cord, and seldom used it (as she rarely wears a kimono), but gradually she found that it helped her to have a 'better *seishin*' (spirit or mind) about her *yakudoshi* and gave her a 'settled spirit' (*kiyasume*). Later another woman explained that in a woman's *yakudoshi* the gift of a five-coloured object, especially something long such as a sash (*obi*) or waist-string (*koshi-himo*) becomes a protection against evil (*yakubarai*), taking away the calamity of a *yakudoshi*, and is usually given by mothers to daughters. The long object symbolizes long life. It might be that the use of a sash is related to the wearing of a *hara-obi* in pregnancy and linked with the idea that a woman's 'calamity' (*yaku*) is taken away if she bears a child in her *yakudoshi*.

c) For his *yakudoshi* a man received from his mother-in-law in Himeji a pair of iron 'cooking chopsticks', about a foot long, which he hung over the front door at the entrance to his house. The chopsticks had been bought from a commercial shop rather than from a shrine but a leaflet enclosed with them stated that according to a local legend from the Himeji district these chopsticks expel evil. It is significant that this gift was given at Setsubun, which by the older calendar was a kind of New Year.[23]

Social pressure to conform to *yakudoshi* observances

One man, Mr. Shimada, described how all those who had been in the same class together at his middle school, who were all of the same age, together went to the Suwa shrine in Iwate prefecture to pray for protection in their *yakudoshi*s. Mr. Shimada's native village is in this area of northeastern Japan and all his middle school class had kept in touch with each other through periodic reunions and the Old Boys' Association. In other years, those of the group whose wives reached the age of thirty-two (which was thirty-three by the traditional *kazoe* system) also went to the same shrine together to pray for protection in their *yakudoshi*s.

Mr. Shimada's case illustrates the continuing importance attached to networks based on friendships involving reciprocal obligations.[24] In this case it was reinforced by their being a common age group. Although they are now dispersed throughout Japan, the very fact that they are the same age serves as a focus for group activity when together they encounter their *yakudoshi* years. It is this network of friendships which often provides the motivation or incentive for purchasing charms or visiting shrines at the time of one's *yakudoshi*. Mr. Shimada's case is a rare one of friends visiting the shrine together as a group, but for other people such networks of closer friends are the ones who are aware of each other's ages and remind each other of approaching *yakudoshi* years. Within these networks there will often be an awareness that such-and-such a person was born, for instance, in the Year of the Dog, so others born in that same year will know that they have *yakudoshi*s at the same time. They may then comment to each other that they should 'take care' and be careful about their health in their *yakudoshi* years. Such statements do not necessarily imply a 'belief' in misfortune occurring during a *yakudoshi* year, but might simply be polite, socially appropriate comments. Nevertheless, their effect is to reinforce in the listener an awareness of his or her *yakudoshi*.

Many informants confirmed the influence of a social awareness that they were approaching or in the time of a *yakudoshi*. They often mentioned the fact that other people said they should 'take care' or visit a certain shrine. Some say that their friends of the same or similar age are the ones who say they ought to visit a shrine, and the social pressure mounts as those in their *honyaku* or *atoyaku* remind those in their *maeyaku* that they should take the necessary precautions.

Pressure can come also from within the family, and be harder to resist. A wife who has already experienced her principal *yakudoshi* is often concerned for her husband's health as he enters his forties. The presence of his principal *yakudoshi* focusses her attention upon those critical years and she may see his performance of the ritual precautions as one way of allaying her general anxieties about his health.

Elderly parents, who have themselves experienced *yakudoshi*s in the past, may exert a further influence. If they are concerned for their child to have special protection in his or her *yakudoshi* they might buy a charm vicariously on behalf of a son or daughter and either post it or take it when they next visit. One elderly mother also paid a priest to recite prayers on behalf of her son in his *yakudoshi*.

*Yakudoshi*s and East Asian medicine

Charms to avert the anticipated dangers of a *yakudoshi* year are preventative rather than 'curative'. The same applies to other kinds of *mamori* charms and to the common prayer at a *butsudan* or *kamidana* that one would have a safe and healthy day. A very similar attitude is often held towards the use of traditional East Asian medicine, the practitioners of which emphasize the 'preventative medicine' which comes through the regular use of herbal remedies, massage or other treatments.[25] It is the same kind of security which comes from being 'forewarned and forearmed'.[26]

Generally East Asian medicine is used for chronic illnesses which are less amenable to treatment by 'cosmopolitan' (so-called 'Western') synthetic drugs, so that those who begin to use East Asian medicine are often aged forty or over.[27] Often they do so because they feel that their bodies are 'deteriorating'.[28] The increasing incidence of chronic ailments among middle-aged and older people is consistent with the common idea that *yakudoshi*s indicate a change in the life-cycle and in bodily health, with a greater susceptibility to illness as the body deteriorates. For men at least, an interest in, or acceptance of, 'alternative medicine' might be triggered off by their *yakudoshi* at the age of forty-two. Otherwise, the *yakudoshi* might be a factor predisposing them to use alternative forms of therapy if they later experience some illness which is not so amenable to conventional 'cosmopolitan' medicine.

Some evidence that there may be a relationship between the experience of a *yakudoshi* and the use of traditional medicine is indicated by a correlation between these among thirty-six people whom I questioned about the use of traditional therapies. Such a relationship is rather clearer for acupuncture and *shiatsu* (a kind of 'pressure-point massage') than for East Asian herbal medicine (*kanpō*). Probably this is because *kanpō* has enjoyed a sudden popularity and is now sometimes prescribed by doctors trained in cosmopolitan medicine. It appears also that a few people might have classified folk remedies as *kanpō*, whereas *kanpō*, strictly speaking, is Chinese herbal medicine with its own complex body of theory and prescription.[29] The relationship between passing one's principal *yakudoshi* and the use of East Asian medicine is indicated by the following tables:

Figure 7.2 The use of acupuncture in relation to *yakudoshi*s

	Male	*Cases*	*Female*	*Cases*
After yakudoshi	For: Lumbago	1	For: Stiff hips and legs	1
	Stiff shoulders	1	Tennis elbow	1
	Twisted ankle	1	Headaches	1
	Nervous temperament (*shinkeishitsu*[30])	1	Child's mis-behaviour (*kan no mushi*[30])	1
	Never used	8	Never used	3
Before yakudoshi			For: Sprained foot	1
			Trapped nerve in hand	1
			Whiplash effect after car acci-dents	1
	Never used	8	Never used	6

Figure 7.3 *Yakudoshi*s and the use of *shiatsu* ('pressure massage')

	Male	Cases	Female	Cases
After *yakudoshi*	For: Muscle ache	1	For: Muscle ache	1
	Stiff shoulder	1	General fitness	3
	Never used	10	Never used	3
Before *yakudoshi*			For: Muscle ache	1
	Never used	8	Never used	8

Figure 7.4 *Yakudoshi*s and the use of *kanpo* (herbal medicine)

	Male	Cases	Female	Cases
After *yakudoshi*	For: Stomach medicine	3	For: Cure for hiccoughs	1
	Overdrinking	1	*Dokudani* infusion during pregnancy	1
	Colds	4		
	Waist pains	1		
	Preventative medicine	1		
	Never used	2	Never used	5
Before *yakudoshi*	For: Gastritis	1	For: Colds	1
	Abdominal distress	1	Muscle ache	1
	High blood pressure	1	Constipation	1
	Recovery from fatigue (after a bicycle race)	1	Child's nappy rash	1
			Slimming	1
	Never used	4	Never used	4

It can be seen from Figures 7.2 to 7.4 that there is a noticeable increase in the proportion of people who try either acupuncture or *shiatsu* at some point after their *yakudoshi*s. *Kanpō*, however, is more popular among younger people too, although the relatively high proportion of women past their principal *yakudoshi*s who have never used *kanpō* is probably due to the fact that they are somewhat younger than the men whose principal *yakudoshi* occurs when they are in their early forties.

As an example of the link between *yakudoshi*s and the interest in traditional therapies, we can go back to the case of Mrs. Kimura, who had wondered whether or not a stomach ache after a row with her husband might be linked with her *yakudoshi*. The following year a friend of hers, of the same age, joined a keep-fit class. Mrs. Kimura decided to join one of the classes too and chose the cheapest, which was a *shiatsu* course. When she later explained her reasons for studying *shiatsu*, she gave as her primary motive her concern about her health following her stomach problems during her *yakudoshi*.

In practice, religious, East Asian and cosmopolitan ('Western') therapies are often used in conjunction with each other. For instance, when Mrs. Yamane was pregnant she attended a clinic practising 'Western' medicine for her ante-natal check-ups and for the birth itself. In the fifth month of pregnancy she bought a *hara-obi* from a local temple and at the same time purchased a 'safe birth' (*anzan*) *mamori* which she attached to whichever of her three *hara-obi*s she was wearing at the time. She returned the *mamori*s to the temple at the following New Year. From a pharmacist she bought some dried *dokudani* herbs to which she added boiling water in order to make an infusion called *senjugusuri* which she often drank during pregnancy. This is said to purge the body of the toxins and 'poisons' which a woman is said to produce in her body during pregnancy. Mrs. Yamane says that she took *senjugusuri* on the recommendation of her mother-in-law, because, she says, 'you tend to believe lots of things when you're pregnant and anxious about the baby'.

What should be the Christian attitude towards East Asian medicine?

I have no doubt that many of these traditional East Asian therapies do 'work' in many cases. However, supernatural cures are also claimed by occult practitioners such as spiritualists, whose attempts to consult the dead are in violation of scriptures which describe such practices as 'detestable' to God (Deuteronomy 18:9-13), and through which God's people would be 'defiled' (Leviticus 19:31).

An expert on deliverance from demonic powers strongly warns against the use of acupuncture. He writes,

> 'We must always look at the PHILOSOPHY which is behind a particular practice... In the case of acupuncture, we find it goes back to Emperor Huang Ti who concluded, through a study of the stars, that harmony and balance exist in the universe. There is a definite input from astrology in this practice. There is a reference to an energy or life force called Ch'i which is supposed to go into the body at birth and out again at death. This flows through the body in two systems, namely Yang—which is the male principle, and represents the sun—and the female principle, Yin, which represents the moon.
>
> Yang and Yin are supposed to flow through the body by a system of canals called the meridians which, in turn, go under the skin and around the body with fourteen main ones linked by fifteen luo canals and forty-seven subsidiary meridians, passing close to the skin at 365 points.
>
> It is not hard to see that just below this practice there is a philosophy involving the sun, the moon, the days of the year.
>
> I firmly believe there are psychic powers behind the practice of acupuncture and even its most innocent form can bring spiritual oppression. There can be a physical healing which takes place, as frequently happens when we use occultic powers in medicine, and with that comes a spiritual oppression.'[31]

On the other hand, a Christian missionary in Japan told me of how a fellow missionary in Taiwan had been cured after treatment by a Christian acupuncture specialist after conventional 'Western' medicine had been unable to help. Though I have some reservations about acupuncture, in the case of *kanpō*, traditional East Asian herbal medicine, it might be possible to reject an associated philosophy while still accepting that certain treatments might in themselves be 'neutral', or even from God. Some Christian missionaries have looked upon *kanpō* with suspicion because of its associations with theories of Yang and Yin, but experimental research into some of the plants used by *kanpō* practitioners has shown that such herbal remedies can actually be more effective than their equivalent 'Western' medicines. This research has shown that trace elements and other molecules hitherto considered unimportant do in fact play a vital role in ingestion by limiting the reaction of the drug in the body.[32] By contrast, many medicines in the West were originally derived from isolating the active ingredients in various plants, and using only those active ingredients, without the mitigating influences of side effects which these trace elements can give. This is why *kanpō* medicine is reputed to have fewer unwanted side-effects. This does not mean that one has to accept also theories such as those about Yin and Yang which have subsequently become associated with such medicines. We might believe that God created plants having these properties as medicines which also in their original form reduce their unwanted side-effects. The side-effects come when man tries to separate what God has joined together.

In these questions, it might be helpful to consider the attitude of the early church towards food sacrificed to idols. Certainly the philosophy behind such a practice was to be rejected. Some New Testament passages are very critical of those who eat such food (Acts 15:20; Revelation 2:20) whereas St. Paul's attitude was apparently more flexible. To Timothy he wrote about 'certain foods, which God created to be received with thanksgiving...For everything God created is good...' (1 Timothy 4:3-5). We might say the same about the herbs used in *kanpō* medicine. However in Romans 14 and 1 Corinthians 8 St. Paul writes that we should not take advantage of our freedom to eat such foods if our actions cause others to 'stumble'. In such cases it may be better to abstain, simply out of love.

CHAPTER
8
Fortune-telling

I T TOOK MR MURATA a long time to decide on a name for his daughter. Several weeks before her birth he had decided that if he had a daughter he would name her 'Yūmiko' because he liked the sound of the name. His problem was deciding how to write it.

Murata-san had bought a book which told him about 'lucky' and 'unlucky' combinations of Chinese characters in a person's name. They depended on the numbers of strokes in each character and how they added up in various combinations. For any syllable in Japanese there are often several Chinese characters (*kanji*) with that pronunciation; also, most *kanji* have both a Chinese and a Japanese pronunciation, which are often very different, and a few *kanji* have more than one Chinese pronunciation.

So there were many different ways in which the name 'Yūmiko' might be written. Murata-san decided on the *kanji* 祐 (with 9 strokes) for the '*Yū*' part, and the common female ending 子 (with 3 strokes) for the '*ko*' part. His problem then became focussed on the appropriate character for '*mi*'.

At first he considered the *kanji* 美, meaning 'beautiful', but this would have produced an unlucky total of 33 for the girl's 'total fate'.[1] He then considered the character 実, meaning 'fruit', which would have given the 'very good' total fate number of 32. However, in a girl's name the character for 'fruit' could carry embarrassing sexual connotations. Finally, Murata-san decided on 見, the '*mi*' of the verb '*miru*', to see: it did not carry much meaning but it produced a total fate of 31 which was considered to be 'very good'.[2]

Mr Murata's own name can be used to illustrate how the different elements in a name are combined to produce different kinds of 'fates', each of which can be 'lucky' or 'unlucky'. (His personal name is 'Akira'.)

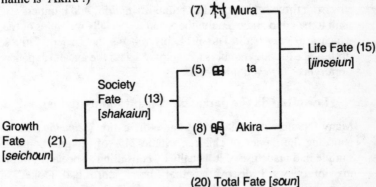

(20) Total Fate [*sōun*]

Names with different numbers of *kanji* in either the surname or personal name are calculated on the same general principles, according to whether a character is the first or last in each part of the name.

For each of these different 'fates'—the 'total fate', 'life fate', 'society fate' and 'growth fate'—there are some numbers which are 'very good', others which are 'good', a third group which are 'bad' (that is, 'to be avoided if possible') and a fourth group which are 'very bad' and 'to be avoided at all costs'.[3] To some extent, these numbers reflect common superstitions. For example, the number 'four' can be read as '*shi*', the same pronunciation as the word for 'death', so for this reason blocks of houses often lack a house number four. It might be that this superstition accounts for the way in which the numbers 14, 34, 44, 54 and 64 are all 'very bad' for the 'total fate' of both sexes—but 24 is exceptional as 'very good'.

The years of major *yakudoshi*s of both sexes (19, 25, 33 and 42) also tend to be in the 'bad' category for boys. However, the numbers 61 and 37 are exceptions, but it might be because these are apparently less known and less widespread than the other major *yakudoshi*s.[4] The same applies to girls, except that 33 is good for them. This might or might not be connected with the common idea that their *yakudoshi* is nullified by their bearing a child in that year—especially if the child is male. It is also possible to read '33' as '*san-san*', meaning 'birth after birth', with reference to fertility, just as during the marriage ritual the bride and groom take three sips from three *sake* cups.[5] For name-divination, odd numbers also tend to be good and even numbers bad, especially multiples of ten, which are 'very bad'. This probably reflects the ancient Chinese preference for odd numbers as compared with the ancient Japanese preferences for even numbers.[6]

How often do the Japanese consult name-divination?

Many Japanese do make use of name-divination (*seimeihandan*) in choosing the names of children. Some 24% of my questionnaire sample had made use of it, usually by consulting a specialist, but in my interviews I discovered that many more had looked at *seimeihandan* books for themselves without seeing a professional fortune-teller. Quite often it is a grandparent who chooses a child's name so the parents might not know if the grandparents made use of *seimeihandan* or not. However, most parents think it highly likely that the grandparents would have made use of *seimeihandan*, and in a few cases they were sure of the fact.

There are also some differences according to the sex and birth order of the children. It appears that the eldest son (*chōnan*) is more likely than others to have his name chosen by reference to *seimeihandan*. The eldest child—especially if a boy—is also more likely to be named by grandparents than are subsequent children. The following table shows the diversity of methods which are used for eldest children.[7]

Table 8.1 Naming methods for eldest children

Choice made by:	Using seimeihandan	Without seimeihandan	Method Unknown
Both parents together	6	8	0
Husband only	21	16	0
Wife only	3	1	0
Seimeihandan specialist, in consultation with parents	13	0	0
Husband's parents			3
Husband's father		1	2
Husband's father, in consultation with parents		1	
Husband's mother	1		
Husband's mother and grandmother			1
Wife's father			3
Wife's mother, in consultation with parents	1		
Wife's mother	1		
Column totals	47	26	9

Therefore, *seimeihandan* was consulted in at least 57% of these cases and the percentage could well be higher if it was consulted also by those relatives whose naming method was unknown. The incidence of *seimeihandan* is even higher when calculated according to its use for at least one child in a household: this is because at least three of those whose eldest children were girls did not use *seimeihandan* when choosing her name but did use it later when boys were born.

As a woman's surname changes at marriage, parents are often less concerned about finding an auspicious name for a girl. *Seimeihandan* can also be used in decisions about a future marriage partner, but it is only as an adjunct to other factors which are considered to be much more important.[8]

A *seimeihandan* specialist is often a Shinto or Buddhist priest, but sometimes the specialist can be a neighbour, relative or friend who has an interest in the subject. However, even the experts can disagree among themselves, as one family discovered. First they went to one Shinto priest who said the name the parents had chosen was 'very good'. Later they checked it also with another Shinto priest, who said the name was 'very bad', and suggested various alternatives. As a result the family became sceptical about *seimeihandan* in general and for their next child they simply chose a name which they themselves liked.

In a few other cases some scepticism arose from perceived inconsistencies between the parents' expectations and the actual experiences of the child. One *chōnan*, for example, suffered from osteomyelitis at the age of nine months and had to be hospitalized for three months. Another boy whose name was chosen by a *seimeihandan* specialist—who said the child would be healthy because of his good name—contracted an illness (called 'Kawasaki disease') when he was four years old. His mother regarded this as inconsistent with the expert's predictions.

These childhood illnesses are closer in time to the naming procedures, so may be more closely connected in the minds of the parents. However, many parents refrained from giving any opinion on whether or not the expert's predictions had come true. They said it was too soon to tell. The overall tenor of a person's life can only be assessed in retrospect, by which time those who named the person are normally dead themselves. If they are not, they may no longer be interested in the question of whether or not a *seimeihandan* specialist's predictions might have been fulfilled.

Why, then, do many parents consult *seimeihandan*? To some extent, they may be conforming to pressure from grandparents or other people, especially in the case of a *chōnan* who might become responsible in the future for ancestral rites. Some pressure might even be exerted by the wife's parents if she follows the custom of returning to her natal home to give birth there. However, grandparental pressure does not appear to be a major factor in the majority of cases, in which either one spouse alone or both parents together choose the name. Some other motivation seems to be influencing them.

This 'other motivation' is often that of *safety*. In many cases, informants expressed this motivation in terms such as:

'I don't particularly believe in seimeihandan, but I consulted it to be "on the safe side", because if my child were to have an accident

and I had not taken care to choose an auspicious name then I would feel guilty or responsible.'

Some people stressed the 'peace of mind' and 'reassurance' which comes from having a name checked by a *seimeihandan* expert. Very often the stress is on avoiding a 'bad' stroke count rather than necessarily finding a 'good' one. Inauspicious stroke counts are 'dangerous' and to be avoided: it is this fear which often motivates people to consult a name-diviner, rather than seeking the positive benefits which are said to come from finding an auspicious name. Such 'positive' benefits are sought in more 'practical' ways such as trying to ensure the child has a good education or trying to leave the child a substantial inheritance.

It is clear that a common motivation behind many forms of divination is a concern with 'safety', in the sense of reassurance about a decision. People are often looking for peace of heart. The word *anshin* which so frequently occurs in these contexts is formed by two Chinese characters. One of them (安) means 'peace' and the other one (心) means 'heart', 'mind' or 'soul'. Fortune-telling is largely an expression of a desire for peace of heart and reassurance. The same kind of emphasis on 'peace' (expressed in prayers for 'world peace') also occurs in several of the Japanese 'new religions'.

Consultation of mediums

In my questionnaire, 13 out of 576 people, or 2% of those who replied to the question, said that they had consulted a medium at some time in their lives. I followed up some of these in my interviews and collected details from three women and four men about the circumstances in which they had gone to a medium. These were:

Questions about the suitability of a prospective marriage partner:	2 cases
Regarding a medical problem:	4 cases
For consultation with the dead	1 case

The woman who wanted to consult with the dead did so after her younger son died in 1967. Shortly afterwards she went to a 60 year old medium in a nearby city who had been recommended by a neighbour. Although no formal fee was demanded, the mother took with her, on the neighbour's advice, a gift of high quality rice and a 'gift' of ¥1,000. Her description of the séance itself was rather vague, focussing on what was said to her:

> '*The spirit became manifest in the medium but at first said nothing. I was overwhelmed by the experience, and especially when the spirit at last did say something, telling me that my friends should look after me now that one of my sons has died. I then made offerings of many bean-jam cakes (manju) and bananas to my son, because he liked such fruit.*'

Two people consulted mediums about prospective marriage partners. One of them was a 36 year old housewife who twelve years previously had been to a medium on 'two or three' occasions to ask about work and marriage. She had already met her present husband but was confused about whether or not she should marry him. '*The medium gave me a kind of special message, and as I listened I felt it was like a miracle: the spirit approved of our marriage so I went ahead with it.*' However, one result of her marriage in a Christian church was that she ceased consulting mediums, because '*my husband hates anything to do with mediums, Shinto or Buddhism, and has stopped me going to such people any more.*'[9]

A twenty-nine year old man had been to a medium in north-eastern Japan, but only accompanying his grandmother. She often consulted mediums, on average once or twice each year. On this occasion, when she was accompanied by her grandson, his elder brother was about to marry and she was concerned to discover whether or not the marriage would work out well. However, the decision to marry had already been made and would not have been substantially affected by the medium's oracle.

Other cases of consulting a medium concerned responses to illnesses and have been described already in chapter seven.

Kokkuri-san

Consultation of *Kokkuri-san* is the Japanese equivalent to Ouija boards. The only difference is that the Japanese use either a tripod of chopsticks or else a coin, within a circle consisting of the 52 'letters' in the Japanese *hiragana* syllabic 'alphabet'. The practice was actually introduced to Japan by Western sailors from America and then spread within Japan during the late nineteenth and early twentieth centuries.[10]

Overall, 4% of my sample admitted to having consulted *Kokkuri-san*, but the percentage is as high as 40% among those aged between 20 and 24 years. It falls to 10% among those aged 25 to 29 and to 4% among those aged between 30 and 34 years. In other words, its popularity is on the increase, especially among the younger generations.[11] It is therefore important for Christian missionaries working among students to be aware of this practice: I was surprised when an experienced missionary who had spent more than a decade in Japan, and who specialized in work among students, looked at my questionnaire and asked me, 'What's this "Kokkuri-san"?'.

The seven people interviewed who had consulted *Kokkuri-san* gave three main reasons why they had done so:

a) to discover if a boy or girl were interested in them
b) to find missing property
c) to avoid feelings of not participating in a group activity in which their friends were involved.

Whatever the present age of those who described such experiences, they had all done it during childhood or adolescence. Two of them had stopped it after becoming frightened, fearing lest they should come under a curse (*tatari*). One of these had heard reports of the fox god, *Inari*, possessing people and making them mentally unbalanced through their consultation of *Kokkuri-san*.[12]

Palmistry

Over 30% of my sample had consulted a palmist at some time in their lives. Often it involved an outlay of ¥2,000 or more. It is particularly popular among those who are of marriageable age. Moreover, its practice seems to be on the increase, because 47% of those aged between 25 and 29 had consulted a palmist at some time in their lives.

Marriage tends to involve greater changes in the lifestyle of women than of men, so it is not surprising to find that 40% of the women but only 25% of the men had had their palms read. One man told me that his palm was read by a computer, which told him that he would have a major illness during his thirties. At the age of thirty-five he was still waiting to see if the prediction would be fulfilled.

Table 8.2 shows the kinds of statements made by palmists:

Table 8.2   Informants' assessments of palmists' statements

Male informants	Female informants
'The palmist's analysis of my past life and my character were accurate, but I can only remember one of his predictions, and that did not come true.'	'I would be 'separated from my first child'—and I did have a miscarriage, in fact.'
	'I would marry a gentle person.'
'He figured out that I was a musician from my soft hands.'	'He said that I lead a hard life, as he saw my rough hands.'
'He said I would have to look after my mother once I reached the age of 26 or 27, but now I'm 30 and my mother's still quite healthy.'	'I asked the palmist if my husband should change his place of work. Now I can't remember what the palmist said but he did change his job and it has worked out alright.'
	'He said that my hands were those of a murderer!' [reported as being an untrue statement!]

'His reading of the past fitted the time I became ill, but…' [from a man with an obvious glandular problem]

'He said that my condition would improve, but so far it has not.'[from the same man]

'My palm was read twice when I was 15, and the predictions about the kind of work I would do and whom I would marry came true exactly: I worked as an 'office lady' after leaving school and I got married at the age of 23.' [This is a very common career pattern for women in Japan.]

It is very difficult to assess the extent to which people 'believe' in palmistry. Often they say that they consulted the palmist '*for fun*' or out of curiosity, although as students or younger people on fairly low incomes they were still willing to pay the relatively high fees demanded. Any prior disposition to 'believe' can be reinforced by a few memorable statements which seem to 'fit' with experience, while many of the more general, non-specific statements are forgotten.

As with *seimeihandan*, scepticism about palmistry can also arise if a prediction does not fit the facts of experience. However, the test usually does not come for several years, by which time the person has often forgotten the details of what was said.

'Western' Astrology

Most of those interviewed about astrology had not consulted a professional fortune-teller but had instead read their horoscopes in a newspaper or magazine. Often they said that they had read their horoscopes '*by chance*' or '*out of curiosity*' when browsing through periodicals left in a doctor's or dentist's waiting room. However, the magazine and book departments of most local stores sell astrological compendia or almanacs for each year, often as pamphlets for each star sign. In many stores, the books on fortune-telling cover at least one or two full shelves containing a wide variety of titles. Several people had bought such books during their teens or early twenties, but had tended to drop such interests in later life as family or work responsibilities took up more and more of their time.[13]

Most people claimed their interest in astrology was more at the level of '*fun*' or '*curiosity*' rather than 'belief'. Only a few people, all of them women, claimed any greater measure of 'belief'. One of these is Mrs Matsumura, whose first marriage had ended in divorce. She says '*it was important for me to make the right decision this time*', and so she consulted both a palmist and an astrologer about her prospective match. Her present husband is very quiet and withdrawn so it might have been difficult for him to find a wife apart from an 'introduction' or an 'arranged marriage'. A friend of his sister's introduced the couple to each other, so the sister acted as a kind of go-between or 'guarantor' for the match. It was Mrs Matsumura who told me that the palmist had said she would marry '*a gentle person*', but it was not clear what other clues the palmist could have been working on.

Another woman says she believes in astrology because a fortune-teller had correctly predicted that she would have a minor traffic accident. Now she consults a weekly horoscope column on behalf of each member of her family '*to see what we have to be careful about*'. A third woman reads her horoscope daily and claims that it correctly predicted illnesses and recoveries in the lives of her children and mother-in-law, although the illnesses concerned were relatively minor ones. She claims that '*if the stars are in the wrong arrangement things will go wrong*', so at the beginning of each year she buys an astrological book to see what the future might hold.

Several others say that they read their horoscopes every week but are less willing to admit to a belief in it. One of these is a lady who supports the Communist party and superficially appeared to have nothing at all to do with religion. She seemed embarrassed to admit that she '*sort of*' believes in astrology and that she thinks the character judgments often fit the people concerned. A number of others restricted their 'belief' in astrology to the area of character analyses rather than prediction of the future.

'Chinese' astrology

The kind of astrology which is more commonly used for character judgment is based on the Chinese zodiacal year of birth. Almanacs (*koyomi*) which include this information, among other material, can be bought at most Shinto shrines, many Buddhist temples and some bookshops.[14]

Among those interviewed, there were several who had consulted such almanacs prior to getting married. They had wanted to check their 'affinity' (*aishō*) according to their respective years of birth by the Chinese cycle. For example, a woman born in the year of the sheep is said to be an unsuitable partner for a man born in the year of the tiger. However, those who consulted *aishō* had already made up their minds one way or the other: those who had already decided on marriage usually said that a favourable *aishō* brought '*reassurance*' but an unfavourable one was dismissed by the claim that they '*did not really believe in*' the *aishō*.[15]

Nevertheless, an indication that many people do pay some attention to these 'animal years' comes from the significant drops in recorded birth rates in 1906 and 1966, years of the 'Horse in Fire Major'. Women born in such years are reputed to be fiery tempered, quarrelsome with their husbands—even to the point of murdering them—and to make 'notoriously bad wives'. Apparently many parents tried to avoid having a daughter in these years lest her marriage chances be jeopardized.[16]

Blood group divination

An increasingly popular kind of divination among younger people is one based on blood groups. There is a widespread awareness of one's blood group because each person's group is tested at birth and recorded in his or her 'health handbook' (*kenkō techō*). Many people also think that one's blood group also indicates one's personality. 'O' people, for example, are said to be cheerful and intelligent, while 'B' people are sociable, creative and think about both sides of a question.

Like character divination based upon one's star sign or the animal years of one's birth, blood groups have become a form of divination among younger people considering compatibility in marriage. The popularity of blood-group divination stems from the way in which it appears to be more 'scientific', but doctors say that there is no medical basis for these claims.[17] Logically, there is little difference between claims that one's personality is shown by one's blood group and similar assertions that it is indicated by the lines on one's palm. Both blood groups and lines on the palms are physical features of the body which are presumably both governed by heredity. There is little reason to assert that one is more 'scientific' than the other.

As for palmistry and astrology, blood group divination is increasingly being used by younger women as a way of gaining an indication of the character and compatibility (in personality terms) of a potential husband. One appeal of blood groups is that they are fixed and immutable from birth. By contrast, some said they had doubts about palmistry because the lines on one's palm can alter during one's lifetime—whereas others said they had confidence in palmistry because the lines do not change!

One man said he was very patient because he belongs to blood group B, and remarked that his fate, blood group, name, the lines on his palm and also hereditary characteristics are all immutable and fixed from birth. His attitude to them all is the same: he is unable to do anything to change them, so he has to live in these circumstances by adapting to them rather than trying to change them.

In the same way, a woman remarked,

> *'I didn't believe in this before marriage, but I think I believe in it now. My husband says I'm quick-tempered, and I suppose I am at times, which is supposed to be a characteristic of 'A' type people like me.'*

The ethical implications of these attitudes are far-reaching but not immediately obvious. In essence, they deflect responsibility for a character weakness away from one's own volition and onto something less amenable to change. Whether one's character is thought to be 'fated' through one's blood group or through the year of one's birth by the Chinese calendar, it is fixed and immutable. Therefore responsibility for negative traits can be evaded by the attitude that *'it can't be helped'* (*shikata ga nai*, or *shō ga nai*). This is a widespread attitude among the Japanese.

This same principle of deflecting responsibility for one's actions applies also to other types of fortune-telling. If one can blame a 'character weakness' on one's sun sign or one's year of birth by the Chinese animal zodiac, then one can avoid responsibility for doing anything about rectifying it. The 'weakness' is apparently immutable. Perhaps this is related to the claim that Japanese society stresses 'shame' more than 'sin', an idea which I shall discuss further in chapter eleven.

Mikuji drawing

The most common kind of divination in Japan is known as *mikuji*.[18] These are printed oracles available at most Shinto shrines, but the mechanics of *mikuji* consultation vary from shrine to shrine. Sometimes it is by taking from a box one of many identically wrapped horoscopes; at other times it is by drawing a numbered stick from a cylinder and then buying the horoscope of that number from a nearby shop in the shrine. It always involves some kind of random selection of a printed horoscope.

Whatever the method, the *mikuji* contains printed oracles referring to a variety of aspects of life such as health, marriage proposal, financial matters or friendships. Some examples include:

[about health]	'Do as your doctor advises.'
	'No illness is to be expected.'
	'Have a check-up.'
[about work]	'Respect the opinions of your seniors (*senpai*) and friends.'
	'Go in the way you have been thinking about already.'
[about marriage proposal]	'Hard at first, alright afterwards.'
	'Look towards the East.' [*i.e.* for a spouse]

At the top of each *mikuji* horoscope the overall fortune of the oracle is announced in terms of three categories: 'very good luck', 'good luck' or 'bad luck'.[19] The possibility of 'bad luck' being predicted caused four women, all aged over forty, to stop drawing *mikuji*s when they began to draw some containing unspecified 'frightening things'. A fifth woman, aged fifty-eight, had never drawn one at all because she did not want to repeat her mother's experience in which some unspecified disaster had befallen the household as predicted in the *mikuji*. These women did not seem to think that the drawing of the *mikuji* caused the ill luck, or that the bad luck would not occur if they did not know about it, but instead they preferred to let it happen anyway without being forewarned.

Another reaction to *mikuji* oracles, reported by six women and two men, is similar to this but allows them to continue the practice. Their attitude is that they refuse to believe any of the bad things which are written but they are glad when anything good is predicted. Such an attitude is consistent with the comment of one informant, who said, '*Japan's kami are gods of convenience*' (*tsugō ga ii kami*): they are called upon if they are needed but are otherwise ignored. In the same way, some people *choose* to believe that which they want to believe in *mikuji* oracles but to ignore whatever they do not want to believe.

A third reaction, reported by five men and four women, is to worry when something bad is predicted, thinking that little or nothing can be done to avert it. All these three types of responses assume that 'fate' is relatively unchangeable. However, some of those who report these reactions, and many others, do pray at the shrine for the god to avert the predicted evil or to bring about the good things foretold.

Prayers of this kind view the *mikuji* horoscopes as warnings or promises *conditional upon human responses*, by prayer for super-human intervention, rather than as unchangeable destinies. Some people then tie up the 'bad' *mikuji* oracles on the branches of trees or bushes in the shrine, or on strings provided for the purpose; they pray for the evil to be left at the shrine and not brought home. The 'good' oracles might be kept in a handbag or somewhere at home. Others, however, also tie the 'good' or 'very good' horoscopes to the branches or strings and pray that the promises on them will be fulfilled. Therefore the act of tying a *mikuji* to a tree can have a variety of meanings, depending on the type of *mikuji*.[20]

Many younger people draw *mikuji* oracles, but they often stop doing so after they get married. By then their questions about marriage have been answered. However, many married people deny that the *mikuji* oracles have any predictive power at all.

About half of those interviewed about the topic gave such denials, saying, for example:

'They are all printed, so cannot be too specific for any individual.'

'The oracles are so vague that by statistical probability some items are bound to come true.'

'Any prediction which 'comes true' is simply one's own inter-pretation of subsequent events.'

Others were prepared to say they *'half believed'* or else implied some belief by their behaviour in ceasing to draw *mikuji*s out of a fear of 'bad' events being predicted. Only three individuals, how-ever, could give specific examples of predictions which they consid-ered to have come true. One said the *mikuji* was accurate in predicting he would have good friends, and another said the predic-tions *'sometimes'* came true when he lost something. The third person gave a small list of fulfilled predictions about losing a purse and a valuable pendant, where her husband would come from, friends visiting *'from afar'* and having no more than three children: she has two, *'both with difficulty'*, and had to wait eleven years for the first. However, it is rare to have more than three children in modern Japan anyway.

Most people say they consult *mikuji*s out of *'fun'* or *'curiosity'* but few seem to take them very seriously. When I asked the high priest of a major Shinto shrine (*jingū*) about his attitude to *mikuji* oracles, he said that they come true *'only if you take them seriously, with all your heart, and not with a casual attitude.'* Probably the few who do have such a serious attitude are more likely to read into subsequent events any possible fulfilment of the predictions.

Other kinds of divination

There are a number of other kinds of divination practised in Japan, including the kinds used in house building which I described in chapter four. One of the more bizarre types of divination reported to me is based upon the shape of one's navel. On Mount Ikoma, between Osaka and Nara, there is one such fortune-teller who inspects his customers' navels! Outside his 'office' he displays pic-tures of the various different kinds of navels which people might have.[21] Even this form of divination, however, is understandable in the Japanese cultural context where attention is paid to the significance of one's navel and the importance of the umbilical cord, as I shall describe further in chapter ten.

The increasing interest in divination

In the above descriptions of different kinds of divination, I have referred to the fact that consultation of *Kokkuri-san*, palmistry, 'Western' astrology, blood group divination and *mikuji* oracles appears to be on the increase. All these are more popular among the younger generations.[22]

It is also clear that many forms of divination are more popular among women than men, and particularly young single women who are considering questions of marriage. On the whole, marriage in Japan involves a greater change in the life of a woman than of a man. Probably for this reason women are much more concerned about making 'the right choice'. In such a major decision, it is a help or 'reassurance' if an 'external' power or source of some kind of supernatural knowledge confirms the decision which the woman is about to make. Usually the decision is made primarily on other grounds, but fortune-telling can be used to further justify that decision. On the whole, divination might be used to confirm a decision or as an excuse to turn down a prospective match in an 'arranged' marriage, whereas in a 'love' marriage divination tends to be used more as a positive confirmation. If the result of the divination is less favourable, it is then more likely to be ignored on the grounds that 'we didn't really believe in it anyway'.

Christian implications

Christians also seek to discover God's will through various means, but regard some methods as acceptable and others as dangerous. The Bible strongly condemns the practices of divination or sorcery, turning to mediums or seeking out spiritists, because those who do so would be 'defiled' by them (Exodus 22:18; Leviticus 19:26b, 31; Deuteronomy 18:9-13). Contemporary experience shows that it usually leads to some kind of demonic control or influence over a person. Often some kind of deliverance ministry is required in order to set the person free from the occult influences. This needs to be done through the authority of Jesus and the power of the Holy Spirit.

On the other hand, we need to be open to God's guidance in legitimate ways. Divination in Japan is largely a seeking after *guidance*. Christians need to be able to offer, and demonstrate in practice, what it means to know God's clear guidance—whether through scripture, divinely appointed circumstances, dreams, visions or other means. Some missionaries and pastors in Japan may take on a shamanistic rôle equivalent to fortune-tellers when they are consulted for guidance and advice. This may lead to an excessive dependency upon the human agent and to a falling away from the church when that person moves on.[23] It is necessary to encourage instead a greater dependency upon the Holy Spirit for his revelations and guidance.

One of the topics which seemed to fascinate Japanese people was how Ruth and I were led together by the Lord. It is not necessary to go into all the details here, but simply to mention that there were several clear and remarkable confirmations that it was God's will for us to marry. Such testimonies of divine guidance have a significant impact among the Japanese, partly because they contrast so strongly with the widespread efforts to seek guidance about marriage partners through occult means.

Other Christians may have quite different stories of divine guidance, but what is important is that they authentically demonstrate the hand of God. Guidance comes in many forms, some more dramatic than others, but most of us can give examples from our own experience. In many ways it is better to present the positive alternative to divination rather than criticising various kinds of fortune-telling.

Some divination, however, is also to do with the future. Christians have at least two counterparts to this. One is eschatological, based on biblical predictions of future events. The other is the testimony of contemporary Christian prophecy, which is admittedly a controversial topic. Without going into the debates here, I shall merely note that I do believe God continues to give insights and warnings about future events, often as 'signs' to confirm other prophetic messages. However, I also believe that there are many people around who receive such messages but do not know what to do with them.[24] The 'famous names' receive attention—and criticism—but God wants to raise up a prophetic people throughout the world among whom such gifts are commonly manifested. He desires to pour out his Spirit on all his people so that their 'sons and daughters will prophesy...' (Joel 2:28). Peter interpreted that prophecy as having been fulfilled on the Day of Pentecost (Acts 2:16-21), but that was merely the beginning. The Holy Spirit still works among us, granting gifts which include prophecy (1 Corinthians 12 to 14). This is because one of his tasks today remains that of telling us 'what is yet to come' (John 16:13).

CHAPTER
9

The cult of the dead

'TEN DAYS AGO I had a dream about my mother's brother. He wanted me to pray more fervently and to perform the ancestral rites for him...I can't now remember his words to me in the dream, or even if there were any words at all, but my strong feeling when I awoke was that this was what my uncle wanted me to do.'

Mr. Kaneda, the speaker, had inherited from his maternal uncle several rice fields and a mountain about twenty miles from Ueno, the sale of which had enabled him to buy his present home. Otherwise, it would have been impossible for him to buy a house in Aoyama on his present salary as a railway conductor. His mother's brother had died childless and had not formally adopted Mr. Kaneda, but as heir of his uncle's property Mr. Kaneda feels a responsibility to maintain the ancestral rites on behalf of his uncle. However, his irregular shifts meant that sometimes he was unable to pray daily at the household Buddhist altar (*butsudan*), so his wife usually performed the rites on his behalf. Now, because of his dream, he is trying to perform the rites more regularly himself.

What Mrs. Kaneda had been doing each evening in front of their *butsudan* was to recite the phrase 'Glory to Amida Buddha' (*Namu Amida Butsu*) for a minute or two and to offer fresh water daily, plus rice if she had cooked any that day. On most days she burned incense and candles, sometimes also changing withering flowers for

179

fresh ones. Mr. Kaneda's uncle had died on the 29th of April, so on the 29th of each month this family also offer sweets at the *butsudan*, and put similar offerings at his grave site.

Families in which there has been no recent bereavement may not have a *butsudan* at present, but once someone has died they will usually obtain one and begin to practise the cult of the dead. Such was the case in the Fujii family of Sakurano, whose first child died at the age of three months from a heart disease. When interviewed fourteen years later, the mother still had an enlarged photograph of the child on the wall of her apartment, even though she had also had two subsequent children. Every day she prays to (or for) the dead child. Perhaps, in a case like this, any Christian approach to the situation needs to minister also to the mother's sense of continuing grief at the loss of a baby.[1]

The *butsudan* itself can take various forms. In urban areas it often consists of a standing cabinet with double doors which are opened whenever the rites are performed. From the outside it sometimes appears to be merely a cupboard set into the wall, whereas in rural areas it can occupy most of a room specially set aside for it. Nowadays *butsudan*s are usually bought from specialist shops at prices well in excess of £1,000 each, but one man in Sakurano had constructed his own small one.

Inside the *butsudan* are stored memorial tablets (*ihai*), each inscribed with the posthumous name of a deceased ancestor. Many *butsudan*s also contain statues or paintings of Buddhist divinities, offering dishes, photographs of deceased relatives and a gong or bell to alert the ancestors of one's presence. Either with the offering dishes or in a drawer underneath the *butsudan* might be kept a rosary and a 'book of the past' (*kakochō*), which contains a record of the dates of death of various family members. Sometimes important family documents are also kept in this drawer, symbolically protected by the ancestors.

Offerings at the *butsudan* commonly consist of some combination of fruit, cooked rice, incense, flowers, water or tea. In theory Buddhist vegetarian principles should preclude the offering of meat, but in practice fish or fowl might sometimes be offered.[2] Foods of which the ancestor was particularly fond, including sweets and chocolate biscuits, may be offered too.

There is wide variation among different families in how frequently they perform the rites and the kinds of offerings they present. For example, Mrs. Minami, a 46 year old Aoyama resident, offers daily a portion of the first rice she has cooked that day, changes the flowers every few days, gives the first (*hatsumono*) of each kind of fruit or vegetable as they come into season each year, and on the anniversaries of each ancestor's death presents special gifts of that person's favourite foods. However, her neighbour, Mrs. Kawasaki, normally presents offerings only on the 16th of each month—the date when her father-in-law died—and in addition at the summer *bon* festival, the equinoxes (*higan*) and New Year. Her offerings generally consist of fruit, rice cakes (*mochi*) and bean-jam buns (*manju*). Even fewer offerings are given by Mr. Tanaka, a 52 year old *shataku* resident. He presents offerings of tea and rice at New Year and at the *bon* festival in August, and in addition gives suitable fruit at *higan*, but he makes no other offerings throughout the rest of the year.

Many families observe special rites at the Spring and autumn equinoxes (both called *higan*) and at the August *bon* festival, when the ancestors are said to return temporarily to this world. In many areas *bon* dances are held to welcome the ancestors. A few days later, the souls of the ancestors may be symbolically escorted back to the other world through the lighting of bonfires or the floating of illuminated model boats out to sea or down a river.[3]

In addition to rites on a daily basis—either every morning or every evening, or both—many families also present special offerings and prayers on the deceased's annual deathday (*shōtsuki meinichi*). This might be, for example, on the 24th of May each year for someone who had died on that day. Some families also commemorate the person's monthly deathday (*maitsuki meinichi*), which in this example would be the 24th of each month. At such times special offerings might be made or a priest might be invited in to recite sutras.

Even if a family remembers a deceased member on each anniversary of the death, on certain special anniversaries close relatives of the deceased come together for a more elaborate memorial rite called a *hōji*. They sit together quietly while a Buddhist priest chants sutras, but often it is also the occasion for a family reunion over a common meal, especially when the members are geographically scattered and rarely see each other at other times. These anniversaries bring together wider kin such as scattered adult brothers and sisters, children and grandchildren. *Hōji* rites are held on periodic anniversaries of death, called *nenki*, which occur on the first, third, seventh, thirteenth, twenty-third, twenty-seventh, thirty-third and fiftieth anniversaries of the death, and sometimes on the hundredth anniversary too.[4]

There are so many individual permutations in the occasions on which which people observe memorial rites that seventy-nine different patterns were found among the 144 people with *butsudan*s who reported the occasions on which they perform rites.[5] Only twenty-five of these seventy-nine patterns occurred more than once.

Virtually 60% of these 144 people perform rites on a daily basis, and a further 12% perform monthly rites on the death dates (*meinichi*) of known ancestors. Another 25% perform rites less frequently than once a month, most of them combining seasonal rites at *bon* or *higan* with occasional rites for individual ancestors on the anniversaries of their deaths. A few people—five in all— said that they never worship at a *butsudan* even though they have one in their homes, but in each of these cases there is somebody else who does perform the rites.

Inheriting responsibility for the rites

Religious rites on behalf of the dead are performed in virtually every family at some time or other. What matters is that *someone* should perform the rites for a recently deceased relative. Traditionally the one responsible for the rites was the eldest son, but nowadays if the eldest son lives at a considerable distance from the family grave sites then another child nearer at hand might take on responsibility for the rites. Those living further away might still perform rites at a *butsudan*, but their visits to the family graves might occur only once a year, or even less frequently.

A widow or widower will normally look after the *butsudan* rites for a deceased spouse, but when the surviving spouse also dies the responsibility is passed on to the next generation. Traditionally the eldest son, who assumed responsibility for the rites, also looked after the parents in their old age. However, he also inherited the 'lion's share' of the parental property while any other siblings received only a small share or nothing at all.[6] There was therefore an economic reward for the eldest son's faithfulness, and to some extent gratitude for this might be an additional motivation for the heir to perform the ancestral rites once the parents have died.

Nowadays, official legislation stipulates that a family's inheritance should normally be divided equally, but in practice the traditional custom remains fairly strong: the eldest son (*chōnan*) still inherits all or almost all of the property. Sometimes the other siblings formally sign away their rights to equal inheritance. In other cases the younger siblings might receive some monetary compensation in exchange for allowing the *chōnan* to inherit the parents' house. For example, one Aoyama man said that formally his eldest brother owned their deceased parents' house in Nagano prefecture but in fact it was unoccupied and all the siblings had the right to use it as a holiday home. In another case, the youngest son among ten siblings inherited the family property because he was considered the 'most suitable'. Sometimes sisters are excluded from the division of the family property because they are now considered to belong to another 'house', that of their husbands.

Whatever inheritance practices are adopted, the *chōnan* almost invariably inherits the *butsudan*, except in cases where his work or other circumstances have taken him away from the parental home and ancestral graves but a younger brother has remained. Inheritance of a *butsudan* continues to reflect the traditional distinctions between a family's 'main' lineage (*honke*) and 'branch' families (*bunke*) which are formed by the splitting off of younger sons. When a family has no children or has only daughters, an 'adopted son-in-law' (*yōshi*) may take on the family's surname and assume all the rights and responsibilities of the *chōnan*. Often the *yōshi* is a younger, non-inheriting son of another family who has married one of the daughters. Mr. Kaneda, whose circumstances were described at the beginning of this chapter, is not actually a *yōshi* but he is a '*de facto*' one.

Eighty percent of the 173 *chōnan*s in my sample either possess a *butsudan* now or else expect to inherit responsibility for one in the future. Most of the remainder either live quite far away from their natal homes or, in a few cases, are Christians of one kind or another. One man is not a Christian himself but is married to a Christian wife who refuses to participate in the *butsudan* cult.

Although inheritance of the *butsudan*s, and responsibility for the rites, is normally passed on to men, in practice their wives are the ones who often perform the rites. To some extent this is on account of the greater amount of time available to the women because of the amount of time their husbands are away from the home while at work. Another influence is the fact that women are normally responsible for cooking the meals, so that putting an offering of rice on the *butsudan* before serving out portions to the rest of the family can easily become a regular habit. Similarly, the changing of older flowers for fresh ones on the *butsudan* is not unlike their other domestic chores for keeping the home generally clean and tidy.

There are relatively few cases in which a man alone is responsible for the upkeep of a domestic *butsudan*. One such man is Mr. Maruyama, whose first wife, by a 'love marriage', was killed in a motor accident. He was left with the care of two young children and married shortly afterwards, this time by an 'arranged' marriage. His *butsudan* enshrines the memorial tablet (*ihai*) of his first wife. Every evening after he returns from work he offers at the *butsudan* some rice which his present wife has cooked for their evening meal, plus fruit and vegetables in season.

It can be seen, from the examples already cited, that almost anybody can be enshrined in a *butsudan*. Mr. Kaneda performs rites for his maternal uncle, Mrs. Fujii for her dead child and Mr. Maruyama for his deceased wife. Several scholars have sought a more appropriate term than 'ancestor worship', in so far as other people besides 'ancestors' may also be enshrined and it is debatable whether or not what is performed at the *butsudan* or grave is properly described as 'worship'.[7]

Grave rites

Closely linked with *butsudan* rites, as another variant of the 'cult of the dead', are rituals performed at grave sites. The three principal occasions for visiting the ancestral graves are at *bon* (15th August) and the Spring and autumn equinoxes (both called *higan*). Some families also include New Year, which means they practise observances in every season.

Families living close to their ancestral graves may visit more often, in some cases once a month. One such family are the Matsuis. Their first child died in infancy but, unlike the Fujiis, they do not have a *butsudan* in their *shataku* apartment. Instead, they gather before the *butsudan* at the home of the husband's parents and then go together to the child's official grave site. In fact, the infant's bones are in a charnel house in the city centre, but after the child died, thirteen years ago, Mr. Matsui's father constructed a special gravestone memorial near his home, not far from Sakurano. The memorial is for both the infant and his great-grandfather. On the second Sunday of each month, a date near to the child's *meinichi* when the whole family can attend, the family clean up the grave and offer flowers, incense, branches of *sakaki* (the sacred tree of Shinto), and sometimes sweets or other foodstuffs. They also hire a priest to read sutras for the child and for his great-grandfather.

It is noteworthy that this dead infant is still referred to as the *chōnan*, and his two brothers born subsequently are taught to refer to the dead child as their elder brother. The two other boys are now aged twelve and ten, and throughout their lives have attended these rites with their parents.

For the Matsui family, it is important to have a site for the memorial observances even if it is not the actual location of the dead child's remains. Sentimentally, it is very important for the surviving relatives to have *somewhere* which they can identify as the place for remembering the dead. The Matsuis are continuing a practice of 'double' graves found in some rural areas of Japan.[8] Another *shataku* family, the Naganos, have three grave sites because their ancestors belonged to the Zen sect of Japanese Buddhism. Their case illustrates the way in which ancestral rites continue to be affected by the traditional distinctions between 'main' and 'branch' lineages in a family.

Traditionally, a family's main lineage was perpetuated through the eldest sons, whereas younger sons might initiate 'branch' lines.

The branch lineage does not necessarily have a *butsudan* of its own until one of its members dies. However, the main temple of Zen Buddhism, Eiheiji in Niigata prefecture, contains at least one piece of bone from the ashes of each deceased member of this Nagano family, of both main and branch families. The Naganos say this is 'so that all the ancestors can be together and not be lonely'. The other part of the ashes of Mr. Nagano's ancestors, up to and including his paternal grandfather are in Tsuruga, on the Japan Sea coast, where the Nagano main line have lived for several genera- tions. Mr. Nagano's father, however, was not a *chōnan*, so, having no claim on the family's property, migrated to Kyoto. There he founded a branch lineage and was buried. Now his son visits this grave at *bon* and *higan*, and, if he has time, on his father's *meinichi* too. He also visits Tsuruga every year when they have a family holiday, not at one of the traditional times for grave visits. It is too far for him to go to Eiheiji very often, but if he has enough time off over New Year he might take his family there. On such occasions Mr. Nagano reports on what has been happening in the family, but does this to his own father and not to the collectivity of ancestors.

Those living further away from their ancestral graves tend to visit less frequently, especially if there is another relative who lives nearer to the graves. One woman from Kyushu sends money to her younger sister and brother-in-law in Kyushu, asking them to visit the graves on her behalf. The money is sufficient to cover the costs of their car journey to a relatively remote part of the island as well as the costs of incense and other grave offerings. She is motivated by personal attachments to her parents, even though she has mar- ried outside the family and theoretically is no longer obliged to perform rites for her own parents. There are also several examples of men who are not *yōshi*s but who perform rites to their wives' ancestors, largely because the graves are nearer to where they are now living. In this way, there is a tendency for geographical prox- imity to take precedence over genealogical priority.

More people visit their family graves at *bon* than at *higan*, largely because there is more opportunity for families to take a holiday in the summer. Overall, 63.5% of informants had visited their ancestral graves at *bon*, as compared with 45% at *higan*. Some men send money to a local priest, for him to perform rites in their absence. For the most part, it is felt that as long as *somebody* looks after the grave, and takes responsibility for it, the obligations to the ancestors are discharged.

Some attitudes towards grave visits are indicated by the replies of seventy people who were asked whether the ancestors would be 'angry' or 'sad' if they did not visit the graves:

Table 9.1   Attitudes expressed towards grave rites

	People who regularly visit ancestral graves (Number = 50)	People who seldom or never visit (Number = 20)
Yes: ancestors are both angry and sad	7 people (=14%)	1 person (= 5%)
No: ancestors are neither	16 people (=32%)	18 people (=90%)
Ancestors are not angry but they are sad	13 people (=26%)	
Ancestors are not angry but are lonely	4 people (= 8%)	
'I would feel guilty inside if I didn't go'	6 people (=12%)	1 person (= 5%)
'I can't say because I go there anyway'	2 people (= 4%)	
'Don't know'	2 people (= 4%)	

To a large extent these beliefs are consistent with people's practices. However, there are a variety of motivations for such rites. Several people initially said it was 'custom' or 'tradition'. Some other reasons given for performing the rites include:

'I go because it is a custom; it is also a good time to go, as the graves need to be tidied up at some time or other, and I suppose I'd feel ashamed if I didn't do it.'

'We received our education from our ancestors, so we should remember them: it's a Japanese tradition.'

'Because we have ancestors we should worship them, and I want my children to do the same for me. I am the *chōnan* and I inherited property from my ancestors, so I should esteem them.'

Kamidana rites

The Shinto god-shelf, called a *kamidana*, often takes the form of a ledge or small shelf set fairly high up on one wall of a room. The choice of preferred room can vary to some extent between different regions of Japan.[9] In Ueno it is commonly in the kitchen or living room, but one household without a formal *kamidana* regard their image of Kōjin, a kitchen god, as the equivalent of a *kamidana*.

Most *kamidana*s contain at least one, sometimes several, amulets or talismans (*fuda*) from a variety of Shinto shrines. There are many types of *fuda* but most commonly they consist of inscribed pieces of paper, sometimes wrapped around a wooden plaque, or else the wooden plaque by itself. The inscription contains the name of the shrine where the *fuda* was bought and might claim to confer some practical benefit such as safety from fire or safety in the home. Certain shrines are famous for particular specialities, such as the 'Iwadani' shrine (a few miles from Nishiyama) which specializes in charms against *yakudoshi*. Other types of charms which might be kept in a *kamidana* include *mamori* amulets for safety and *chimaki* charms kept from the Ueno festival.

The range of items offered to the *kami* at the *kamidana* is not dissimilar to those offered at a *butsudan*. They include fruit, incense, flowers and rice, though rice was only reported as being presented to the *kami* at New Year. There are, however, a few notable differences between what is offered at the two types of household shrine.[10] Some of the offerings peculiar to a *butsudan* or *kamidana* among Ueno informants are as follows:

Table 9.2   Offerings peculiar to *butsudan*s and *kamidana*s

Kamidana	Butsudan
Salt	Bean-jam buns (*manju*)
New Year foods (*o-sechiryori*)	Biscuits or sweets as favourite foods of a particular ancestor
Sakaki branches	*Shikimi* branches
Seaweed	
Spiced *sake* (rice wine)	
Cuttlefish	

As for *butsudan*s, there is also a wide variation among different families in the occasions when they practise *kamidana* rites. A few families make offerings to the *kami* on only the first and fifteenth days of each month, and a couple of others which have daily *kamidana* rites put out special offerings (such as *sake* instead of water) on these days. Essentially these days mark the beginning and middle of the month and by the older lunar calendar would have occurred every fourteen days.

Among the 152 people possessing a *kamidana* who reported the pattern of their rites, about 40% worship on a daily basis. There is also a great variety in their occasions for worship. In all, 21 patterns occurred more than once, accounting for 73% of my cases, but another 41 different patterns occurred only once each.

New Year is an especially important time for *kamidana* rites. Some 95% of these informants practise some kind of *kamidana* rites then. Ten people who perform daily rites also singled out New Year as a time for special ceremonies, and another twenty-seven people worship only at New Year. These figures are not surprising because the New Year is strongly associated with Shinto.

What is more surprising, however, is the fact that twenty of the 152 respondents claimed to perform *kamidana* rites on the death dates of *ancestors*—that is, on a *meinichi* or *nenki*. This goes against the conventional stereotype that ancestors are revered at the *butsudan* but Shinto deities at the *kamidana*. Even in relation to ancestral rites there is some overlap in functions between the *kamidana* and the *butsudan*.

However, in ten out of these twenty cases the informants also possess a *butsudan* and it is likely that they perform rites at both on the same day. One person left blank the question about *butsudan* ownership but wrote 'Yes' for having a *kamidana*: probably he does not have a *butsudan*, but he does perform rites as if to ancestors. Another three might have been referring to their parents' practices, as they indicated on their forms that such people were responsible for the rites; however, this does not explain why their parents perform *kamidana* rites on the death dates of ancestors. The six remaining people who do not possess *butsudan*s but perform *kamidana* rites for ancestors reported their patterns of rites as follows:

Table 9.3   Ancestral rites practised at some *kamidana*s

No. of cases	New Year	Every evening	Monthly meinichi	Nenkis
1		X		X
3	X		X	
2	X			X

One of these six people refused to be interviewed about *kamidana* rites, saying that her husband was the one who knew more about his *ancestors*—a significant word in this context. Two others, however, allowed me to interview them about such matters.

Mrs. Yamamoto, aged forty-five, lives in one of the *shataku* apartments. From childhood, she says, she had been taught to revere the ancestors: her parents had both a *butsudan* and a *kamidana*. She says that '*Kamisama*' ('God') and '*Hotokesama*' (either the Buddha or ancestors) are both 'very old ancestors' who, together with the more recent ancestors, 'are protecting the family so we can pass each day happily'. Like most others, she does not distinguish between *Kamisama*, *Hotokesama* and the ancestors (*go-senzosama*), but instead she groups them together by saying they all—'but especially the ancestors'—have this protective function. The recent ancestors, in her view, 'have much more influence, power and relevance': it is for this reason that she gives 'thanks to the ancestors every evening' at her *kamidana*.

As her parents are still alive, Mrs. Yamamoto's most recent ancestors are her grandparents. On the occasions of their *nenki* rites, (when the family gathers together for a *hōji*), she also prays specifically to these ancestors at her *kamidana* and she presents special offerings of rice, *sake* and *sakaki* branches, like she does at New Year. When she prays her feelings are primarily ones of thanksgiving, and every night she gives thanks to the ancestors for keeping the family safe during the day. She also includes petitions for health and safety, especially for her husband at work in the factory.

The other family interviewed who perform ancestral rites at a *kamidana* belong to a minority of 'out and out Shintoists'.[11] Originally this family came from the Miyazaki area of Kyushu, where, they say, there is a local Shinto group who are not Buddhists but perform only Shinto memorial rites which take place ten days, fifty days and one year after a person's death.[12] My informant's father is now ninety years old but migrated to the Kansai area at the age of twenty-two, in search of work. He was the second son of a Shinto family, the Ōtsubos, but he was adopted as a *yōshi* by his mother's sister and her husband, who were childless. In this way he changed his surname from Ōtsubo to Yamashita, and later inherited the Yamashita *kamidana* after his mother's younger sister died in 1941.

In this *kamidana* are *ihai*s of the Yamashita ancestors who were revered at their *kamidana*. There are now ten *ihai*s there, but the informant's father does not perform any rites for the earlier ancestors whom he never knew. To a limited extent he does them for his adoptive parents, his aunt and her husband. The only person for whom he does perform specific rites is his eldest son, who died at the age of twenty on the 7th January 1949. Now on the seventh of each month—his son's *meinichi*—Mr. Yamashita makes an offering of *sakaki* at his *kamidana* and performs the usual Shinto 'prayer' of two bows, two handclaps and one more bow. When other family members are at home they join him in this. This same rite is also performed on the first of each month (but not the fifteenth), so automatically includes New Year too. However, these ones at the beginning of each month are not to a particular individual but to the collectivity of *kami*.

There is therefore some overlap, in practice, between the functions of *butsudan*s and some *kamidana*s, in so far as ancestors may be revered at both. This is similar to the lack of distinctions made by most informants between Shinto shrines and Buddhist temples, and between the imputed functions of *kami*, *hotoke* and ancestors. All 'protect' or 'watch over' the living members of the family, who make very little distinction between their functions except to say that the ancestors (*go-senzosama*) are in some way 'nearer'. In particular, they are thinking of those who died within living memory.

'Substitute *butsudan*s'

Instead of a formal *butsudan*, some people keep substitute memorial places in their homes. One of these is Mr Tanaka, who was one of ten children but was adopted into the Tanaka family as a *yōshi*. He lives in a small *shataku* apartment and keeps the *ihai* of his real and adoptive parents in a cupboard along with an assortment of other paraphernalia such as books, pens, correspondence, binoculars and his camera. Some of these fell out when he opened the cupboard to show us the *ihai*. Four times a year he sets up the *ihai* and makes offerings to them.

The Suehara family of Aoyama have what they call a *zushi* instead of a formal *butsudan*. Mr Suehara's father was a Buddhist priest who grew up in a temple and was expected to follow the 'family business' by becoming a priest too. However, he became critical of some of the formality and life-styles of those in the temple and he submitted proposals to simplify the management of the institution. Because these proposals were rejected, Suehara-san was put in a position in which he felt unable to remain in the temple organization. He left and became a school teacher while one of his nephews took over his place in the temple.

This nephew also took over responsibility for the Suehara ancestral cult. For this reason, the Suehara *zushi* in Aoyama contains no *ihai* of Suehara-san's parents, only their photographs, and this is one of the reasons why Mr. Suehara prefers the technical term *zushi*. However, the *zushi* does contain one *ihai*, that of their dead daughter. Mementoes of the parents and particularly of the deceased daughter are kept in the drawer underneath the *zushi* along with Suehara-san's rosary. Every day he and his wife pray at the *zushi* and offer fresh rice: Mrs. Suehara usually takes away and eats the old rice of the previous day, whereas many younger families throw away the old offerings.

Their thirty-five year old son prays there about once a week, 'for a very short time'. Sometimes he puts his hands together, bows and says '*Namu Amida Butsu*' (Glory be to Amida Buddha), but more usually he simply says '*Man man chan*', a children's version of the same phrase which he has been taught since childhood. His twenty-nine year old wife prays for just a few seconds each morning, saying '*Ohayō gozaimasu*' ('Good morning'), and often in addition prays for peaceful relationships with her mother-in-law, safety in the home (*kanai anzen*), or 'absence of illness, life without disasters'.[13]

Five other families, all living in Aoyama, also possess some kind of 'substitute *butsudan*'. One man (who was not available for interview) wrote '*ihai*' on his questionnaire next to the question about *butsudan* possession, leaving the question blank because of not being sure what to reply. The other four people with 'substitute' *butsudan*s gave no indication on their questionnaires of the existence of these memorials, but information about these practices only came to light when they were interviewed. It is therefore likely that others also have such memorial places in their homes.

In the bedroom of Dr. and Mrs. Satō there is a table set by itself against one wall. On it, the photographs of the deceased fathers of both Dr. Satō and his wife are displayed prominently, each in its own frame. In front of the photographs is a small dish containing a few sweets as offerings. Next to the photos are fresh flowers, a *fuda* from a shrine and their daughter's recent graduation certificate.[14] Whenever the family is given any unusual delicacy (*mezurashii mono*), it is first offered at this 'substitute *butsudan*'. On such an occasion, Mrs. Satō says words such as, 'Look, father, Mr. X has brought this' and bows towards the photograph. The food may be left there for a few days before being eaten by the family. Every so often Mrs. Satō changes the flowers: when she does so, she claps her hands together and bows towards the photographs.

A similar practice occurs in the Kobayashi family. This is a three-generational household where the husband's father—like Dr. Satō—is a second son. The elder Kobayashis live with their son, daughter-in-law and grandchild, and say that there is not enough room in the house for a 'proper' *butsudan*, or even for larger photographs. Instead, they remember the parents of Mr. Kobayashi senior by daily offering water before two small photos. However, they do have a 'proper' *kamidana*, which Mr. Kobayashi senior inherited as a second son when his elder brother inherited responsibility for the family *butsudan*.

Another Aoyama family also keep photographs of deceased parents on a special shelf and regularly change the flowers next to them. This husband is also a second son. They consider their practice of keeping these photographs next to some regularly changed flowers to be 'usual', but they do not place any food offerings there and deny bowing or praying before the photographs.

The Sakashita family of Aoyama denied having a *butsudan* when they filled in their questionnaire, but when interviewed said that they keep with them in the house an *ihai* of the husband's parents. Because the parental home in Nagano prefecture is now unoccupied, 'it would be bad if there were a fire and the *ihai* were destroyed'. This reflects the idea among some people that the ancestors actually live in the *ihai*.[15] However, the Sakashitas also ensured that all was safe in this respect because when they moved to Ueno they asked the local temple in Nagano prefecture to perform a special ceremony to transfer the ancestors' souls from the *ihai* into the temple. Although Mr. Sakashita is the *chōnan*, he now considers there to be no need to perform the rites, present offerings or pray to these *ihai*, because they have become 'just pieces of wood without a soul in them'.

These cases show how the ancestral cult extends considerably beyond the formal limits of *butsudan* ownership, to include the possession of *ihai* and 'substitute *butsudan*s' as well as grave rites and rituals performed at *kamidana*s which are directed towards ancestors.

*Yakudoshi*s and memorial rites: structural parallels

A number of authors have shown how there is a structural parallelism between the timing of rites after birth and after death.[16] Sometimes the parallels are strained or distorted, particularly with reference to some major *yakudoshi*s based upon word plays (particularly the one for forty-two). Nevertheless there still remains a general parallelism, especially if one also includes the minor *yakudoshi*s at (usually) three-year intervals which are not differentiated by sex. These parallels are shown in figure 9.4.

Figure 9.4   Parallel cycles in 'life' and 'death' rites

Yakudoshis	Nenkis	Days of rites after death Buddhist	Shinto	after birth (Shinto)	Other rites
1 year	1 year				Shinto one year memorial rite
4 years	3 years				7-5-3 rite
7 years	7 years	7 days		7 days	
10 years			10 days		
13 years	13 years				
16 years	17 years				
19 years					(Adults' Day?)
22 years	23 years				(Adults' Day?)
25 years					
28 years	27 years				
33 years	33 years				(*Miyamairi* on 33rd day)
		35 days		35th day	
37 years					
40 years					
42 years					
46 years					
49 years	(49 or) 50 years	49 days	50 days		
52 years					
53 years					
58 years	100 years			100th day	
		First *bon*		First New Year	

This parallelism further reinforces the way in which Shinto and Buddhism complement each other. There is some 'division of labour' but not necessarily differences of function, because through the appropriate rituals each 'religion' mitigates the effects of certain critical stages in the 'life' and 'death' cycles. During life, the crises are the *yakudoshi* years; in death the risk is that one might become an 'unattached spirit' (*muenbotoke*) if the proper rites are not performed at regular intervals—although relatively few people nowadays are overtly motivated to perform memorial rites out of fear lest the ancestor become a *muenbotoke*. The full cycle of ancestral years is often completed by the thirty-third year: at that time, the individual ancestor may become a member of the collectivity of ancestors and no longer receives special individual rites.[17] In the same way, the newborn child becomes a recognized member of the community after thirty-three days. Some households do continue memorial rites until the fiftieth or hundredth *hōji*. However, in all cases the final *hōji* becomes a kind of 'weaning' for the ancestor who no longer receives special, individual food offerings but shares with the older ancestors the common food offered to them all collectively. Like a child, the ancestor passes through certain developmental stages from an early existence which is highly dependent on others (lest the ancestor become a *muenbotoke*) to full 'maturity' as a well-established ancestor. In this process Shinto and Buddhism—despite being two different 'religions' at a formal level—merge at a practical level into two complementary parts of the same Japanese religion.[18]

Christian perspectives (a): Filial piety

The Confucian value of filial piety is one of the motivating influences behind the ancestral cult. However, it is also consistent with a considerable amount of biblical teaching. The ancestors of the Jews occupied a prominent place in the Old Testament and—as in Japan—there was a cherished idea of being buried with one's fathers (Genesis 47:30; 50:13, 25; Exodus 13:19; 1 Kings 2:10; 11:43; 14:31; 15:8 *etc.*). The different generations of a lineage may be linked together in blessing or curse (Exodus 20:5; 1 Samuel 2:30-36; 2 Samuel 7:12-16)—although the fact that Jesus became accursed for our sakes (Galatians 3:13) means that many modern Christians pray for the power of ancestral curses to be broken through repentance and the cutting off of demonic influences through the family line.

An emphasis on the importance of filial piety can be seen in the New Testament too. Jesus denounced in his Jewish society a lack of filial piety towards both human parents and our spiritual parent (Mark 7:9-12). Moreover, the instruction in 1 Timothy 5:4 ('...to put their religion into practice by caring for their own family and so repaying their parents and grandparents') is accurately rendered into Japanese by the technical and traditional vocabulary used for expressing filial piety.[19]

We all have a 'Heavenly Parent' who created each of us and towards whom we have a responsibility of filial piety (*oyakōkō*). It is not enough to show *oyakōkō* (filial piety) towards earthly parents if at the same time we commit *oyafukō* (lack of filial piety) towards God. True filial piety involves more than mere outward conformity to social expectations, which becomes hollow hypocrisy unless it is accompanied by sincerity of heart. A Japanese Christian suggests that writing to one's parents or visiting them while they are still alive, taking them out to dinner, giving them a massage and so on are ways in which Japanese Christians might demonstrate their filial piety in more meaningful ways than by mere observance of rites connected with the *nenki* anniversaries, *higan* or *bon*.[20]

Christian perspectives (b): The theology of heirship

Another of the motivating pressures behind the Japanese performance of ancestral rites is a sense of obligation towards those from whom one has inherited property. To some extent this is illustrated by the Kaneda family, described at the beginning of this chapter. During the interview, Mr Kaneda had to leave the room to answer a telephone call, so we asked his wife for her views. She expressed her opinion that 'nothing survives death and the body just dies naturally', but 'although I don't believe in a life after death it is my responsibility to my husband's mother to perform these rites. Having possession of the *butsudan* means that I have to do the rituals to fulfill my responsibilities as wife and daughter-in-law. It is not exactly an obligation (*giri*) to my husband's maternal uncle, because I never knew him...but if my husband were to die before me I would do these rites as *giri* to him.'

It should be remembered that the Kanedas had inherited from this uncle several rice fields and a small mountain; it was only because of this inheritance that they could afford to live where they do now. A sense of obligation on account of having received inherited property is one of the factors which has traditionally motivated eldest sons to perform rites for those ancestors.

In the Old Testament there are numerous references to inheritance, especially regarding the land of Israel as an inheritance. However, the New Testament quite often refers to the concept of inheritance as a metaphor for God's blessings, particularly that of salvation. Jesus spoke to his followers about their 'inheritance, the kingdom prepared for you since the creation of the world' (Matthew 25:34). On another occasion, he was asked, 'What must I do to inherit eternal life?' (Luke 18:18).

There is far more to the concept of inheritance than is realized by some modern Christians, who tend to underestimate the significance of the word 'inherit' and treat it as if it were merely equivalent to 'receive'. Firstly, 'inheritance' presupposes that a death has taken place. 'In the case of a will, it is necessary to prove the death of the one who made it, because a will is in force only when somebody has died' (Hebrews 9:16-17). We are familiar with the term 'last will and testament' but we rarely think about what we mean when we speak of the 'New Testament'.

Secondly, an inheritance is usually motivated by love. This is certainly the case for the inheritance which God gives us. 'In his great mercy [God] has given us new birth into...an inheritance that can never perish, spoil or fade—kept in heaven for you...' (1 Peter 1:3-4). Therefore we give thanks to the Father, who has qualified us 'to share in the inheritance of the saints in the kingdom of light' (Colossians 1:12).

Thirdly, an inheritance is normally received as a free gift, not as a reward for services rendered. This aspect is very important in the Japanese cultural context, where there is a feeling that one has to try to repay favours received. To some extent, this motivates the ancestral cult, as an attempt to repay such favours. Christians recognize that we can never repay what God has given us, but can only receive it with gratitude. God freely gives us this inheritance because he has adopted us into his family as heirs (Romans 8:14-17; Galatians 4:6-7). Each one of us is, in effect, God's *yōshi*.

It might be unwise to push the analogy too far, because all human metaphors have their limits. Certainly this one is complicated by the Resurrection of Jesus. Nevertheless, we might say, in a traditional Japanese context, that Jesus is the *chōnan*, the 'appointed heir of all things' (Hebrews 1:2), who voluntarily gave up his rights in order that others might be adopted as *yōshis*. Through his death, establishing his will and testimony, his own rightful inheritance has been bequeathed to us, if we are willing to receive it.

There is even more to our inheritance, however. God looks

after his heirs and even appoints angels as 'ministering spirits sent to serve those who will inherit salvation' (Hebrews 1:14). Moreover, right now God has given us his Holy Spirit as a 'deposit, guaranteeing what is to come' (2 Corinthians 5:5). It is he who enlightens us to know the riches of our 'glorious inheritance' and God's 'incomparably great power for us who believe' (Ephesians 1:17-19). With the Holy Spirit, we are 'sealed for the day of redemption' (Ephesians 4:30), but what we experience now of the Holy Spirit is but a small proportion of our final inheritance. In 2 Corinthians 5:5, the Holy Spirit is compared to a 'deposit', but what is to come is far greater. Even now, the Holy Spirit is producing in us the fruit which God desires (Galatians 5:22-23) and is granting us his power (Acts 1:8) and a variety of spiritual gifts (Romans 12:6-8; 1 Corinthians 12:4-11, 27-28; Ephesians 4:11-13). However, these and other blessings are merely the 'deposit' or first instalment of our greater inheritance when we 'receive the full rights of sons' (Galatians 4:5).

CHAPTER

10

Memorialism

ALTHOUGH EVANGELICAL CHRISTIANS tend to assume that religious belief ought to be reasonably consistent with practice, this is not necessarily the case in Japan. The same *practice*, of ancestral rites, can have a variety of *beliefs* associated with it. Simply because a person performs rituals as if to ancestors doesn't necessarily imply even a belief in an afterlife.

In the general questionnaire, 18.4% of the men and 29.3% of the women replied 'Yes' to a question asking if they believed in a life after death.[1] Another question asked about belief in a personal spirit which survives death, and to this question 28.6% of the men and 40.2% of the women replied 'Yes'.

Among the 100 people later interviewed in depth, there were initially three broad responses to a question on the afterlife, as follows:

1 A soul or spirit survives	36 people
2 'Don't know'	28 people
3 Death is the end	36 people

However, this was later followed by a more specific question about heaven and hell, which produced a wider spectrum of answers. How these replies relate to these earlier responses is shown in the next table:

Table 10.1 Beliefs expressed about what happens after death

	Neither heaven nor hell	Both heaven and hell	Heaven but not hell	Don't know	Reincarnation	Other
Something survives	7	13	6	4	5	1
'Don't know'	7	3	5	11	0	2
Death is the end	18	2	2	3	1	10
Totals	32	18	13	18	6	13

A number of comments might be made about these figures:

a) Among those who initially said, 'Something survives', seven people subsequently denied any belief in a heaven or hell; they did not offer any alternative concept of an afterlife, such as reincarnation.

b) To some extent, these people might be identified with the six who affirmed a belief in a heaven but not a hell. In fact, only three of those in this category explicitly stated such a belief, whereas the other three preferred to speak of an undifferentiated afterlife. Logically, a belief in an undifferentiated afterlife is incompatible with the judgement implied in the idea of there being both heaven and hell. One woman clearly expressed the reason for her preferring to believe in an undifferentiated afterlife: she said, 'If I believed in a heaven and a hell, I would have worries (*fuan*) about where my father is, but the idea of an undifferentiated afterlife appeals because it gives me peace of heart (*anshin*)'.

c) Among those who initially said that nothing survives, there were some who appeared to have altered their minds when confronted by a more specific question on heaven and hell.

d) Five of the six who expressed a belief in reincarnation were from rural backgrounds, but the six were equally divided between men and women. One of these women said the spirits return to Mount Osore in Aomori prefecture.[2] Another said she thought the souls were probably 'recycled', using the same term as for recycled paper. When her husband asked where she got this idea from, she replied, 'I just thought of it myself'.

Four others mentioned a belief in reincarnation when the first, more general, question was posed, but they gave other answers when asked more specifically about heaven and hell.

e) Similar apparent inconsistencies in beliefs have been reported by other researchers.[3] Therefore these results are not peculiar, but instead illustrate widespread attitudes.

f) Almost all those who expressed a belief in heaven and hell said that it is one's own conduct which determines where one goes after death. None of them mentioned the ritual conduct of one's own descendants. Two women mentioned the Buddhist concept of Emma-san, the lord of hell, who decides where one goes. The three people to mention faith as something which affects one's salvation were all Christians, two of them Roman Catholics.[4] At least five people belong officially to the Pure Land sect of Buddhism, which in theory stresses salvation by faith rather than by works, but none of these mentioned faith as a determining factor. This further illustrates findings by other researchers that there is a widespread lack of acquaintance with formal Buddhist doctrine. In Ueno this sometimes extends to an inability to name the Buddhist sect to which one formally belongs: such knowledge is not important until one becomes responsible for arranging a funeral, but such people do know the name of the temple which performed funerary rites for a grandfather.

g) Many people said they had 'never really thought about such things before', so they often seem to express the first idea which comes into their minds. Some people might express some belief if pressed about a specific doctrine, such as that of heaven and hell— which is an orthodox one for most branches of Japanese Buddhism. However, for the most part such a belief tends to be of little importance for their daily lives.

h) Examples of replies in the miscellaneous 'other' category include 'one becomes absorbed into the world of nature' and 'one becomes a star'. Some others will be quoted shortly.

i) Even among those who possess a *butsudan*, there is no clearly defined pattern of beliefs in an afterlife:

Table 10.2   Beliefs in an afterlife among *butsudan* owners

	Neither heaven nor hell	Both heaven and hell	Heaven but not hell	Don't know	Reincar-nation	Other
Something survives	1	2	1	2	3	0
'Don't know'	2	1	0	2	0	0
Death is the end	5	0	1	0	0	1
Totals	8	3	2	4	3	1

Among *butsudan* owners, there are fewer apparently 'inconsistent' replies, and in fact these are largely the result of tabulating survey data. They are not so clearly inconsistent when the nuances are obtained in an interview situation. Their actual replies were:

'I don't really know what happens after death but while I'm alive I try to do good works to avoid going to hell...Yes, I do believe in heaven and hell.'

'Nothing in particular happens after death...I don't believe in hell but I'd like to go to heaven.'

What is rather more striking is the fact that seven people who possess a *butsudan* also claim that death is the end. Moreover, of the seven *butsudan* owners who say this, five perform rites every day. Two of these perform rites to or for a deceased spouse and one to deceased parents; the other two join a co-residential mother-in-law in rites for her deceased husband. Why do people continue to perform rites when denying a belief in any afterlife?

Motivations for ancestral rites

There are many motivations for ancestral rites, whether performed at a *butsudan*, grave site or *kamidana*. For some people, worship might be expressed as primarily for the benefit of the spirits of the dead. In Ueno this was most explicitly mentioned by those belonging to the Sōka Gakkai.

Another motivation relates to the idea that the dead might become vindictive. 'Unattached spirits' (*muenbotoke*) are particularly feared in this regard. However, in Ueno only one person explicitly mentioned the possibility of supernatural punishment (*bachi*) if the rites were not performed. In this case, *bachi* was thought to take the form of illness or disasters affecting the household. However, in different contexts several others also mentioned the idea of *bachi* as a result of doing something bad to living people (rather than to the dead).

Occasionally guilt can become a motivation for ancestral rites. This is the case for a man whose first wife died in a car accident and who feels guilty that he had let her drive at that time rather than driving himself. Some people might also feel guilty if they neglected to perform ancestral rites.

Some people view the rites as an expression of thanks for favours received from the ancestors. This can be either in terms of spiritual protection or else in terms of their past contributions to the household.

Ancestral rites can also be viewed as expressing a kind of 'pledge' to the ancestors that one would conform to certain moral standards'.[5] This 'ethical' view of ancestral rites was expressed by Mr. Tanaka, who said, 'When in front of my *ihai* it has never entered my head to consider what happens when I die. It is just a matter of ethical values for the living to remember the deceased and to learn self-control through practising the rites'. Among those interviewed, Mr. Tanaka was the only one to express this view clearly, but he himself is hardly representative of most Japanese people: on his questionnaire he called himself a 'Christian' because twenty years previously he had been a Catholic for one year and a Protestant for three, after which he ceased to have any further contacts with Christianity.

A much more common attitude towards ancestral rites is that of *respect* for the ancestors. Often these feelings are mixed with those of *gratitude* towards the ancestors for what they have done. This is one of the reasons why the term 'worship' is often inappropriate as a description of the ancestral cult.

There is also a commonly expressed idea that the ancestors, *hotoke* or *kami* are those who 'watch over' and protect the household. Sometimes children are told that they should not do wrong because the ancestors or *kami* are 'always watching'; this seems to be a milder version of the threat of *bachi* ('divine punishment') as a means of disciplining children. Nevertheless, even for a number of adults the concept of the ancestors as 'always watching' can become 'internalized' and affect their behaviour, prompting them towards observing that which is expected of them.[6]

Among those who rarely or never perform ancestral rites of any kind, there might be 'theological' rationalizations to explain their conduct. For instance, one man says, 'The spirits are with you wherever you go, so you don't need to go to the graves'. When he travels in an aeroplane he prays at take-off and landing to the spirit of his dead father.

Very occasionally, personal experiences might incline a person towards more cynical attitudes. A possible instance of this is a twenty-six year old Nissen blue-collar worker who throughout the interview displayed a very cynical attitude towards ancestral rites. Towards the end of our time together he told us how his parents had separated only a few weeks after he was born and were divorced sometime afterwards. Such experiences probably colour attitudes towards one's ancestors.

Memorialism

These motivations for ancestral rites cover the majority of cases but not all of them. There still remain at least seventeen people who deny the existence of any afterlife but who nevertheless continue to practise some ancestral rites. Of these, five perform *butsudan* rites—four of them daily and one weekly.[7] Another nine perform grave rites regularly each year, one of them on a monthly basis. Of the remaining three, one performs *butsudan* rites when he visits his parents, and as *chōnan* expects to become responsible for the rites in the future. Another occasionally performs grave rites at *hōji*s and the third, Mr. Yamashita the younger, performs *kamidana* and grave rites for his older brother if he is at home when his father performs the rites.

All of these people deny a belief in any afterlife but they continue to perform rites as if to the ancestors. When asked why they still practise the rituals, their unanimous answer is that what is important for them is not the existence of the ancestor but rather the *memory* of that person. How they expressed this concept differed to some extent. For instance, seven of these people—of which five were women—stressed the importance of *feelings*. They said that 'the ancestors are in one's own feelings' or 'I do the rites in order to esteem the ancestors properly in my own feelings (*kimochi*)'. Others, mainly men, tended to stress the importance of *memory* or *recollection*. They tended to use terms such as *omoide* ('reminiscence'), *natsukashii* ('nostalgic') or *kinen* ('commemoration'). Others, who are less specific about their rejection of an afterlife but stress the value of memorialism, put up to at least 20% of my sample the numbers of those who perform ancestral rites for the sake of memory. These common attitudes are well illustrated by the case of Mr. Yamazaki, a forty-one year old schoolteacher who as *chōnan* will inherit his parents' *butsudan*.

Each summer holiday Mr. Yamazaki visits his parents for about ten days or so. There he prays each day at their *butsudan*, which, he says, gives him a 'feeling of security'; however, he never prays at his parents' *kamidana*. Once a year, at *bon*, he visits the graves of his father's parents and grandparents, and that of his father's brother who was killed in the war while still unmarried. At the graves Yamazaki-san reports to the deceased relatives about any major family events, and he gives thanks to the ancestors for his family's health during the previous year. He also lights candles and incense sticks and places fresh flowers there, whereas at the *butsudan* he offers rice daily—'to help my mother when she does it'— and changes the flowers every few days.

However, Yamazaki-san says 'nothing at all' happens after death and that there is no heaven or hell. When asked where his ancestors might be, he replied, 'In my imagination', and again denied the existence of any spirits which survive death.

He then went on to explain about his attitudes to the rites:

'I pray and make reports at the *butsudan* and graves in order to reflect on my life and to watch my steps in future. As the ancestors are supposed to be enshrined (*matsurarete iru*) in the *butsudan*, I imagine in my mind that they will come and listen to me.' Although at present he claims that he puts the offerings on the *butsudan* in order to help his parents—'and that's as far as it goes'—he also admits that he will most likely continue to offer the rice, water and incense on a daily basis when he himself inherits responsibility for the *butsudan*. He does not think that the offerings are 'eaten' by the ancestors or benefit them in any tangible way, but he says that the performance of these ritual acts 'evokes a nostalgic feeling and nostalgic thoughts in memory of my forebears'. These sentiments are assisted by the presence, in the same room, of photographs showing the deceased relatives. As there are many kinds of memories, he is unable to specify exactly which ones are evoked, but the ritual serves as a reminder to recall thoughts of his ancestors, and, in the future, more specifically of his parents.[8]

Various other examples could be cited, including that of the younger Mr. Suehara who denies any belief in an afterlife but prays weekly at his family's *zushi*: he says its 'only meaning is to remember my older sister, but not in a concrete form—just a feeling related to her'. These and others attach more importance to the *sentiments* associated with the practices of memorialism than to any beliefs about what might happen after death.

The importance of *memorialism* is also brought out by the commonly expressed attitude that these rites are directed primarily towards those ancestors who were personally known to the person conducting the rites. For example, a thirty-eight year old woman said, 'There are seven *ihai*s in the *butsudan*—those of my great grandparents, my grandparents and of my father's three brothers who were killed in the war. But my grandmother was the only one I knew when she was alive, so when I pray at the *butsudan* I can visualize only her. That's why I pray to all the ancestors but only give thanks to my grandmother.' Others expressed very similar attitudes, saying that they only bother with the memorial rites for those they knew personally, or that they specially focus their attention on such ancestors. After a while, the more distant ancestors lose their individuality and merge into the collectivity of relatively undifferentiated *hotoke*.[9]

The importance attached to one's 'native place'

The importance attached to memorialism is expressed also in strong emotional attachments to one's 'native place'. The Japanese term *furusato* ('native village') can be applied now to both rural and urban places of origin. It normally tends to evoke fond, nostalgic memories. Various writers have commented on this. Spae, for example, writes that 'The Japanese grow very attached to the places where they were born and have lived, to the countryside, and to their native soil...'.[10]. Graburn comments that 'Japan enjoys a special concept of nostalgia, *kyōshū*, a nostalgic dreaming of the homeland, or *natsukashii*, a somewhat sad longing for an ideal harmonious context, often placed in the personal or historic past'[11]. This word *kyōshū* (郷愁) is formed by the character for 'rural area' (郷) plus one for 'sad, nostalgic thoughts' (愁), the compound indicating that the nostalgia or memories are directed particularly towards the rural area from which one originated. Another word for 'nostalgia', *kaikyō*, is used particularly for feelings directed towards one's *furusato*. The cultural importance attached to these concepts is further reinforced by the fact that there is a more literary synonym for *furusato* (故里), namely *kokyō* (故郷). As mentioned in chapter one, there is a tendency for each language to have a proliferation of words clustering around topics of importance for its own culture.

These widespread feelings affect behaviour in a variety of ways. For instance, Dr. Satō gave various practical reasons for choosing to live in Aoyama, such as the cost of building land, but then added what to a Westerner might seem to be a minor consideration. He said that he was attracted to this house because on a summer's evening he loves to sit in his garden where he can watch the fireflies and listen to the frogs in the rice valley below. (In Japan frogs are said to 'sing' rather than 'croak'.) This is because as a child he enjoyed going to a house which his father had rented on the outskirts of Kyoto, where for the first time in his life he heard the croaking of frogs and watched the rice being planted. His choice of a house site is therefore influenced to at least some extent by these childhood memories.

Similarly, two girls who graduated from the same university in Kyoto and who now work at the same place in Osaka described how they had to go to Kyoto for an afternoon appointment. As they had the morning free, they decided to walk around their old university campus—rather than visiting one of the many places of interest around the city. At the university they did not even go to greet any of the staff, but simply walked around it and had lunch at a cafe which they had frequented in their student days—all for the sake of 'the memory' (*omoide*).

These kinds of feelings can even become one of the motivating forces behind the attachment to Shinto. Spae continues his comments on the importance of the *furusato* and the Japanese attachment to their native soil by noting that 'all these familiar things and places become personified. Through a projection of one's affections, nature seems to return one's love. A profound and beneficial empathy sets in between man and his surroundings....These surroundings take on the shape of the numinous; they are worshipped and...by a mysterious osmosis they put him in touch with the divine.'[12]

If Spae's observations (or intuitions perhaps) are valid, they suggest that the concepts of *furusato*, memory, nostalgia and *omoide* take on a new meaning or are transformed into what is normally thought of as 'Shinto'. The personification of natural features such as mountains, trees or rocks is associated with Shinto rather than Buddhist thought, but this investigation into the spheres of memory, nostalgia and their related concepts began with an examination of the ancestral cult which is normally associated with Buddhism. However, at what are now primarily Buddhist ceremonies—*bon* and *higan*—many Japanese physically return to their native villages, especially at *bon* when they meet together with the ancestors who also return to the places they have known in their physical lives. There the generations meet together in a 'reunion', in the place where the ancestors lived and also where the very trees and hills 'take on the shape of the numinous', 'are worshipped' and put the inhabitants 'in touch with the divine'. At the *furusato* Shinto and Buddhism merge. Both might be seen as in some sense manifestations of the sense of attachment to one's native soil and of the associated feelings of 'nostalgia' and 'memorialism'.

These same feelings further feed into other forms of religious or quasi-religious behaviour. For instance, a Japanese student of anthropology at a British university brought with him as a safety charm an embroidered pouch containing sand from his father's grave. He treasured it because it evoked memories of his father.[13] Similarly, a section manager at the Nissen factory always keeps in his wallet a photograph of his dead father, because, he says, 'it means my father is with me all the time'. Functionally, the photograph is not dissimilar to a safety charm, but this man feels he has no need for a formal charm because each day he prays at his *butsudan* and *kamidana*; some mornings he also prays at the Nissen company shrine.

These observations also have relevance for Japanese Christianity. For Japanese Christians similar kinds of feelings can become attached to 'the place of their spiritual birth'. How these sentiments can affect church growth is described by Yamamori with reference to the migration of Japanese Christians from one city to another. He writes, 'Even where there was a church of his own denomination [in the city to which he had moved], his intense loyalty to the place of his spiritual birth prevented him from joining the church and being active in it. After moving to the new city, he would keep in touch with his home pastor for a while, but the various pressures causing membership leakage would soon catch up with him, and he would become a loss to the church'.[14]

It is difficult to find a solution to these problems. Yamamori's comments are made in the context of his observation that even the presence of a church of the same denomination in the new locality is not sufficient to avert this trend: the United Church of Christ in Japan—the largest Protestant denomination—'experiences today much loss by migration'[15].

Idealistically, we might hope that a solution could come through reinforced teaching about a Christian's loyalty being not to a particular community or place on this planet but rather to Christ, because 'our citizenship is in heaven' (Philippians 3:20). Those who regard themselves as 'aliens and strangers on earth' show that 'they are looking for a country of their own' and 'longing for a better country—a heavenly one' (Hebrews 11:13-16). If these kinds of concepts could be fused with, and transform, the strong Japanese attachments to their 'homeland' or 'native place', a major step forward could be achieved in overcoming the denominationalism which often continues to frustrate co-operative ventures in Japan.

Fortunately, this is a problem which is widely recognized, and more and more Christians in Japan are seeking to rectify it as they try to work together across denominational boundaries. Their aim is to transform perceptions of the kaleidoscope of different denominations from that of an inchoate mess into something like a beautiful stained glass window through which the light of Christ can shine while refracted in many different ways. In doing this, however, it is also necessary to confront spiritual bondages of jealousy and control which certain pastors can actually exercise over their church members by expecting those who have moved away to continue tithing to that church or to receive videotapes of services.[16]

There are not only theological but also sociological considerations to take into account. Many Japanese Christians who move to different cities do not settle easily into new churches because it takes considerable time and effort to develop meaningful new relationships. In the new environment they might not feel welcomed by the local Christians, or might feel that they are relatively neglected by the local pastor. Such perceptions might be distorted, but they still influence how the Christians feel about the new situation.

At the same time, there often continues to be a strong emotional attachment to the one who led them to Christ. Sixteen years after she became a Christian, a Japanese lady still refers to my wife in glowing terms as the one through whom she came to faith. Such sentiments are related to the strong attachments which often develop in Japanese society between a 'teacher' (*sensei*) and a 'pupil' (*deshi*): this is especially so if the relationship involves close personal contact of the kind found, for example, in traditional arts like flower-arranging. Regular Bible studies together can produce a similar kind of bonding. Where such interaction continues, it can be a source of great strength, but its weaknesses appear in a mobile society where 'pupils' move elsewhere and need to find another 'teacher'. Often the inflated sentiments attached to the original 'teacher' mean that others seem not to match up to expectations. While these kinds of problems can occur also in the West, they seem to become exacerbated in Japanese society. It seems that the problem is compounded by the emotional attachments which stem from the bonding to one's 'place of origin' (whether physical or spiritual), and which are often expressed by various types of 'memorials'.

Memorialism in apparently non-religious aspects of Japanese culture

Memorialism is a widespread value in many other spheres of Japanese culture. For example, all Japanese hospitals give to mothers after childbirth the tip of the child's umbilical cord which was attached to the infant's naval area before the cord was cut. Most families preserve this fragment in a special box. When asked why they keep it, mothers give replies such as, 'Because the hospital gave it to me, and as it was a part of both myself and the child I cannot throw it out'. Often they say, 'I keep it as a souvenir, or commemoration (*kinen*)'. Some added that they regard it as a 'proof' that the mother and child were once connected.

Two of the eleven women asked about this practice took the idea further, into a religious sphere. One of them said that the umbilical cord indicates one's 'connection with the ancestors'. The other said she had heard that the cords of the children should be put in a mother's coffin when she dies, so that the cord would also go into the afterlife and remain as a link between the deceased mother and her children. In a number of families the umbilical cords of daughters are given to them when they get married, and remain as symbols of their links with their original families.

Other memorabilia of birth are also very common, including the preservation of a child's first hand or foot prints. In some families the hair from a child's first hair cut, or a few strands of it, might be used to make a special calligraphy brush because the hairs have tapering rather than jagged ends. Many mothers also keep diaries of their children's development, tending to do so more conscientiously at first than later.

The practice of diary writing, in general, has been described as a 'Japanese obsession'.[17] It is 'so much to the Japanese taste that their number today is uncountable'.[18] Many diaries focus on reminiscence, memory and reflection on one's inner feelings, written down at a later point in time.[19] For some women, the diaries are channels for expressing their inmost thoughts and feelings— important in a culture where they often feel inhibited from doing so verbally. One woman told me how she keeps all her old diaries and each year, at New Year, looks back through them and thinks about the past. A tradition of diary writing, by both men and women, goes back at least a thousand years and includes many famous literary works.[20] The same tradition might even be expressed in the 'I' novels of the twentieth century.[21] Diaries, or parts of them, may be sent to other people as messages, so that exchanging diaries is 'not an unusual form of courtship'.[22] It can also be used in some psychotherapy, but I have not yet heard of any Japanese Christian pastors using it as an aid in counselling.

Photography has become a well known part of Japanese culture, but the form of the photographs also emphasizes memorialism.[23] An outing might be commemorated by a group photograph which often depicts in its background not the beautiful countryside visited but instead the name of the station where they alighted or the door and name plaque of the hotel where they stayed. These 'markers' are symbolic of the whole trip. They are not intended so much to evoke memories of the scenery but rather of what it felt like to arrive at the place and to be there as a group with these people.[24] They evoke sentiments related to the people rather than the place.[25]

In this context, it is pertinent to note common attitudes towards the Shinto 7-5-3 ceremony, when girls aged seven or three and boys aged five are dressed up in kimono (for the girls) or smart clothes (for the boys) and taken to a Shinto shrine. There they sit with their parents while a priest recites prayers and performs a ritual purification over them. Afterwards all the families take photographs of the children in the shrine precincts. However, when parents with children who had been through these rites were later asked how important they considered the ceremonies to be, many laid stress on the commemorative photographs:

Table 10.3   Attitudes of parents to the 7-5-3 ceremony

'It has "some" religious meaning, if only because it takes place in a Shinto shrine.'	5 people
'It is important for its own sake to preserve the custom for the next generation.'	3 people
'Not important at all'	16 people
'The only importance is the taking of photographs'	17 people
'It is important only as a memory'	1 person

These comments about commemorative photographs were all spontaneous remarks without any prompting, and indicate the attitude of the majority of people. Most people said the photographs were important for 'evoking nostalgia' on the part of the children when they were older. A particularly interesting comment by several parents, especially mothers, was that the photographs were a 'proof' of the parents' love. Examples of such comments are:

'One day my children will say, 'My parents did this for me' and will be glad it was done for them.'

'The photos are to show the children they are loved very much.'

'The photographs provide some proof which the children can see of how much we love them.'

This 'proof' is expressed not only in the parents going to all the expense of buying expensive clothes and paying for the ceremony performed, but also in the tangible 'proof' of this as demonstrated through the photographs. Often at New Year the family looks back through their old photograph albums and evoke the memories of such times, when the photographs serve as 'proof' of the parents' love.

Christian implications

'This is how God showed his love among us: He sent his one and only Son into the world that we might live through him.' (1 John 4:9)

The New Testament is also concerned with proofs or demonstrations of God's love. Ultimately, it is demonstrated through Christ's sacrificial death on the cross, a price far greater than any of the fine clothes which Japanese parents buy for their children when they attend the 7-5-3 ceremony.

God the Father demonstrates his love through a far greater sacrifice, that of his only Son, in order that we might become adopted into his family. Jesus, the Son, demonstrates the same love in voluntarily laying down his life: 'Greater love has no-one than this, that one lay down his life for his friends' (John 15:13).

Christians, too, commemorate this supreme sacrifice. The Communion service is a ritual memorialization of Christ's sacrifice. 'Do this in remembrance of me', Jesus instructed his disciples (Luke 22:19). These instructions were carried out by the early church, who thereby continued regularly to 'proclaim the Lord's death, until he comes' (1 Corinthians 11:26). In a tangible form, it is a ritual 'replay' or 're-enactment' of an event in order to evoke memories. The same kind of 'replay' is practised by the Japanese year by year when they look through their old photograph albums—although Christians see the death of Christ as having a far greater significance, and some might find it offensive even to compare it to the memorialization which comes through photo albums.

Nevertheless, the Bible often refers to the importance of memorials in one form or another. God instituted the rainbow as a sign and memorial of his covenant with Noah (Genesis 9:12-17). He revealed himself to Moses as Yahweh, 'the name by which I am to be remembered from generation to generation' (Exodus 3:15). The Passover festival became established as a commemoration of God's deliverance for his people when he brought them out of Egypt (Exodus 13:1-16, especially verses 9, 14 and 16). Later, the feast of Purim was instituted in order to commemorate another deliverance for the Jews, so that the memory of those days should not die out among their descendants (Esther 9:28).

Jesus declared that the woman who anointed him with perfume had 'done a beautiful thing' and that 'wherever this gospel is preached throughout the world, what she has done will also be told, in memory of her' (Matthew 26:13). The older branches of the Christian church have continued this custom of memorializing certain saints of God whose piety is considered to be worthy of special commemoration.

Whatever their views on such memorials for other Christians, virtually all Christians are united in recognizing the importance of the Communion service as a time for special remembrance of the sacrifice of Jesus. It would seem that this service is particularly suitable for expressing, in a Christian form, the importance which the Japanese attach to memorialism. However, my observation of Protestant churches in Japan is that they actually celebrate Communion rather less frequently than do Protestants in the West. Most Protestant churches do hold a Communion service once a month, though it may be less frequent in pioneer situations. Roman Catholics, however, continue to observe the Mass on a weekly basis in Japan, as they do elsewhere.

To some extent, Protestants might be wary of being misunderstood because of certain external similarities between the Eucharist and Japanese ancestral rites.[26] Both involve memorialism for the death of a beloved one, and both involve the symbolic sharing of food. However, the Japanese practice contains relatively little hope for a reunification with the beloved one, even despite the idea that at *bon* the spirits of the ancestors are said to return to this world. By contrast, the Christian Eucharist is also a celebration which looks forward to the Second Coming of Christ (1 Corinthians 11:26). It is also a foretaste of the time when we shall celebrate together with Jesus in his Father's Kingdom (Matthew 26:29).

Japanese Funerals

The question of appropriate forms of memorialism is most acute at the time of a funeral. To a large extent, Christian funerals in Japan tend to be modelled on Buddhist forms, but with significant differences. I shall therefore describe both typical Buddhist funeral rites and Christian equivalents, which might vary to some extent between different churches.

The death of a person initiates a period of ritual pollution in a home, so the *kamidana* is often closed or else covered over with a cloth. The main funeral rites usually take place at home just two or three days after the death, avoiding a *tomobiki* day lest a friend be drawn into death too. The first ceremony at which a Buddhist priest usually officiates is the *nōkanshiki*, when the body is put into the coffin. A Christian equivalent to the *nōkanshiki* involves the pastor reading from the Bible and saying a few prayers.

On the evening before the main funeral there is a wake (*tsūya*) for relatives and closer friends of the deceased person. At this time one or more Buddhist priests recite sutras and the relatives line up to light a candle or incense stick as a symbolic prayer to or for the deceased. A Christian equivalent is the *zenyashiki*, a full-length funeral service which includes a sermon but without any eulogies or offerings of flowers. Being outside of work hours and open to anybody to attend, the *zenyashiki* is often better attended than the main funeral itself.

On the following day is the principal Buddhist funeral rite, the *sōshiki*, which a wider circle of friends and acquaintances may attend. They arrive dressed in black or at least wearing a symbolic black armband. First they go to a table covered with a white cloth, often with a white awning above it too, which has been specially erected outside the house where the funeral takes place. There the visitors hand in a special type of envelope containing money (often about ¥5,000), with the amount and the name of the donor marked on the back. Members of the deceased's family record these details in a book so that a return gift (not of money but of something like crockery or ornaments for the house), of a value roughly one half that of the monetary gift, can be sent afterwards to the donor. All visitors are also given a standard small gift, often a hand towel in a small box, plus a sachet of salt. The salt is for the guests to sprinkle over themselves as a ritual purification when they return home.[27]

In the area where I did my fieldwork the names of those donors who have given a substantial contribution of money before or during the wake are inscribed on large boards erected outside the house. These remain up until after the funeral, sometimes until the following morning. Afterwards, until the forty-ninth day, the ritual pollution of the home is indicated by the affixing of a sticker with the character 忌 (*ki* or *imi*), meaning '[period of] mourning', above the door of the house.

During the funeral itself most of the visitors remain outside the house, in the street, while the priests chant sutras for half an hour or more. Usually those waiting are silent, but some men might light cigarettes or exchange occasional quiet comments among themselves. Towards the end of the ceremony the names of the principal mourners are announced and these people then go in to burn incense and pray to the deceased. Then the wider group of friends and acquaintances go in to do the same (not in any fixed order except that those nearer the house start off). Each person burns a pinch of incense and bows towards where the priests are chanting next to the covered coffin. Most participants bow their heads and put their hands together in prayer for a few seconds.

About an hour or two after I attended a funeral for a young man, I asked one young woman what she prayed or felt at that time. She replied that she simply said 'Sayōnara' ('Goodbye') to her dead friend. An older man told me that he just reflected on what kind of person the young man had been but he did not offer any specific prayers to him.

After burning the incense and praying, the mourners return to the street. Some of the dead person's relatives might offer the gift of a packet of cigarettes for anyone who wanted them. Shortly afterwards, the priests leave the house and are soon followed by those who bear the coffin.

Christian funeral services are usually held in a church and include conventional Christian prayers. Because it is a worship service to God, care is taken to avoid giving any impression that the deceased's spirit is present or is being ministered to by the ceremonies. In contrast to Buddhist rites in which the words of condolence or eulogy (chōji) are addressed in the second person to the deceased person, in Christian funerals 'everything concerning the deceased is in the third person and is directed towards the mourners'.[28]

However, in many denominations there is also a concern for rectifying the image of Christianity as a religion which destroys respect for the ancestors. Although handbooks and other literature on funeral services produced by the United Church of Christ in Japan, Lutherans and other denominations make it clear that the funeral 'is not worship of the dead or prayer for the happiness of the dead', there remains the problem of how best to express this without appearing to be rude or disrespectful towards the dead.

Therefore many churches conclude the Christian funeral with a special farewell ceremony similar to the Buddhist one. The mourners pass by the coffin, but, instead of offering incense, they usually place a flower in the coffin or at a table which has been specially brought in for this purpose.[29]

Japanese Christians have differing opinions about this custom. Some see it as merely 'courteous greetings necessary in a Japanese context' whereas others take a more cautious attitude which questions where the boundary might be between this practice and the offering of foodstuffs (as at a *butsudan*). A number of Japanese Christians therefore regard it as a 'dubious practice which should be abandoned'.[30] What is important in this context is not the meaning of the custom to the participant but how it is *perceived* by those outside the faith.[31]

After the funeral, the coffin is put in a hearse to be taken to the crematorium.[32] Only the deceased's close kin are present at this final disposal of the body while the other visitors disperse to their homes. Prior to the placing of the casket into the oven, there may be a brief Christian ceremony with a scripture reading and prayer, perhaps a hymn too, but Boyle reports that 'this appears to be a Christian innovation'.[33]

After the bones are brought out from the furnace, and before the ashes are buried in a graveyard, the family members select from the skeletal remains some bones, or parts of bones, and place them in the funeral urn. Chopsticks are provided for this task. This can be a very moving or traumatic time as relatives select bones which might hold special memories for them: these individually selected bones are then interred in the family grave.[34] Later there might be a brief Christian memorial service at the church, with the crematorial urn and ashes also present, but usually attended only by relatives and close associates of the deceased.[35]

The family of non-Christian Japanese gather again on the seventh day following the funeral, when a Buddhist priest recites sutras in front of their *butsudan*. Similar observances are held by some families on each subsequent week up to and including the forty-ninth day, but most families observe only the rites for the seventh, thirty-fifth and forty-ninth days. The forty-ninth day marks the principal 'lifting of pollution' and some people say that at this time the spirit of the dead (*reikon* or *tamashii*) becomes in some sense an ancestor (*hotoke*).[36] Among Christians, the ashes may be kept at home for a few weeks, usually on a kind of family altar with a cross, a Bible and other Christian symbols. Then a mutually convenient time is decided upon for a brief interment service to be held at the grave.[37]

Non-Christian families keep a note of the contributions made by each visitor to the funeral and later send an appropriate return gift (*kōden kaeshi*). Boyle remarks that this custom can sometimes be burdensome and one which 'many Japanese would like to lessen'. One possibility might be to contribute to a charity in memory of the deceased, another might be to send out a booklet about the memories of the deceased person which could include, for example, 'things the deceased wrote, words from family and friends', photographs and so on. One family which did this had printed on the cover Hebrews 11:16 ('. . . they were longing for a better country—a heavenly one. Therefore God is not ashamed to be called their God, for he has prepared a city for them.').[38]

Often a Christian memorial service is held about the time of the first anniversary after a person's death, and on other anniversaries it is 'by no means unusual' for Japanese Christian families to ask their pastor to hold private services for a deceased relative. These may be held either at home or in a church, perhaps with a few close friends of the deceased also present. When such services are not annual events, they seem to occur on or near the times when *hōji* rites would be held by non-Christian Japanese families. At least some Japanese Protestants also visit their family graves at *higan* and/or *bon*. Those who do not have a memorial altar in their homes may nevertheless keep photographs of deceased family members in a prominent position in their homes and put in front of the photos gifts of fruit and vegetables which they have received.[39]

Japanese Roman Catholics in some areas have developed further Christian parallels to the traditional Buddhist rites. At the beginning and end of their funerals the priest often offers incense before the coffin (and altar) with the comment that it is 'in honour of the corpse of the dead as a sanctuary of the Holy Spirit'. A mass for the dead is offered at the funeral, is offered again on the third, seventh and thirtieth days afterwards, and then again every year on the anniversary of the person's death. In the village of Saga, in Kyoto prefecture, Catholic homes have either a normal *butsudan* or else a substitute *butsudan* and the priest performs *hōji* rites according to the traditional Buddhist pattern. The Catholic church has a special hall (called the *ihai-do*) for the tablets of the departed, where at *bon* and on All Souls Day the Catholic priest conducts Holy Mass particularly for the sake of the dead. In general, the church seems to have become a kind of new Buddhist temple by taking over from Buddhism the performance of rites for the dead.[40]

Commenting on these kinds of practices, Berentsen notes that in the New Testament

> 'the unequivocal emphasis is all the way on the assurance of salvation through faith in Christ in joyful expectation of the resurrection. In this perspective there is no need for prayers, masses, or offerings of any kind. To resort to intercessions for the well-being of departed Christians...cannot but obscure the vital doctrine of justification through faith with its corresponding assurance of salvation for Christ's sake alone...
>
> In the name of accommodation, to adopt liturgical intercessions for pre-Christian and non-Christian relatives may give an immediate impression of Christian concern for the ancestors. However, it may in the long run produce a much deeper uneasiness and doubt as to the fate of the departed than is the case when they are simply and faithfully entrusted into God's mercy. How are we then going to avoid the idea that their salvation is—after all—dependent upon our intercessions?...In other words, we will be moving effectively in the direction of making man an indispensable agent of salvation for the departed.'[41]

Many Japanese are interested in questions about what happens after death. They have heard many ideas but are not sure what to believe. Once I told a Japanese woman how one of the influences in my becoming a Christian was my examination of the historical evidence for the resurrection of Jesus. She was so interested in knowing what evidence there was that she did not notice that her legs had 'gone to sleep' underneath her (while we were kneeling at a low table in her living room). I also explained how Christ's victory over death can give us more confidence in his authority to tell us about events after death. In Japan there is a widespread interest in what happens after death: Christians need to be able to discuss these issues frankly and also to address questions about the interpretation of near-death experiences.

Rose, an Orthodox monk, warns Christians to be 'extremely cautious' in interpreting the 'visions of heaven' seen by dying and dead people. However, in Japan, as in the West, there is a widespread curiosity about such experiences. Studies in the West have shown that, in general, near-death experiences tend to be *either* (1) 'heavenly' experiences or encounters with a 'presence' who might be described as a 'being of light', *or* (2) meetings with the spirits of what are regarded as dead relatives, *or* (3) 'hellish' experiences, the memory of which the mind often seems to suppress shortly afterwards. I suggest that the sharp distinction between categories (1) and (2)—which never seem to occur together—might parallel the strong contrast between experiences of the presence of God and those of the presence of the dead reported while a person is still in this life. Experiences of the presence of God have been shown to be associated with higher than average levels of psychological wellbeing and expressed satisfaction with life. By contrast, experiences of what are regarded as 'the presence of the dead' are often reported by those who have been involved with spiritualism. In my research among nurses in Leeds I discovered that among those nurses who had tried to contact the dead through a spiritualist medium there were lower than average levels of psychological wellbeing and of personal satisfaction with life. Moreover, using a statistical technique known as the 'analysis of variance', I found that the differences in levels of psychological wellbeing were statistically significant.[42]

The Communion of Saints

Though often motivated by memorialism, Japanese ancestral rites in practice also express an *interrelatedness* between the living and the dead. While *motivations* of respect and memorialism may have several Christian parallels, many Christians see dangers in the *expressions* of these motivations as reflected in offerings and prayers to or for the dead. One danger with these practices is that

Christians may unwittingly open themselves to influence from the spirits of the dead. Those who venerate such spirits—whether Buddhists or Christians—can become enslaved by them. From a Christian perspective, it would seem that behind the ancestral cult are spirits of death and other kinds of demonic forces which seek for themselves the worship due to God alone.

However, 'even though Christianity cannot talk of a reciprocal interdependence between the living and the dead as is the case with the ancestral rites, it confidently talks of an interrelatedness between the two in a way which should enable any Christian to understand and sympathize with the quest for community across death prevalent in ancestor worship.'[43] This 'interrelatedness' is expressed in the Christian doctrine of the 'communion of saints', about which many Christians are reminded when they read the Apostles' Creed.

The 'communion of saints' has applications both in space and time. At any one time, Christians here on earth belong to the worldwide 'body of Christ' which incorporates many different cultural expressions (Romans 12:4-8; 1 Corinthians 12:4-31; Galatians 3:26-29; Ephesians 4:3-16 *etc.*). What is not so clear is the extension of this concept across time to include different generations of believers, both living and dead. However, on the mount of transfiguration Jesus was talking with both Moses and Elijah. They were not only representatives of the law and the prophets whose messages were fulfilled in Christ, but were also believers from past generations whom God had sent to talk with Jesus about his own imminent 'exodus' (Luke 9:30-31). After highlighting examples of faith among people of previous generations, the letter to the Hebrews draws the conclusion that 'therefore, since we are surrounded by such a great cloud of witnesses, let us...run with perseverance the race marked out for us' (Hebrews 12:1). The same writer encourages us not only to 'fix our eyes on Jesus' as our example but also to remember our leaders and 'consider the outcome of their way of life and imitate their faith' (Hebrews 12:2; 13:7).

Japanese Christians have done this in a Japanese way by commemorative anniversaries. 'Among the churches that trace their origin to a specific individual, one can find several that hold, annually or at stated times, a memorial service on or near the death anniversary of the founder.'[44] Protestant educational establishments have the same practice, as illustrated by Dōshisha University which continues each year to hold services at the grave of its founder, Niijima Jō, on the anniversary of his death, on the day commemorating the founding of the University and at the beginning of each academic year so that new students can be 'introduced' to the founder.[45] Many churches hold annual memorial services for members who have died, which are sometimes attended by non-Christian relatives for whom such services are their only connection with the church. The timing of such services varies among different local churches, commonly occurring on the first Sunday in November, at the time of *bon* or at Easter.[46]

Japanese culture is in many ways closer than Western culture to the biblical standard of respecting and giving honour to one's parents and forebears (Exodus 20:12; Mark 7:9-13; Ephesians 6:1-3).[47] McGavran points out the importance of genealogies in the Bible and suggests that Japanese Christians ought to set an example to non-Christians by knowing a lot about each of their ancestors and cultivating a greater sense of family history. He suggests that their names could be placed in a conspicuous location in the house as *reminders* of the ancestors but not as objects to which prayers are addressed. Instead, family devotions could include prayers thanking God for the family, perhaps stimulated by the reading together of a section from a family history which could be compiled. Alternatively, another kind of Christian daily ritual might be developed which would 'remember, honour and exalt the ancestors more than the Buddhist bowing before the *butsudan* does'. A Christian ritual of this kind would 'take more time and be more costly' but would have the aim of showing that becoming a Christian 'builds family loyalty more effectively than anything else now being done in Japan' and that becoming a Christian means becoming a *better* son, daughter, husband or wife.[48] In this way, Christianity could be seen as coming not to abolish but to fulfill the traditional Japanese values of filial piety and respect for those in the family who have gone on ahead.

From the Meiji Restoration until the end of the Second World War the government tried to promote an ideology according to which the Emperor, as the direct descendant of the gods, was head of the supreme 'main lineage' (*honke*) from which all other Japanese families were 'branch lineages' (*bunke*).[49] Even though most people pay their respects only to ancestors in their own branch, and rarely also to those in the lineage from which their *bunke* split off, there are cases in which some households do continue to revere ancestors from the *honke* too. The Emperor system's ideology extended this much further and demanded the respect and fulfilment of duties which came from the supposed moral obligations towards the Emperor.[50]

Beyond the Emperor, however, God is the one from whom 'all fatherhood'—or his 'whole family'—in heaven and on earth derives its name (Ephesians 3:15). 'God is the rightful head of human *families*' and his authority 'is derived through *fatherhood*'.[51] 'Jesus...was the son, so it was thought, of Joseph, the son of Heli...the son of Seth, the son of Adam, the son of God' (Luke 3:23, 38). In this sense, all families are descendants of Adam, the 'son of God'.[52] St. Paul refers to 'one God and Father of all, who is over all and through all and in all' (Ephesians 4:5), while Malachi 2:10 says, 'Have we not all one Father? Did not one God create us?'. The same point is brought out by Jesus himself, when he said, 'you have one Father, and he is in heaven' (Matthew 23:9). Therefore the Japanese cultural emphasis on giving honour to the founders of one's family (and which for a time was extended to the Emperors too) is truly fulfilled when we each give to God the glory due to him alone as the real founder and head of every family.

CHAPTER
11

A Sin and *Shame Society*

Japan as a 'shame society'

THE HAYAMA CONFERENCE is a regular event which brings together missionaries belonging to many different missions from all over Japan. In 1982 the main theme of this conference was 'Guilt, Shame and Grace in a Unique Culture'.

Missionaries to Japan have been very influenced by the idea that the Japanese are motivated more by feelings of 'shame' than by concepts of 'guilt' or 'sin'. This is one of the problems which they mention when they try to explain how hard it is to convert Japanese people to Christianity. It is supported by the observation that the Japanese have no word equivalent to the Western notion of 'sin': *tsumi*, the word which is normally used to translate 'sin', also means 'crime'.[1] Missionaries and Japanese pastors have to explain its theological meaning. To some extent, St Paul might have had a similar problem in the Graeco-Roman world, as indicated by his use of a variety of metaphors for sin. The Greek work for 'sin' (*hamartia*) originally meant 'missing the mark', but St Paul also used words such as 'disobedience' (Romans 5:19) and 'transgression' (Romans 4:15) or 'trespass' (Romans 5:18,20). John referred to sin as 'lawlessness' (1 John 3:4). Jesus spoke of various kinds of sin as 'evils' which 'make a man "unclean".' (Mark 7:20-23).

This notion that Japanese society is a 'shame society' whereas the supposedly Christian Western countries are 'sin societies' might also be justified theologically. It appears to be consistent with the distinction between Japanese polytheism (or whatever it might be!) and Western monotheism. Concepts of sin before a single, supreme and holy deity are obviously inapplicable in a society where people believe in many deities.

There are moral consequences too. A common stereotype of the Japanese businessman is that he may appear morally upright when at home but have looser moral standards when away on a business trip. He is very concerned about 'face' within his own social group (especially the family and work groups) but can do what he likes when he is an anonymous stranger. Although this scenario seems also applicable to many nominally 'Christian' Westerners, there nevertheless does seem to be a particular emphasis upon 'face' and fear of 'losing face' in Japan. Shame (*haji*) is 'based on the judgement of others...Standards of morality are outside oneself and, although they do not entirely take away the conscience of guilt and sin, they tend to warp it and drown it in the exterior criteria accepted by the community'.[2] Japan has therefore been characterized as a 'shame' society in which moral and social order is maintained by social pressure and fear of 'losing face' publicly. This moral and social control is preserved through the avoidance of shame, whether that shame is for the individual, the family or the institution to which the person belongs. Such shame is openly acknowledged as something to be avoided.

Shame lends power to gossip and also generates the fear of it: one is ashamed if the neighbours are gossiping about something which one has done and of which they disapprove. It then becomes difficult to go out and meet people if one is aware that one's behaviour is the subject of local gossip. This produces at least two results: one is reclusive behaviour among those who try to avoid social contacts, the other is a tendency to reveal little about oneself to one's neighbours and to keep topics of conversation relatively superficial. Another possible result is a kind of paranoia which reads references to oneself into innocent comments or glances. Children are often disciplined by the comment, 'Neighbours are watching whatever you do' (that is, in a judgmental fashion).[3] Personal honour and that of one's family are at a premium.

If some very shameful deed does become publicly known, there are few ways to escape it. Some people might be able to move away from the area, but often there are economic constraints which make it difficult to move too far away. Those living in company housing or with relatives sometimes have few other options available. Sometimes remaining in a community can be made even more uncomfortable if one is ostracized by the neighbours: ostracism was a traditional social sanction in many villages and even today can sometimes be used as a powerful weapon to punish those who are public nuisances in a neighbourhood.

For some people, the only remaining alternative is suicide. This was the option chosen by one Japanese family who lived not too far away from us. Their son was in the same school class as the son of Kimura-san, one of our friends, who told us what the neighbours thought had happened:

'The boy had been caught stealing and everyone knew this. It seems as if the father hit him, but he must have hit the boy too hard and somehow killed him. In any case, the parents then decided on a mass suicide. They took the dead boy and his sister to the family's hut in the mountains. Then they killed the sister and both parents hung themselves while embracing each other. When the children did not turn up at school, the school made investigations and contacted the police, who eventually found the family in the woods.'

Whether or not the details of this reconstruction are accurate (and the facts are consistent with details published in the national and local press), this is the version that the neighbours believed. Another neighbour stressed what to her were the salient details:

'The boy's crime was public knowledge and brought shame upon the whole family. They could not face the public shame and gossip, so needed to escape it somehow. I don't know whether the father intended to kill his son or if it were just an accident, as some say, but it solved the problem of the family's shame.'

Suicide has a long association with honour and shame in Japan. It was used as an honourable end for a defeated *samurai* warrior, and an extension of this tradition was the emergence of *kamikaze* suicide pilots during the Second World War. For the *samurai* it expiated the shame of defeat and provided an avenue for honour to be redeemed. Some of these associations still cling to the practice, but its primary purpose in the cases cited above seems to be an escape from public shame. The alternative would be to face the gossip of the neighbours, which for many Japanese seems to be a worse fate than suicide.[4]

To some extent, this practice might be associated with a common idea that death is the end and that there is no afterlife. In our interviews we asked all informants if they fear what happens after death. Almost all said 'No', although some admitted to a fear of the process of dying. One 58-year old woman appeared uneasy at the question but denied any fear of death itself. Two men who did admit to some fear were a young Roman Catholic man and a man whose own father had died when the informant was six years old: this man fears sudden or unexpected death and he prays to his father when he travels in an aircraft.

On the other hand, there are some Japanese who regard suicide as a weak man's way out of a situation. Such an attitude is reflected in one informant's personal philosophy of a three-tier afterlife in which the lowest tier is occupied by those who had committed suicide. In a Shinto context, suicide is ritually polluting through its associations with death. It is commonly considered that suicides who leave no living descendants may become 'wandering spirits' (*muenbotoke*) or 'hungry ghosts' (*gaki*).

Therefore people are reluctant to buy a house in which a suicide has taken place, for fear lest it might be haunted. One such house, in which the wife had committed suicide five years previously, had been on the market for most of that time and had still not been sold. Neither could the owner attract tenants despite his asking a cheap rent for it. The husband of the woman who had committed suicide had lived there for about a year after his wife's death but had then moved out to live in an apartment where he hoped to escape from the associations connected with the house. He thinks that eventually he might have to pull the house down and have another one built if he is unable to sell or rent it in its present condition.[5]

A relatively high proportion of Japanese suicides are schoolchildren who either fear the shame of failing an examination or else had received poor results in important examinations and were then too ashamed to face their parents or classmates. Reports of such suicides occur not infrequently in the Japanese press and reflect the associations between suicide and shame.

The idea that Japan is predominantly a 'shame society' rather than a 'sin society' seems to have the authority of an expert on Japanese culture, the anthropologist Ruth Benedict.[6] Her work was commissioned by the U.S. government during the Second World War in order to help them better understand their enemy. She was therefore unable to conduct fieldwork at first hand in Japan but instead had to rely on travellers' reports and accounts given by Japanese immigrants in the U.S.A. (Many of these might have been second-generation Japanese.) Her work has been strongly criticized as relying too much upon normative statements about ideal behaviour instead of actual observation of real behaviour. Moreover, her characterization of Japanese culture, based on information derived from immigrants who have lived for some time in the U.S.A., has been criticized as reflecting feudal and pre-war values which may no longer be relevant.[7]

Contemporary feelings of shame and guilt

In characterizing a society as predominantly motivated by 'shame' rather than 'guilt' or 'sin', we are dealing with an aspect of culture which is not easily amenable to direct observation or testing. It is extremely difficult to penetrate the mind and feelings of other people when dealing with deep-seated emotions such as guilt. This makes any hypothesis such as Benedict's essentially untestable. We are left with indirect clues and reported feelings as the only basis for inference. Unsatisfactory as it is, this is the kind of data which I tried to elicit in my questionnaire.[8]

Table 11.1 tabulates the replies which were given on my questionnaire in response to the question, '*In which of the following circumstances would you feel ashamed, if the deed were known to others?*'.

Table 11.1   Expressed feelings of shame in various circumstances

	'Yes'%	'No'%	'Neither'%	Number of respondents
Stealing	99.1%	0.5%	0.5%	659
Lying	94.7%	1.7%	3.6%	658
Adultery	92.9%	1.7%	5.4%	632
Premarital sex	56.4%	24.2%	19.4%	640
Disloyalty to a superior	76.5%	6.4%	17.0%	652
Betrayal (of one's group)	93.5%	1.5%	5.0%	658
Not repaying a debt	93.5%	2.7%	3.8%	657
Speeding in a vehicle	55.1%	21.6%	23.3%	644
Neglecting one's parents	87.6%	3.6%	8.9%	643
Illegal parking	56.0%	21.4%	22.5%	639
Having an abortion	77.9%	8.1%	14.0%	592
Forcing one's wife to have an abortion	75.0%	10.3%	14.7%	496
Not helping a friend in need	83.9%	3.8%	12.3%	652
Not helping a stranger in need	74.5%	6.2%	19.3%	648

On the whole, these figures suggest that most Japanese do feel a sense of shame if they are publicly known to have committed these kinds of acts. As is probably true also of the West, fewer people report feelings of shame about illegal parking or speeding than they do about theft or lying. However, are there feelings of guilt in addition to those of shame? Are Japanese people more likely to report feelings of shame than feelings of guilt? Or do they feel both? Table 11.2 shows the responses of the same people to the question, '*In which of the following circumstances would you experience a feeling of guilt, even if the act were not known to anyone else?*'.

In general, it can be seen that most people report feelings of *both* shame *and* guilt for each of these items. If they feel shame, then they also feel guilt, and *vice-versa*. There are relatively few people who feel shame but not guilt. *These figures indicate that it is misleading to characterize Japan as a 'shame society', with the*

Table 11.2   Expressed feelings of guilt in various circumstances

	'Yes'%	'No'%	'Neither'%	Number of respondents
Stealing	98.6%	0.6%	0.8%	662
Lying	83.1%	4.6%	12.3%	657
Adultery	88.7%	3.5%	7.9%	635
Premarital sex	44.4%	30.9%	24.7%	644
Disloyalty to a superior	69.8%	8.2%	22.1%	648
Betrayal (of one's group)	94.8%	0.6%	4.6%	657
Not repaying a debt	96.8%	1.1%	2.1%	657
Speeding in a vehicle	47.2%	27.5%	25.3%	651
Neglecting one's parents	85.4%	3.6%	11.0%	644
Illegal parking	54.1%	23.1%	22.8%	649
Having an abortion	78.5%	5.6%	15.8%	606
Forcing one's wife to have an abortion	77.8%	7.2%	15.0%	487
Not helping a friend in need	81.7%	2.6%	15.7%	656
Not helping a stranger in need	68.7%	5.2%	26.1%	654

implication that guilt is not so strongly present. Instead, Japan appears to be both a 'guilt' and a 'shame' society.

The Japanese term which was used in the above question to elicit responses about 'a consciousness of guilt' was the term *tsumi no ishiki*, which means a 'consciousness of *tsumi*", the word which has been translated as either 'sin' or 'crime'. By focussing on the *consciousness* of it, and feelings associated with it, I attempted to elicit responses describing what in the West might be termed 'guilt'. In the wording of the question, shame was assumed to be public but guilt to be private.[9] It is significant that these respondents said they would feel a sense of guilt *even if their actions were not known to others*. This indicates that shame ('public guilt') does not necessarily in itself produce guilt (as 'private shame').

How valid is such data?

The questions posed in my questionnaire are admittedly hypothetical, and answers might not reflect real behaviour. However, four considerations do indicate that responses to the questionnaire *do* reflect actual attitudes and feelings.

Firstly, where observation has been possible it has borne out the answers written by these same individuals on their questionnaires. A good example is the behaviour of a couple who had conceived their first child about three months before they married. During the early days of my fieldwork, and about six months before this questionnaire was distributed, the husband pointed out this fact to us very openly while we were having a meal at their home. He had no need even to mention it, let alone point it out after a relatively short acquaintance with us; in fact, he appeared proud of the fact. By contrast, his wife blushed conspicuously and averted her eyes. Six months later, when they filled in my questionnaire, the husband replied 'No' to both questions about feelings of shame or guilt regarding premarital sexual relations, whereas his wife independently answered 'Yes'.

Secondly, the fact that a wide variety and significant percentage of respondents independently gave similar answers does suggest a general consistency in attitudes and feelings. This is particularly the case for the 'No' answers, which go against accepted normative standards and therefore probably reveal actual feelings. 'Yes' answers might reveal actual feelings too, but might to some extent be conforming to expected attitudes and opinions.

Thirdly, the questionnaire was administered in strictest confidence, with brown envelopes being provided for the return of the completed questionnaires, in order to assure complete confidentiality.

Fourthly, I discovered later (either in collecting the questionnaires or in conducting follow-up interviews) that a number of respondents had not noticed our address on the introductory page and had not seen us around the neighbourhood so had not realized that we lived locally. Therefore when filling in their questionnaires they were writing their answers anonymously—as far as they were concerned—and had our assurances that the information would be treated in utmost confidence.

When filling in the questionnaire most respondents had no idea at all about our own ethical values, so I consider it unlikely that their responses were influenced too much by a desire to express values which would be considered acceptable to a foreigner, or to disguise any unfavourable impressions of Japan. Some Japanese who had visited England or America were not inhibited by 'politeness' from expressing to us negative opinions about their experiences. One woman who expressed such opinions but was also very concerned lest Japan should be given a bad image nevertheless gave answers in her own questionnaire which would not be in accordance with a desire to please a foreigner or to represent Japan in the best possible light.

The replies of those who did know us well enough to be influenced by a knowledge of our possible reactions to their answers actually strengthen my confidence that the questionnaire results are not seriously distorted by such influences. There is very little discernible trace of such influences, and the replies tend to conform closely to the overall pattern which has been tabulated already.

Cultural influences on replies

A number of the questionnaire items referred to values which are particularly esteemed in traditional Japanese culture, including loyalty to one's group, loyalty to superiors and the repayment of social and monetary debts. It is noticeable that the three items about which most guilt is expressed are stealing, 'betrayal action' and not repaying a debt. It is noticeable that many people said they would feel guilty about 'betrayal actions' and not repaying debts, but fewer said they would feel guilty about disloyalty to a superior.

Another traditional Japanese value is said to be the care of one's parents, as expressed, for example, in the ancestor cult. In practice, there are cases reported in which elderly parents are neglected, but the high value placed on caring for parents is still reflected in the 85% who said they would feel guilty if they neglected their parents. Some of those who replied 'No' or 'Neither', or who left the question blank, might no longer have parents alive, or else might have other siblings who are responsible for the care of living parents. Nevertheless, many younger sons answered 'Yes' to this question too.

De Vos has shown that in certain contexts, such as the choice of a marriage partner, underlying feelings of guilt can be powerful influences on Japanese behaviour. He argues that this is a guilt which results from feelings of having hurt one's parents through a failure to live up to their expectations, rather than being a guilt which comes from feelings of having transgressed a divine commandment.[10] This may be the case for some of the situations represented in my questionnaire, but it is less likely to apply to all of them, as suggested, for example, by the responses to the item about not helping a stranger in need.

In theory, the Japanese 'group ethic' means that greater emphasis is placed on honouring obligations to others within one's own group than on helping those who are outside one's group. From this perspective, it is not surprising that more people should say they would feel guilty about not helping a friend in need than about not helping a stranger in need. Nevertheless, the fact that almost 70% said that they would still feel guilty about not helping a stranger in need would seem to indicate that values are not so particularistic. In addition to group sentiments, there are also more general, though perhaps not so strongly felt, moral feelings regarding conduct towards strangers.

The discrepancy between helping friends versus strangers in need is consistent with attitudes towards gift giving. Table 11.3 contrasts the percentages of incomes which are given to charity with the percentages spent on gifts to acquaintances outside one's own family; these gifts include traditional mid-year and year's-end gifts to teachers or superiors.

Table 11.3 Percentages of income given to charity or as gifts to non-kin

Percentage of income	Given to charity [No. of replies = 442]	Spent on gifts [No. of replies = 543]
Nothing at all	48.6% of respondents	2.8% of respondents
Less than 0.1%	5.5% of respondents	
0.1%	14.7% of respondents	
0.1% to 0.5%		7.8% of respondents
1.0%	21.7% of respondents	
Between 1% and 10%	7.7% of respondents	79.3% of respondents
10% or more (up to 30%)	1.8% of respondents	10.1% of respondents

Attitudes towards premarital sexual relations are rather more complex. During the Edo period, and more recently too in some parts of Japan, young men often used to sleep with their girlfriends and decide on marriage once her fertility was proven. This custom of *yobai* declined after the Meiji Restoration while the former *samurai* custom of arranged marriage became more prestigious among other social classes.[11] Opportunities for premarital sexual relationships became scarcer, especially for those who married by *miai* ('arranged') marriage. Several female informants who married prior to the early 1970s claimed that they were virgins at marriage. Nowadays premarital sex is generally discouraged by parents, who try to keep a strict control over their daughters' evening activities, but it nevertheless occurs among those living away from home. The number of young unmarried couples living together 'suddenly increased' in large cities after the 1969 students' revolts, when students of both sexes barricaded themselves into university buildings for a few months.[12] In at least two households of Aoyama, the wife was pregnant when she got married.

For some reason there was a noticeable drop in the numbers of people who were willing to answer the question on adultery, even though they systematically answered the other items.[13] Traditionally it was not uncommon for wealthy men to have mistresses or concubines, but nowadays most men cannot afford the expense of maintaining such women in addition to their own wives. Prostitution as such has been outlawed, but instead certain kinds of 'bath houses' have become almost equivalent to brothels.[14] Liaisons between married men and other women are said to be 'not too uncommon', and were known or suspected in at least four households in the area which I studied.

Traditionally, unwanted children, especially girls, were sometimes abandoned after birth, but during the twentieth century abortion has become preferred to infanticide. Nowadays it is rare for families to have more than three children: in the area which I studied, the only family with four children had the last two as twins.

Mizuko kuyō, memorial services for aborted babies, were originally for miscarried babies, but they now include aborted children too. About forty women attended one service which I witnessed, but they were coming and going at intervals because the temple was performing such services every hour (on the hour) during that week. Only two teenage girls were present, one of whom was accompanied by her boyfriend and parents. All the other women were middle-aged. My impression was that they had aborted an unwanted child after they had already borne their 'quota' of children.

Afterwards one of these middle-aged women told me she had wanted to keep the child but her husband had 'made' her have an abortion. Three years later her conscience had been pricked by seeing in a newspaper and local buses advertisements for the memorial services. She then felt she 'ought to attend'.

The abortion figures in my tables are not fully clear because of a confusion arising over the two forms of the question. As only women can, strictly speaking, 'have an abortion', I included an item for men to fill in whether they would feel guilty or ashamed about making their wives have one. However, many respondents answered both questions. The figures relating to guilt feelings are as follows:

Table 11.4 feelings of guilt regarding abortion

Having an abortion

	'Yes'%	'No'%	'Neither'%	Number of respondents
Males	73.7%	7.8%	18.4%	358
Females	85.5%	2.4%	12.1%	248

Forcing one's wife to have an abortion

	'Yes'%	'No'%	'Neither'%	Number of respondents
Males	75.5%	8.4%	16.1%	392
Females	87.4%	2.1%	10.5%	95

These figures still show that the great majority of people, whether men or women, do feel guilty about such actions. Their sense of guilt about abortions is partly reflected in the practice of *mizuko kuyō*.

Other moral attitudes

In another question, I asked respondents to give their opinions on a variety of topics. These included 'pin-ball machines' (*pachinko*)—a popular form of petty gambling—and 'no-pantie coffee shops' where the waitresses wear mini skirts without underwear underneath.[15]

Some explanation may be required for my inclusion of 'cartoons' (*manga*). The term covers a wide variety of cartoons, many of them innocuous or satirical, but some can be pornographic or offensive in what they portray. Some comic strips 'have introduced sado-masochism..., overt eroticism..., and realistically portrayed violence...In both boys' and girls' comics, scenes of nudity, kissing, lovers in bed, homosexuality, and scatology are frequent.' Another strip 'always involves defecation and the toilet'.[16]

Table 11.5 shows the overall pattern which emerged: the items at the top of the list are on the whole regarded as more acceptable than those at the bottom.[17]

Table 11.5   Moral values and attitudes

	'Good'%	'Bad'%	'Neither'%	'Don't Know'%
'Cartoons' (*Manga*)	31.6%	3.7%	60.7%	4.1%
Pachinko	27.4%	5.8%	63.4%	3.5%
Betting [on horses]	12.3%	18.8%	62.6%	6.2%
Pornography	8.7%	25.6%	55.9%	9.8%
Premarital sex	7.1%	27.8%	55.7%	9.5%
Drunkenness	7.3%	40.2%	48.2%	4.3%
Divorce	3.3%	34.0%	48.8%	13.8%
'No-pantie coffee shops'	5.8%	45.6%	37.1%	11.6%
Homosexuality	2.7%	48.1%	24.8%	24.4%
Abortion	2.3%	60.1%	28.8%	8.8%
Bribery	1.7%	78.4%	16.3%	3.7%
Adultery	1.2%	79.5%	13.5%	5.7%

Bribery and adultery are clearly evaluated as the worst items in this list, which is consistent with the findings given above regarding guilt feelings. However, the ranking is also indicative of other social and cultural values.

The first three or four items can be classified as kinds of hobbies; certainly a number of people listed *pachinko* as one of their hobbies, and gambling games such as *mahjong* are also popular. Many adults read *manga* books for light reading while travelling, and even relatively serious newspapers sometimes carry sketches or drawings of a mildly pornographic nature. Pornography is sold in vending machines and can sometimes be given as gifts to male guests leaving a party. All these are generally viewed as matters of personal choice involving one individual alone and not particularly affecting others.

However, the next five items do involve two (or more) people who voluntarily participate in some act and should in theory face the consequences themselves without involving others. Some people wrote in comments that these were acceptable as long as no third party were involved.

Such a third party is involved in the three items regarded as the worst offences on the list. Adultery involves the breaking of an existing formal promise and might therefore be regarded as rather more serious than using a bribe in order to obtain a particular agreement in the first place. Both adultery and bribery are on the whole viewed as somewhat more serious than violating the rights of an unborn child, especially as such violation might be rationalized away on medical or economic grounds.

Therefore these moral attitudes in Japan do seem to be very closely related to the 'group ethic'. They also involve considerations of personal responsibility and the rights of others. Such considerations are mediated through one's conscience, which can be dulled rather more easily by personal actions unknown to most other people. The conscience is less easily dulled when a third party is unjustly or involuntarily involved. In these circumstances shame of public knowledge and guilt from individual knowledge reinforce one another.

Guilt and Shame in a Christian perspective

Timothy Boyle presents a very interesting attempt at communicating the Christian gospel in terms of 'shame' rather than guilt.[18] He notes that most references to shame in the Bible are in the Old

Testament, where, he claims, the Hebrew culture was 'a very group oriented culture similar to the Japanese culture in this and several other respects...Sin itself was seen more in terms of defilement and uncleanness to be removed by purification than has usually been recognized in the West. The sin of one person affected all and was like a pollution in the land...[as illustrated by the sin of Achan in Joshua chapter 7]. ...These all point to a shame orientation rather than a guilt orientation, and thus shame is a far more important concept in the Bible than most Western readers have been aware.'[19]

Boyle goes on to discuss how the sin of Adam and Eve could be interpreted in terms of 'Original Shame': they sought to hide their shame in an inadequate manner by fig leaves, but God provided a better 'covering for shame' through the [implied] first sacrifice of an animal (Genesis 3:21). Although human righteous acts are as 'filthy rags' (Isaiah 64:6), it is God who provides 'garments of righteousness' (Isaiah 61:10). In the New Testament there are promises of new white clothes which are available through Christ (Revelation 3:4, 18; 7:9, 13-14).[20]

Moreover, in a Japanese context the head of a family or of a company may take responsibility and publicly apologize for the shame brought about through the misdeeds of a junior member. Hence it could be said that 'God takes responsibility for our shame' and, through Christ's incarnation and very shameful form of death, God takes a 'deep bow' like that of an apologetic superior who in such circumstances might even bow lower than would be expected of someone in his position. In a Japanese context, suicide is a possible outcome of such a situation: Boyle suggests that, although Jesus did not commit suicide, the voluntary nature of his death—in which he was fully in control—might be seen in a similar light.[21]

It is God himself, however, who is the one against whom there has been an offence as well as being the one who might take responsibility for the shame on behalf of his family. Ultimately all human metaphors are inadequate in themselves as complete expressions of what the atonement represents, but each expresses a relevant aspect of it. Just as the metaphor of redemption is readily understood in a slave-owning society, but is not so appropriate for other kinds of social structures, so Boyle's depiction of the atonement in terms of shame is more appropriate for some cultural contexts than for others. Within the Japanese context, he found it to be more effective when there has already been an adequate communication of the concept of a Creator God.[22]

Nevertheless, from the data presented previously in this chapter it can be seen that feelings of *guilt* as well as shame are in fact widespread in Japanese society. It is not enough simply to characterize Japan as a 'shame society' and to assert that guilt feelings are less common among the Japanese. Rather, *both* feelings appear to be very common, even though certain moral attitudes and values are still influenced by the Japanese so-called 'group ethic'.

At the Hayama conference mentioned at the beginning of this chapter, Clark Offner presented a very useful paper on 'the place of shame, guilt and grace in Japanese religions'. In it he noted his awareness of how Benedict's distinction between 'shame' and 'guilt' cultures relied on nineteenth-century material, and in this sense is 'dated'. Later, Offner remarks, 'In probing Japanese feelings of shame, Benedict did not go far enough. She stressed the outward or public shame, but overlooked...internal or private feelings of shame'.[23] He also noted how difficult it is in practice to distinguish feelings of guilt from those of shame. I do not wish to imply that missionaries are unaware of these problems or that all of them believe in the validity of Benedict's distinction.[24] On the other hand, Benedict's book is still much more widely known than the criticisms of it. There is still a tendency for missionaries on furlough to speak at their deputation meetings about the difficulties of communicating the gospel in Japan because of the way in which the Japanese are motivated by shame rather than guilt.

Concepts of a Supreme Being

If Japan is traditionally polytheistic or 'animistic', even perhaps to some extent 'nihilistic', how do these feelings of guilt arise? What moral law or rule is being broken in order to produce such guilt, since in the absence of rules there can be no feeling of guilt at having broken them?

In fact, many Japanese *do* believe in some kind of 'Being above man and nature' who might be analogous to a conception of a

Supreme Being. Such a belief was asserted by 63.3% of the 651 people who answered my question on this topic. Only 20.7% expressed a definite disbelief in such a concept, and these were mainly those whose wartime experiences seem to have made them generally more cynical.

In practice, however, my questionnaire item about a 'Being above man and nature' did not differentiate easily from concepts of Shinto *kami* or Buddhist *Hotoke*, even though I tried to capture Shinto animistic-type beliefs in a separate question on 'a spirit within man and nature'. I also asked about ideas of a personal spirit or soul. Table 11.6 shows the 'Yes' responses to these questions, broken down by sex:

Table 11.6   Miscellaneous beliefs

Do you believe in the existence of:

	Men	Women
a) A Being above man and nature	60%	69%
b) A spirit within man and nature	34%	44%
c) A spirit within each person	52%	64%
d) A personal spirit which survives death	29%	40%

Possibly related to the idea of some kind of supreme being is the concept of supernatural punishment for wrongdoing. I asked about this, using the Japanese term *bachi*, which does not connote the Christian concepts of judgement. Answers to this question were as follows:

Table 11.7   Attitudes towards *bachi*

Question: *'If you were to do something bad, do you think divine punishment would befall you?'*

	Yes	No	Don't know
Men:	50%	22%	28%
(Number = 404)			
Women:	64%	13%	23%
(Number = 252)			

These kinds of beliefs are relatively vague and nebulous but are found in most, and possibly all, religious systems of the world. All of these beliefs are professed more by women than by men. However, the specific manifestation or understanding of a concept such as *bachi* differs considerably from one person to another. Among thirty-four people questioned in my interviews about their attitudes towards *bachi*, the main attitudes to it were as follows:

(1) *Bachi* is manifested as injury or illness as a result of neglecting the ancestors: five people
(2) It is injury or illness as a result of more generalized bad conduct: another five people
(3) A definite cause and effect in human relationships (*e.g.* 'If you betray someone you yourself will be betrayed.'): eight people
(4) One experiences psychological suffering, or a guilty feeling (which one man expressed as 'a feeling of not being forgiven'): seven people
(5) *Bachi* is mainly a threat to children, to make them behave: three people—one of whom also saw *bachi* partly in terms of category (2).
(6) 'Don't know', or 'the form of it is unpredictable': two people
(7) Other replies: four people. Their replies were as follows:
   (a) A woman with three daughters and no sons who considered herself 'not overblessed', but she did not go as far as calling it *bachi* because that would impute guilt or responsibility to herself.
   (b) A woman influenced by the Jehovah's Witnesses who viewed death and judgement as forms of divine punishment, but, contrary to attitudes (a) and (b) above, she did not see injuries or lost property as forms of *bachi*.
   (c) A woman whose father-in-law's cousin lived with his cousin (father's sister's daughter) without being married to her. In the village where they live their relationship is regarded by their neighbours as incestuous even if it is not legally so. Their first child died in infancy, their second is mentally deficient and their third is normal. The villagers and some of the family regard these misfortunes as *bachi*. This man is also regarded by the villagers as being pos-

sessed by the spirit of Ryūjin, the dragon god, from whom he claims to receive visions and revelations.

(d) A man whose car turned over on the way back from a Shinto shrine after he had bought a *mamori* in defiance of Sōka Gakkai teachings regards his experience as a form of *bachi* which nevertheless led to his conversion to the Sōka Gakkai. He had bought the *mamori* from a Shinto shrine but had gone no more than ten kilometres when his car overturned and crashed. He escaped unharmed, but the first thing he did was to throw away the *mamori*. Shortly afterwards he joined the Sōka Gakkai, a Buddhist 'new religion' which condemns Shinto as a 'false religion'.[25] (This is an exceptional case in which a motor accident was attributed to the purchase of a *mamori*.)

The attitudes towards *bachi* are varied, but those towards 'a Being above man and nature' are somewhat more consistent. To some extent the ideas of *bachi* are linked to the concept of some kind of supreme moral order in the universe. Although my question about a 'Being above man and nature' did not ask if people thought the Being might also *be morally concerned*, the idea of *bachi* in folk religion does embody vague moral concepts. This might be seen either in material terms—such as 'if a man is a thief he becomes poor'—or in spiritual terms regarding a judgement in an afterlife. Therefore the concept of *bachi* needs to be seen also in the context of beliefs about some kind of 'Being above man and nature' who (or which) might be held responsible for upholding that moral order.[26] Perhaps such a belief (or even 'feeling') that a supreme Being does exist in some form might account for the widespread feelings of guilt which my informants reported.

This widespread 'belief' or 'feeling' about the existence of a kind of supreme being might also be related to the Japanese concept of 'conscience' (*ryōshin*). Unlike the idea of 'sin', *ryōshin* is an indigenous and universally understood concept. The question of the origin of one's conscience would explain the guilt feelings which are widely reported. As far as I am aware, the existence of a 'conscience' has not been explained satisfactorily by psychological theories of a 'super-ego', because these still recognize the role of religious beliefs in forming such a 'super-ego'. To some extent, 'conscience' can be moulded by the laws and customs of a society, but breaking such a law still produces guilt even if the transgression is not known to others. Theories that social laws become 'internalized' might account for the existence of a conscience to a limited extent, but fail to explain the ways in which ideas about moral absolutes may demand higher standards of morality than those required by society. Prophets who uphold such higher standards have often been rejected by their own societies.

The philosophical search for an origin of human 'conscience' still remains elusive unless it is recognized as a recognition of the standards set by a morally concerned Supreme Being. Christians believe that 'conscience' is a God-given attribute of human nature which directs humanity towards God's supreme moral standards. As St. Paul expressed it:

> 'When Gentiles, who do not have the law, do by nature things required by the law, they are a law for themselves, even though they do not have the law, since they show that the requirements of the law are written on their hearts, their consciences also bearing witness, and their thoughts now accusing, now even defending them.' (Romans 2:14-15).

In this way, it makes theological sense to assume that the Japanese *do* have a strong sense of 'guilt'. Theirs is *both* a 'guilt' *and* a 'shame' society. Human cultures can indeed channel ethical values in such a way that certain moral absolutes can be ascribed greater importance than others, and the latter might be 'conveniently' violated until conscience becomes numbed in those areas. However, a 'prophetic' figure can then emerge who seeks to restore violated moral absolutes.

Those communicating the Gospel of Jesus need to be such prophetic figures. To do so, they need to to address their message to the voice of conscience which is already within the Japanese people. Rather than espousing 'foreign' values, the Gospel in Japan should address what is already recognized by the Japanese people themselves as areas of moral failure and guilt. In this way, the 'inner' voice of 'conscience' agrees with the 'outer' voice of the spokesperson for God. At the same time, we may pray for the work of the Holy Spirit to 'convict the world of guilt in regard to sin and righteousness and judgment' (John 16:8).

CHAPTER

12

Aspects of Church Growth

WHY HAVE SOME Japanese churches grown faster than others at various points in history? What kinds of people have different denominations tended to attract? Why were they attracted to Christianity? What perceptions of the churches have been held by non-Christian Japanese? These and other related questions are crucial to an understanding of the place of Christianity in Japanese society today. This chapter is intended as a general overview in which I shall particularly highlight some of the many factors which have facilitated or hindered church growth in Japan.

Early Encounters

The year 1549 is generally regarded as the year in which Christianity was first introduced to Japan.[1] It was then that Francis Xavier and two other Jesuits arrived in Kagoshima, on the south coast of Kyushu; they were later joined by other Roman Catholic missionaries. During the following decades, there was an apparently rapid increase in the numbers of Christians, so that by 1614 the number of Christians amounted to about 300,000. This represented about 1.5% of the Japanese population at that time—about three times as much as the proportion of church members in the Japanese population today.[2]

Among the various factors facilitating this growth could be mentioned the following:

a) At first, Christianity seems to have been regarded as simply another branch of Buddhism, rather than as a completely alien religion. This impression was conveyed by their unfortunate use of terms with strong Buddhist connotations when seeking Japanese translations for concepts such as 'God', 'heaven' or 'soul'. For example, for 'church' Xavier used the word *daidō-ji* (connoting a Buddhist temple), for 'heaven' he used *jōdo* (connoting the 'Pure Land' teachings in the Pure Land sects of Buddhism), for 'priest' he used *sō* (connoting a Buddhist monk or priest) and for 'God' he used *Dainichi* or *Hotoke*. In 1551 he discovered that the Buddhist term *Dainichi*, which he had thought was the equivalent of 'God', in fact made the notion of a Trinity unimaginable to the Buddhist priests. 'It did not indicate a Creator but some pantheistic notion. Furthermore, occult symbolism gave it sexual overtones.' Xavier therefore imported the Latin (or Portuguese) term *Deus* and used this 'foreign' term, even though some of his audience mockingly distorted this into '*Dai-uso*', the 'Big Lie'.[3]

b) In contrast to their policies in some other countries, the missionaries to Japan made a conscious effort to adapt themselves to Japanese customs such as styles of dress and etiquette. However, it appears that Xavier himself had little knowledge of the Japanese language and that the Jesuits did not train many Japanese missionaries.[4]

c) Where possible, they sought audiences with powerful feudal lords, under whose patronage they were allowed to operate.[5]

d) For these feudal lords, the missionaries brought with them valuable gifts such as clocks, richly bound books or muskets. The Japanese were also fascinated by aspects of Western medical knowledge and Christianity also 'became a kind of exoticism or ornamental accessory for the progressive *samurai*'.[6]

e) Usually the missionaries were accompanied by traders with other exotic commodities. It appears that in some cases the feudal lords ordered their populations to convert to Christianity *en masse* as an inducement to the missionaries and traders. If no traders came, however, the lords might order their subjects to revert back to their former religions. Therefore 'it was loyalty to their superiors that kept the fidelity of believers... It is not a miracle that there were over 700,000 Christians, nor that the whole number could disappear overnight... The Western religion disappeared quickly because it had no root'.[7]

In general, it appears that the popular understanding of Christianity in this period was often relatively superficial. Nevertheless, there were a number of Japanese who did embrace Catholicism in all sincerity and trained for the priesthood. The strength of devotion among a substantial proportion of the Christians is further shown by the effects of the subsequent severe persecution of Christianity. Some were willing to die for their faith, while many others clung onto it in secret and passed on their Catholic traditions to their descendants.[8] For about two and a half centuries (from roughly 1614 until 1865) families of 'hidden Christians' (*kakure kirishitan*) survived in parts of Kyushu and adjacent remote islands. Officially, they had to become parishioners of a Buddhist temple and to participate in the forced public denunciation of Christ by treading on an image of him. Nevertheless, at home they continued to preserve various Christian traditions, even though by the time they were 're-discovered' in 1865 it appeared that over the centuries these traditions had also been influenced by aspects of Japanese folk lore and other ideas.

Some Christian influence from this period might have survived in an unexpected form, in a Japanese custom which is normally thought to be associated with Zen Buddhism—namely, the tea ceremony, which developed after the introduction of Roman Catholicism in the sixteenth century. The master of the tea ceremony who taught it to Toyotomi Hideyoshi (one of the three warlords influential in the unification of Japan) was a close associate of Takayama Ukon, a well-known Christian feudal lord. In the tea ceremony itself 'the concepts of equality and humility were quite different from the general culture at large, and... the symbolisms of the tea ceremony resemble Christian concepts very closely. For instance, all differences in social status are disregarded within the tea house. Everyone is equal, and the door of the house is made very low so that all have to stoop in humility to enter.... No weapons are allowed...Outside the house, the stepping stones, the water basin and the stone lantern all symbolize a willingness to be of service: the stones to be trod upon, the water to remove dirt, and the wick of the lantern to be consumed that a little light might fall. Also, the ceremony itself is similar in form to the Christian Holy Communion, as the participants sit in contemplation while a single cup of ceremonial tea is passed around and small, sweet-tasting cakes are shared. Interestingly enough, some of the tea cups from this period have the symbol of a cross on them.'[9]

During the sixteenth century, it seems that Christianity was attractive partly because it was accompanied by Western knowledge and goods. However, this became a liability towards the end of the century and in the first half of the seventeenth century, when those who were uniting Japan began to see Western influence as a threat. In 1600, Tokugawa Ieyasu gained control of Japan after the battle of Sekigahara by defeating a coalition of feudal lords whose fiefs were predominantly in outlying areas of the country. Among the more powerful of these lords were those from Kyushu, whose contacts with the West remained a threat to the Tokugawa regime. These political considerations seem to have been among the main reasons for the almost total exclusion of foreigners (apart from a few strictly limited Dutch traders) and the suppression of Christianity.[10]

Characteristics of Japanese Christianity between 1859 and 1939

Japan was forced to open up again to more contacts with the West after Commodore Perry arrived with U.S. Navy gunboats in July 1853. Six years later both Roman Catholic and Protestant missionaries arrived, even though the anti-Christian edict of 1614 was still officially in effect. The first Orthodox missionary arrived in 1861.

I shall not dwell on the histories of individual denominations in Japan, concerning which a number of books have already been written.[11] Rather, I shall briefly summarize general characteristics of Japanese Christians and some significant patterns of church growth, particularly as revealed by Yamamori's detailed study of eight different Protestant denominations during this period.[12]

From 1859 to 1872 there was virtually no church growth. This was largely because the missionaries were confined to certain parts of the country, most of them were unable to communicate well in Japanese, and they were still restricted by the official edict against Christianity. After the public notices banning Christianity were removed in 1873, church membership grew slowly until 1881. By then the number of Japanese Christians was no more than 4,000 but already their general characteristics revealed patterns which have prevailed right up to the present day.[13] Some of these features are as follows:

1) At first the Christians were drawn primarily from among the sons of the former *samurai* class who studied in the mission schools and were the most easily accessible to the missionaries. The *samurai* had lost the privileges which they had enjoyed under the Tokugawa régime, so that, in comparison with other classes, the younger *samurai* became less attached to traditional social norms. Both the early American Protestant missionaries and their Japanese converts 'came from religiously conservative groups who felt themselves losing status in their home lands'.[14] The Japanese converts, however, had political ambitions for Japan to become a respected member of the international community, and Christianity seemed to them to be one of the factors which might have helped the West to become politically and economically dominant. Moreover, these sons of the *samurai* were the intellectuals of the day who could read the Chinese version of the Bible before the Japanese one was available. For the most part, Japanese Christians were drawn from the educated, urban population.[15]

However, the social characteristics of these early Christian converts 'have sown seeds of such highbrow nature in Japanese Christianity that they have erected a barrier against the broad propagation of Christianity among the common people'.[16] Because most of the early Protestant converts came from bureaucrats of the samurai class who had served under feudal domains which had been affiliated with the deposed shogunate, there developed in Japanese Christianity 'a certain aloofness from the establishment... Once a body of believers had been drawn from the urban middle class, and once these people had organized and established churches, they promptly made of their churches miniature closed societies. People of other classes, coming into contact with these cliques, felt shut out and rejected. Aware that they constituted a suspect minority group, church people considered their churches as citadels that protected them from a hostile administration and accordingly developed close-knit ties among themselves. In the process they brought into play the conscious distinction between insiders and outsiders typical of Japanese groups, and their churches became even more tightly closed societies.'[17] Several studies by different scholars have shown how in subsequent decades there continued to be a conspicuous tendency for Christianity to be confined largely to the urban, educated, white-collar classes.[18]

2) The tendency for Christianity to be confined mainly to the educated urban classes stems largely from the initial pattern of conversions through mission schools. This pattern prevailed at least until the Second World War, with a large proportion of converts being those who attended Christian schools or colleges. In the 1930s, for instance, those who became Christians through attending Christian schools accounted for approximately 37% of all those baptized by the American Baptist Church in Japan.[19]

Nowadays the influence of Christian educational institutions is probably not as great as in the pre-war period, but even today there remains a psychological legacy from the emphasis upon educational approaches. For many of the early converts Christianity was 'conceived more as an ethic than a religion and, if a religion, it was more as the religion of the head; Christianity to most converts was something to be learned as one studied the subject of American history or mathematics.'[20] After graduation from the mission school, or after going to church for a few years, such converts also 'graduated' from Christianity.[21] 'Just as easily as they caught hold of a new faith... they were quick to let it go when the current fad went out of style or the new one competed for its allegiance.'[22] Japanese Christianity had 'become an independent world where one could enjoy a distinctive atmosphere and a complicated theology. The desire to 'know' Christianity became far stronger than the impulse to convert people to it. Christianity became a self-contained and even self-satisfied world of elaborate ethics and exotic dreams.'[23]

That Japanese Christianity continued in the 1930s to have an emphasis upon 'head knowledge' was confirmed by Iglehart, who wrote,

> 'In Japan Christianity is still largely a teaching, as is indoctrinated into individuals, slowly and thoroughly until one by one they accept it. The tradition is that no one is to be very emotional and that even if a travelling evangelist does awaken a spark of warm feeling under which decisions are made, this must be followed by months of intellectual training before one can really be said to have entered the Christian life. This may in part account for the fact that before the churches have got around to making the link-up following an evangelistic meeting, all but one or two percent of those signing cards have cooled to their former indifference, and are lost to the church'.[24]

3) The exposure to Christianity through educational institutions was also partly responsible for the generally younger ages of most converts. In the late nineteenth century conversions (or at least baptisms) tended to occur between the ages of sixteen and twenty-three. Many converts were baptized as students, and others shortly after graduating from school.[25] This pattern persisted until after the Second World War: 'In both prewar and postwar periods...persons between the ages of twelve and twenty-two were most responsive to the Christian faith'.[26] Yamamori's study of ten churches in Kyoto showed that 61% of those baptized were of school age and a further 13% were aged between twenty-three and twenty-six.[27] Today it is widely recognized that students constitute one of the sections of Japanese society which is most responsive to the Christian gospel. (To a large extent, this is a pattern found also in the West.)

4) In the mid-nineteenth century Japanese men had more opportunities than women to study Western education, so this early period was exceptional in having more male than female converts.

However, by the early twentieth century there was a shift from male to female predominance in the church. Before the Second World War, the ratio of men to women was two to three.[28] (This trend has continued into the modern period too, as I shall discuss more fully in chapter 13.)

It was again through education that many women also became Christians. From 1870 (when the first school for girls was opened) until the turn of the century (when the Japanese government began to promote schools for women) 'the history of education for women in Japan' was 'almost identical with the history of the Christian schools for girls. In 1905, Christian high schools for girls represented 70% of the total number of girls' schools'.[29] In the late nineteenth century most women who became Christians were graduates of mission schools for girls.[30] Since then the proportion of girls' schools and colleges which are Christian has continued to drop, so that by 1930 it was less than 5%, but some of them, such as Dōshisha University in Kyoto, have continued to have a high academic reputation.

5) To a large extent, evangelism was left to the professional clergy. Yamamori suggests that this could be a cultural legacy of Buddhist and Shinto services in which lay people are passive recipients. Missionaries and pastors were regarded as the trained specialists on Christianity. For the predominantly white-collar Japanese Christians, the heavy emphasis placed on learning meant that many of them had a view of Christianity which was psychologically coloured by traditional Japanese attitudes towards the 'master-disciple' (*sensei-seito*) relationship. This reinforced the monolithic leadership structure of most Japanese churches.[31] (Remnants of these attitudes still seem to be common today.)

6) Christianity continued to be seen as a 'Western' religion, and this impression continued to be reinforced by styles of worship and music. A report published in 1932 observed:

> 'The missionaries who went out in the early nineteenth century had grown up in the circles of the Protestantism of that period and they could hardly be expected to approach their task with their minds detached from rigid forms and molds, or with princi-

ples of truth so free and fluid that they could find and absorb new ways of expressing their truth and new forms of incarnating it. They carried with them a set of pre-formed doctrines which seemed to them essential to Christianity and they felt at the same time that they were the bearers of a sacred church model.

The result was that they put down a foreign-made system upon the minds of their converts. They ignored in large measure the...habits of the people among whom they worked.

...When we...consider the quality of community worship in the rank and file of the churches there are some high peaks of attainment but a general level which runs fairly low.... In general...the pastors and leaders...seemed to us too apt to pray at great length in a conventional manner. The periods of prayer on many occasions seemed to be a time of formalism instead of being a time of fused and heightened group-consciousness...

Church music in...Japan is almost wholly western in type. There are gratifying signs in the new hymnals of an awakening of interest in the music of the land and of its people. Yet much patient work must be done by the small groups interested, if there is to be any large place for indigenous music in the churches of...Japan.'[32]

Patterns of Church Growth

Yamamori's study also provides many useful insights on patterns of church growth during this period. Some of the principal patterns were as follows:

1) In general, periods when there has been a political and social climate of openness to the West, at least among the educated classes, helped to produce more rapid church growth. 'Modernization' rapidly became mixed in with a superficial 'Westernization' among some urban intellectuals. An interest in, or openness towards, Christianity was another component of this limited 'Westernization'.

Because Christian schools were seen as channels for gaining access to Western education, the fastest growing churches during some periods were those with affiliated schools. Hence, for example, between 1882 and 1889 memberships of the Congregational and Presbyterian churches grew from about 1,000 and 2,000 respectively to about 9,000 members each, whereas denominations like the American Baptist Church, which concentrated on evangelism rather than education, showed relatively little growth.[33]

2) Even during periods of anti-Western feelings, such as the 1890s and the 1930s, there continued to be many conversions. However, in most denominations the effect of these conversions was lost because of a high rate of membership 'leakage' among existing Christians. Hence, for example, the Congregational church during the 1890s gained an average of 662 members per year, but lost an average of 620.[34] During both pro-Western and anti-Western periods, many churches suffered considerably from membership leakage. A probable reason for this was the individualistic, 'one by one' approach to evangelism whereby converts lacked the supportive networks of Christian relatives. Most churches were made up of people who were the only Christians in their homes.[35] The large proportion of Christian women married to non-Christian men were particularly likely to internalize their faith and to sever ties with the church.[36]

3) Most church membership loss was not through death but through loss of interest, a reduction in fervour or so-called 'backsliding'. 'There seems to be a vicious cycle of people coming in, staying a few years, and leaving.'[37] However, there were significant differences between denominations in their rates of membership leakage. Between 1906 and 1915, for instance, the Methodist church had a leakage of 66%, calculated by comparing that decade's baptismal total (13,536) with its decadal loss of 8,961. In the same period, the Southern Baptists baptized 648 people but lost 178, giving them a much lower leakage rate of 27%.[38]

4) Periods of anti-Westernism in the political and social climate did not necessarily hinder church growth. For instance, during one of these periods, the 1890s, the Episcopal and American Baptist churches more than doubled their memberships and the Methodists experienced slight but significant growth. However, the Congregational and Presbyterian churches had high rates of membership leakage (94% and 84% respectively), mainly because these denominations had a high proportion of 'fair weather Christians' who had been converted through these churches' educational

establishments. The effect of the less favourable political climate was to exacerbate membership leakage in denominations which were more susceptible to it.[39] Similarly, in the 1930s 'some churches were battered' by the adverse environment but 'others apparently remained unaffected by it'. The fact that all churches continued to register considerable gains through baptism during the 1930s 'proves that adverse environmental causes do not prevent growth and that the main problem lies elsewhere'.[40]

5) Another significant, and contrasting, development was the rapid growth of the Holiness Church during the 1920s, which 'soared up through the others like a spacecraft taking off for the moon'. In actual figures, the communicant membership reached 2,987 by 1924 and then climbed rapidly to 19,523 by 1932.[41] In percentage terms, its growth rate was 97.7% between 1917 and 1923 but then rose to 286.3% between 1924 and 1930.[42] Several of its characteristics strongly contrasted with those of the traditional denominations:

a) In contrast to the denominations in which converts 'learned' Christianity in an intellectual fashion, converts in the Holiness Church 'had a radical religious experience' and could not contain within themselves the joy of their salvation.

b) A stress on immediate conversion meant that the convert's original zeal was not lost during 'months of intellectual training' before they could be said to have entered the Christian life. Instead, the new convert was quickly taught the fundamentals of the Christian faith and encouraged to communicate this faith to others.

c) The Holiness Church actively sought the conversion of whole families as units and encouraged members to bring their relatives and friends into the faith.

d) In contrast to denominations predominantly made up of white-collar intellectuals, many members of the Holiness Church were blue-collar workers, merchants and employees in small businesses.

e) The Holiness Church had a multiple leadership structure which emerged from amongst the ordinary membership. Their seminary in Tokyo had minimal entrance requirements: applicants should have experienced rebirth, should be able to read and write, and be at least eighteen years old. The Church took seriously the doctrine of the priesthood of all believers, and encouraged the formation of house groups led by ordinary church members.[43]

f) There was also an emphasis on reaching various social groups which had been relatively neglected by the other denominations—such as lepers, 'outcaste' *burakumin* people, Korean immigrants in Japan, poor people in Tokyo, Japanese emigrants to Brazil, California and Korea, native Formosans in Taiwan and Russians in Manchuria and Siberia. 'In the midst of each of these groups churches were planted'.[44]

The impact of the Second World War

Japan's defeat in World War II had a noticeable impact, at least for a while, on the psychological and religious consciousness of the Japanese people. The shock of defeat after many heroic sacrifices on behalf of a supposedly divine Emperor, followed by the Emperor's renunciation of his claims to divinity, made many Japanese people rethink their presuppositions—not only about religion but also about ethics and life in general.[45]

Miura Ayako, who was a young primary school teacher at the time of the defeat, describes its impact upon her own thinking:

> '...When the defeat came...it was...a major event in my own life and for the entire Japanese nation....
>
> We had to go right through the State-authorised textbooks and correct them.... First we took out the book on ethics and I instructed [the children] as I had been ordered.
>
> 'Please cross out page 1, columns 2 to 5.' As I spoke, the tears slipped down my cheeks....
>
> It was too painful to be in charge of the children. What did it really mean to order them to correct their books in this way? Had Japan been wrong until now? If Japan had not been wrong, was America wrong? If one was right, which was wrong?
>
> ...Because I was a teacher I had to know. Were the corrected textbooks right, or had they been right before?...If everything I had taught so wholeheartedly was wrong, I had simply wasted

those seven years. And then again, there was a big difference between wasting time and being wrong. If I had been wrong, I should apologise on my knees to the children. Indeed, in the circumstances, just as soldiers committed suicide after the surrender, so we teachers should apologise to the children by taking our own lives.'[46]

The American occupation of Japan and the new Constitution—which officially separated religious institutions from the State and promised freedom of religion—provided greater freedom not only for Christianity but also for some of the so-called 'new religions'. Some of these had been started during the nineteenth century, and in some cases had suffered repression during the pre-war period, but after the Second World War there was a significant growth in both the numbers of new religions and their individual memberships. Faced with the American occupation and the various economic problems connected with war and its aftermath, many people were at least temporarily disillusioned with some of the older religious ideas and some were open to alternatives.[47] To at least some extent, an interest in the new religions—and even in Christianity for a while—may have been stimulated by the psychological shocks from defeat in war and the Emperor's renunciation of any claim to divinity. Many Christians discerned the hand of God in the defeat of what they regarded as a demonically-inspired régime and in the greater opportunities for evangelism afforded by General McArthur's appeal for missionaries.[48]

The psychological impact of the defeat was felt especially strongly by those who were in their teens or early twenties at the end of the war.[49] Their diminished practice of New Year shrine visits and more frequent choice of non-religious or Christian weddings possibly reflected their disillusionment with Shinto.[50] Even thirty-five years after the end of the war, this generation still tended to be much more sceptical about many different religious beliefs than those who were younger or older, as indicated by their responses to several items on my questionnaire:

Table 12.1   The impact of the Second World War on aspects of religiosity

Years of birth (in 5-year age bands)

	1921 -1925	1926 -1930	1931 -1935	1936 -1940	1941 -1945	1946 -1950	1951 -1955	1956 -1960	1961 -1965
a) Belief in:									
A being above man and nature	71%	47%	57½%	57%	73%	65½%	57%	65½%	53%
A being within man and nature	73%	47%	27½%	23%	38½%	37%	36%	49%	53%
A personal spirit	86%	75%	46%	50%	59%	59%	55%	50%	60%
A spirit which survives death	57%	41%	25%	22%	25%	35%	37%	40%	40%
Life after death	43%	33%	17%	8%	24%	19%	22%	41%	48%
Bachi ('divine punishment')	73%	41%	42%	55%	50%	57½%	56%	61%	60%
Belief that science will eventually explain all mysterious things	13%	29%	10%	12½%	8½%	10%	13%	17%	7%
b) Disbelief in:									
Ghosts*	93%	100%	92½%	81%	82%	88%	83%	64%	60%
Fireballs*	79%	61½%	74%	60%	51%	54½%	54%	31%	33%
UFOs*	57%	73%	61%	49%	50%	49%	33%	24%	20%
c) Practice of:									
Mamori possession	67%	71%	44%	71%	78%	74%	68½%	66%	71%
Hatsumode	87%	69%	66%	78%	78%	82%	75%	72%	80%
d) Marriage by:									
Shinto rites	64%	47%	69%	77%	76%	83%	88½%	80%	100%
Buddhist rites	7%	0%	9½%	6½%	5%	3½%	6%	8%	0%
Christian rites	0%	13%	7%	3%	8½%	3%	1½%	6%	0%
Non-religious rites	29%	40%	14%	13%	10%	10½%	4%	6%	0%

* Owing to the high proportion of 'Don't know' responses to these items in section (b), the 'No' answers, indicating definite disbelief, are clearer than the 'Yes' answers.

This generation's increased scepticism was particularly notice-able for items which might imply the possibility of some kind of personal spirit and of an afterlife. Moreover, even thirty-five years after the end of the war, there is a noticeable drop in the possession of *mamori* safety charms among those who were in their later teens in 1945, whose outlook on life might have been most profoundly affected by the dropping of atomic bombs on Hiroshima and Nagasaki. They recognised the impotence of *mamori* charms in the face of the devastating force of an atomic bomb.

Post-war growth

In general, it appears that church growth in Japan has been helped by periods of positive attitudes towards the West but hindered by more negative periods. The effect of defeat in war and occupation by the Americans was ambivalent. On the one hand, the crushing of national pride and the humiliation of a foreign occupation might have led some to resent the propagation of Christianity, which many continue to see as a 'foreign' religion. On the other hand, many people questioned their assumptions and were at least intellectually aware of the religion of the Americans. The new constitutional guarantees of freedom of religion and the fresh wave of missionaries gave a greater impetus to the church. For a while there seemed to be significant church growth, but 'after a brief outcropping of 'rice Christians' who visited the churches only for the purpose of getting some 'occupation things', growth stopped and even declined. Christian leaders had prepared no better spiritual food than an imitation of European and American Christianity'.[51]

The growth rate for both Roman Catholic and mainline Protestant churches peaked in about 1950 and then severely declined.[52] Although the United Church of Christ in Japan did attract a substantial number of new members between the end of the war and 1960, most of the gains were offset by a recurrent problem of membership leakage and by the departure of dissatisfied splinter groups.[53]

From 1980 to 1988 the number of Protestant churches grew from 5,918 to 6250, and in 1991 reached 7,076.[54] During the 1980s the older Japanese churches recorded 'only modest growth', as illustrated by the United Church of Christ in Japan which between 1977 and 1987 showed a 5.2% growth, from 189,587 to 199,425 members. During this same period 'significantly higher growth rates' were recorded by Japanese churches which have 'identified more closely with American evangelicalism', but their higher percentage growth needs to be seen in the context of their lower absolute numbers. For instance, the Southern Baptists grew by 15.8% from 24,345 to 28,195 members while the Assemblies of God reported a 69.7% increase in membership, from 5,821 to 9,879 members.[55] Between 1984 and 1988 the Pentecostals had a growth rate of 34%, whereas all the other 'mainline' denominations had rates between 1% and 13%.[56] Relatively rapid growth is also reported among the churches founded by Paul Yonggi Cho's Korean missionaries, but, with a few exceptions, their converts are mainly ethnic Koreans resident in Japan and Japanese spouses of Koreans.[57]

Groups such as the Unification Church ('Moonies'), the Jehovah's Witnesses and the Church of the Latter-Day Saints [*i.e.* Mormons] also reported rapid growth between 1966 and 1982.[58] Two other rapidly growing groups were indigenous Pentecostal-type movements, the *Iesu no Mitama kyōkai* (Spirit of Jesus Church) and the *Makuya* (Tabernacle [of Christ]).

Indigenous forms of Japanese Christianity

Most of this chapter has focussed on official, denominational Christianity, because these are the most obvious and numerically dominant forms of Japanese Christianity, about which information is more readily available. However, some of the more significant developments have come from those expressions of the faith which appear to be less influenced by Western models.

Probably the most important of these is the 'non-church' (*Mukyōkai*) movement. Its roots lie in the teachings of Uchimura Kanzō, who was baptised in 1878. He and six other Christian students at the Sapporo Agricultural College formed a 'little church of seven brothers' who met three times a week with a rotating leadership and a simple structure to their meetings. Later disillusionment with the effects of denominationalism, both in Japan and the U.S.A., led to the development of Uchimura's distinction between '*ecclesia*' and 'church'. He argued that the original *ecclesia* was a fellowship of believers who had chosen to model their lives after Christ, but over the centuries this original *ecclesia* developed into an institutional church with a specialised hierarchy and distinctions between priesthood and laity. The *Mukyōkai* say that an institution (with its organisation, creeds and rituals) was substituted for the true fellowship of Christ, and that this was as true of Protestantism is it was of the Catholic and Eastern churches.[59]

Uchimura was careful not to establish another 'church'. Instead, the *Mukyōkai* consists of independent Bible-study groups which generally meet in private homes or in rented halls. There is no national headquarters and no official membership statistics are kept. A 'rough survey' in the 1970s indicated 91 groups in Tokyo, 46 in other cities and 247 in small towns and villages. The rural groups averaged five to ten members whereas urban groups averaged thirty-five members.[60] However, I once attended a special *Mukyōkai* gathering in Kyoto at which probably at least two hundred people were in attendance.

My own impression confirms Caldarola's findings that the *Mukyōkai* has more male than female members—a noticeable contrast to the situation of many Japanese churches. Each group is structured around a Bible teacher who has a number of disciples. Although the *Mukyōkai* has traditionally appealed to the Japanese intelligentsia, the movement has more recently begun to enjoy considerable success also in the countryside, especially among farmers—that is, among some people who have been less responsive to organized Christianity.[61] For instance, influenced by Uchimura Kanzō or the *Mukyōkai*, in north-eastern Japan an elderly farmer who studied the Bible by himself had taught himself Greek in order to read the New Testament in its original form.[62]

Uchimura Kanzō's personal involvement with both spiritual with social concerns was 'what made him so fascinating and compelling to his audience, the Japanese people'. Similarly, one of his followers, Professor Yanaihara Tadao, published a Christian periodical named *Kashin* ('Good News') which 'alone against all difficulties and harassments, continued its criticism [of the government] all through the war years and into the post-war period'.[63]

In the post-war period, a small group of *Mukyōkai* Christians with Pentecostal leanings formed a group called the 'Original Gospel Movement' (*Genshi Fukuin Undō*), more popularly known as the *Makuya* ('Tabernacle'—*i.e.* of Christ) movement. Like the *Mukyōkai*, they rejected all institutionalized forms of Christianity such as constitutions, clergy, liturgy, membership rolls or church buildings and their Christianity was focussed around Bible study groups in private homes or rented halls. After 25 years of existence, the *Makuya* had about 500 groups with an estimated total membership of about 60,000—four times as great as the number of Japanese converts among all the Western Pentecostal groups together during more than fifty years.[64]

Makuya's most effective method of evangelism has been through miracles: many members were converted through the miraculous healings of themselves or of family members. Often at their meetings there are public testimonies of healings or other works of God in people's lives.[65]

In contrast to most Christian denominations, the *Makuya* Tabernacle 'appeals primarily to people of lesser education and lower social status: its membership is composed of unskilled or semi-skilled labor, lower white-collar workers, and small businessmen. University graduates, professionals, primary and high school teachers constitute only two or three per cent of the adherents...' Caldarola claims that '*Makuya* is the only movement to indigenize Christianity—traditionally an upper-class religion—in the Japanese lower classes.'[66]

However, there are also 'a number of other indigenous movements that have made similar cultural adaptations, and at least one of these, the *Iesu no Mitama Kyōkai* (Spirit of Jesus Church) has met with equal or better success [than *Makuya*] in attracting members from among the less educated population'.[67] Its founder, Murai Jun, had been a pastor in the Japan Bible Church (*Nihon Seisho Kyōkai*) but in 1941 refused to join the United Church of Christ in Japan. In that same year his wife received a revelation giving the name by which their church was to be known. There was little significant growth until after the Second World War, but by 1958 they had 28,000 members, making this group into the third largest Protestant denomination in Japan. 'All of this was achieved without the direct assistance of foreign missionaries. This church continued to grow steadily on into the 1970s and has reported phenomenal growth for the past decade'.[68]

The statistics, however, need to be viewed critically. In 1989 the church claimed a membership of 420,000 (as compared with a total of 460,000 for all other Protestant bodies). However, a member of their church in Katsuta, Ibaraki prefecture (with a claimed membership of 26,000) says that the active membership is only about one percent of that figure, whereas the reported figure of 78 members for the congregation in nearby Mito is accurate.[69]

The *Iesu no Mitama kyōkai* is a charismatic form of Christianity in which 'speaking in tongues, anointing with oil, dancing in the Spirit, miracles of healing and revelations from God are all basic components of everyday religious life'.[70] Their pastors have a relatively high status and power because the laity 'has no official role in the church government'.[71] A distinctive feature of the church is the practice of baptism on behalf of the dead, instituted on the basis of 1 Corinthians 15:29. The interpretation of this verse has been the subject of considerable debate among Christians.[72] While rejecting Buddhist forms of ancestor veneration as idolatry, the *Iesu no Mitama kyōkai* has nevertheless found a Japanese Christian substitute manner in which to express their concern for the departed.[73] Whether or not they are correct in their theology, the appearance of the *Iesu no Mitama kyōkai* upon the Japanese church scene has great significance as an attempt to develop a more indigenous form of Japanese Christianity.

In comparison with most other denominations, both *Makuya* and the *Iesu no Mitama kyōkai* represent more indigenous forms of Japanese Christianity. Both of them have charismatic styles of worship and ministry. They are also among the fastest-growing Christian denominations in Japan. However, this does not necessarily mean that they should be emulated uncritically. Like all churches, they have their strong and weak points. Some of their doctrines and practices are either controversial or at least questionable.[74] Nevertheless, they represent significant attempts to develop forms of Japanese Christianity which are apparently more indigenous than many other denominations. They have been growing rapidly and, compared with most other denominations, have been able to attract more people from the lesser educated and working class populations. Even if *Makuya* and *Iesu no Mitama kyōkai* have some questionable doctrines and practices, it seems to me that there are many aspects of their faith and lives which could provide positive examples for other Christians.

Church growth at the local level

At the level of local congregations, rather than of denominations, there are many local variations. Though there are no doubt exceptions, the following broad generalizations seem to apply to many churches.

On the whole, the emphasis has often been on the conversion of individuals rather than family groups. Several commentators have remarked that Christianity in Japan might have had more impact if it had been introduced with a greater sensitivity to family structures.[75] The high proportion of individuals—or low proportion of families—in Japanese churches means that the 'pastoral care required per member tends to be much greater in Japan' than, for example, in America (where a church of 100 members might be drawn from perhaps 25 to 40 families). One result of this higher proportion of unrelated individuals in Japanese churches is that the maximum size a group can reach and still maintain intimate fellowship is when there are about thirty to fifty active members. 'Therefore, subconsciously, members often do not want to pay the price of seeing their fellowship grow much larger. Likewise, on the subconscious level, they realise that their portion of the pastor's time will be reduced'. The pastor also 'feels he has reached the limit he can handle', so there is a widespread tendency for the growth rate of many churches to level off when there are between fifty and one hundred members.[76]

One solution to this problem involves the training of lay leaders for house groups or other kinds of small fellowship structures. (Such structures are well developed in *Makuya* and in a number of the rapidly growing Buddhist 'new religions'.) A strong support group is especially important when those who became Christians at school or university start work. Studies have shown that about half of those who became Christians as students drifted away from their faith after graduation. One reason is that their faith is regarded by parents and colleagues as merely one kind of the temporary radicalism common among students which can no longer be so easily tolerated once the students enter the general work force.[77]

Some fast-growing individual churches from a variety of different denominations have also been described by Rob Gill of the

Japan Church Growth Institute.[78] The individual circumstances of each church vary, but often they seem to place a high emphasis on the importance of prayer and the training of lay leadership. Some have introduced major changes to their styles of worship. 'The fact that no rapidly growing congregation studied by such groups as the Japan Church Growth Institute is pastored by a non-Japanese missionary (and that almost none were even started by missionaries) may be significant' too.[79]

It therefore appears that the main growth areas of contemporary Christianity in Japan are among the more indigenous types of churches. A religion which in the popular mind is still largely regarded as a 'Western' one is growing better when it has been able to shed at least some of the Western cultural forms which were imported alongside the gospel of Jesus Christ. Perhaps in this sphere too there is an example of a common stereotype of the Japanese as people who can adopt, adapt and improve on the ideas which they have taken from the West. In technological expertise and some aspects of industrial management the West is now beginning to learn more from the Japanese: perhaps the day is coming when the Western church will become more open to learning from Japanese Christians too. In theological circles there is already widespread appreciation of the writings of Kitamori Kazō and Koyama Kosuke, and at a more popular level the novels of Christian writers such as Endō Shūsaku and Miura Ayako have an influence in many parts of the world. Perhaps some organizational features of the *Mukyōkai* might be of relevance for newly-developing churches in countries with a dispersed Christian population. God wants every culture to contribute to the worship of heaven (Revelation 5:9; 7:9), but each culture has an important contribution to make towards the enrichment of Christ's Kingdom here on earth too.

CHAPTER

13

Characteristics of Contemporary Christianity

Religious practices

AT LEAST A THIRD of the Japanese population in some areas have visited a Christian church at some time in their lives, if only to attend a wedding or funeral. Between a quarter and a third of the population possess Christian literature in their homes, and at some time in their lives have read it either regularly or occasionally. However, official statistics, based on church membership figures, show that less than two per cent of the Japanese population are Christians.[1] Sociological surveys, on the other hand, consistently show a rather higher percentage who call themselves Christians.[2] This is because many of those who have attended a Christian school or university feel more identified with Christianity than with any other religion. They therefore call themselves 'Christians'.[3]

Even if we call them 'nominal' Christians, it is still significant that they themselves are willing to classify themselves as Christians in a questionnaire. In my own survey, only 176 people claimed to have any religion at all, as follows:

Table 13.1   Professed religious allegiances

Buddhists:	104 people = 15.6% of the sample
Shintoists:	29 people = 4.3% of the sample
Christians:	38 people = 5.7% of the sample
'Another religion':	5 people = 0.7% of the sample

Adherents of 'new religions' such as Tenrikyō or Ōmotokyō claimed to belong to 'another religion', whereas adherents of the Sōka Gakkai counted themselves as Buddhists. However, these figures do include some double counting because eight people claimed to have more than one religion. Six of these were simultaneously Shintoists and Buddhists, one was both Buddhist and Christian and one man subscribed to all three religions together.

Most people, however, feel that they do not have any particular religious affiliation. They therefore deny having any religion at all. These people, accounting for almost three-quarters of my sample (73.6%), nevertheless may visit Shinto shrines at New Year, buy *mamori* charms, worry about their *yakudoshi* years, observe ancestral rites at a family *butsudan* or participate in other kinds of 'religious' activities.

In theory, the Christians in my sample came from a variety of different denominations, including Roman Catholic, Russian Orthodox, Methodist, the United Church of Christ in Japan, the *Mukyōkai* and an independent evangelical church. They include several regular church-goers and others who in the past have had some Christian connections and might still attend church for certain major festivals. Sometimes the children of Christians continue to call themselves Christians too, even though it might be many years since they attended a church. Even if many of these are 'nominal' Christians, however, they are still in many ways representative of Japanese 'Christianity' as it is actually practised among those who call themselves 'Christians'.

If one looks at claimed affiliations, there appears to be some kind of consistency between practice and belief. For example, 65.5% of the twenty-nine Shintoists have a *kamidana* but only 5% of the Christians have one. However, if we take *practice* as the principal index and claimed affiliations as secondary, these differences seem relatively minor. The distribution of these practices among the various religious affiliations, or lack of affiliation, is roughly proportional to their overall sizes in the sample. For example, Shintoists account for about 4% of the sample, Christians for about 5% and the non-religious for about 74%, but among those who possess a *mamori* charm the percentages are virtually the same—proportional to the size of each group. This is shown by Table 13.2.

Table 13.2   Claimed religious affiliations, or none, correlated with various religious practices

	Shintoists (Number = 29)	Buddhists (N. = 104)	Christians (N. = 38)	Non-religious (N. = 491)
Proportion of overall sample	4.3%	15.6%	5.7%	73.6%
Possession of a *kamidana* (N.=162)	11.7%	17.9%	1.2%	68.5%
Possession of a *butsudan* (N.=152)	5.3%	34.2%	2.6%	57.9%
Possession of a *mamori* (N.=431)	3.7%	14.8%	4.6%	76.1%
Having drawn a *mikuji* (N.=579)	4.3%	15.5%	4.5%	75.1%
Having 'done astrology' (N.=168)	4.2%	14.3%	6.0%	75.0%
Having consulted a palmist (N.=185)	7.0%	14.6%	5.4%	73.0%
Having consulted a *seimeihandan* specialist (N.=146)	8.2%	19.2%	1.4%	70.5%
New Year shrine visit in 1981 (N.=510)	4.3%	16.5%	2.7%	75.7%
Grave visit at *bon* in 1981 (N.=410)	4.4%	17.6%	3.9%	73.7%
Pay attention to *yakudoshis* (N.=322)	4.3%	17.4%	3.7%	73.6%
Having 'prayed by oneself' [at a time of crisis rather than out of habit] (N.=349)	6.9%	17.2%	9.5%	65.9%

As might be expected, a higher than proportional number of those with a *kamidana* call themselves Shintoists, and likewise for those with a *butsudan* who classify themselves as Buddhists. On the whole, however, there is relatively little association between practice and claimed religious affiliation beyond fairly obvious connections such as those relating to domestic altars. For most practices, their overall distribution is approximately proportional to the overall distribution of these groups.

One of these Christian families regularly attend the local church of the United Church of Christ in Japan (*Nihon Kirisuto Kyōdan*), the main Protestant denomination. (It was formed in 1941 through the forced merger of virtually all the Protestant denominations operating at that time in Japan.[4]) I asked the wife why they also have *mamori* charms and subscribe to other non-Christian practices. She appeared embarrassed by my question and said that she knew the Bible prohibits such things 'but my own opinion is that it is important to follow these traditional customs too'.

Other studies show similar results. For instance, among David Reid's sample of 251 Christians, a quarter said that there was a *butsudan* (or equivalent) in their homes. Those with a *butsudan* also participate more fully than those without one in household and community rituals for the dead.[5] Other studies have also shown that a high proportion of Japanese Christians continue to practise various kinds of Shinto and Buddhist rites and sometimes also folk religious observances such as worship of the sun or moon.[6]

Sometimes these practices are performed reluctantly or out of a sense of obligation, especially in homes where a minority of the family members are Christians. For instance, Boyle reports how after the death of the father of a Christian young man, who was the eldest son, 'a tremendous amount of pressure was applied to him by his non-Christian relatives to fulfill his filial duty of enshrining his father's soul' in a *butsudan*.

Although this went against his Christian faith, 'in order to avoid an acrimonious family spirit, he reluctantly consented to allow the altar to be placed and Buddhist services held in his home'.[7] Whereas the first Japanese Protestants tended to destroy their *butsudan*s and *kamidanas*, later generations became more accommodating by introducing substitute *butsudan*s or by continuing to maintain *butsudan* rites intact.[8] The effect has been a continuing receptivity to demonic influences from Shinto and Buddhist practices. Such demons can often be passed on through families.

Political allegiances

In my questionnaire I also asked which political parties people support or had voted for in the last national or local elections. Ten different parties were mentioned by the 72% who had voted, but my overall results were skewed by the fact that virtually all the *Nissen* employees had voted for the party supported by their union. The company union belongs to one of the conferations of trade unions called Dōmei (short for *Zen Nihon Rōdō Sodomei*) which supports the Democratic Socialist Party (D.S.P.). In the Sakurano *shataku* estate, only 12% of the men voted for parties other than the D.S.P., although 14% did not vote at all. Similarly, most of the *Nissen* employees living in the owner-occupied estate which I call 'Aoyama' also voted for the D.S.P. Because of this support, a D.S.P. candidate from *Nissen* is virtually guaranteed a seat on the local council—and can thereby help to influence local government decisions when it comes to regulations about industrial pollution and other matters.

Those in Sakurano who voted for other political parties did not publicize their dissent but kept it to themselves. This was true also of two men belonging to the Sōka Gakkai who voted for the political arm of their religious organization, the 'Clean Government Party' (*Kōmeitō*), but from fear of criticism did not tell their neighbours that they had not voted for the D.S.P.

In Aoyama the pattern of voting was closer to that of the nation as a whole, with more people voting for the ruling Liberal Democratic Party. The L.D.P. is a Conservative party, the D.S.P. more in the centre and the Socialist Party further to the left than the D.S.P. Among those in both estates who voted at all, or answered the question on their political allegiances, there were eighty-seven Buddhists, twenty-one Shintoists and thirty-one Christians. Their voting behaviour among the three main parties is shown in Table 13.3.

It is true that the Shintoists are split evenly between the D.S.P. and L.D.P., but this is largely because of the *Nissen* union influence which has created a disproportionately large D.S.P. block in my sample. Six of the eight Shintoists who voted for the D.S.P. live in the *Nissen shataku*. Nevertheless, taking the figures overall, it can be seen that on the whole Shintoists tend to be more right-wing, Buddhists more in the centre but Christians more left-wing.

This correlation between Christianity and left-wing political

Table 13.3   Political support according to religious affiliation

	'Left wing' (Socialist Party)	Centre (D.S.P.)	'Right wing' (L.D.P.)
Percentage of Shintoists	4.8%	38.1%	38.1%
Percentage of Buddhists	11.5%	41.4%	31.0%
Percentage of Christians	19.3%	58.1%	12.9%
For comparison:			
Percentage of 'non-religious' people (Number = 370)	13.5%	52.2%	24.3%
Total votes for each party as a percentage of the total sample of 667 people	10.0%	38.7%	19.5%

parties can be traced back to the early twentieth century, when many founding members of the Social Democratic Party, the Japan Federation of Labour and the Japan Farmers' Union were active Christians.[9] The socialist movement in Japan owes some of its beginnings to Christianity, because 'as the Christian teachings of love for one's neighbor and human equality were considered in relation to existing economic disparities, many Christians came to think of socialism as a means for the expression and application of Christian ideals and became leaders of Japan's first labor movements.'[10]

During the twentieth century several historical factors have combined to reinforce a suspicion of right-wing politics among many Japanese Christians. Prior to 1945 the attitude of the Japanese government towards religious organizations was that they should be at the service of the State. For this purpose Buddhism was favoured during the Tokugawa period and Shinto from the Meiji Restoration until 1945, whereas Christianity was subject to relatively stricter kinds of control or repression. During the 1930s, for instance, some Christian leaders were imprisoned or mistreated by the authorities because of their refusal to participate in 'patriotic' rituals such as the singing of Shinto hymns in church, attendance at Shinto shrines or bowing towards an image of the supposedly divine Emperor. After 1945 the Americans insisted on a new Constitution which guarantees the 'separation' of religion from the State—but many Japanese Christians have continued to be suspicious of the conservative government's sincerity in upholding this Constitution. There have been a number of court cases over the issue of whether or not public organizations or individuals should participate in an official capacity in certain Shinto rituals. Verdicts delivered by the courts, particularly by the Supreme Court, have shown a tendency for the re-assertion of traditional, pre-war attitudes towards the unity of religion and the State. Shinto rites in particular are often regarded as 'customs' which are 'not religious': therefore their performance by public officials does not violate the Constitution.[11] Because many Japanese Christians are suspicious of such tendencies they may tend to have political views which are not right-wing.

A study by David Reid also confirms this tendency for Japanese Christians to support left-wing political parties.[12] It is particularly noticeable among those without a *butsudan* in their homes, an indirect indication that those with left-wing political views may also be those with an orientation towards life or religion which is much more heavily influenced by their Christian faith.

These findings raise a number of questions about the ways in which missionary strategy has been related to Japanese felt needs. Aikawa and Leavenworth note, for instance, that

> 'for those who were engaged in evangelical activities, a purely spiritual version of Christianity was quite enough, and they almost completely failed to relate it to politics and economics; but for most people Christianity was regarded as a new teaching of society, a new social ethic, or social policy. Two negative qualities resulted. From the former the aloofness of Japanese Christianity was born, and from the latter came a lack of dynamic and commitment on the part of adherents. Many outstanding Christian novelists and leaders of the social movement therefore left the church after a few years of earnest church life.'[13]

Christians in Japan have certainly been very active in the field of social work. 'To people who had heretofore been neglected and even despised in Japanese society, the Christians extended helping hands. Believing in human equality and in charity towards all, they led the way in social welfare by establishing and supporting institutions to care for the destitute, the lepers, the physically handicapped, the mentally retarded, delinquents, prostitutes, and other people in need. Gradually, as the government assumed responsibility in this area and organized public facilities to care for such people, the influence of Christianity waned. Nevertheless, the social work programs of groups like the Salvation Army are still pointed to as models for the organization of social welfare work.'[14]

A concern for the alleviation of social ills often leads to a recognition that, in addition to caring for the symptoms, it is necessary also to attack the institutional and legal supporting structures. For example, Japanese Christians were among those who advocated the introduction of legislation to curb prostitution and in at least one case to oppose the use of nuclear weapons at an American air base—although the implementation of such laws was influenced by many other factors too.[15] These kinds of social and political activities may also have been expressions of a Japanese perception of Christianity as a kind of new social ethic, a view which is consistent with the biblical model demonstrated by the Old Testament prophets who were prepared to speak out on issues of politics and social justice.

However, this is at variance with another perspective which has been held by some other Christians in both the West and Japan. This is the view that somehow one can separate 'politics' from 'religion', and that the latter should not interfere with the former.[16] In this context, a missionary with long experience of Japan expressed to me his opinion that the missionary task is to 'preach the gospel, not to change the culture'—although he thought that resulting social changes would follow in due course later.

In all societies there is a complex interlinkage between the different aspects of social life which for analytical convenience we label as 'politics', 'economics', 'religion', 'medicine', 'family life', and so on. It is therefore unrealistic to expect these various elements to function in isolation from each other, although the degree of interlinkage between particular components may be stronger or weaker in different societies.

In Japan 'significant religious developments have tended to coincide with periods of social and political unrest'.[17] However, since about 1970, the emergence of 'new religions of magic and miracle' have apparently accompanied significant socio-economic change. This is not to say that social change in itself causes the emergence of new religious organizations but merely that there seems to be a linkage between the two.[18] Actually, the spiritual forces behind the religious systems have remained of the same kind but their forms of manipulation and control have changed in accordance with different social or political situations. The more overt expressions of demonic activity had at one time been focussed around mediums such as those on Mount Ontake, but in the nineteenth and twentieth centuries shamanic-type individuals (mainly women) have founded 'new religions' which have a greater appeal to the urban Japanese. In recent decades demonic 'possession' activity has simply become more overt among not only the leaders but also the laity in some of these cults.

In the context of political and social changes, we need to ask what God has been doing. Behind many political developments on earth there are spiritual battles going on in the heavenly places. Christians can have a profound influence on these political and economic developments not only through active political involvements but also, at an even more significant level, through intercessory prayer. Japan's defeat in the Second World War opened up a spiritual vacuum into which many competing ideologies have flocked.[19] As the Holy Spirit has been renewing the church to be better equipped for this situation, there have been corresponding developments also among the opposing spiritual forces.

Education and social class

On the whole, Japanese Christians tend to be better educated than those belonging to other religious groups. In the neighbourhoods which I studied, 63% of the Christians, 52% of the Shintoists and 32% of the Buddhists had received some kind of university education. Partly this may be due to the fact that some who call themselves Christians do so because they had attended a Christian university.

For the most part, there continues to be a tendency for most churches to be middle-class. Sometimes this pattern is reinforced to some extent by the common missionary practice of using English classes for developing contacts, who therefore tend to be drawn more from the educated upper middle classes.[20] A contrasting pattern, in which there was little or no missionary input, is found among denominations like the *Makuya* Tabernacle and the *Iesu no Mitama kyōkai*, which have greater numbers of working-class converts. Other working-class Christians can be found among Roman Catholics in northern Kyushu: there many people had become Christians during the sixteenth century and some families had retained some kind of a Christian tradition as 'hidden Christians' during more than two centuries when Christianity had been officially repressed.[21]

Sexual composition of the churches

An impression gained from visiting a number of churches in Japan, and confirmed by various missionary reports, is that there are more women than men among Japanese converts to Christianity.[22] This is shown even in my relatively small sample from two urban neighbourhoods:

Table 13.4   Sexual distribution among claimed religious affiliations

	Shintoists	Buddhists	Christians	Others	'Non-religious'
Men					
(N. = 409)	3.9%	15.5%	2.9%	1.2%	76.0%
Women					
(N. = 258)	5.0%	15.1%	10.1%	0.0%	69.8%

[The higher number of male respondents is because many households in Sakurano received only one questionnaire rather than two from their local community representative and the men often thought it was their duty as *Nissen* employees to fill in the questionnaire.]

It can be seen from Table 13.4 that Christians account for less than 6% of my total sample but for about 10% of the women represented in it. A number of factors might be cited for this, including the following:

a) Most of those who claim to be Christians trace their allegiance to their having attended a Christian school or university. Many of these have a high female intake, especially some of the older-established colleges and universities which in the later nineteenth century were virtually the only institutions of higher education available for women in Japan.[23] It may be that some women who through their education have had more contact with Christianity than with any other religion might continue to call themselves 'Christian' on a questionnaire.

b) It might be that a contact with Christian education has pre-disposed some women to seek help from Christian pastors at times of domestic crisis or other personal problems. Table 13.5 shows that approximately equal proportions of men and women reported having consulted Shinto or Buddhist priests—usually for the pur-pose of arranging weddings or funerals—but conspicuously more women had consulted Christian pastors or missionaries.

Sometimes they had done so regarding problems such as a child's truancy from school or a husband's suspected infidelity. To at least some extent, this is because the Christian pastor or mission-ary is perceived as being outside of the social networks of gossip and as someone whose advice and confidence is respected. Some-times the Christian worker is also regarded as giving more practical advice than that given by other religious specialists. (I came across no cases of Shinto or Buddhist priests being consulted for marriage counselling or similar kinds of personal advice.)

Table 13.5　Consultation of priests, pastors or missionaries

	Men	Women
Consultation of:		
Buddhist priest	20 = 5.6%	11 = 5.0%
Shinto priest	9 = 2.5%	6 = 2.8%
Christian pastor or missionary	8 = 2.2%	13 = 6.1%

c) A common method by which missionaries gain contacts is through English classes, which often attract middle-class women as a leisure activity. In general, missionaries tend to have relatively fewer contacts with Japanese men, who are often involved with their work and have less interest in cultivating contacts during their leisure time with Christian workers. There is a need for a greater variety of male-oriented social and leisure activities to be developed within many Christian churches, and perhaps for the preaching to be orientated more towards masculine interests.[24]

d) To a large extent, Christianity has generally been concentrated among the intelligentsia of the upper middle classes because of Christian educational facilities such as schools and English classes. Typically the men from such social classes tend to join either large corporations such as *Nissen* or government bureaucracies, where male networks in the sphere of work can sometimes take priority over other networks in the sphere of leisure and church; such pressures often pull Christian men away from the churches. In the executive stream of such firms they are also likely to be moved from one place to another. Unless they have a church of their own denomination in the new area to which they are moved, they might not seek out a church of a different denomination. Particularistic loyalties to the micro-group (the denomination) can sometimes take precedence over generalized loyalties to the macro-group (the wider church) in spite of the fact that all owe their loyalty to Jesus Christ as the 'Head of the body' (Ephesians 4:15-16). Under such circumstances men might drop out of active church involvements. Their wives, however, seeking a network of friends in a new environment, might actively seek out a church of some sort. Their desire for Christian fellowship can also at times help to overcome possible reservations about joining a church of a different denomination.

e) In many Christian churches there is a tendency for a 'one man band' kind of leadership to develop. This is focussed on the pastor or missionary. Sometimes the missionary intends to let local lay Christians take on responsibilities for various activities after they have 'matured' sufficiently in the faith. However, this can also give the impression that the leader is holding on to power in the church and does not want others to take over his or her role. It might be that a lack of opportunity for taking responsibility or for organizing or leading church activities can discourage some Japanese men from active involvement in the churches.

For instance, it is not too uncommon for a congregation's membership to drop noticeably after a missionary leaves to go on furlough. This is a problem especially if the missionary has an attractive personality which attracts people but does not necessarily sustain their loyalties to the church after the missionary has left. Those who do remain loyal to the church are often the women.

It is important for pastors and missionaries to train up potential leaders by allowing them to take on responsibilities for small tasks and gradually being given greater tasks. They must also be given the freedom to make mistakes, and to learn from their mistakes. It is a wise leader who is willing to entrust appropriate responsibilities to those who are learning and allow them to learn in the process, as Jesus did with his disciples (Luke 9:1-6, 10; 10:1-24).

Moral issues

In chapter eleven, I discussed aspects of Japanese morality as reflected in questionnaire responses. For some items on my questionnaire, such as stealing and lying, almost everybody said they would feel both ashamed and guilty about such behaviour. There was therefore no difference according to religious groups either.

However, even for some items in which there is a greater spread of opinions there was actually no statistically significant difference between Christians and non-Christians. I stress this fact because it is at variance with what one might expect from looking merely at doctrinal differences between Christianity and Japanese religions or Japanese traditional values.

This lack of differentiation between Christians and non-Christians applied to feelings of guilt about disloyalty to a superior, speeding, illegal parking, having an abortion, not helping a friend in need and not helping a stranger in need. It continued to apply also in the responses to questions on feelings of shame regarding disloyalty to a superior, having an abortion, not helping a friend in need and not helping a stranger in need.

Although there was no statistically significant difference between Christians and non-Christians in their responses to the question on feelings of guilt regarding illegal parking or speeding, those who answered 'Yes' to this question accounted for 65.5% of the Shintoists, 54% of the Buddhists, 47% of the Christians and

43% of the 'non-religious' majority. It is noticeable that the Christians' responses were more like those of the 'non-religious' people. The same pattern is found in the responses to the question on whether or not people have feelings of shame in situations of illegal parking or speeding. Their responses are tabulated in Table 13.6:

Table 13.6   Feelings of shame regarding illegal parking or speeding

Illegal parking

	'Yes'%	'No'%	'Neither'%	Blank%
Shintoists	62%	17%	14%	7%
Buddhists	68%	15%	14%	2%
Christians	47%	24%	24%	5%
'Non-religious'	50½%	21%	24%	4½%

Speeding in a vehicle

	'Yes'%	'No'%	'Neither'%	Blank%
Shintoists	72%	10%	10%	7%
Buddhists	67%	14%	16%	2%
Christians	42%	26%	26%	5%
'Non-religious'	50%	22%	24%	4%

For illegal parking, the difference between the religious groups is almost, but not quite, statistically significant, but for speeding in a vehicle it does turn out to be a statistically significant difference.[25] Buddhists and Shintoists are more likely to feel ashamed of speeding or of parking illegally, whereas Christians and 'non-religious' people are less likely to feel shame about such actions.

Neglecting one's parents is one other item in which Buddhists in particular, and to some extent Shintoists, stand out as having significantly different values from others.[26] However, this result is obtained only by amalgamating the 'No', 'Neither' and 'Blank' responses and then comparing these with the 'Yes' replies. Such a result is not particularly surprising, because Japanese Buddhism, as far as the ordinary person is concerned, is closely connected with the ancestral cult. If somebody has responsibility for maintaining the Buddhist rites for the family's deceased ancestors, the wilful neglect of such a responsibility is often regarded as shameful. Of course, my question was intended to elicit feelings about the neglect of living parents, but in the Japanese cultural context it is clear that attitudes towards parents are coloured to some extent by the ancestral cult (and vice-versa), and that this is more likely to be an influence on those who regard themselves as Buddhists.

There was only one item among these questions in which Japanese Christians stood out as being significantly different from others. This was in their attitudes towards premarital sexual intercourse, regarding which Japanese Christians are much more likely to express feelings of both guilt and shame. Statistically, the correlation is highly significant.[27] The relevant figures are presented in Table 13.7:

Table 13.7 Feelings associated with premarital sexual intercourse

a) *Expressed feelings of guilt*

	'Yes'%	'No'%	'Neither'%	Blank%
Shintoists	59%	24%	14%	3%
Buddhists	47%	23%	26%	4%
Christians	68%	5%	24%	3%
'Non-religious'	40%	33%	24%	3½%

b) *Expressed feelings of shame*

	'Yes'%	'No'%	'Neither'%	Blank%
Shintoists	62%	24%	10%	3%
Buddhists	66%	15%	15%	3%
Christians	74%	5%	18%	3%
'Non-religious'	50%	26%	20%	4½%

Christians are conspicuously different from others in their expressed feelings about guilt or shame regarding premarital sexual intercourse, but it is possible that this difference has little direct connection with their religious beliefs. Instead, this apparent difference between religious groups could also be accounted for by differences in the responses of men and women. Statistically, the correlation between guilt or shame feelings regarding premarital sex is as significant for male- female differences as for religious differences.[28] Women are much more likely than men to express feelings of guilt or shame about such activities. In view of the high proportion of Japanese Christians who are women, the differences between Christians and non-Christians in their feelings of guilt or shame about premarital sex could also be accounted for by significant differences between the sexes themselves.

I also found that in cross-tabulating other moral attitudes with professed religious affiliations, there was no significant difference according to religious identifications with regard to attitudes towards cartoons (*manga*), *pachinko*, drunkenness, abortion and bribery. For no-pantie coffee houses the difference was not statistically significant either, but it was very close to being so.[29] Christians, and to a large extent also Buddhists, tended to see no-pantie coffee houses as 'bad', whereas the Shintoists and the 'non-religious' tended to have more neutral attitudes towards them.

Regarding betting on horses, however, there was a statistically significant correlation whereby Christians in particular, and to some extent Buddhists, were much more inclined than the 'non-religious' to consider such gambling to be 'bad'.[30] For divorce, the attitudes of Shintoists and of Christians were close to statistically expected values, given their proportions in the overall sample. Buddhists, however, expressed much more negative attitudes. Comparing the Buddhists with all other groups combined, the difference is highly significant.[31] Might it be that Japanese Buddhists place a greater emphasis on family relationships than do other Japanese people? Certainly the fact that most of these Buddhists have a Buddhist ancestral altar (*butsudan*), the upkeep of which in many households is the wife's responsibility, at least indicates that Japanese Buddhists have regard for the preservation of some kind of relationship with deceased relatives. Might something of the same psychology also affect their attitudes to relationships among living family members?

In their views about pornographic literature, Christians were much more negative than the other groups, to such an extent that the correlation was very significant. However, this too could be attributed to the high proportion of Christians who are women, because there was also a highly significant correlation whereby women had much more negative views than men about pornography.[32] Christians were also more negative than others in their views about premarital sex, but again this could be attributed to the much stronger links with male-female differences, whereby women expressed much more negative views than men about premarital sexual relationships.[33]

All those who claimed to have a religion, but especially the Christians, tended to see homosexuality in morally worse terms than was the case for 'non-religious' people. In this case, it is more useful to cite the actual percentages:

Table 13.8 Moral attitudes towards homosexuality[34]

	'Good'%	'Bad'%	'Neither'%	'Don't Know'%
Shintoists	3.4%	51.7%	20.7%	20.7%
Buddhists	4.8%	52.9%	15.4%	25.0%
Christians	0.0%	65.8%	15.8%	18.4%
'Non-religious'	2.4%	44.4%	27.1%	24.6%

A similar pattern can be seen in responses towards the item about adultery, whereby religious people tend to see it in morally worse terms than do 'non-religious' people. The relevant percentages are as follows:

Table 13.9 Moral attitudes towards adultery

	'Good'%	'Bad'%	'Neither'%	'Don't Know'%
Shintoists	6.9%	86.2%	3.4%	0.0%
Buddhists	1.9%	82.7%	7.7%	4.8%
Christians	0.0%	89.5%	7.9%	2.6%
'Non-religious'	0.8%	75.4%	15.1%	6.1%

For both homosexuality and adultery, the differences are statistically significant.[35] This raises questions about Professor Ronald Dore's observation that 'matters of sexual conduct... are not made the centre of Japanese morality as they frequently are of the Christian'.[36] At a doctrinal level, this may well be the case. However, it would appear as if those professing to have a religion, whether it be Shinto, Buddhism or Christianity, do have stronger views about these areas of sexual conduct than do the 'non-religious' majority. Perhaps it is simply that the majority who claim no particular religious affiliations also tend to be less definite about their moral views.

It appears that these Japanese Christians are not particularly distinctive in their moral views. In most respects they are similar to the 'non-religious' majority, except in a few attitudes, particularly towards sexual matters, in which the statistics are affected by the relatively high proportion of women among them. These findings indicate something about the moral attitudes of those who profess to belong to Christ in Japan, even though many of them are those whom other Christians might regard as having a 'nominal' faith.[37]

Similarities and contrasts between Christianity and the 'new religions'

The 'new religions' in Japan have mushroomed both in variety and in numbers of adherents, particularly since the Second World War. They came more into prominence during the 1950s, so that by the early 1960s there were 171 of them officially registered with the Ministry of Education, having a total claimed membership of over eighteen million people.[38] One of the most famous of these is the Sōka Gakkai, which alone has at least three times more Japanese adherents than has Christianity.[39]

There are a number of similarities and contrasts between Christianity and the 'new religions'. Both of them, for example, appeal more to women than to men. Statistics on the proportion of women in some of the 'new religions' range from 58% for the Sōka Gakkai to 62% in Mahikari and as high as 66% in the 'Salvation Cult' studied by Lebra, in which 80% or more of the 'active members' are women.[40] In Reiyūkai too, 'women predominate in all ranks except the highest, the branch leaders'.[41] Christianity, as another form of 'organized' religion, fits into this overall pattern, but if my own sample of Christians is at all representative, the fact that 68% of them are women is still rather higher than for the 'new religions' as a whole.

Whereas Christianity has been a religion more for educated upper middle-class people, the 'new religions' have tended to appeal primarily to lesser educated, lower middle-class people. Later some of them have spread to a more limited extent among the upper middle classes.[42] It is not surprising therefore to find that 68% of the Buddhists in my sample had not received any university education, as compared with an average of 53% in the sample as a whole. Both of the two Sōka Gakkai men living in the *Nissen shataku* had been educated up to high school level only. The Sōka Gakkai adherents living in Aoyama also lack a university education and are employed in smaller, less prestigious businesses. One man, for example, is a draftsman in a small metal company. Another is the manager of a garage who rents rather than owns both the garage and his home in Aoyama.

To some extent, the spread of these 'new religions' has been facilitated by a simplification of Buddhist doctrines into easily memorized formulae requiring relatively little intellectual effort.[43] This is also characteristic of forms of worship which require little intellectual effort to understand, such as the repeated chanting of the phrase 'Glory be to the Lotus of the Supreme Law' (*Namu Myōhō Renge Kyō*) by Sōka Gakkai adherents.[44] By contrast, a stereotype of Christ which has been expressed to me by a number of non-Christian Japanese is that they consider Christianity 'difficult to understand' because they consider the Bible to be couched in archaic language: the existence of modern translations into everyday Japanese is not generally known. Moreover, some who have attended church services have sometimes been put off by encountering the use of classical language in hymn books, which can be unintelligible to those unused to such language.[45]

Some of the 'new religions', particularly the Sōka Gakkai, have in the past had a reputation for being rather 'forceful' and persistent in their proselytizing zeal—rather like the Jehovah's Witnesses have been in the West and to some extent in Japan. This style of evangelism is not necessarily a good thing, but I mention it only because it contrasts with the more 'softly, softly' approach which seems to be adopted by many Christians.

There is a tendency in some Christian churches for leadership to become focussed mainly around the pastor or missionary rather than being more widely diffused. By contrast, Dale's study of a 'new religion' known as Risshō Kōsei-kai shows how active lay leadership is developed through small groups, known as hōza, which are for counselling and teaching.[46] These groups for fellowship, discussion and counselling often minister to practical problems of everyday life rather than teaching abstract doctrine— though a certain amount of doctrine is included in an easily understandable form illustrated by frequent anecdotes.[47] I have heard that Dale has adopted a similar practice in a Christian context, with very positive results. Within the Sōka Gakkai, a well-developed lay leadership structure within a tightly knit web of relationships formed through 'vertical, horizontal and diagonal' social groupings is one factor responsible for a lower rate of membership leakage than that which has plagued Christian churches.[48]

The 'effervescent spirit' in Sōka Gakkai group meetings 'fills the individual members with zeal', and their worship 'on all levels helps the members heighten their sense of vocation—...which is none other than the winning of new converts'. By contrast, the Japanese understanding of Christianity 'as a matter only of the head and not of the heart has often made Japanese Christians timid in their witnessing activities'.[49] For these and other reasons the growth rate for Christianity in Japan has been considerably less than that of the 'new religions'.[50]

Spiritual warfare

Many of the 'new religions' have also incorporated an emphasis on miracles such as healing: some are openly critical of religions which simply preach and have no miracles.[51] Testimonies of miraculous healing are often used in their advertising, and attract people's interest or curiosity.[52] This is a feature which has been developing also in many charismatic churches throughout the world, but there still remains a certain resistance to it among many mainline denominations of Japan. One mission, for instance, tends to send its charismatically-minded missionaries to Tokyo but to keep the non-charismatic ones in its principal area of operations in order to avoid problems with non- charismatic Japanese pastors in that area. Policies such as this have sometimes led to what I call 'mission shock', as illustrated by a personal communication from a missionary couple working with that mission:

'It is probably fair to say that most people called to church-planting come to the field with the expectation of planting churches where there is as yet no other church; it has therefore been hard to come to terms with the tendency for churches to be started in towns or suburbs where there are other churches, albeit of different denominations. If we had wanted to further a denomination we would not have joined [this mission]!

...In Britain we were able to come to terms with the anti-charismatic stance of [the church association with which the mission is affiliated] on the basis that it was cultural, and we should join in with what God is doing wherever we are, rather than pressing our views on certain issues. Now we are here we realise that there is no cultural reason not to have charismatic churches, and that God is doing a great deal in Japan in and through them! It would have been helpful to have been told this before we came, even if our decision to come would have remained the same.'

I should stress that this example may not be representative of missions throughout Japan in general, but it does illustrate the kinds of attitudes which are apparently very widespread. Such attitudes are probably connected with the way in which Christianity in Japan has often been seen as a religion 'of the head rather than of the heart'—leading to a more suspicious attitude towards practices which may be 'trans-rational' (rather than 'irrational'). Questions of theology, of mission organization or of church practices are important in their own way to a certain extent, but they are not the most fundamental problems. The real issues are those of spiritual warfare. If I seem at times to be critical of certain practices in the Christian church or missions in Japan, I desire to express these in love as the admonitions of a friend in order to help fellow Christians in our common task of promoting the Kingdom of God.

In this battle, we are fighting not against 'flesh and blood'—nor against church attitudes or mission structures—but against the unseen forces in the heavenly realms. We are severely handicapped if we try to fight without divine revelations about the nature of the conflict. Moreover, we need to use the weapons which God has entrusted to us. Unfortunately, the church in Japan has tended to neglect these supernatural gifts, whereas many of the Japanese 'new religions'—as well as various forms of the older religions—

have an openness to spiritual revelations and spiritual power. Unfortunately, among them the channels of revelation which God intended for communication with himself have often been usurped by demons. These religions in themselves testify to the fact that supernatural revelations and spiritual power are fully part of the indigenous Japanese religious scene. In advocating an increased openness to this dimension, I am not trying to foist yet another 'Western' model upon the church in Japan, but instead to highlight the real nature of the spiritual battle in which we are involved. God is the one who gives his gifts, and he may grant them in different ways according to the local situations. Our task is to be willing to let him use us in whatever ways he knows are the most effective.

Aikawa and Leavenworth relate a story which was told about Father Organtino, a Roman Catholic missionary to Japan in the mid-sixteenth century. He had a feeling that spirits lurking in the mountains, woods and houses were always intent on preventing the spread of the gospel in Japan. Then he had a vision of the indigenous gods of the country. One of them, a minor deity, told him how they absorb but change the foreign gods out of all recognition into Japanese ones. This spirit concluded by commenting, 'Perhaps in the long run, your Christian God will be changed into an indigenous god of this country. As Chinese and Indian gods were once changed, the Western god must likewise be changed. We spirits of the land are always haunting you in the trees, in the wind that passes over a rose, or even in the twilight which lingers on the walls of temples. We are here everywhere and always. Beware of us, beware of us!'[53]

In many ways, Japanese Christianity has already succumbed to these spirits. At least, those who claim to be 'Christians' often participate in religious practices and have moral values which are hardly distinguishable from those of their neighbours. However, when we recognize who the real enemies are, we can fight the real battles.

This spiritual warfare involves power encounters using God-given tools such as prayer, fasting and ministries of deliverance from evil spirits connected both with people and with places. For example:

'While I was speaking to a group of students in a Japanese house one night, one of the young ladies suddenly cried out. She told us that her closest girl-friend in secondary school had become so taken over by the spirit of the Fox, that she had become the school fortune-teller. Then she began to swear and curse so much that she was stood down from school. She eventually went insane, and was committed to a mental institution. The girl then cried out, 'That spirit has come to me'. I immediately went to her, and took authority in the name of Jesus Christ, and it left her. As it did so, a young man on the opposite side of the room said, 'I saw it go out of her'. Another young lady immediately cried out for help because she became oppressed. She too was freed...'[54]

Ministries of deliverance are essential in Japan because of the demonic influences which continue to affect many Japanese Christians. At the same time, however, an understanding of spiritual warfare and an openness to the power of God's Holy Spirit needs to be coupled with a sympathetic understanding of the local culture. In chapter fourteen I shall discuss a number of possible approaches to the communication of the Christian message in culturally sensitive ways. Although these are presented in an 'intellectual' fashion, I should stress that such approaches are insufficient in themselves unless they are also coupled with a life-changing experience of the power of God in each person's life.

CHAPTER

14

Communicating the Christian Gospel

ALL CHRISTIANS, AND missionaries in particular, hope to communicate the good news about Jesus in terms which are comprehensible and culturally relevant. However, Boyle notes that 'typically, the preaching of the gospel in Japan has been a 'sender oriented communication'—that is, communication done from the reference framework of the communicator (in other words, using Western cultural understandings and thought patterns). What is needed is 'receptor oriented communication'. One of the principles of communication theory is: 'What is understood is at least as dependent on how the receptor perceives the message (plus the paramessages) as on how the communicator presents it.' Thus, in order to effectively communicate the Good News of God's message to all human beings everywhere, it must be done in each culture's own thought patterns and symbols...History has shown that when presented in primarily Western thought patterns and concepts, relatively few Japanese have understood the message properly and accepted it as God's communication to them as Japanese.'[1]

Various attempts to communicate the gospel in culturally sensitive terms have already been undertaken by a number of Japanese Christians. Japanese theologians such as Kitamori Kazō have sought to do this in one way; writers such as Endō Shūsaku have approached it in different ways.[2] The indigenous Christians are usually the best people for this task, but many of them are hampered in this by the fact that 'even when communicated by Japanese Christians, the Western thought forms and styles learned from the missionaries have generally been predominant'.[3]

Nevertheless, Christians from other cultures may still have an important role as *catalysts* by being able to notice relevant features of the culture which native people take for granted.[4] This was St. Paul's approach in Athens, but a similar principle also characterized the parables of Jesus: he made use of familiar features of his human culture in order to communicate truths about the 'culture' of God's Kingdom. My intention in this book has been to use my training as a social anthropologist in order to develop further insights which may be of relevance in at least certain situations.[5] 'In presenting each of these ideas, it is hoped that readers who are involved in crosscultural ministry to and with the Japanese can gain insights into how their own formulation of the gospel message can best be done in their own given situation. Some formulations will be helpful in certain situations while not being very relevant in others...'[6]

Throughout this book I have tried to bridge the gap between an academic study of Japanese religion and the practical needs of missionaries and other Christians. In doing so, I have fallen between two stools. On the one hand, I have violated the pretence to academic 'neutrality' which most anthropologists try to convey. On the other hand, I have probably offended a number of missionaries by questioning their assumptions about missionary strategies in Japan.

In doing this, my purpose has been a very practical one. I am not seeking to be iconoclastic merely for the sake of it, but because I believe that to a large extent the slow growth of the church in Japan can be attributed to the way in which Christianity has been presented. Change needs to begin with the 'household of God', and this can indeed be painful at times. Perhaps it is a tendency to become more critical of failings perceived in those people or institutions close to one's own heart which leads me to express some criticisms. However, in doing so, my desire is that those seeking to communicate the Way of Jesus to the Japanese might question some of their own assumptions and the values which they had taken for granted.

Throughout this book I have been making some practical recommendations about ways in which the Christian gospel might be more effectively communicated in terms which are relevant to ordinary Japanese people. Some of my suggestions are tentative; others are more definite. It is up to the Christians of Japan to decide what they will do with these ideas.

However, suggested new 'methods' are insufficient in themselves unless one establishes meaningful and close relationships with one's Japanese friends. This demands time and effort. For non-Japanese Christians, it involves taking a lower place and learning from the Japanese how to behave appropriately in Japanese society. In order to develop such relationships, and the trust which goes with it, missionaries may need to refrain from 'jumping in' and thrusting their message on the listener at the earliest opportunity. Such behaviour may seem 'effective' in terms of forcing the listener to 'hear the gospel'—who listens merely out of politeness to the foreigner—but this does not captivate the heart. Real relationships are like flowers which need time to grow and need to be nurtured tenderly.

Many of my suggestions in this book are also relevant to those seeking to share their Christian faith with Japanese people living outside Japan itself. For the most part, these expatriate Japanese still hold the same values and beliefs concerning issues such as safety and security, purity and pollution, memorialism and age. (Actually, those for safety and security are the opposite side of the same coin to the values concerning purity and pollution. Similarly, a concern with memorialism is to some extent an extension (or mirror image) of concerns with a person's age).

In this book I have tried to indicate a number of customs and beliefs which Christian missionaries might turn to good use. At a formal level it might involve Christian counterparts to certain traditional rituals. However, this is because at a deeper level there are certain deeply engrained attitudes and values in the culture which in themselves are not necessarily anti-Christian but which need to be expressed appropriately. If a concern with memorialism or a respect for age is not expressed appropriately in a Christian manner, there is a danger that converts will be tempted to express these in a non-Christian manner.[7] Nevertheless, it seems that in themselves some of the motivations (of memorialism or of respect for age) which lead people to emphasize these dimensions of life are not only wholesome but are in many ways more biblical than contemporary Western Christianity tends to be.

In this final chapter I would like to discuss some other possible approaches to communicating the Christian message. My model is largely inspired by Don Richardson's book *Eternity in their hearts*, which shows how traditional customs or beliefs in various parts of the world have become stepping stones for communicating the Christian message in culturally relevant ways.[8]

This raises a very difficult question about the tension between 'syncretism' and 'enculturation'. 'Syncretism' is generally seen as something negative, an undesirable mixture of religious elements, whereas 'enculturation' is something positive, a way of presenting the Christian gospel in a culturally sensitive manner. Trying to achieve 'enculturation' without falling into the pit of 'syncretism' is likely to be an extremely hazardous task.

A Japanese name for God

This dilemma is raised even as soon as one tries to find a term for 'God' in Japanese. It was a difficulty encountered in the sixteenth century by the Jesuits when they tried to use the Buddhist term 'Dainichi' as a translation of 'God', which they later abandoned in favour of the Latin or Portuguese word 'Deus'.[9] When Protestant missionaries came to Japan in the nineteenth century, 'there were no appropriate words already in existence that were not already loaded with incompatible meanings. Thus, they either had to create a new word or try to revamp the meaning of an existing word.'[10]

Nowadays most Christians use the term *Kamisama*, which is the Shinto term *kami* plus the suffix *-sama* (merely an honorific term of address which is more polite than *-san*: perhaps rather like the difference in English between 'Esquire' and 'Mister'). '*Kamisama*' is often used also in addressing Shinto gods (*kami*). For instance, one day I observed a group of kindergarten children who, escorted by their teacher, entered the park surrounding a Shinto shrine.

They went up to the shrine where together they were taught to say, '*Konnichi wa, Kamisama*' ('Good day, *Kamisama*').

The Christian use of the term *kami* 'has made accurate communication of the gospel message even more difficult'.[11] At the very least it is confusing, and requires Christians to imbue the word with a new set of concepts. It necessitates teaching converts and potential converts what Christians believe about the nature of this God. 'Once this terminology became firmly fixed, about the only choice left was to modify *kami* with various adjectives such as *tenchisōzō no kami*'.[12] Others prefer to use terms such as the opening words of the Lord's prayer ('Our Father in Heaven': *Ten ni imasu watashitachi no Chichi*) in public situations and an informal equivalent such as *Ten no Otōsama* in ordinary conversation.

Perhaps the Christian use of '*Kamisama*' for 'God' could even be labelled 'syncretism'. On the other hand, what better term is there to use? Richardson cites a number of other cultures where there was an indigenous concept of a Supreme Deity whose attributes were so similar to those of the God of the Bible that missionaries could use these indigenous terms as they were. In Korea they used '*Hananim*', in China '*Shang Ti*'. What could they use in Japan?

The nearest possible indigenous concept which I have been able to discover is the figure of '*Ame-no-minaka nushi*' who is mentioned in the ancient Shinto traditions as a kind of original deity. The problem is that this deity is a rather shadowy figure, not described or given clear attributes. Nevertheless, a Shinto priest named Deguchi Nobuyoshi (1615-1690), who served at the Geku ('Outer shrine') at Ise, attempted to establish 'a religion verging on monotheism, in which the ancient 'Heavenly Central Lord' [*Ame-no-minaka nushi*] was regarded as the supreme deity'. Later, the Shinto scholar Hirata Atsutane (1776-1843), who was influenced by reading Christian literature even while it was still officially prohibited, also tried to promote a version of Shinto monotheism focussed on the figure of *Ame-no-minaka nushi*.[13] For him at least, this deity was a possible candidate for a Supreme God. Moreover, this deity was also associated with two others in an original triad. These other two were known as the 'High-Producing' [*Taka-mi-musubi*] and the 'Divine-' or 'Mysterious-Producing' [*Kami-mi-*

musubi]. This first triad 'vanished without leaving posterity' and were followed by a series of similar ones who were 'generated spontaneously independently from one another'. Before one identifies the first triad with the Christian Trinity, it should be noted that the deities accompanying *Ame-no-minaka nushi* 'seem to have symbolised the male and female principles of generation and are sometimes identified with the Divine-Male (*Kami-rogi*) and the Divine-Female (*Kami-romi*)' who are frequently invoked in Shinto rituals.[14] Moreover, another scholar has suggested that this primal triad is actually a Japanese version of a Chinese triad consisting of Ultimate Reality and its two principles of Yin and Yang.[15]

Actually, *Ame-no-minaka nushi* means 'the Lord in the Sky' and carries the same basic meaning as terms for 'Sky Lord' or 'High God' which Richardson cites from other cultures and which have been used by Christians as the name for God. The Chinese term *Shang Ti*, 'The Lord Above', carries a similar connotation. There is also some uncertainty among Japanese scholars whether *Ame-no-minaka nushi* is the same as, or distinct from, another deity known as the 'Eternal-Land-Ruler' (*Kuni-toko-tachi*). The meanings of these terms nevertheless bring out connotations to do with the 'Lord of Heaven and Earth'. In Japanese such an expression could be rendered as *Tenchi no shu*, and indeed a very similar term is used in a Japanese translation of Psalm 121:2, which refers to the 'Maker of heaven and earth' as *Tenchi o tsukurareta Shu*.

In chapter eleven I mentioned that 63% of my respondents asserted a belief in some kind of a 'Being above man and nature'. When I later asked people why they held such a belief, their replies were of four main kinds, as follows:[16]

1) An ontological argument that 'there are many things we cannot do', or 'many things man does not know'—and therefore, as one person put it explicitly, 'nature is so great there must be a God'. Most people left the conclusion implicit, saying that there are 'many things science can not explain', or else they referred to man's limited power or knowledge. Of the fifty-four people questioned on this topic, answers of this type were given by thirty-three respondents—that is, 61% of them. This 'ontological' approach tends to be favoured by the women, as it was mentioned by 73% of the thirty

women versus 46% of the twenty-four men. Similarly, over 70% of my questionnaire sample (70.5% of the men, 72% of the women) replied 'No' to a question worded, 'As Science progresses, do you think it will explain all mysterious things?'. Only 13.5% of the men and 9% of the women actually replied 'Yes' to this question, the remainder opting for the 'Don't know' response.

This ontological argument for the existence of some greater power is a more emotional and intuitive approach than the following one, which was mentioned by only four people, of whom three also mentioned this ontological argument.

2) A teleological approach which referred to natural scientific laws and the cycle of nature, which are inductively used to reason that there must be a Creator. Examples include references to the constant revolution of the planets, the annual cycle of flowers and plant life, with each blossoming in its own turn, and a more general ontological/teleological comment that 'there must be something to keep things going'.

3) An experiential awareness of a 'greater power' governing and directing one's experiences in life. Some people referred to 'miracles' in their lives: two men suffering from ill health said it is 'a miracle that I exist' and 'my own existence depends on *Kamisama*'.

One woman mentioned a premonitory dream about her mother's death. Another referred to the birth of children as a miracle: this was a woman who had to wait eleven years for her first child. Others were more vague about 'unexplained mysteries because *Kamisama* looks after you, so that wonderful things often happen'. Two men working for *Nissen* referred to experiences which they could not have planned for themselves, one of them attributing the way he had been moved around by the company to the workings of a 'greater power', which he identified with Fate. A few others, mainly *shataku* workers in the blue-collar and shop-floor foreman ranks, referred to jinxes and omens as evidence of a greater power. Examples of such jinxes or omens were:

(a) A man who says that if he breaks a cup early in the morning he feels all day that something else will go wrong at work. He therefore takes special care to avoid injuries.

(b) A man who said that if things go badly at work one day he avoids drinking the same kind of green tea again in the morning, but if things go well he drinks the same kind of tea again the following morning.

(c) A man who first met his wife at the funeral of a common relative of theirs; their go-between when they got married said, in jest, that it was a 'jinx'.

4) Four men and one woman asserted a belief in a greater power by reference to the authority of scriptures (whether Christian or Sōka Gakkai) or books on religious education. In addition one Christian man made a remark which is obviously influenced by his religion but does not fit into any of these four categories, namely 'All people feel a need for moral absolutes'.

Whatever term one uses to refer to a supreme being, an understanding of these attitudes may have relevance for Christian apologetics in Japan. To some extent, there may be differences in the emphases which might be appropriate for different sexes and social classes.[17] In addressing women, for instance, one's approach might need to include not only 'logical', teleological arguments but also an appeal to their sense of awe and intuitive feelings.

The appeal of Nature

The teleological arguments mentioned above rely largely on perceptions of order in the natural world. In Japan there has been a tradition of nature worship whereby certain mountains, trees, the moon and other features of nature have been imbued with divinity and worshipped. 'Japanese emotions are nature emotions', partly 'because they are powerfully influenced by nature in general and by every surrounding aspect of it in particular...This total affectivity carries within itself the seeds of a natural mysticism...'[18]

One thirty-year old woman whom I interviewed described how she sometimes prays to the moon, especially when she sees the full moon or crescent moon. Sometimes she makes requests but sometimes she merely puts her hands together and stands in adoration or admiration 'because the moon is beautiful'. A few others mentioned how they 'greet' the moon. Another woman described how sometimes she prays or worships when she gazes at a majestic local mountain.

'...When you look up to the sky and see the sun, the moon and the stars—all the heavenly array—do not be enticed into bowing down to them and worshipping things the Lord your God has apportioned to all the nations under heaven' (Deuteronomy 4:19). Even though Christians are forbidden from worshipping what God has created instead of worshipping the Creator, there is nevertheless a place within Christianity for an appreciation (rather than worship) of natural beauty. Perhaps this element of Christianity needs to be demonstrated more in the Japanese context.

An example of this is given by Boyle, who describes the use of Japanese aesthetics in the six feet or so between the front of their church and the pavement. To one side of the church entrance they placed a large boulder of the kind used in Japanese gardens, with a sign in front of it displaying the words of Psalm 18:2, 'The Lord is my rock, my fortress and my deliverer; my God is my rock, in whom I take refuge'. On the opposite side of the church entrance they created a fountain by setting up a solid, round granite basin about 50cm. across and 30cm. deep—the kind used for pounding rice in—on top of a pedestal with colourful stones cemented around its base. Water flowed through a split bamboo trough into the basin, from which it overflowed and ran down over the rocks at the base. On the front of the basin they printed the characters 命の泉 (*inochi no izumi*, 'the fountain/spring of life') and behind it they placed a large sign displaying the text of John 4:13-14 in which Jesus spoke of his gift of a 'spring of water welling up to eternal life'. Boyle notes that the church received many positive comments about the fountain, which provided an 'excellent conversation starter' as well as displaying a relevant scripture for drinkers to contemplate.[19]

The place for an appreciation of nature in the way one communicates spiritual truths was expressed earlier this century by a Japanese Christian named Kagawa Toyohiko, who wrote:

'So strong is the instinctive feeling of the Japanese for nature that if Christ had not been a nature-lover I question whether they would have found it possible to give him their hearts' fullest and finest devotion.

Paul and Peter impress the Japanese as being over-importunate. Christ pointed to the lily of the field. He lifted his eyes to the birds of the air. He called our attention to the evening glow, the soil by the roadside, the wheat, the tares, the fig tree and the lamb. For this reason the Japanese leap to an understanding of Christ.'[20]

Again, we are pointed back to the way in which Jesus taught. Just as he used the language of 'clean' and 'dirty' to express spiritual truths, so also he used nature as the source of many of his illustrations. One illustration I have found useful in communicating to a Japanese lady the concepts of resurrection and of 'new birth' is that of a caterpillar which enters the 'tomb' of the chrysalis but then becomes a beautiful butterfly.

Conventional sermons in the West tend to be much more 'logical' and step-by-step in their structures. By contrast, the sermons and parables of Jesus were much closer to the Japanese *haiku* poetry, or even the Zen Buddhist *kōan* sayings, which often express a thought in 'condensed' picture language without spelling out the meaning. For 'those who have ears to hear', the inner truths may need to be worked out afterwards.

'The parables of Jesus are powerful because they powerfully echo the longings in the hearts of those who suffer injustice...

Echo, *hibiki* in Japanese, is important in *haiku*, the shortest form of Japanese poetry, consisting of seventeen syllables. *Haiku* is an echo of what is in the heart of nature. It is the resonance of humanity in the busy life of the marketplace and the village square. It is the *hibiki* of what lies deep in the human heart... *Haiku* is the *hibiki* of life... That is why it always consists of short verses, with one pair hitting something and the other pair acting as its resonance.

In this sense, the soul of a parable must also be *hibiki*. With a parable you hit the deepest spots in the life of a people, and in an instant you get the *hibiki* of it in their hearts. In this sense the soul of theology must also be *hibiki*... Jesus could have surpassed Basho as a master of *haiku*. He had the natural instinct to learn from nature and apply it to human life...'[21]

As examples of Christ's use of *haiku*-like forms, Song shows how Matthew 6:26 and 6:28-30 can be arranged in the styles of *haiku*:

> 'Look at the birds of the air;
> they do not sow and reap and store in barns.
>
> Your heavenly Father feeds them.
> You are worth more than the birds!'
>
> 'Consider how the lilies grow in the fields;
> they do not work, they do not spin.
>
> Even Solomon in all his splendour was not attired like them.
> Will not God all the more clothe you?'[22]

The use of poetry and literature

Another original and positive approach in this area is that of Dr. Patrick McElligott, a missionary whose doctorate was on the eighteenth century Japanese poet Kobayashi Issa. Often in his preaching the interest of his audience is aroused by his quotations from Issa or other Japanese writers. McElligott has also questioned the use of 'Western', 'logical' sermon structures in a Japanese context. His reasons are worth quoting at length:

> '[In Japanese theatre]...a list of basic scenes...became the kernel of the plays and the chief centre of interest. These basic scenes which commanded the importance that in other theatres is taken by the plot, are called 'scenes of emphasis' and vaguely correspond to the Western idea of climaxes.
>
> The context of much of the traditional theatre of Japan comes from the world of Japanese literature. The great works of Japanese literature...are at first a disappointment to the Western reader. The diaries describe a variety of completely unrelated incidents with no apparent unifying factor. The *Tales of the Heike* is episodic rather than epic, and books like *The Pillow-book of Sei Shanagon*, *Tsure, Tsure Gusa*, and *The Tales of Ise* contain no logical structure but seem to be strings of little incidents or comments upon trivial things. The appeal of these works is not to the intellect but to the emotions...Logical

sequence in the Western sense is not the object of the presentation...

It is my conviction that this mode of communication should at least be considered in the structure of our preaching. Most of us have sat for years under consistent expository preaching, and were taught hermeneutics and apologetics at Bible school or seminary along principles based on Western ways of thought which have, as their basic principles, logic, consistency, and the building up of a case that leads to a clear conclusion. The appeal to the emotions is seen as legitimate, for most of us, in a secondary sense. Most Japanese pastors are taught similar principles in Bible colleges and seminaries here in Japan. Little or no reference is made to the modes and methods of communication to an audience which we find in literature and the other arts in Japan.

Not for one moment am I suggesting that we go for an all out non-logical appeal to the emotions in our preaching. But I do feel that in our sermon preparation we should pay more attention to 'scenes of emphasis' which primarily appeal to the emotions, and describe those scenes in ways that build up to a climax with which the listener can identify emotionally, and from that point apply scriptural truth related to the passage to a heart that is already moved. The Scriptures, particularly the historical passages of the O.T. and the Gospels in the N.T., are full of such scenes: 'The Prodigal Son', 'The Widow of Nain', the woman taken in adultery, the blind men sitting by the wayside. In fact, all the Gospel stories where people meet Jesus contain scenes which can be presented so as to arouse the emotions in a legitimate way. Even when preaching from the Epistles such Gospel scenes should be utilised to illustrate truth. I often feel that much of my preaching falls short because it so easily becomes an explanation of truth rather than a demonstration of truth.'[23]

McElligott also makes good use of comparisons and contrasts between Japanese literature and the Bible. For example, there are *haiku* verses which speak of the transience of life by comparing it with the fleeting beauty of the cherry blossom, which is in bloom for about a week before its blossoms begin to fall. Two such *haiku* verses from Issa are:

'Ohiru hana ya sude ni onore mo kudari saka.'

'The blossoms fall and scatter
I too
Am already in decline.'

'Shinijitaku itase itase to sakura kana.'

'Get ready! Get ready to die
Say
The cherry blossoms.'[24]

A similar imagery from nature to indicate the transitoriness of life is used by the prophet Isaiah:

'All men are like grass,
and all their glory is like the flowers of the field.
The grass withers and the flowers fall,
because the breath of the Lord blows on them.
Surely the people are grass.' (Isaiah 40:6-7)

However, the next verse, which repeats the same imagery, goes beyond that of the Japanese poets, who merely note the transience of life and are unable to point to any hope afterwards. Isaiah, by contrast, points beyond this transience to that which is eternal:

'The grass withers and the flowers fall,
but the word of our God stands for ever.' (Isaiah 40:8).

Similarly, McElligott notes how in their literature the Japanese are always looking up to the hills and mountains, but receive no help from there. For example, he quotes this verse from Fujiwara Shunzei:

'Oh this world of ours
There is no way out!
With my heart in torment
I sought the mountain depths
But even there the stag cries.'[25]

McElligott contrasts this with the sentiments of Psalm 121:1-2, which also look to the mountains, but see beyond them to the source of real and lasting help:

> 'I lift up my eyes to the hills—
> where does my help come from?
> My help comes from the Lord,
> the Maker of heaven and earth.' (Psalm 121:1-2)

While fully endorsing McElligott's approach, I would also suggest that more popular forms of literature might be more appropriately used by those seeking to communicate to working class and lesser educated people. Already considerable use is made of books by Christian novelists, such as *Shiokari Pass* or *A Heart of Winter* by Miura Ayako (some of whose novels have been made into popular films).[26] There are several other Japanese Christian novelists, poets, painters, dramatists and formal dance artists who have been trying to communicate their Christian faith through the arts. Some of these are fairly popular but others more 'highbrow'—such as using the dramatic forms of the *Nō* theatre to portray the Resurrection of Christ or the conversion of St. Paul.[27]

A favourite television show features a feudal lord named Mito Kōmon who, disguised as an old man, regularly travelled around his domain uncovering corruption and championing the oppressed. The show is based on the real exploits of Tokugawa Mitsukuni (1628-1700), who did do such things. Other popular television stories, such as Tōyama Kinsan, similarly depict a sovereign ruler who lowers himself to become like a commoner in order to experience their lives and to help them. Boyle has used these ideas as illustrations of certain aspects of the Incarnation of Christ.[28]

The God of the *Kamikaze*

These similarities and contrasts between Japanese and biblical concepts are not dissimilar to St. Paul's approach in Athens, when he preached about an 'Unknown God'. There he too quoted from a Greek poet, who wrote, 'In him we live and move and have our being' (Acts 17:28), but the poet in question was Epimenides. This Epimenides was the one who was responsible for the erection of 'anonymous altars' in and around Athens in order to stop a plague.

The line from Epimenides which in Acts 17:28 is quoted by St. Paul in fact follows almost directly on from another line from Epimenides which Paul quotes in Titus 1:12, where he refers to Epimenides as a 'prophet'.[29]

Some have questioned St. Paul's use of this approach in Athens, pointing to the apparently limited number of converts (Acts 17:34), and have suggested that this is why Paul afterwards in Corinth 'did not come with eloquence or superior wisdom'; instead his message and preaching 'were not with wise and persuasive words, but with a demonstration of the Spirit's power' (1 Corinthians 2:1-4). Nowadays this could be polarized as the difference between intellectual apologetics and a 'signs and wonders' approach. Personally, I feel that both approaches are necessary. In a cross-cultural situation, it is right to make use of concepts which point to God's prior working in that culture, as Paul did in Athens. It is necessary to speak in terms to which the people can relate, and if possible to show the Christian gospel as a fulfilment or completion of what they already knew about God. This is what Christianity did in relation to Judaism, and what Paul sought to do in Athens. On the other hand, this also needs to be complemented by 'a demonstration of the Spirit's power', perhaps through healings or other miracles, so that our preaching becomes a demonstration of truth rather than merely an explanation of truth.

Richardson suggests that the weak point in St. Paul's sermon in Athens was not his use of the 'Unknown God' or his references to Greek poetry but rather a logical flaw in verse 31 where Paul 'mentioned the resurrection of the man God authorized to judge the world *without first explaining how and why He had to die in the first place*.'[30] In addressing the Greek philosophers, Paul had to set out his case very logically, which he had done up to that point, but then he jumped a step. Among the philosophers of Athens it was important to proceed logically: this was an opposite cultural setting to that of the Japanese theatre with its concentration on 'scenes of emphasis'!

Nevertheless, we might ask whether or not in Japan, as in ancient Greece, there was some historical event which was interpreted as a time of national salvation through the agency of an 'Unknown God'. I would suggest that such an event might have been the occurrence of typhoons which in the thirteenth century averted the threatened Mongol invasions of Japan.

The Japanese referred to each of these typhoons as a 'divine wind' (*kamikaze*)—the term used in the Second World War by *kamikaze* suicide pilots. This *kamikaze* has become part of the Japanese national tradition—the islands were divinely protected from the Mongolian armies which had already subjugated China and other parts of Asia.

However, when I have asked Japanese people which god sent this *kamikaze* they do not know. One man suggested it might have been Amaterasu Ōmikami, the goddess who was the founding ancestress for the Imperial line and who is particularly associated with the Japanese nation.

I then suggested that whichever God saved Japan must have been a far greater God than one who is concerned only with Japan. The same God also saved Europe from the Mongols. Europe would almost certainly have fallen to the Mongol Empire too but was saved through the sudden death of Ögedei, Genghis Khan's third son, who was at that time the Mongolian 'Khakhan' ('Khan of khans'). The Mongolian armies had to return to Mongolia for a council to elect a new Khakhan. It was only this event which saved Europe, because the Mongols almost certainly would have defeated the remaining European forces, just as they had already defeated the Russians and Hungarians and had swept right across to the Adriatic Sea. Surely the God who was protecting both Japan and Europe was much greater than a deity like Amaterasu Ōmikami who is really concerned mainly with Japan? The God who stopped the Mongolians from invading both Western Europe and Japan was the same God who 'made every nation of men, that they should inhabit the whole earth; and he determined the times set for them and the exact places where they should live' (Acts 17:26).

> 'He makes nations great, and destroys them;
> he enlarges nations, and disperses them' (Job 12:23).

The *Discovery of Genesis*

Kang and Nelson have written a fascinating book entitled *The Discovery of Genesis in the Chinese Characters*.[31] In it they argue that some of the 'basic' Chinese characters display in a pictorial form the same traditions as are recorded in the early chapters of the biblical book of Genesis.

For example, there is a character for 'boat' which is drawn as (舟), depicting in stylized pictorial form a boat with a rudder and two oars. However, the character for a 'big boat'—or ship—is depicted as this same character with two other elements added to the right of it:船 Instead of using the character for 'big' (大) and adding that to the one for 'boat'—which might be a logical way of depicting a ship—the two extra characters used are those for 'eight' (八) and 'mouth' (口). In other contexts, as in the word for 'population' (人口)—which is written as a person (人) plus the character for mouth (口)—the 'mouth' character can represent people. So, according to Kang and Nelson, the Chinese character for ship actually embodies the idea of 'eight men in a boat'—that is, Noah's Ark!

Kang and Nelson reinforce their theory by claiming that the early Chinese were monotheists, worshipping the one god, Shang Ti, whose name is now used by Chinese Christians as the name for God. More academic sources are so not clear in asserting that the early Chinese actually were fully monotheistic, but they do leave the possibility open.

When I first read Kang and Nelson's book I was a little sceptical, wondering if they were reading too much into the characters. However, on reflection I felt that there were a couple of aspects to their theory which were not discussed in their book but which actually made me more convinced that they could be right.

Firstly, I remembered that when I had taken a course in Archaeology during my first year at University one of the lecturers mentioned a debate over the beginnings of bronze technology in China. Chinese archaeologists like to say that bronze technology was discovered independently in China at the beginning of the Shang period, whereas non-Chinese scholars say that the technique was imported from the Middle East. As evidence, they cite the fact that

Shang period bronze artefacts in China are of a relatively high quality, but there are no earlier prototypes for these. There is therefore no evidence of an independent development of bronze technology in China, and it is more likely that the techniques were originally brought to China from the Middle East.

The most likely route for such knowledge to flow was along what later came to be called the 'Silk Road' through Central Asia. If technological knowledge could be passed along such a route, why not religious traditions? Indeed, why not stories of the kind recorded in Genesis?

Secondly, I considered the statistical probability of combining the 214 basic elements (called 'radicals') in the Chinese characters in order to make something which is meaningful by reference to the book of Genesis. If there are only three radicals in a character, as in the example given above of a ship (Noah's Ark), then the statistical probability against combining these three radicals 'by chance' is 214 x 214 x 214, which comes to 9,800,344. In other words, it is highly unlikely that they would have been meaningfully combined merely by chance alone.

This is further reinforced when one considers the range of other characters which Kang and Nelson interpret in the light of the book of Genesis. Some of them, such as the one for devil, are far more complicated than the simple example given above of three radicals together.

Of course, nobody can say for certain that one explanation for the origin of the characters is 'better' than another, because such theories were developed long after the characters themselves had come into use. For example, a more conventional theory for the 'ship' character sees the 'eight' radical (丿\) as a simplified version of the one for 'river' (〕﹔). By this theory, a 'ship' is a larger boat which sails in the mouth of a river (and perhaps out to sea) rather than remaining upstream.

Nevertheless, the cumulative evidence in favour of Kang and Nelson's hypothesis is quite compelling because it relies on a variety of different characters. Some of them are much more difficult to explain away by other interpretations: for instance, why should the character for 'forbid' be represented as two trees plus an ideograph denoting God? It makes more sense in the light of the Genesis account.

Boyle notes that Kang and Nelson's book 'takes a very literalistic view of Genesis, but that is not at all necessary to the thesis that similar stories were brought into China with the advent of civilization... All of this only amounts to circumstantial evidence that the ancient Chinese had similar stories about the origins of humankind as are found in Genesis, be that interpreted as literal history, symbolic "poetic history"... or fanciful mythology'.[32]

Boyle also suggests a number of other Christian interpretations for characters which Kang and Nelson do not discuss. For instance, the character 聖 meaning 'holy' contains the radicals for 'ear', 'mouth' and king: Boyle notes that for a person to be 'holy', someone must be king of that person's ears and mouth.[33] Similarly, the character 義 for 'righteousness' contains two parts: the upper part is the symbol for a lamb, the lower part is the first person pronoun 'I'. In other words, the message means: 'Under the lamb, I am righteous'! This interpretation of the character has also been used effectively in China, where the Chinese were unable to supply an answer to the question, 'Which lamb must we be under in order to be righteous?'; the Christians, however, were able to suggest an answer from the New Testament (John 1:29; Revelation 13:8).[34]

These interpretations of characters for 'holy' or 'righteous' were respected even by those who were dubious about the supposed links with the book of Genesis. On the whole, Boyle reports that almost all the feedback he has received has been positive and that lay people have been particularly fascinated by the ideas. He notes that this approach has also proved useful among Japanese-Americans, who 'really identified with these interpretations, somewhat in the sense of being part of their "roots".'[35]

Spiritual Warfare

These cultural 'springboards' for the Gospel at least help to attract the attention of an audience even if they do not necessarily lead directly to conversions. They prepare the ground and help people to recognize that what is preached is not a 'foreign' religion but a 'fulfilment' of their own. This was the case for the early Christians converted from Judaism. It was probably also the case for the Dionysius mentioned in Acts 17:34 who was one of those converted after St. Paul's speech on Mars Hill, and who, according to a second century tradition, became the first bishop of Athens.[36]

On the other hand, there is the danger of falling into syncretism. Some traditions might be so tainted by unhelpful connotations that they are no longer suitable as vehicles for communicating Christian truths. For example, I have been told that the lion statues guarding Buddhist temples in Japan usually depict one lion with his mouth open and the other one with his mouth shut because they are pronouncing the sacred mantra 'OM', which consists of the first and last letters of the Sanskrit alphabet. I would hesitate to use this as a 'springboard' for speaking about Jesus as the 'Alpha and Omega' (Revelation 1:8), which are the first and last letters of the Greek alphabet.

There does come a point at which there is some conflict. Jesus came to fulfill the Jewish traditions, and to establish the Kingdom which had already been predicted in Daniel 2:44. However, this was not merely a ministry of bringing new interpretations to old customs. Before long, he was demonstrating the power of the Kingdom of God in casting out demons and healing the sick (*e.g.* Mark 1:21-34). Shortly after sending out his disciples to do the same (Matthew 10:1-8), he announced that from the days of John the Baptist onwards the 'Kingdom of heaven has been forcefully advancing, and forceful men lay hold of it' (Matthew 11:12). This advance against the invisible forces of darkness was accompanied on the visible level by opposition from the religious authorities who were threatened by this ministry and by the political forces which eventually allowed the executions of both John the Baptist and of Jesus.

In Japan too it is necessary to proclaim the Kingdom of God but in doing so one is likely to encounter opposition. It might be through human agencies but the real enemies are demonic ones. Jesus sent out the twelve with authority to heal the sick and cast out demons (Luke 9:1). Later the seventy (or seventy-two) reported that even the demons submitted to them in Christ's name: then Jesus announced that he saw Satan fall like lightning from heaven, and that he had given his followers authority 'to overcome all the power of the enemy' (Luke 10:17-21). Christ's commission today needs to be done in the power of his Holy Spirit (Luke 24:49; John 20:21-22) and involves training other disciples to do the same—as part of all that Jesus commanded (Matthew 28:20). His instructions to preach the gospel, heal the sick and cast out demons (Matthew 10:7-8; Luke 9:1-2) are still today essential aspects of Christian ministry both in the West and in Japan. After listening to lectures on the deliverance ministry, Rev. Paul Benedict, a missionary with 35 years of experience in Japan, remarked, 'You have shown us why we were so unsuccessful in our ministry when we first came to the country. We were trying to cut down trees with baseball bats!'[37]

Experiential Evangelism

John Wimber's book *Power Evangelism* has influenced many Christians around the world.[38] It basically argues for an incorporation of 'signs and wonders' ministries as part of our evangelism. However, the examples given in the book are mainly to do with either healing or special revelations from God. Such revelations may include either 'words of knowledge' or prophecy. Certainly St. Paul was referring to prophecy when he wrote in 1 Corinthians 14:24-25, 'if an unbeliever or someone who does not understand comes in while everybody is prophesying, he will be convinced by all that he is a sinner and will be judged by all, and the secrets of his heart will be laid bare. So he will fall down and worship God, exclaiming, "God is really among you!".'

This passage tends to imply that Christians—indeed the Christian community as a whole—will be receiving such revelations on a regular basis. Some might say that 'Power Evangelism' is all very well for those who need healing, or about whom such revelations have been given, but what about other people? Either we need to become much more open to receiving revelations from God, or else we have to hope that they are influenced by what they see of healings and 'words of knowledge' relating to other people. Otherwise, we have to pray that they will be brought into the Kingdom of God through more 'conventional' evangelistic approaches.

More recently, God has been bringing to my attention another approach to evangelism, which I believe complements both the 'conventional' evangelistic approaches and also what has come to be known as 'power evangelism'. I call this approach 'experiential evangelism'. Essentially it assumes that many people are already aware of a 'spiritual' side to their lives, and that such experiences can be 'stepping stones' for relating the Christian message to them. Sometimes the experience is of a demonic nature, and requires deliverance (*e.g.* Acts 16:16-18).

On the other hand, there are 'positive' experiences through which God prepares people too. In the Bible there are several cases of God revealing himself to *Gentiles* through dreams and visions, preparing their hearts and minds for a human messenger to bring the interpretation or fulfilment of such revelations. Examples include the interpretations of dreams given to Pharaoh and Nebuchadnezzar or the fulfilment of the vision given to Cornelius (Genesis 41; Daniel 2 and 4; Acts 10). All of these also required the obedience of human 'men of God': Joseph, Daniel or Peter. A similar pattern can be seen in the experience of Saul on the road to Damascus, who also needed the ministry of Ananias. I therefore suggest that *Christians should begin to pray for God to speak to people in 'supernatural' ways in order to prepare their hearts and minds to become more receptive to the Gospel.* Then we should ask God to lead us to those whom he has already been preparing in advance. This might involve listening to specific instructions from God of the kind which he gave to Cornelius about where to find Peter or to Ananias about where to find Saul (Acts 9:10-12; 10:3-6).

Let me conclude by giving a specific example of how a Japanese woman came to Christ through a vision of Jesus. In this case, it was through her being present when the Holy Spirit was invited to come and minister to a group of Christians. I shall quote from a letter dated 6th May, 1989 which was written to me by William Bussman, one of those present at the time:

'An older Japanese woman, Buddhist, spoke no English,...was visiting her daughter, from Japan, in San Antonio, at Randolph AFB, Texas. Her daughter, the wife of an Air Force member, was attending a Lay Witness Mission, sponsored by the Air Force Chapel, on March 4–6, 1988. Her mother attended with her.

The circumstances were as follows: Karen and I were leading a small group ministry on prayer on the morning of March 5th, for about ten women. We called the Holy Spirit, and the mother had clear manifestations of the Holy Spirit which continued for about 10–15 minutes. When the Spirit lifted, she told her daughter in Japanese, who translated to us, that Jesus had come personally to her and testified about Himself. She immediately received Christ as her Lord and Savior. She was filled with joy and great happiness. We spoke with her through her daughter several times during the remainder of the weekend and her joy remained.'

NOTES

Preface   The Anthropologist

1 See, for instance, Platt 1976:113-122 or Evans-Pritchard 1951:83-5. For a discussion of this problem with particular reference to Japanese religion, see Reid 1991: 59-68.

2 Southwold 1983:8

3 See also Geertz 1973:193-233

4 Burridge 1969:4, footnote 2

5 Evans-Pritchard 1962:45

6 Southwold 1983:8

7 Schmidt 1931:6, cited by Evans-Pritchard 1965:121 and Southwold 1983:61

8 Van Der Geest 1990:589-590, 595-6, 598, notes 3 and 4

9 Aikman 1991:17

10 Otis 1991:85

11 Aikman 1991:16-17

12 The Romanization I am following is that used by Kenkyusha's New Japanese-English Dictionary (1954), whereby macrons indicate long vowels except in the case of a final long 'i', which is usually doubled. (It is a modified version of Hepburn's (1867) Romanization, having alterations such as *mitsu* for 'three' instead of Hepburn's 'mitsz' or *mizu* for 'water' instead of 'midz'.) However, following the precedents of earlier writers such as Norbeck (1970:iv), I omit macrons for principal geographical names such as Tokyo, Osaka or Kyushu (which more strictly should be Tōkyō, Ōsaka and Kyūshū).

13 Generally I use simpler forms of Japanese words without their honorific prefixes, such as *mamori* instead of *o-mamori*. An exception, following Kenkyusha's dictionary, is the retention of the secondary honorific prefix *mi* in (o-)*mikuji*.

14 This research was sponsored by what is now the Economic and Social Science Research Council of Great Britain, for whose sponsorship I would like to express my thanks.

15 How my wife and I viewed the response rate was also influenced by our Christian faith. After we had distributed the questionnaire, one of our

314

neighbours came round and told us how some of our questions (on education, moral values and so on) were far too personal—especially as we were neighbours and we had asked people to fill in their names and addresses too. In her opinion, probably no more than 20% of those approached would fill in such a questionnaire.

However, just at that time, we were sent a tape from our church in England. It contained a sermon by our minister, who pointed out how the harvest of thirty, sixty or a hundred times what was sown (in Matthew 13:23) was far greater than would have been expected from 'normal' crop yields. This encouraged us to pray for many more people to fill in the questionnaire. We were encouraged also by the words of Psalm 27:13, 'I am still confident of this: I will see the goodness of the Lord in the land of the living.'

During the next few days a number of people returned their questionnaires themselves through our letter box. Then, after a week or two, we went around collecting in the forms. As we returned with bags full of completed forms, our neighbour kept asking how we were doing!

16 Obtaining the co-operation and help of the *jichikai* (more generally known as the *chōnaikai*) has much wider ramifications for many kinds of religious activities. Boyle (1986:22-23) stresses the importance of getting to know in advance the local *chōnaikai* Chairpersons, especially in areas where elderly Christians reside, in order to explain to them the 'distinctives of a Christian funeral' and to ask for their co-operation if a death occurs among any of the local Christians. He writes that this 'could prove very useful in increasing the visibility of the church as well as making it seem a little less foreign'.

17 I am grateful to the Japan Foundation for a Dissertation Fellowship which enabled me to develop my research further from 1983 to 1984 while I was a Visiting Fellow at the National Museum of Ethnology in Osaka.

Chapter 1 Safety First

1 Berentsen (1985a:82-83), among others, notes that the fear of *tatari* (a 'curse' by malevolent spirits seeking revenge) is greater in the case of an abnormal death. Reader (1991a:44-45) discusses contemporary cases of misfortunes being attributed to the spirits of a dead ancestor or of an aborted foetus.

2 Brief descriptions of this and other religious rites were originally published in Lewis 1986a and to a more limited extent in Lewis 1986d.

3 Douglas 1966:35.

4 This paragraph condenses ideas in sociolinguistics known as the Sapir-Whorff hypothesis: a popular introduction to their ideas is given by

Trudgill (1983:24-27). Moeran (1984:252, 259-264) discusses the concept of 'key words' in Japan.

5 Kamata 1982:58-59, 96-97, 109-110 *etc.*

6 Dore 1973:244-245

7 Lo (1990:23) mentions similar 'safety first' signs and 'pep talks' on safety at another Japanese factory.

8 Reader 1991a:54

9 To some extent such concerns might be linked in with the presence of earthquakes and typhoons in Japan; however, an explanation only in such terms seems to be over-simplistic because *all* cultures face certain common types of dangers, whether these be from aspects of the environment, wild animals, human enemies or whatever. Ben-Dasan (1972:11) notes that because of Japan's insularity and abundant water resources 'the Japanese have always known complete security', as compared with nations such as Israel. Paradoxically, their 'excessive safety and security have turned the Japanese into a cloistered people who panic when faced with crises of even minor severity' (p.22), so that many of them might have become 'incapable of coping with the unexpected' (p.24). Perhaps it is this characteristic which seems to express itself in the strong concern with safety and security which is manifested in many aspects of Japanese religion.

10 For such reasons, and others, my wife and I felt we had to get rid of an expensive silk-robed doll which had been given to us but which had apparently come from a Buddhist temple.

11 Dr. Patrick McElligott, an experienced missionary in Japan, comments,
'It would be unthinkable for most Japanese to throw out a Buddhist altar with the household rubbish or unwanted furniture. Such an action would almost certainly bring unnecessary recriminations from the neighbours... A Buddhist home altar can be as large as a wardrobe and is almost always the joint property of a family or a group. A Shinto god-shelf is not normally as large as a Buddhist home altar but it is usually family property, not personal property. Unless the new convert is the head of the family the disposal of an altar would not come within the scope of his or her responsibility. The new convert's problem is that of relating or not relating to this symbol of family respect and unity.

Even when the head of a local household is converted he is not generally free to dispose of an altar unless he has purchased one for his own immediate family only. If there are younger brothers or sisters in the extended family the converted head of the family will normally ask one of his younger brothers or sisters to take on the family altar. Only if they all refuse, which would be very unlikely, would he then be free to dispose of it. Buddhist home altars and Shinto god-shelves are invariably destroyed by burning.'

12 Even the 'secular' manifestations might nevertheless be motivated in many cases by fears which can lead people into bondage to spirits of fear.

13 On the whole, I prefer to use the term 'non-religious' rather than 'secular', because the latter tends to imply that there has been some sort of transition from the 'religious' sphere to the 'secular' one (Tamaru 1979:91). For many of the practices described in this book, there is inadequate historical evidence to show whether there has really been 'secularization'—or merely the substitution of certain expressions of religiosity for others.

Chapter 2   Industrial Mission

1 A brief description of this rite and of others described in this chapter was first published in Lewis 1986a.

2 The *ema* prayer plaques on which people write inscriptions at many Shinto shrines may also be substitutes for an earlier practice of horse sacrifices (Reader 1991b:25-28).

In ancient Shinto, a 'Great Exorcism' rite took place on the last day of the sixth and twelfth months. In this rite, a priest read off a long prayer listing the sins or crimes (*tsumi*) of the kingdom which were then ritually transferred on to 'heavenly narrow pieces of wood' and 'heavenly sedge reeds' which were thrown into a river to be carried away by the current (Earhart 1974:163-166). Commenting on this ancient rite, Boyle (1986:49, note 38) remarks that it sounds very similar to the ancient Jewish Day of Atonement (Leviticus 16) but he was unaware of any contemporary Japanese custom of this kind. However, he thinks 'it would be interesting to find out, as this may also provide a bridge of communication as it did with the Jews. Jesus, the Lamb of God, became the 'scapegoat' who once and for all bore away the sins of the people. Could he not also be the 'heavenly narrow piece of wood' that took onto himself the sins (pollutions) of the Japanese?'.

3 Corwin 1967:156-159. On p.159, note 10, he gives a modern example of *ikenie*: he writes that a business executive might offer his daughter in marriage to another business associate's son, in an effort to foster stronger business ties, and that such an action might be described by others as offering his daughter as an *ikenie* for business.

4 Lewis 1986a and 1986d.

5 See, for example, Reader 1991a:73-76; Rohlen 1974:41; Abegglen 1973:140; Matusek 1986:169-175; Hashimoto 1962:13.

6 Sue Behague, personal communication.

7 Dr. Patrick McElligott, personal communication.

8 Nakamaki 1990:131-132

9 This is also mentioned by Hoshino and Takeda 1987:310.

10 Joya 1958:562-563. Otis (1991:108) cites a similar kind of practice in ancient Babylon but he also remarks, in the context of similarities between the Japanese *daijōsai* and ancient Babylonian rites, that, 'It is not known if the similarities...arise from specific historical contact between ancient Japan and Babylonian culture, or were simply choreographed by related, spiritual powers' (p.101, note 13).

11 Joya (1958:563) also notes that this eye-opening service is observed as a 'popular custom' in the painting of eyes onto *Daruma* dolls. (See also Reader 1991a:37).

12 Lewis 1986a:273

13 Lewis 1989:121-124; 1987:36-40; 1990:112-120

14 See, for example, Wimber 1986:130; Subritzky 1986:118-119, 123-124.

15 In Japanese: '*hontō ni wa, shinkō shite imasen*'. He does it as 'part of my work' (*kaisha no shigoto*).

16 In Japanese: '*kamisama ga mamotte iru*'.

17 In Japanese: '*seishin o tōitsu suru*'.

18 Lewis 1986a:269-270.

19 In Japanese, his words were: '*Kaisha no gyōji desu kara, shikata nashi ni sanka shite imasu.*'

20 Watanabe 1989:281. At the *Nissen* factory, the door of the large outdoor cabinet-like structure which used to be opened daily for corporate prayers to the Emperor now remains shut, but the Emperor's portrait is said to be still inside.

21 Warriner 1983:50

22 Kinoshita 1983

23 Patrick McElligott, personal communication

24 Laymen's Foreign Mission Inquiry 1932:252

25 Ben-Ari 1990:105-107

26 Germany 1967:109-113, 127-128

27 Patrick McElligott, personal communication

28 A more controversial approach is that advocated by Hayashi Minoru (1988:367-369), who notes that 'the real meaning attached to 'bowing' in the Japanese context is more of 'paying or showing one's respect' than of worshipping the one to whom one bows'. He sees the custom as largely a reaffirmation of group identity rather than idolatry, because 'if a person does not bow, it signifies that he/she does not belong to the group. His/her act will be perceived as an act of insult and contempt toward the group'. Citing the precedent set by Elisha's response to Naaman in 2 Kings 5:17-19, Hayashi argues that 'God knows the dif-

ference between the outward form and its real meaning. In the case of Naaman, to bow down meant that he was showing submission and loyalty to his king. It did not mean that he was worshipping Rimmon...Therefore, God understands and forgives Japanese Christians if they bow before an idol in the course of their duty to their company or office.'

29 Patrick McElligott, personal communication. Another example he mentioned is a firm called Thornton Preserves.

Chapter 3 Shrine and Temple

1 However, an increasingly popular form of leisure activity in Japan is to go around some of the old pilgrimage routes. (Some new ones are being introduced too.) Noda (1983) indicates the spiritual influence which a pilgrimage exerted upon her—a third-generation Japanese American, who called herself a 'non-Buddhist' (pp.174-5). Having initially felt that she 'had to' go to Shikoku in order to perform a pilgrimage there, she later discovered that 'the journey was as much an inner one as an outer one' (p.174), because she 'travelled through three realms (mind, body, heart; present, past, and future)', and sometimes entered 'a fourth realm of freedom' (p.183).

As a kind of hobby, some of those who participate in pilgrimages or visits to temples like to collect on a hanging scroll the official stamps of the temples they have visited. One of those I interviewed showed me such a scroll depicting the goddess Kannon, around the edge of which were the stamps of about fifty different temples. This man reckoned that he visits about twenty different temples a year. In my sample there were four others who visit temples or shrines as a 'hobby'—and therefore tend to go to them more frequently than do most other people. Two of these families go every week (one of them to temples, the other to Shinto shrines), one goes 'once a week at most, sometimes less frequently' and the fourth had visited about thirty temples and shrines while on holiday the previous year. Two of these families had bought statues of Buddhist deities: one was a statue of the goddess Kannon to which the man sometimes prays in his home, and the other was a statue of Miroku Buddha which a man bought for his wife and to which she prays if she is worried about her children when they are late home from school.

2 Reader 1991a:2

3 See, for instance, Kitagawa 1966:201-202; Anesaki 1963:334-335; Holtom 1938:56-57; Norbeck 1970:45,49.

4 Elsewhere (Lewis 1989:143-146) I have noted a connection between

musical or artistic abilities and a receptivity to divine revelations in a Christian context.

5 The discrepancy between the total number of religious adherents and the national population varies a little from year to year: Morioka (1975:4) stated that the number of religious adherents was 1.7 times the national population, but in 1985 the multiple was 1.84 (Reader 1991a:6) and in 1988 it was about 1.55 (Reid 1991:20).

6 McFarland 1967:18. For example, numbers of 'Shintoists' might be based upon approximations of how many people visit a certain shrine at New Year, but there are families who visit more than one shrine. The high priest of a major Shinto shrine told me that he had no idea how many thousands of people visited his shrine at New Year. All he could say was that their car park, with a capacity for 3,000 cars, was in constant use and that thousands of others came by public transport.

7 Namihira 1976:358, 367; Ooms 1967:289-291

8 Yanagita 1970:56

9 Perhaps one might even see in this certain parallels with the views of some scholars who say that in Japan the group takes precedence over the individual in public settings, whereas individualism tends to be restricted to the private domain.

10 Joy Hendry (personal communication).

11 I am here writing in what anthropologists call the 'ethnographic present'. This is a convention within cultural anthropology whereby one writes in the present tense but in fact refers to the time when one's fieldwork took place. In the present context, this is the period from 1983 to 1984, but the amount stated here has probably risen now owing to inflation.

12 Dore (1958:345) found this to be the case in the immediate post-war period, and my experience of contemporary Japan suggests that it is also the case now.

13 Benedict 1946:271.

14 Befu 1971:104; Singer 1973:27; Reader 1991a:25-27; Earhart 1974:9-13 (taken from Holtom 1938); Earhart 1984:49-54; Hashimoto 1962:36

15 Ono 1962:7. He continues, 'Also regarded as kami are the guardian spirits of the land, occupations, and skills; the spirits of national heroes, men of outstanding deeds or virtues, and those who have contributed to civilization, culture, and human welfare; those who have died for the state or the community; and the pitiable dead. Not only spirits superior to man, but even some that are regarded as pitiable and weak have nonetheless been considered to be kami.' More detailed studies of *kami* include those in English by Holtom (1940) and in Japanese by Iwata (1979).

16 Berentsen 1985a:96. The Agency for Cultural Affairs (1972:38) notes that only those *kami* with human characteristics have been introduced into formal shrine worship, whereas the *kami* of plants, animals or places might be appeased in specific rites like the *jichinsai* without having formal shrines dedicated to them.

17 Befu 1971:104

18 Berentsen 1985a:88-89; 1985b:268

19 Berentsen 1985a:81

20 Dore 1958:313, 434, 457 (note 257). He also refers to deceased known relatives as 'close-relative *hotoke*' in order to distinguish between them and 'the ancestors' in general, which he refers to as 'ancestor *hotoke*'.

21 Befu 1971:112-113; Davis 1980:128

22 Davis 1980:31; Reader 1991a:44-5, 206-7

23 See, for example, Wimber 1986:122-3, 132, 205-6; Subritzky 1986:39, 41, 46-48, 61-62, 67, 118, 123-124, 192-194; Lewis 1989: 117-120, 339; Lewis 1990:112.

   When certain demons manifest they can cause animal-like behaviour in people who might, for example, slither like a snake or bark like a dog (Subritzky 1986: 43, 45, 94, 126, 144-5, 146). Blue (1987:86) also mentions a woman who felt 'as though cats and dogs were running out' of her chest when she was healed of atrial fibrillation (rapid, irregular heartbeat) after her pastor and daughters commanded 'this evil rhythm' to leave her body.

24 Smith 1974:56

25 *Ibid.*, pp.146, 183; Plath 1964:303. Those whom Plath (1964:301-4) refers to as 'the departed' would be the *shirei*, *nii-botoke* and *senzo* or *hotoke* in my modified version of Smith's schematization.

26 At some Buddhist temples this concern with memorialism can also be extended to the performance of memorial services for broken needles—an example of which I witnessed at a temple on the outskirts of Kyoto—and for other animate or inanimate objects which have been of service to man, including eels eaten in a restaurant, discarded dolls and used printing blocks (Reader 1991a:45-6). A temple in Okayama prefecture held a memorial service for the six million pieces of dried cuttle fish produced each year by local factories (Hashimoto 1962:13).

27 Matsudaira 1963:185-6; Smith 1974:41; Hashimoto 1962:39-40

28 Agency for Cultural Affairs 1972:123. [Note that the *tama* is here said to be given at birth rather than at conception: to a certain extent this idea might have at times influenced attitudes about the acceptability or otherwise of abortion.]

29 Dore 1958:435

30 Blacker 1975:43; Devereux 1989:35, 36, 149

31 One of these had seen the fireball in a graveyard 'among the trees' while the other specified that it was 'a place where people had died without a purification having been performed (*o-harai sezu ni*), perhaps a place like the former battleground where the *Nissen* factory now stands. Both of these informants (one male, the other female) said their experiences were 'very frightening' so they ran away.

32 Southwold 1983:12, note 27

33 Bowen 1954:44

34 From a sixty-six year old man quoted by Beardsworth (1977:40-41). Another account (on page 41 of Beardsworth's book) describes an 'extremely brilliant ball of light' which was seen indoors, in a bedroom. About three or four weeks later—a time span similar to the one in the West African example which I quoted—the experience was repeated but 'this time the ball of light was surrounded by an equally intense line of light round the circumference just a short distance from it'.

35 Gardner 1986:72

36 In 1904-1905, at the time of a revival associated with Mary Jones, there were various kinds of light phenomena in north Wales, including a globe over a chapel where a service was taking place (Devereux 1989:64-69).

37 There is a widespread interest in UFOs and other paranormal phenomena among Japanese young people (Reader 1991a:234-235).

38 Tanya Denisova, personal communication. The article was entitled 'UFOs—envoys of Satan' (NLO-poslantsy Satany) in the Moscow newspaper *Golos Vsyelyennoi*, April 1991, pp.1-3.

39 Devereux 1982:227-228; 1989:77-78, 104, 158; 1990:121, 135-137, 144.

40 Devereux 1982:221-225; 1989:111-112, 118, 126-127, 133,135, 142-143, 149, 152, 203-225. Moody (1976:72-3) quotes a hospital patient who described how a 'ball of light, almost like a globe' appeared to him and showed him in advance what would happen to him after his imminent operation. The patient (or his disembodied consciousness) was led by the 'ball of light' to another part of the hospital, and was conducted there by holding on to what appeared to be a 'hand' which extended out from the 'ball of light'. However, when the patient was not using the spiritual hand 'the spirit went back to the circular pattern'.

41 Devereux 1989:135, 219-220 and especially 1982:224 (a being which 'did not appear to be three-dimensional' and 'gave the...impression of being hairy all over. Its head was mounted directly on its shoulder...The arms ended without hands almost like a single finger which curled inwards. In each of these curved 'hooks' it held what I can only describe as a glowing rod. Each was about eight to ten inches long and

thicker than the average pencil. They glowed red as if with heat. Its legs were straight, but disappeared from the knee down...').

42 Otis 1991:90 However, sightings often seem to be associated with geological faults or earth movements, leading Devereux (1982:201-202) to interpret the phenomenon as a discharge from the earth which in certain circumstances takes on a form within the atmosphere and becomes visible 'by ionization or some other photon-emitting process'. [Many sightings occur at night, when the lights are more conspicuous, but at night one is less likely to see a 'patch of absolute darkness'—such as was observed in the Longdendale valley at a place called the 'Devil's Elbow'—which 'may simply be the obverse face of the process producing light' (Devereux 1989:90, 207)]. My own personal hunch is that a spiritual being of some kind which interacts with parts of the electromagnetic spectrum might become a 'nucleus' which attracts and concentrates any discharge produced by earth movements. It functions rather like the particles of dust around which raindrops coalesce from water vapour in the atmosphere. Therefore the *sightings* are more common under certain specific circumstances but normally the spiritual beings (whether demonic or angelic) remain hidden from our view.

43 Lowell 1894:1-15; Blacker 1975:159-161; Hori 1968:141-179; Hori 1975:237; Dore 1958:331-332

44 Ono 1962:100-101

45 *Ibid.*, p.3

46 Befu 1971:95

47 Agency for Cultural Affairs 1972:29-32; *cf* Spae 1972:25-26

48 See Crump 1989. In an afterword to the paperback edition (Oxford University Press, 1991, p. 224) Crump notes that the enthronement ceremonies were regarded as part of the Emperor's 'private religion'.

49 Information from David Swain, who also noted that about 100 citizens' groups were formed to deal with this issue.

50 Oshima 1990:223

51 Undated bulletin entitled *Japan—A Call to Prayer*, produced by the Japan Evangelistic Band, Portsmouth. Emphasis as in the original.

52 Nishikawa 1990:135; Oshima 1990:222

53 Crump 1989:100, 107

54 Blacker 1981:79; 1990:180, 188

55 Otis 1991:92

56 Koyama 1982:83-85; Watanabe 1989:275-281

57 Crump 1991:15. Certainly the government was concerned about the security aspects of these rituals, but the heavy police presence in Tokyo, with armoured cars and riot shields, at the time of the *sokui no rei* ritual

held ten days before the *daijōsai*, is described by Crump (p.14) as a 'case of massive over-reaction'.

58 Bownas 1963:40.

59 A nationwide survey in the same year put the percentage at 56% (Asahi Shinbun 1981).

60 The Japanese word *kokoro* means 'heart', 'soul', 'mind' or 'spirit', among other nuances.

61 Theoretically, the *bachi* would normally be limited to the individual transgressor or her household. Although her family joked about it affecting her companions, they also denied any belief that this would in fact be the case.

62 It is significant that those aspects of the 'Western' Christmas which have been adopted in Japan are those which had existing Japanese parallels at New Year. New Year is traditionally a time for the sending of greetings cards, the giving of gifts to certain individuals (particularly money to children), parties and the putting up of pine decorations next to the front door of one's house. Special foods are traditionally eaten at New Year, so Christmas cake is an extension of this practice to a different setting a few days previously. The Japanese word for 'carol' (*karoru*—a loan word from English) refers to 'Jingle Bells' and 'Rudolph the Red-nosed Reindeer'—which are played *ad nauseam* in shopping precincts—but specifically Christian songs are generally unknown outside the churches. The few Japanese greetings cards available for Christmas (and often printed in English, primarily for foreign residents) usually contain words such as 'Season's Greetings' rather than 'Happy Christmas', and invariably have traditional Japanese artwork on the front rather than any biblical motif. Many people buy a 'Christmas cake' (usually a thin sponge topped with thick icing), those with children often play Santa Claus, and a few families also buy plastic Christmas trees. Many companies hold Christmas parties, which, because wives may be invited to them, are regarded as more 'democratic' than the traditional end-of-year *bōnenkai* parties which only professional women such as waitresses, *geisha*s and entertainers are allowed to attend (Plath 1974:268).

To some extent the exclusion of more specifically religious elements from the Japanese Christmas might be attributed to the secular attitudes to Christmas among the Western public, with religious vestiges further stripped away upon reaching Japan. However, the importation of so many other facets of Christmas (such as Santa Claus *etc.*) virtually intact suggests that there has been a filtering out of any 'religious' elements and an adoption only of those features which had existing Japanese parallels.

Confirmation of the non-religious nature of the Japanese Christmas comes from the comments of several people who wrote in the margin of my questionnaire 'Christmas is not religious'. This was in response to a question asking if they considered it religiously strange that the same person should participate in (Shinto) New Year shrine visits, (Buddhist) grave rites and Christmas. Out of 662 respondents, only 15% saw these categories as exclusive rather than inclusive of one another. Rather than seeing this as evidence of 'syncretism', however, it seems that a variety of practices may be adopted which are consistent with existent cultural values but are regarded as merely 'customs'. In this sense, the Japanese Christmas is indeed 'non-religious'.

63 Reader (1991a:62-66) has a fuller description of what happens at a shrine during New Year.

64 Several other popular 'customs' are generally regarded as hardly religious even if they might at one time have had religious elements. Examples include the festivals of Chinese origin on the third of the third month (Girls' Festival), fifth of the fifth month (Boys' Festival), seventh of the seventh month (Tanabata) and ninth of the ninth month (Chrysanthemum Festival). With the shift to the Gregorian calendar these are now observed on the 3rd of March, 5th of May *etc.* but the Chrysanthemum Festival has fallen out of use because most chrysanthemums bloom in October rather than September. The Girls' and Boys' Festivals are celebrated by families with daughters or sons respectively and both involve the setting up of a dais on which are placed expensive feminine dolls for the Girls' Festival and *samurai* warrior dolls in armour for the Boys' Festival. Often the maternal grandparents buy the Girls' Festival dolls and paternal grandparents buy them for the Boys' Festival, but there are many exceptions in individual circumstances. Carp streamers (*koi nobori*) are also flown from poles outside the home during the Boys' Festival. Tanabata on the 7th of August is said to derive from a Chinese legend about the weaving girl who on account of 'the bliss of marital relations with the cowherd boy...neglected her task of weaving' so that as a punishment 'she and her lover were separated eternally by the Milky Way and are allowed together only on this one night a year' (Saso 1972:26; Hendry 1986:40-41). In some rural areas tall Tanabata decorations are put up outside houses, but in urban Japan the children make smaller decorations at school by attaching paper streamers to branches of wood which may be put up in the entranceway of the homes for a few days or a week. These may also include a card on which the child writes a kind of prayer or promise to the effect that he or she will 'work hard and be good'.

Most families see these 'customs' as devoid of religious significance, but behaviour strongly resembling religious action is shown by some families who bow down in front of the Girls' or Boys' Festival displays when they first place a kind of 'offering' of special rice cakes wrapped in seasonal leaves on the front row of the dais. they do not regard this as a 'prayer' but more as a kind of 'greeting' (*aisatsu*) or 'custom' and are often unsure why they should continue the practice. There is also a widespread saying that the Girls' Festival display should be taken down within a week after the festival or else the girl will not be married and will be 'left on the shelf' like the dolls. In Japan these 'customs' are not normally regarded as 'religious', whereas in China they coincided with Taoist and other festivals of a more overtly religious nature: the Birthday of Hsüan-t'ien Shang-ti (third of third month), the festival initiating the summer solstice (fifth of fifth month), the Festival of the Seven Young Ladies (seventh of seventh month) and the Birthday of T'ai-tsu Yeh, the 'naughty god child' (ninth of ninth month). Tanabata also coincides with the 'Opening of the gates of hell' when the 'hungry orphan souls with no offspring are thought to wander about, looking for sustenance in the visible world' (Saso 1972:26). This has parallels in the Japanese *segaki* rite around the time of the midsummer *bon* festival (Smith 1974:19-20, 42-43).

65 However, there are relatively few references to Setsubun in descriptions of rural life such as those by Embree (1946), Smith (1956), Beardsley, Hall and Ward (1959), Dore (1978), Smith (1978) or Hendry (1981), so there remains a question about the degree of importance attached to it even in rural areas.

66 Michael Pye (personal communication) tells me that in some areas of Japan the order of the expression is reversed to 'In with good fortune and out with the devil!', but neither of us know of any significance in this variant. Reader (1991a:34-35) describes the Setsubun rite at a Buddhist temple where the cry referring to demons is changed to *oni mo uchi* ('demons also in'), 'representing the Buddhist view that all existence can be transformed and made good'.

67 For a description of the Gion *matsuri*, see Bownas (1963:76-89).

68 Jeremiah 50:39a, referring to Babylon, is translated by the N.I.V. as 'So desert creatures and hyenas will live there...'. The Good News Bible renders this same verse as 'And so Babylon will be haunted by demons and evil spirits...'.

69 This was mentioned at a training course on 'Claiming the Ground' which is periodically run at Ellel Grange and Glyndley Manor, Christian healing centres in England.

70 Otis 1991:87

71 Ruth and I had not been in Japan very long before we visited Mount

Hiei, a mountain to the northeast of Kyoto—guarding the city's 'devil door' (*kimon*)—on the top of which is a famous Buddhist temple. In the past it was one of the strongholds from which 'warrior monks' used to march out to battle. Around the mountain's lower slopes are a number of Shinto shrines. As we walked around through the woods near these shrines we found ourselves bickering about trivial things in a way which was unusual for us. After a while it dawned on us that it might have something to do with the spiritual atmosphere of the place. We sat down and prayed together. Then the bickering stopped and we felt free from the influence of what had been affecting us.

We soon learned to pray for protection when we entered Shinto shrines or Buddhist temples. However, on one occasion when we were walking through Kyoto with our British pastor and his wife, who had come from England to visit us, we decided to go for a picnic under the cherry blossoms in Maruyama Park. To get there, we passed through the entrance to the Yasaka shrine, but we were in the middle of a conversation and I did not want to interrupt it by suggesting we pray together. I can't remember whether or not I prayed quietly by myself, but as we walked I found myself distracted by some of the pretty Japanese girls. Later, when I mentioned this to Ruth, she pointed out that the Yasaka shrine is right next to the *geisha* quarters. (The *geisha* are traditional entertainers who did also supply sexual favours for their special clients.) Later, I read how 'in earlier times, dancing girls, who also provided sexual services, used to be found in temples and shrines' (Hendry 1981:20). Another anthropologist mentions that 'a few decades' before his study *bon* dances 'were the traditional occasions for sexual licence' (Norbeck 1954:161-162). The same was true also of some pilgrimages during the Edo period (Davis 1992:55-56).

On another occasion I attended a *bon* dance in the Shinto shrine nearest to where we were living. Before I went, and while I was there, I prayed for protection for myself but I did not particularly think of praying for protection for Ruth. She was already asleep by the time I got home that night, but after I came to bed she experienced horrible nightmares throughout the whole night.

One New Year's Day Ruth and I went to the local *Nissen* shrine where we could watch from the outside as one family visited it to say their prayers. Later we went to the largest and most prestigious shrine in the city. We prayed for protection as we walked in the outer precincts of the shrine and saw some of the fortune-telling stalls. In particular, we were concerned for the protection of our unborn child, as Ruth was in the early weeks of pregnancy. We prayed particularly for the baby's protection, as well as for ourselves. When we both got as far as a particular doorway into the inner part of the shrine, we both felt that we had come far enough and that it was not right at that time for us to go any further into the shrine. We turned back.

I do believe Christ has the authority and the power to protect us, but also that it is foolhardy to go deliberately into a 'highly-charged' spiritually dangerous place such as that shrine at New Year unless there is a good reason to do so and others are praying too. A few months later I returned to that shrine with a Japanese acquaintance who had arranged for me to meet the shrine's high priest. (Ruth was at home.) The high priest took me into the innermost sanctum of the shrine, to which the public do not normally have access, and showed me the place where the emblem of the *kami* (the *go-shintai*) was kept. Before doing so, however, he told me to sit down on a bench. Suddenly I realized that he was performing a Shinto 'purification' or 'exorcism' ceremony (*harai*) over me. I just prayed silently for protection, and I believe the Lord was indeed protecting me.

These two incidents at the same shrine, a few months apart, illustrate how we need to listen to what God is saying in a particular context. At the 'spiritually charged' time of New Year we felt unable to proceed beyond a certain boundary, especially while Ruth was pregnant, but a few months later I went much further into the shrine and even had a *harai* performed over me. Therefore I prefer to avoid being dogmatic about whether or not Christians should go to such places. (Missionaries have different opinions about whether or not Christians should enter Shinto shrines or Buddhist temples. I have heard of one mission which carried out an open air evangelistic meeting in the grounds of a Shinto shrine, conveying an attitude which other missionaries have felt was not in good taste. Another missionary family told me how they would have preferred their teenage daughter not to have spent the night with some of her friends in a building belonging to a Buddhist temple, but it was there that the young girl ended up sharing with her friends about Christ.) What I do believe, however, is that it is necessary to be sensitive to the Lord's voice in these matters and to pray for his protection.

I recognize also that my experiences could easily be dismissed by a sceptic. Certainly they are anecdotal, and a couple of these accounts could be misconstrued as trying to blame demons for what was simply personal sin. Nevertheless, as such experiences mounted up we realized that we did need to pray seriously against the forces of darkness associated with these places and to claim Christ's protection when I visited such locations in the course of my research. In this context, it may be relevant to note the form of words used by a non-Christian anthropologist in telling us how he had once attended a Nō play at a Shinto shrine, where, as it grew dark, 'you could feel the spirits fall'.

72 For further information on territorial spirits and how to pray against them, see, for example, Wagner (1991), Dawson (1989) and Otis (1991).

73 Otis 1991:95

Chapter 4   Unless the Lord builds the House...

1 Hendry (1981:217) records that some households in Kyushu protect the internal corner of the *kimon* by placing there either the family's Buddhist altar (*butsudan*) or their Shinto god-shelf (*kamidana*).

2 I have heard one missionary refer to the *jichinsai* as a 'ground breaking ceremony', but the literal meaning of the Chinese characters used for the word conveys the idea of 'ground pacifying ceremony'.

3 For a fuller description of this rite in a rural setting, see Hendry 1981:218-9. She also mentions offerings and prayers at the corner where the *kimon* would be, but only one of my informants—a recent migrant from a nearby village—attached importance to this aspect of the ritual.

4 Patrick McElligott, personal communication.

5 Lewis 1986b:178. Such attitudes are related to the idea that one is liable to particular dangers if one becomes 'out of place': they are therefore connected with the concepts of purity and pollution to be described in chapter six.

6 Picken (1980:33) sees the emblems as symbolic of prosperity (or fertility, in their original agricultural context). However, only one of my urban informants, after some thought, offered such an interpretation. He said the emblems are symbols of an 'abundant harvest'.

7 See Richardson 1981. (Pages 14-25 discuss Epimenides and the altar to the unknown god.)

8 In a symbolic sense the rice [of Japan] and the lamb [of the Jews] 'become identical'. Moreover, '...the Jews regarded domestic animals as the basis of life to such an extent that the lamb became a symbol of God and the Saviour of the world. Raising animals was a holy duty, and slaughtering them the work of priests. But the very lack of contact with nomadic traditions bred in the Japanese the idea that four-legged animals were generally impure and that people who slaughtered them were outcasts. It is only to be expected that these disparate approaches manifest themselves in differences of philosophy.' (Ben-Dasan 1972:30, 33-34). [Note that these ideas are actually being presented not by a Jew but by a Japanese author named Yamamoto Shichihei writing under the pen-name of 'Ben-Dasan': I am grateful to David Swain for confirming what had long been suspected about this book.]

9 In stressing the *symbolic* nature of sardine skeletons and other emblems

which point towards a much deeper truth, it is necessary to proceed beyond the symbols to an examination of that truth. If this is not done carefully, there is a danger of enforcing a widespread Japanese attitude that all objects of worship are intrinsically 'the same' in being of only secondary importance. 'There is a very well known proverb in Japan which reads and translates as..."Iwashi no atama mo shinjin kara": "Even a sardine's head may become an object of worship through faith and sincerity". What this proverb means is that the object of faith is of considerably less importance, virtually of no importance at all. What is important to the Japanese is the subjective feelings of the worshipper. Faith and sincerity in the heart of the worshipper can make even a sardine's head worthy of worship! It is therefore not surprising that...most people had no idea at all what the meaning of the sardine was. It would not matter to the average Japanese what the precise religious meaning of almost any object of worship is. Such meaning is of minor importance. The performing of the act, for most people, is the critical factor. The actual efficacy of the act is not in relation to the object worshipped but in direct proportion to the sincerity of the worshipper, and that is a personal affair.' (Patrick McElligott, personal communication).

This widespread Japanese attitude could certainly cause problems in developing 'redemptive analogies' in Japan if one remains merely at the level of symbols. I therefore stress the importance of going beyond the symbols to the deeper truth which they represent. This too is something with which the Japanese are familiar in art, poetry and even in enigmatic Zen Buddhist sayings, which use symbols or word-pictures to depict more abstract concepts. Jesus did the same in his parables and metaphors. Rather than arguing over the symbols themselves, it is necessary to use them simply as channels for communicating more important spiritual truths.

10   See Shillony (1991:134-142) for further details of these kinds of theories. Among those who may be confused or misled about the historical details of the life of Christ there is also a claim that Christ's tomb is located in the village of Shingō (formerly called Herai) in Aomori prefecture, where one local family claims genealogical descent from him (Tebēcis 1982:355-360).

11   For instance, the Israelite laver might correspond to Shinto washing places and there are parallels in terms of the holy place, the use of incense and the presentation of offerings (if rice cakes correspond to shewbread). Noel Gibson (personal communication) mentions that one Shinto shrine has a seven-branched candlestick and quotes Dr. Robert West as claiming that Japan's first god was 'I AM'.

Chapter 5   A Time to be Born...

1 Wagatsuma 1983:247.

2 Ohnuki-Tierney 1984:80

3 See, for example, Hoshino and Takeda (1987) or Bardwell Smith (1988)

4 Ohnuki-Tierney (1984:79)

5 From a medical point of view, according to an English doctor, the sash is unlikely to have any effect on the size of the child unless it were worn so tightly as to be extremely painful, which it is not. Ohnuki-Tierney (1984:184) also mentions 'custom' and 'because it feels good' as further reasons for wearing the sash.

6 Ohnuki-Tierney (1984:182) found that almost all of her sample of 149 women had used a sash, except for a few who had used a corset or girdle instead.

7 She said that if the child were a girl one should go on the 100th day, but there is no known reason for this difference. It appears to be related to ideas of how long ritual pollution after childbirth lasts for each sex of child: see also Bownas (1963:68-69)

8 Of course, such children are born now and again, but there has been a tendency for children with Down's syndrome, for example, to be relatively secluded and kept from public view on account of a certain 'shame' felt by their families.

9 One variant mentioned is that the character inscribed is that normally used for dog (犬), which resembles that for 'big' (大) but with the addition of an extra stroke: the implication is that this is connected with the Day of the Dog, when the *hara-obi* is put on, and is therefore symbolic of the birth having been an easy one. Such an explanation seems unlikely for a rite conducted after birth (rather than beforehand), whereas the widespread use of the character for 'small' on female babies makes more sense when in contrast to 'big' for boys. Moreover, the normal character for dog (犬) is replaced by a more specialized one (戌) for referring to the year of the Dog, although in practice the more usual character (犬) is widely used on greetings cards and prayer plaques (*ema*) commemorating the Year of the Dog.

10 Hendry (1981:201-3) describes *hatsu-miyamairi* in a rural context.

11 Lock 1980:218-9.

12 Ohnuki-Tierney 1984:185-7

13 These percentages, and those in table 5.1, are derived from my questionnaire filled in by 667 people, not all of whom had children. The figures on which table 5.2 are based are as follows:

Overall percentages of children receiving *miyamairi* rites

	First child	Second child	Third child
Mother's natal home	*260*	*168*	*22*
(or nearby hospital)	315	212	27
Father's natal home	*31*	*29*	*10*
(or nearby hospital)	36	31	10
Couple's own home	*145*	*119*	*39*
(or nearby hospital)	179	184	63
Other locations	*28*	*14*	*4*
	37	27	9

14 Norbeck 1952:271-3; Bownas 1963:69
15 Embree 1946:182-3; Hendry 1981:201
16 Bownas 1963:70; Norbeck 1955:118.
17 Ohnuki-Tierney 1984:.28
18 See, for example, Vickery 1986.
19 A congregation of the United Church of Christ in Japan offers a service of 'blessing infants' when they are 100 days old—the traditional time of weaning—and also regularly performs a blessing of the children just before communion services so that the children will 'feel more a part of things' (Boyle 1986:84-85).
20 Boyle 1986:85, footnote 72; see also Warriner 1983:48.
21 Bownas 1963:40, 39-56. Ben-Ari (1991:89-90) describes a more traditional Adults' Day rite, from a village on Mount Hiei near Kyoto.
22 See, for example, Beardsley, Hall and Ward 1959:288-290, 311-312; Norbeck 1953:373-384.
23 Hendry 1989:44; see also Hendry 1986:56.
24 Nakane 1970:26, 59, 129.
25 Cole 1971:76, 78, 84-88; Dore 1973:98*ff.*; Clark 1979:114-119.
26 Dore 1973:24.
27 Dore 1973:46-53, 60-67; Rohlen 1974:63-73, 192-207; Cole 1971:149-150.
28 Compare also Nakane 1970:35-37.
29 Aikawa and Leavenworth 1967:33.
30 Coleman 1984:106.
31 Hugh Trevor, personal communication. He further writes, 'I myself never use *sensei* of missionaries on...scriptural grounds, but use it concerning Japanese pastors, so as not to cause offence'.
32 Commenting on these remarks Dr. Patrick McElligott, an experienced missionary, observed, 'In actual fact, even though I am the pastor of a church here, whenever I meet men of the church in a social context (like a game of ten pin bowling for example), they sometimes drop the '*sensei*' title in favour of the more familiar 'san'...But in public, espe-

cially in the local church, if a church member called the pastor '*san*' it would be considered by all who heard it as a mark of disrespect. It would create a considerable problem—a greater problem than the one created by the use of the word '*sensei*' in the first place. The title '*sensei*' is more an expression of respect than the recognition of a position of authority, although the latter meaning is also included. The 'status' content of the word can be a fellowship barrier but in my opinion not a barrier of the magnitude that necessitates the abandonment of the word in the churches.'

33 Boyle 1986:73-75.

34 *Ibid.*, pp.74-75.

35 Nakane 1970.

36 Befu 1980; Mouer and Sugimoto 1980; Mouer and Sugimoto 1986:99-155. For instance, it is argued that the model applies more to large government bureaucracies or business corporations than to small firms or other small groups. The model also focusses especially on the male-dominated formal structures and ignores the large proportion of the Japanese population who are housewives. Criticism has also been levelled at the *ideology* of 'one great big happy family' which is connected with the 'group model' of Japanese society and has been popularised through stressing concepts such as 'harmony' (*wa*). Real conflict *can* and *does* occur at times in such organisations despite their ideology of 'harmony'.

Chapter 6 Purity and Pollution

1 See, for example, Herbert 1967:76-78; Holtom :1938:29-30; Ohnuki-Tierney 1984:35-39; Blacker 1975:41-42; Lock 1980:25-26.

2 Ohnuki-Tierney 1984:36-37; Aston 1974:294, 302; Philippi 1959:45-49.

3 Namihira 1974:231-9; Fujita 1983:362-3; Hoshino 1983:186; Itō 1983:253-4; Davis 1992:239-240

4 Namihira 1974:239-244

5 Namihira 1976:367

6 Ohnuki-Tierney 1984:30

7 Ohnuki-Tierney 1984:29

8 Lock 1980:89

9 McKean 1981:109-110

10 Hendry 1989:624-633.

11 Hendry (*ibid.*,p.630) sees these customs as further stages in 'unwrapping'.

12 Ohnuki-Tierney 1984:30

13 Wheelwright 1983:116

14 Yanagita 1970:125

15 Hashimoto 1962:22

16 Beardsley, Hall and Ward 1959:454-6, 463.

17 Norbeck 1954:62, 92-3, 120, 134-5, 152

18 Russell 1935:214

19 Herbert 1967:119, 308; Holtom 1938:11, 127; Ono 1962:5, 13, 23; Singer 1973:25.

20 Befu 1974:210

21 See Yanagita 1970:52.

22 Lock 1980:88

23 Norbeck 1954:148, 150

24 Befu 1974:210-211

25 Hendry 1984:215-217; 1986:75

26 David Turton, personal communication. An understanding of this common Japanese attitude had a very useful application in 1983, when my wife, Ruth, and I were allowed to attend a language school specially set up for missionaries in a provincial city of Japan. Half of the teachers at the school were Christians and half were not. Before each class, the students had to fetch the portable tape recorders from a cupboard and afterwards to put them away again. Once, as Ruth was going past that cupboard, she heard an older teacher say to a new one, 'Don't go in there—it's dirty.'

We then realized how unwittingly the missionaries had been offending the Japanese teachers, who had been too polite to say anything about it. Some time previously, there had been a problem when the wires for plugging the tape recorders into the mains electricity sockets had often become tangled up. Then a senior missionary had come up with an apparently logical and simple solution, which was to fold up the wires and keep each one separate by inserting them into the left-over inner tubes of used toilet rolls. Unfortunately, trainee missionaries at the language school had for a long time accepted this practice and not realized that it was offensive to the Japanese. Fortunately, however, this cultural gaff was rectified because we pointed it out to the senior missionary who was the director of the language school.

(This incident also illustrates how junior missionaries can become *socialized* into certain attitudes and ways of behaving which they assume are acceptable and right because they imitate more experienced missionaries.)

27 See also Lock 1980:89-91.

28 See also Ohnuki-Tierney 1984, chapter two.

29 Dore 1978:30-31, 67-8

30 Douglas 1966:35

31 Lock 1980:89

32 Hendry 1981:135; Lock 1980:90-91
33 Hendry 1981:134-5; for further information on the *burakumin* see De Vos and Wagatsuma 1966. Discrimination against *burakumin* was also found among certain Japanese Christians but since 1975 the United Church of Christ in Japan has been trying to eliminate such discrimination (Francis and Nakajima 1991:73).
34 Davis 1980:22, 24, 36*ff*.
35 Lock 1984:126-129
36 Bownas 1963:68
37 Befu 1971:106; Bownas 1963:65-66; Davis 1992:242
38 Oto 1963:47
39 Lock 1980:90
40 Hendry (1981:241) defines *sengachi* as a day when 'a venture started early is likely to succeed' and *sakimake* as a day when 'important ventures should not be left until late'.
41 Hendry (*ibid.*) defines *shakkō* as 'a dangerous day when high noon is the only safe time'.
42 For further discussion of this concept see Douglas 1966.
43 Corwin 1967:152-155

Chapter 7   Illness and 'Calamitous Years'

1 Namihira 1976:357
2 See Ohnuki-Tierney 1984:159-164.
3 Blacker 1975, chapter 6; Norbeck 1954:83, 134-7; Befu 1971:112-3; Namihira 1974:239
4 Blacker 1975; Offner and Van Straelen 1963; Davis 1980:161; Dale 1975:18; McFarland 1967:74
5 Offner and Van Straelen 1963; Dale 1975:119-120, 133, 144-6; Davis 1980
6 Reid 1991:30-31
7 For a discussion of such explanations, see Gardner 1986:23-41, who also provides cases of Christian healings which cannot be 'explained away' so easily.
8 See Lewis 1990:120-122. Some specialists on deliverance ministries say that when a person has received 'healing' from an occult practitioner, it is necessary to cast out both the demon of apparent healing and also the demon which caused the illness before ministering God's healing for the person.
9 Lewis 1986e and 1989. [I did not regard myself as particularly involved in the 'charismatic' movement when I commenced this research but I became increasingly involved as I saw for myself what was happening, analysed 1890 questionnaires, conducted follow-up interviews with a

random sample of 100 people and consulted medical specialists about various cases.]

10 Lewis 1989:215-228.

11 Further details which are omitted in the following summary are included in my article on *yakudoshi* (Lewis 1986b).

12 Lewis 1986b:170. [On pages 170-171 I explain why I challenge a comment by Norbeck (1955:118), who doubts this 'folk' etymology.]

13 The table is reproduced from Lewis 1986b:169.

14 Lewis 1986b:172

15 Kamata 1982:121, 124

16 Lewis 1986b: 175-6

17 *Ibid.*, p.176

18 *Ibid.*, pp.176-177

19 *Ibid.*, pp.172-173 In a nationwide survey in 1981, responses to a question on paying attention to *yakudoshi*s were: 'Yes' 51%, 'No' 48% and 'Other replies' 1% (Asahi Shinbun 1981).

20 Lewis 1986b:174-175

21 *Ibid.*, p.177

22 The term *yakuyoke* can refer to variety of protective charms, not necessarily only those against the effects of a *yakudoshi*.

23 Two women and one man who normally visit shrines at Setsubun said that in their *yakudoshi*s they also bought an extra charm or said an extra prayer also at Setsubun.

24 See Dore 1958:255, 259

25 Lock 1980:204, 245-6

26 See Benedict 1946:22-24

27 Lock 1980:99-100

28 *Ibid.*, p.141

29 The four 'folk cures' which were cited as *kanpō* remedies are: (a) the use of ginseng for slimming, (b) the use of persimmon leaves in a cure for high blood pressure, (c) the use of boiled *dokudani* (Houttuynia cordata) plants during pregnancy, and (d) the use of an extract of plum for abdominal distress. An unspecified cure for hiccoughs might also be included in this list.

30 Both *shinkeishitsu* and *kan no mushi* are what anthropologists call 'culture-bound' illnesses. *Shinkeishitsu* is a nervous complaint whereas *kan no mushi* is a 'disease' which is said to cause children to misbehave. For further details see Lock 1980:95-96, 223, 258.

31 Subritzky 1986:138-139

32 Lock 1980:136

Chapter 8 Fortune-telling

1 His authority for this was at variance with that given in a book on name-divination by Takasugi (1978), according to whom 33 is 'bad' for boys but 'good' for girls. As Murata-san consulted Takasugi's book, perhaps he simply looked at the wrong page and made a mistake.

2 Again, his authority is different from that of Takasugi, who considers 31 to be 'very good' for boys but 'bad' for girls. Unless Murata-san were by mistake looking at the list for boys' names, these conflicting interpretations of numbers show the contradictions between different schools of name-divination. The fact that specialists differ among themselves on 'good' names is confirmed by Haak (1973:208), who mentions 19 as a 'good' number, whereas Takasugi puts it in the 'bad' category.

3 I am here following Takasugi (*op.cit.*)

4 See, for example, Norbeck 1955:107 or Hendry 1981:208. (Hendry mentions the age of 60 as a male *yakudoshi* in the area of Kyushu which she studied, but on page 209 she also refers to the age of 61 as a *yakudoshi*.)

5 Bownas 1963:70

6 *Ibid.*, pp.32-33

7 This table is taken from Lewis 1988:124; other parts of this chapter also reproduce parts of that same article. For further information on different forms of name-divination see Crump 1992:68-73.

8 One appeal of the 'new religion' named Risshō Kōseikai is that it allows married women the liberty to choose a new (more auspicious) name (Crump 1992:73).

9 This woman's Christian background is worth noting. She said, 'I was brought up in an Anglican church school, where I met friends who went to church and Sunday school...Buddhism has lots of idols that are prayed to...which were much criticised and opposed at that time by the school, so I preferred the Christian belief without idol worship, and believed that it could be the true way to follow. But as a Japanese person I was *interested* in all the fortune-telling things too...When I was a student I was incredibly interested in it...and at a shrine did lots of divination by my date of birth (*seinengappi*), and to some extent I think that one comes true...When we got married in a church I spoke with the pastor a couple of times about the wedding arrangements, but nowadays I don't go to church. Our eldest child was ill at the time when he was due to have his *miyamairi*, so we had him baptised at 'Nishiyama' Protestant church, where I was baptised, as we hadn't done any other celebration for him, but we did do the 7-5-3 ceremony for him.'

10 *Nihon Minzoku Jiten* 1971:259

11 According to Miyata (1990:246-7), interest in *Kokkuri-san* is particularly prevalent among younger women.

12 A missionary told me of a man living near him in Kyoto who every morning used to howl out of his window like a fox. The missionary wondered whether this man were possessed by *Inari*.

13 See Lewis 1986c:126-127 for further statistics on how younger people are more likely to consult either palmistry or astrology, and are more likely to express a belief that the position of the stars at birth can indicate one's personality.

14 For further details see Picone 1986 or Crump 1992:80-89.

15 Ueda (1974:188) notes, 'In some cases people 'lie' in such a way that their replies are recognized by the listener as lies. For example, when a *nakōdo* ('go-between') has to decline an *omiai* ('marriage meeting') reasons will often be given which have nothing to do with the parties involved personally—in order to spare the other's feelings. For example, the *nakōdo* may say that the prospective couple should not be married because of an *uranaishi* (a fortune-teller sometimes consulted when drafting plans for a new house) who said that the houses of the two families were not properly oriented to each other.'

16 Dore 1958:447, note 150; Hendry 1981:242; Crump 1992:85; Haak 1973:110

17 Nakahara and Fuke 1985:11. Fuller details about the popular interest in 'blood group divination' are provided by Yamaguchi (1985).

18 Those who had consulted a *mikuji* at some time in their lives accounted for 89% of my sample and 76% of a nationwide one (Asahi Shinbun 1981).

19 Crump (1992:77) notes that there can be six categories whereby the 'good' and 'bad' types can be further subdivided into great, medium and minor categories, but the frequencies adjusted so that the auspicious types are more common than the inauspicious ones.

20 See also Joya 1958:597-598; Crump 1992:77-80.

21 Eisei Kurimoto, personal communication. Patrick McElligott (personal communication) reports a man interviewed on national television who had devised a method of fortune-telling from the shape and texture of women's breasts: he apparently also had customers for his services.

22 See Lewis 1986c:126-130 for statistics which indicate this.

23 Patrick McElligott (personal communication). He notes that another weakness in this tendency may arise if a counsellee feels threatened through thinking that the pastor knows too much about intimate personal details. By contrast, the anonymity of a fortune-teller is less threatening.

24 Lewis 1990:144

Chapter 9   The Cult of the Dead

1 There has been some debate among Christians about what is variously
  referred to by terms such as 'healing of the memories' or 'inner healing'.
  Although some 'inner healing' practices might be questionable, it is
  clear that God does also bring definite healing to certain people through
  the healing of painful memories. I have discussed these issues in greater
  depth elsewhere (Lewis 1989:69-116; Lewis 1990:133-141).

2 Smith 1974:91.

3 Hashimoto 1962:19-20; Smith 1974:101-103.

4 See also Smith 1974:95. Reader (1991a:91, 252) notes that in the Sōtō
  sect of Buddhism about 24% of the temples cease performing memorial
  services before the 33rd anniversary of death, 26% cease after 33 years,
  37% after 50 years, 9% after 100 years and almost 4% continue beyond
  100 years.

5 Compare Smith 1974:106-113.

6 T.C. Smith 1959:45-6; Nakane 1967:6-9; Fukutake 1967:42; Beardsley,
  Hall and Ward 1959:236-240.

7 A recent discussion of this issue is that by Berentsen (1985a:27-28), who
  remarks that to translate the Japanese term *suhai suru* as 'venerate'
  rather than 'worship' in order to tone down the religious implications in
  the English word 'worship' would 'not do justice to its inherent meaning...The word *suhai* implies a recognition of supernatural power on
  the part of the object of "worship", a recognition that the object of
  suhai is superior to man and is in a position to control the life of the
  "worshipper".'

8 See Smith 1974:75-78; Mogami 1963

9 Nakamaki 1983:72-74

10 Compare Smith 1974:91. (My list differs from his on a few items.)

11 Dore 1958:313.

12 The technical terms for these are *tōkasai*, *gojūnichisai* and *ichinensai*
   respectively.

13 This is a more literal translation of a common expression, *mubyō
   sokusai*, which has the connotations of 'a perfect state of health' (Kenkyusha's dictionary 1954:1146).

14 This might not only be to show the ancestors, but might also be a
   reflection of the traditional custom of keeping important documents in
   the drawer underneath the *butsudan*.

15 Hashimoto 1962:10; Smith 1974:65-67.

16 See, for example, Ooms 1976:71-73; Namihira 1976:358; Hendry
   1987:131-133; Crump 1992:104-106. Boyle (1986:22, note 19) states that
   the Jōdōshinshu sect of Buddhism calculates the *nenki* by the traditional

system of counting which is the same as that generally used for reckoning *yakudoshi*s.

17 Plath 1964:303

18 To some extent, Christianity has also been absorbed into this overall religious framework through the occasional choice of Christian weddings as a more 'Western' alternative to Shinto ones.

19 Berentsen 1985a:227-228.

20 Kobatake 1982:654, cited by Boyle 1986:32

Chapter 10   Memorialism

1 Literally, 'a post-death world' (*shigo no sekai*).

2 See Blacker 1975:83, 159.

3 See, for example, Dore 1958:325-328; Ooms 1967:292ff. and Smith 1974:215-6.

4 The Protestant mentioned faith without qualification. One Roman Catholic said 'faith and one's own conduct', while the other gave the opinion that 'faith' could be in any god, not only the Christian one.

5 Dore 1958:322.

6 In the same way, neighbours are often said to be 'always watching' one's social conduct: this in turn affects people's attitudes and behaviour towards neighbourhood relationships. See Benedict 1946:151, 173, 222-4, 272; Kasahara 1974:402

7 This is the younger Mr. Suehara, whose family *zushi* is here counted as a *butsudan*.

8 '*Ryōshin o omoidasu yosuga to suru tame ni Butsuzen de oinori shimasu.*'

9 Smith (1974:56) depicts the stages in the regular progression of the souls of the dead as being: *shirei* (spirits of the newly dead), *nii-botoke* (new buddhas), *hotoke* (buddhas), *senzo* (ancestors) and *kami* (gods). My informants in Ueno, however, would tend to place *senzo* (ancestors) nearer than the Buddhas (*hotoke*) and some would not particularly distinguish between *hotoke* and *kami*. Their conceptualization is more like: *shirei, nii-botoke, senzo* or *hotoke*, then Buddhas or *kami*. The terms are relatively blurred in Japanese partly because the term *hotoke* refers both to ancestors and to Buddhas.

10 Spae 1971:76

11 Graburn 1983:63

12 Spae 1971:76

13 Reader (1991a:189) notes how gifts of *mamori* may be given as tokens of friendship to relatives or friends, including those leaving for another country.

14 Yamamori 1974:80-81. This problem dates back at least as far as the

beginning of the twentieth century, as shown by Yamamori's quotation from a Christian missionary of that period, who wrote:

'Influenced by a not unnatural sentimentality, many are loth to remove their membership from the place of their spiritual birth; and under the present non-cooperative arrangement, the pastor or missionary hesitates to urge them to leave their own churches and seek membership in another denomination. For a time they are kept in touch with the pastor or missionary by letter, but sooner or later communication ceases; and their whereabouts becoming unknown, the record is marked "dropped".' (Yamamori 1974:80, quoting from *The Christian Movement in Japan* (1903), p.63.)

15 Yamamori 1974:80

16 Noel Gibson, personal communication

17 Benedict 1946:274

18 Janeira 1970:75

19 See also Kimura 1983.

20 Keene 1971:31ff.; Janeira 1970:75, 81-3; Kimura 1983; Ueda 1983); Yuasa 1983

21 Nakamura 1969:11, 66-8, 130-131

22 Lebra 1976:124

23 Ben-Ari (1991) provides a more detailed analysis of the place of photography in modern Japanese life, and how it relates to wider themes of 'nostalgia'.

24 I am grateful to Dr. Patrick McElligott for these insights.

25 See also Graburn 1983:49-50.

26 Berentsen (1985a:208) remarks that 'it is no liturgical coincidence...that in the old Church the practice very soon developed of celebrating the Eucharist as part of the funeral. Nor is it surprising that when the intercessory prayer for the dead developed in a liturgical setting, it developed exactly as part of the Eucharist liturgy.'

27 See also Ohnuki-Tierney 1984:25, 37.

28 Boyle 1986:18

29 Berentsen 1985a:170; Boyle 1986:18-19. [Berentsen refers to the final farewell as the *kokubetsushiki*, but Boyle uses this term as equivalent to the main funeral service itself. Boyle states that a flower is given to each mourner who comes forward to 'pay their last respects' and that this flower is then placed 'on a tray, on top of the casket or in the casket as the situation calls for. This is called the *kenka* and takes place just before the doxology or benediction'. He also comments that there is 'nothing inherently wrong' in the use of incense, in so far as it has had a long usage in Judaism and Catholicism—and, I would add, in

Orthodoxy too—but in Japan it is better avoided on account of its Buddhist connotations of consoling the spirits of the dead.

30 Berentsen 1985a:170-171

31 See also McGavran 1985:303, 312-313

32 Boyle (1986:20) notes that at this time there may be a brief Christian ceremony called the *shukkanshiki*, but this is rarely observed.

33 *Ibid.*, p.20. This rite is called the *kasōzenshiki*.

34 I am grateful to Dr. Patrick McElligott for bringing to my attention the importance of this *shukkotsu* ritual. He further comments, 'It is not difficult to imagine how such a practice reinforces the concept of "memorial" in the hearts of the Japanese'.

Other descriptions of funerals available elsewhere include those by Reid (1991:103-4) and Berentsen (1985a:32-34).

35 Boyle 1986:20

36 Dore 1958:317, 435. I was told that this 'lifting of pollution' on the forty-ninth day is referred to as *ki-age*, but Smith (1974:51, 95) calls it *imi-ake*, an alternative rendering of the same written characters.

37 Boyle 1986:21

38 *Ibid.*, pp.24-25

39 Reid 1991:114-115. He also remarks (p.114) that 'in all probability' these Protestants also 'address themselves...not in prayer but in speech, uttered or unuttered' to the person represented by the photograph.

40 Berentsen 1985a:145-6, 167, 203

41 *Ibid.*, pp.203-204. He also notes, however, that 'Luther did not object to private prayer for the departed, and some Lutheran funeral liturgies have developed a more specific prayer for the dead' (p.204). Rose (1980:197-200) presents an Orthodox perspective on this issue.

42 See Rose 1980:57-58; Grey 1985:30-72; Ring 1980:67-68, 190; Hay 1987:173-174; Lewis 1990:112-120.

43 A number of Orthodox and Catholic churches, and some Protestant ones, do practise prayers *for* the dead, rather than *to* the dead. This might be an important distinction, although some Protestants would deny the need for either kind of prayer. McAll (1982) describes how prayer for certain deceased ancestors can produce apparently beneficial results (such as healings) among those who practise Eucharists for their deceased relatives. Among many Protestants this is a controversial practice which seems to be too similar to Oriental ancestral rites—or the experience of Yoshioka-san, who was told in a dream that his prayers had released the spirits of some wartime soldiers who had died on Guam. Whatever one's position on this issue, it is clear that the effects of such prayers seem to be similar to those which come from conventional exorcisms. However, it is also similar to the spirit

appeasement practices of several Japanese new religions, in which the spirits are often placated by prayers and offerings so that they become 'dormant'—no longer manifesting through illness *etc.*—but are not cast out.

44 Berentsen 1985a:210

45 Reid 1991:117-118

46 Boyle 1986:14-15. Berentsen (1985a:212) remarks that this kind of 'Christian reinterpretation of the quest for continuity and community' seems to be 'meaningful far beyond the Japanese context'. He suggests that 'many churches in the West have a lot to learn from this way in which Japanese churches, through repeated commemorative gatherings, cope with the pastoral problem of grief and mourning' and 'are witnessing to the significance and hope' of the communion of saints.

47 Berentsen (1985a:161) notes that the commandment to honour one's father and mother needs to be understood in the context of the commandment to serve the one God alone (Exodus 20:3).

48 McGavran 1985:312-316. Boyle (1986:12) cites Marwin (1976), who advocates a similar kind of approach in addressing the situation of a Christian son or daughter in a traditional home which values the ancestral rites for their strengthening of family ties. In such a situation the Christian might make deliberate use of the existing *kamidana* and *butsudan* by there offering in an audible voice prayers of thanks to the 'Creator God of the Universe' for the ancestors and all that the family now possesses because of the diligent work of the ancestors. The Christian could also pray in the name of Jesus for the entire family and for the special needs of family members. The same could be done at the grave sites which the Christian would help to maintain. However, Boyle comments on this approach that 'if Japan were a new mission field with no long history of conflict with ancestor worship... such an approach would work very well. The problem, however, is that one isn't working in a historical vacuum, and thus such an approach would likely be interpreted as too compromising by many Christians with a "vested interest" in confrontation with ancestor worship. There is also the risk of misunderstandings by those outside the Christian faith as well. Thus, there would certainly be an element of risk involved, and this approach... would not be appropriate in all situations... but judging from some other experiences relating to Christian encounter with ancestor worship, such an approach has good possibilities provided it be done with tact and prayerful forethought'.

49 Dore 1958:94; Davis 1992:21

50 In post-war Japan people no longer acknowledge such indebtedness to the Emperor (Dore 1958:223), but this has not affected the much more

deeply-rooted, essential concepts of discharging one's obligations towards those from whom one is indebted or has received favours.

51 Otis 1991:88 He further observes that, by contrast, 'Satan is in general control over human *systems* (*kosmos*—kingdoms and structures)', which is 'achieved through the *volition of men*'. In this we can see the ways in which human manipulation of the Emperor cult sought to replace the rightful fatherhood of God over the Japanese nation.

52 However, Christians believe that the prophecy in Isaiah 9:6, referring to an 'Everlasting Father'—which in a Jewish cultural context we might render as 'Everlasting Patriarch'—was fulfilled in Jesus. He said about himself that 'Before Abraham was born, I am' (John 8:58). In this sense, we might say that Jesus is the true patriarch to whom the Christian should render all honour and glory. A different imagery is used in Hebrews 2:10-18, which depicts Jesus as our brother and states that 'both the one who makes men holy and those who are made holy are of the same family' (v.11).

Chapter 11   A Sin *and* Shame Society

1 Corwin 1967:152-153; Boyle 1986:38. To some extent, depending on the context, there can also be a similar ambiguity in the words *tsumiishiki* ('a consciousness of *tsumi*') and *yūzaikan* ('a feeling of having *tsumi*'), both of which have been used to translate 'guilt'.

2 Spae 1971:74

3 Kasahara 1974:402; Benedict 1946:221-222

4 Ministry to such situations will often involve deliverance from spirits of suicide and death.

5 In such situations Christians need to be prepared for ministries of exorcism.

6 Benedict 1946:222-224, 286-289

7 Stoetzel 1955:16-17, 185. 193

8 To some extent Benedict's informants might have told her what she wanted to hear—a problem common to many anthropologists! This kind of bias might be less pronounced in my questionnaires because they were filled in when most informants had no personal acquaintance with me or knowledge about my views.

9 At the risk of over-simplification, 'sin' might be described as a special case of guilt, involving a belief that one's guilt is known to an omniscient deity.

10 De Vos 1974:121-122, 136. Sometimes a mother may try to induce feelings of guilt in a child by acting out the pain and suffering which the child has caused her—an attitude of 'Look what you've done to me'.

Sometimes a child whose parent has died may carry feelings of guilt if the child regards the death as punishment for his or her own behaviour.

11 Hendry 1981:24, 121-122; Goode 1963:329; Dore 1958:107-108

12 Sofue 1983:19-20

13 To some extent, this may be attributable to unmarried people who thought the question did not apply to them. A few women might even have considered that this question only applies to men, as the Chinese character used in the word for 'adultery' depicts 'three women'.

14 Buruma 1984:104.

15 Buruma 1984:111-112. These coffee-shops became more popular in the early 1980s.

16 Lent 1989:234. (Such pornography may also give access to spirits of lust.)

17 However, men and women gave conspicuously different answers to certain items. Women tended to have a more negative view of abortion, adultery, premarital sex, pornography, drunkenness, gambling and 'no-pantie coffee houses'. Divorce, however, did not fit this pattern: almost half of both men and women evaluated it as 'neither good nor bad', but of the other half slightly more men than women viewed it as 'bad'. (The difference is not very great: 36.6% of the men versus 29.9% of the women.) This tendency probably reflects the gradual increase in opportunities for women to enter various parts of the labour market both before and after marriage, although they still suffer from discrimination in salaries and promotion prospects. Younger and more educated women tend to give views about divorce in the 'Neither' or 'Don't Know' categories.

There is little difference between the sexes in attitudes towards bribery, but those who consider it to be 'Good' are mainly aged between 26 and 44: they are people who are more likely to gain favours from superiors through the giving of substantial seasonal gifts.

18 Boyle 1986:33-53

19 *Ibid.*, p.40

20 *Ibid.*, pp.42-45

21 *Ibid.*, pp.47-51

22 *Ibid.*, pp.52-53

23 Offner 1982:32, 42-43

24 MacLeod (1982:17) and Sytsma (1982:47) are also aware of these issues.

25 Already he had been under some pressure from relatives to join the Sōka Gakkai. Although this incident might have precipitated his decision to join them, it is possible that the account has been embellished somewhat for the sake of Sōka Gakkai's propaganda.

26 At a 'folk' level several other elements of monotheism have also been present in Japan (Dore 1958:355, 459, note 287).

Chapter 12   Aspects of Church Growth

1 Although Nestorian Christianity spread as far as northern China, there is no evidence that it reached Japan. Before 1549 Portuguese traders might also have communicated some scraps of information about Christianity.

2 Agency for Cultural Affairs 1972:76

3 Muller 1967: 10-11

4 Elison 1988:14, 34

5 *Ibid.*, p.25

6 Aikawa and Leavenworth 1967:63

7 *Ibid.*

8 The fact that some Japanese Christians were willing to die for their faith may have far-reaching spiritual consequences. Otis (1991:157-158) records how one night in 1983 the entire population of an Algerian village received dreams, visions and angelic visitations telling them about Jesus. In retrospect, it seems significant that this village was located very close to the place where Raymond Lull, a Spanish missionary to the Muslims, had been martyred in 1315. Otis stresses the importance of intercessory prayer over the years in triggering this divine visitation. I suggest that something similar could happen in southern Japan too if more Christians seriously pray.

9 Boyle 1986:86, citing Ehara 1978:1-3. Boyle notes that although he had not yet had an opportunity to try to develop a Christian tea ceremony, many who had never previously realized these connections appreciated this interpretation of the meanings of the tea ceremony.

10 A convenient pretext was provided by the Shimabara rebellion of October 1637, after which many Christians in the area were massacred.

11 See, for example, Huddle (1958), Laures (1954), Tucker (1938), Cary (1909), Van Hecken (1963) or, more generally, Iglehart (1959).

12 Yamamori 1974. Although Yamamori's study is limited to Protestant denominations, I believe that many of his findings (perhaps with appropriate modifications) would apply also to Catholic and Orthodox churches in Japan.

13 Yamamori 1974:31-32, 135. (Although Yamamori's study stops in 1939, many of these trends are still evident today.)

14 Howes 1965:337-8

15 Lee 1967:161-163; Yamamori 1974:32-36. There was a brief period of rural responsiveness from about 1877 to 1887, but those who did become Christians in rural areas were mainly literate, self-employed (middle

class) farmers who were among the rural élite and were more open to new ideas (Yamamori 1974:36-38). Where the church did manage to spread in rural areas, it tended to be confined to the more educated rural élite, including ex-*samurai*, and to spread largely through links of kinship and friendship (Morioka 1975:120-123).

16 Aikawa and Leavenworth 1967:67
17 Agency for Cultural Affairs 1972:75
18 Yamamori 1974:55, 57, 61, 78, 79, 94, 101-4, 135, 137, citing Pieters 1912:120, Fisher 1922:204 and Jaeckel 1955:195. (Compare also Lee 1967:105.) For instance, the following figures, taken from Jaeckel's study, show the disproportionate number of white-collar workers among the Japanese Christians, as compared with the general population of Japan at that time:

	Proportion of General Population	Proportion of Christians
Farmers	50%	2%
Labourers	27%	3%
Fishermen	3%	0.05%
Middle class/intelligentsia	20%	94.05%

Since 1953 the proportion of farmers has considerably declined, while the middle classes have grown, but Christian church members still account for no more than about 1% of the overall population.

19 Figures cited by Yamamori 1974:108
20 *Ibid.*, p.57
21 Lee 1967:24-25
22 Yamamori 1974:79
23 Aikawa and Leavenworth 1967:69
24 Iglehart 1932:75, cited by Yamamori (1974:120).

In 1932 the report of the Laymen's Foreign Mission Inquiry observed,

'... Very many of the churches... in the Orient are strikingly conservative in thought. They were formed at a time when a precise and definite theological system of doctrine was generally stressed as vitally important, and this theological emphasis has remained up to the present time a dominant feature of these conservative churches. This excessive occupation with theological doctrine has kept such churches out of touch with trends of thought and intellectual problems in the world around them. Churches of this sort appeal only to a certain type of mind. Students in the main leave them coldly alone and are apt to be turned against Christianity if this is the only kind of Christianity which they know. It seems to them too often a complicated religion of words and phrases, dealing with the issues of a former age, not a living force for the moral transformation of the world and for the remaking of the present social order. There is, too, a pietistic tone in the Christianity of many of the churches, with a tendency to hem life about with legalistic rules and regulations, many of them negative in character.' (p.86)

25 Yamamori 1974:56-7

26 *Ibid.*, pp.123-125

27 *Ibid.*, p.125. Lee (1967:74) reports a similar pattern.

28 *Ibid.*, pp.56, 94-5, 127. Openings for female leadership in the church may have been produced as a positive side-effect of this sex ratio. The Laymen's Foreign Mission Inquiry (1932:275-276) commented that:

'In many churches in the Orient women have equal voting rights, hold the position of elders and deacons, assist at Communion and serve as ushers. In Japan there are two licensed women preachers in the Presbyterian Church, one of whom is taking examinations for ordination. Women in the Orient are members of provincial and national Christian councils and may act as church delegates in most of the churches. In their official status women have received more complete equality in many churches in Asia than has been accorded to women in churches in the West.'

29 Bunce 1955:158

30 Yamamori 1974:56

31 *Ibid.*, pp.127-8. Differences in the growth rates of various denominations may also have been influenced by the extent to which church administration was transferred to a national leadership. By 1888 the faster-growing churches (Presbyterian, Congregational and Methodist) had, respectively, forty-three, twenty-seven and twenty-two ordained national leaders, whereas the slower-growing Episcopal and Baptist churches, after about thirty years' work in Japan, had only half a dozen ordained Japanese ministers (Yamamori 1974:50, 54-55)

32 Laymen's Foreign Mission Inquiry 1932:89, 90.

Unfortunately even today there is still in some churches a tendency for many hymns to be difficult to understand because of their use of many old-fashioned words. For instance, one Sunday my wife and I asked a non-Christian Japanese lady (who was regularly coming to church with us) about the meaning of a refrain at the end of each verse of one of the hymns which we sang on a number of occasions. The refrain was '...*nare-o ba, nare-o ba*'. Her reply was, 'I haven't the faintest idea.'

Shocked by this realization that our Japanese friend could not understand what we were singing about in church, we asked a Japanese

Bible college student what '*nare-o ba*' meant at the end of each verse in that hymn. He replied, 'I *think* it means this, but I'm not totally sure.'

We then asked a missionary who was not only fluent in modern Japanese but had also studied Classical Japanese in depth. He immediately told us what the expression meant. (It is taken from Classical Japanese but although it is taught at sixth form level in most high schools, a great many people would no longer remember it. To some extent it was used to fill out the music and to enhance the 'poetic feeling' of the hymn. Although most of the hymn can be understood without knowing this expression, it is nevertheless not understood by most Japanese and therefore does obscure the meaning of the whole hymn to some extent.)

This hymn book which contains the '*nare-o ba*' hymn is one of two hymn books widely used by Protestant churches throughout Japan. Both of them contain many hymns which are translations from English or German but retain the same Western tunes. However, sometimes the vocabulary or expressions employed can be so obscure or incomprehensible to most ordinary Japanese people that the meanings of the hymns are lost on them, as we discovered when we decided to invite some of our Japanese friends to a Christmas celebration in our home. In a Christian bookshop we found some books of Christmas carols, translations of English ones. 'At least we know what these mean', we thought. However, when we tried to teach them to our Japanese friends we discovered that they found the words virtually incomprehensible. Not only had the translations tried to fit into the English tunes by using some unusual words, but the meanings were made even more obscure because the hymns were not written in Chinese characters but in the Japanese 'syllabic alphabet' (*hiragana*).

33 Yamamori 1974:49, 55, 57

34 *Ibid.*, pp.74-5, 78-82

35 This pattern also tends to be perpetuated today in many churches, to such an extent that in 1992 some Japanese Christians visiting our church in England commented in surprise that in England whole *families* go to church together.

36 Yamamori 1974:79, 98-99, 125-6, 128

37 *Ibid.*, p. 126

38 *Ibid.*, pp.98-99.

39 *Ibid.*, pp.72-82

40 *Ibid.*, p.114

41 *Ibid.*, p.118

42 Marwin 1983:191, 282. In the same tables Marwin provides comparative data from other denominations, as follows:

Denomination	Membership increase		Percentage increase	
	1917-1923	1924-1930	1917-1923	1924-1930
Presbyterian	6,755	8,656	21.4%	22.6%
Methodist	7,050	13,180	45.6%	58.5%
Congregational	c.2,532	c.6,567	11.5%	26.7%
Episcopal	1,375	3,668	7.7%	32.0%
OMS Holiness Church	1,375	7,967	97.7%	286.3%
American Baptist	633	623	17.3%	14.5%
Southern Baptist	787	913	84.6%	53.2%
Disciples of Christ	627	596	62.7%	36.6%
Seventh Day Adventist	c.82	c.365	27.9%	97.0%

43 Yamamori 1974:128-133

44 Marwin 1983:289. It is not clear whether or not Russians or other non-Japanese ethnic groups are included in the membership figures cited, or to what extent the figures are influenced by the inclusion of such groups. Compared with the Japanese, Russians might be expected to be more 'responsive' to Christianity because of their at least nominally Orthodox background (despite the atheistic influence of Communism).

45 Tsurumi 1970:183-189

46 Miura 1970:14-15

47 Frank Buchman, founder of the 'Moral Re-Armament' Movement, arranged for seventy-six key Japanese leaders (politicians, industrialists, bankers and labour union leaders) to attend meetings in Caux where they were profoundly influenced by what they saw and heard. Some of them renounced their previous enmities with each other and many of them resolved to build Japan on a new basis. The mayor of Hiroshima, for instance, in announcing his intention to re-establish his city as a 'pattern for peace', quoted Buchman as saying 'Peace is people becoming different' (Lean 1985:388-390).

48 See Koyama (1984:3-56) for a detailed discussion of the way in which the idolatry centred around the imperial cult led to the destruction of Japan. A few quotations may illustrate his general theme:

'The subject of this book is...idolatry...Was the fate of Japan in some way related to the violent growth of the emperor worship?' (p.3)

'The Glory of the Emperor that Reaches to the Four Corners of the World...was the essence of the national ideology...All other spiritual and physical forces were devoured by the imperial force so that it could grow unchallenged. It was a pagan "theology of glory".' (p.17)

'This parochial god who never criticised his own people was attractive. But it proved to be most destructive to the people of Japan. And Tokyo became wilderness...' (p.24)

'The spirits of the imperial ancestors were unable to protect the nation and the nation was destroyed. For the first time, in a serious manner, the Japanese people's faith in their own tribal gods was shaken...' (pp.33-34)

'...I cannot say that it was by the American military might alone that Japan was destroyed. At the same time if Americans were to claim that the United States had acted on behalf of God to execute justice upon earth by destroying Japan, I would feel the name of God had been taken in vain. Japan destroyed herself primarily by her own idolatry. This...is congruent with the spirit of the words of Jeremiah: "before the fierce anger of the Lord".' (p.56)

49 Stoetzel (1955) analyses the psychological and attitudinal differences between the Japanese youth in 1951-1952 and older generations.

50 Dore (1958:309) confirms that the defeat led to a decrease in visits to shrines, in the number of *kamidana* in private homes and in the frequency of rites at them. He also records how at the end of the war one man tore his *kamidana* from the wall and stamped on it. Though Shinto wedding ceremonies are now the norm, those living in rural areas have sometimes had simple wedding ceremonies at home which they describe as 'non-religious'. Nowadays Christian weddings have again become more 'fashionable'—partly for economic reasons—and may account for 15% to 20% of weddings in large cities like Tokyo and Osaka (Mullins 1990c:51).

51 Aikawa and Leavenworth 1967:94; compare Lee 1967:86-87.

52 Mullins 1990c:47

53 Lee 1967:48; Burton-Lewis 1990:22

54 Ogata 1990b:23; Mitsumori 1992:10

55 Mullins 1990b:11. However, he also notes that 'while there are a number of socio-historical studies of church growth in Japan prior to the second world war, similar comparative studies of contemporary Japanese Christianity are few indeed'.

56 Ogata 1990a:37, citing *Japan Update*, Vol.3, No.1, April 1989

57 Mullins 1992:155-156, 160, 161

58 Ogata 1990a:34, citing an unpublished paper by Hugh Trevor entitled *Church Growth and O.M.F. in Japan.*

59 Caldarola 1979:40-47, 50-53

60 *Ibid.*, p.68

61 *Ibid.*, pp.115-116

62 Saeki 1967:95-96

63 Koyama 1982:97, 107

64 Caldarola 1979:192, 198, 206
65 *Ibid.*, pp.199-202
66 *Ibid.*, pp.198, 208
67 Mullins 1990a:355
68 *Ibid.*, pp.356-357
69 Burton-Lewis 1990:21
70 Mullins 1990a:361
71 *Ibid.*, pp.358-359. Mullins regards the high status of the pastors as 'significantly related to the growth of the movement'.
72 For a detailed discussion of different understandings of this verse, see Berentsen 1985a:193-6. Another interpretation of 1 Corinthians 15:29, not mentioned by Berentsen, is suggested by Leith Samuel (personal communication), who writes, 'This verse always puzzled me until one Sunday evening when I was baptising a post-graduate student...The gist of his testimony was: 'I am here because my mother died recently. She lived the Christian life consistently before my eyes. She prayed earnestly for my conversion. I only turned to Christ after her death. I am here to declare publicly that I wish *to take her place* in Christ's church militant here on earth.'

'Baptised for the dead'? I checked to see if the Greek preposition *'uper* would stand being translated as 'to take the place of', and found I was far from pushing it! It makes very good sense to me in the context.'
73 Mullins 1990a; Berentsen 1985a:193.
74 For instance, established churches regard the *Iesu no Mitama kyōkai* as heretical because of its heterodox views on the trinity (Mullins 1991:60), and many would question its interpretation—or at least application—of 1 Corinthians 15:29. Caldarola's account of *Makuya* ascetic practices, particularly their fire-walking rite at a large gathering in Tokyo, immediately reminded me of descriptions of such ceremonies in a Shinto context (Lowell 1894:47-57; Blacker 1975:251). Various theories have tried to account for fire-walking and other ascetic practices, such as a physiological explanation in terms of the brain's releasing into the blood stream a hormone called endorphin which acts like morphine in reducing the transmission of pain signals to the brain. However, more extreme displays of lack of sensitivity to heat or pain usually occur in the context of demonic 'possession'. Most Christians are highly suspicious of fire-walking and many would regard it as an activity which opens the person to demonic influence.

On further reflection, however, I began to wonder whether this rather bizarre *Makuya* ritual might be about as justifiable biblically as the handling of snakes in some American churches. Both are regarded by most Christians as extreme, but also tolerable in the sense that the practice might be supported on a questionable scriptural basis. The interpretation of Mark 16:18, which led to the emergence of so-called 'snake-handling cults' in the USA, might be supported by the way in which God protected Paul from a snake-bite on Malta (Acts 28:3-6)— although Paul did not deliberately put himself at risk in the way that some contemporary Christians have done. Similarly, there is the biblical case in which God protected Shadrach, Meshach and Abednego when they were thrown into the blazing furnace (Daniel chapter 3), which can be tied in with the promise in Isaiah 43:2 that 'when you walk through the fire, you will not be burned; the flames will not set you ablaze'. Many Christians would prefer to interpret this verse metaphorically rather than literally, although there was indeed a literal example of it in the case of Shadrach, Meshach and Abednego. The previous lines in Isaiah 43 refer to similar promises when the people pass through 'the waters' and 'rivers', and for these too there were literal examples at the time of the Exodus and at the crossing of the Jordan river (Joshua chapter 3). In a similar manner, some Christian churches practise communal foot-washing, in accordance with John 13:14, whereas others regard this verse as a more general call to servanthood rather than an instruction to be taken literally. Although most Christians would not regard Mark 16:18 or Isaiah 43:2 as justifications for the practices of the American snake-handling churches or *Makuya* fire-walking, they would nevertheless recognize that those who do interpret these verses in such a literal way are sincere Christians who love Jesus.

75 *e.g.* Boyle 1986:68-70 ; Aikawa and Leavenworth 1967:70; McGavran 1985:303
76 Boyle 1986:72-3, 76.
77 *Ibid.*, pp.77-78.
78 Gill 1990:13-15
79 Burton-Lewis 1990:23

Chapter 13   Characteristics of Contemporary Christianity

1 Colligan 1980:80-81, 84-85; Agency for Cultural Affairs 1972:257-261; Hendry 1987:114.
2 Basabe 1968:53; *cf.* Stoetzel 1955:191
3 The Agency for Cultural Affairs (1972:76) describes these as 'latent believers', and includes among them those who had gone to church in their youth, and perhaps been baptized, but are no longer currently active. Another survey showed that 7% of respondents in the Kyoto-Osaka region, and 13% in Kyushu, had been to a Christian mission school, where 96% of them had attended at least one lecture on religion

and 69% had attended a religious ceremony or event. However, many respondents had stopped going to church when they graduated from their Christian schools (Colligan 1980:66-69, 82). An NHK survey in 1981 showed that as many as 12% of the Japanese population were sympathetic to Christianity (Kabira 1983:53, 55-56; Mullins 1990c:48.)

4 Further details on the *Nihon Kirisuto Kyōdan* are given by Huddle (1958:196-202) and The Agency for Cultural Affairs (1972:81, 218).

5 Reid 1989:264, 269; 1991:125, 132

6 Morioka 1975:130-131; Berentsen 1985a:139-141

7 Boyle 1986:8-9

8 Reid 1991:109-115; Berentsen 1985a:139

9 Cooper 1983:309

10 Agency for Cultural Affairs 1972:85

11 Reid 1991:35,37,39,45, 50, 54-56

12 Reid 1989:278; 1991:145

13 Aikawa and Leavenworth 1967:69

14 Agency for Cultural Affairs 1972:85

15 Lee 1967:118-119. Dore (1958:159-161) notes how in a more general sense deference to 'Western' standards of morality led to a curbing of the more openly promiscuous sides of traditional Japanese life from the Meiji period onwards. Some of the reforms included the 'cleaning-up of rural phallicism and ritual promiscuity', edicts against public nakedness or mixed bathing in public bath-houses and the introduction of laws against concubinage. In the pre-war period an attempt was made to make 'adultery by the husband a grounds for divorce equally with adultery by the wife... The chief upholders of this new morality were middle-class women... The growth of the ideal was largely a manifesta-tion of feminist aspirations... The Christian terminology of 'purity' and 'soiling' which (male) educators of women had gratefully seized on in their inculcation of feminine chastity, recoiled on its users.'

16 I suspect, but cannot at this stage prove, that these different theological positions are in themselves associated with differences in political orien-tation, whereby right-wing Christians tend to argue for a separation of religion from politics whereas left-wing Christians take a more 'inter-ventionist' approach. Whether it is the theological position or the political orientation which comes first and influences the other is a further issue.

17 Reid 1991:6-19; the citation is from page 19.

18 *Ibid.*,pp.30-32

19 Otis (1991:35, 37) writes of *kairos* moments in history—'extraordinary events flowing out of heavenly vials of vintage intercession'—which 'tend to create spiritual vacuums'.

20 Colligan (1980:84-85) notes that possession of Christian literature is higher among white-collar and better educated people, the rate being as high as 55% among college or junior college graduates.

21 Agency for Cultural Affairs 1972:78-9

22 Although Colligan (1980:92) states that in his sample there was 'no variation in the rate of Christian membership on the basis of sex', he also records that 'generally young, unmarried women seemed to be much more familiar with Christianity' (p.54).

23 Bunce 1955:158

24 Derek and Lilian Cook (1982) suggest that men (at least in the West) respond more to preaching about 'the Kingdom, the power and the glory' and about how they can *do* something significant in Christ's Kingdom.

25 For the correlations given in table 13.6 for illegal parking, the 'chi-square' significance level is such that, when the 'Neither' and Blank responses are amalgamated, $\Sigma=12.5793$, with six degrees of freedom: this is just marginally short of the $\Sigma=12.6$ level at which $p=0.05$. For speeding, however, the correlation is statistically significant, whereby $p=<0.025$. ($\Sigma=16.7429$ with six degrees of freedom, again amalgamating the 'Neither' and Blank responses.)

26 For both shame and guilt feelings, $p=<0.05$.

27 For both shame and guilt feelings, $p=<0.005$.

28 For both shame and guilt feelings, again $p=<0.005$.

29 This correlation is statistically 'noticeable', in so far as it is marginally short of being significant but might turn out to be statistically significant if a larger sample were obtained. [$\Sigma=12.4973$ with six degrees of freedom; $p=0.05$ when $\Sigma=12.6$.]

30 $p=<0.025$. By what might be simply a statistical quirk in a relatively small sample of Shintoists, they turned out to be more in favour of this form of gambling than other groups. It must remain a matter for conjecture whether or not this has any connection at all with the way in which *mikuji* oracles at Shinto shrines are selected by a random choice, in which one hopes to pick a 'lucky one'.

31 $p=<0.005$.

32 Correlating with religion, $p=<0.005$ ($\Sigma=19.0705$ with six degrees of freedom). When correlated with the sex of the respondents, again $p=<0.005$ [$\Sigma=23.2276$ with three degrees of freedom]. In both cases the correlation is so significant that it goes off my cumulative chi-square distribution chart, but the actual significance level for the correlation by sex is greater than that by religion, suggesting that the correlation by sex is the more significant variable. [In both cases, these figures have been reached by amalgamating the 'Neither', 'Don't know' and Blank

responses. This was partly because of the smaller numbers in these categories and partly because there was a tendency for women to prefer 'Neither' and for men to prefer 'Don't know': however, when these two categories were combined, the responses by each sex were very close to expected values.]

33 For links with religion, $p = <0.1, >0.05$, which means that the difference is statistically noticeable but not statistically significant. However, correlating attitudes to premarital sex with male-female differences, the result is highly significant: $p = <0.005$. [$\Sigma = 19.3496$ with three degrees of freedom, omitting 15 blank replies, or else $\Sigma = 14.6988$ with two degrees of freedom if the 'Neither', 'Don't know' and Blank replies are all amalgamated.]

34 In tables 13.8 and 13.9, where percentages do not add up to 100% it is because of blank responses.

35 For homosexuality, $p = <0.05$. For adultery, $p = <0.025$.

36 Dore 1958:386

37 In describing these people as 'Christians' I have followed their own designations. It is a sociological rather than a theological classification because some of these 'Christians' either held unorthodox theological positions or else tended to 'compromise' in some way with prevailing moral attitudes or with non-Christian religious customs. One man who seemed not to 'compromise' at all was a self-employed potter who regularly studied his Bible and who claimed to spend up to thirty hours per week in evangelism: he belonged to the Jehovah's Witnesses.

38 Thomsen 1963:17

39 Hendry 1987:117

40 White 1970:62; Davis 1980:161; Lebra 1976:235

41 Hardacre 1984:64. In her sample, 56% of the questionnaire respondents were women (p.234).

42 Ikado 1968:107-8; White 1970:63-5; Offner and Van Straelen 1963:104, 243-5; Dale 1975:52-3, 55-6

43 Thomsen 1963:20-22; White 1970:31, 36

44 Basabe 1968:32

45 I should stress that this is a popular stereotype of Christianity and that Christians need to take account of this stereotype, whether or not they consider it to be a fair representation. Colligan (1980:82) also mentions some who stopped going to church because they did not agree with the teachings or because they found Christianity too formal.

46 Dale 1975:65 Similarly, at Sōka Gakkai home meetings 'the members are encouraged to share their personal experiences ...Without fear of rejection, the member can unload a burdened heart about a drunken

husband, nagging mother-in-law, or financial difficulty...' (Yamamori 1974:147).

47 Dale 1975:120-145

48 Yamamori 1974:149

49 *Ibid.*, pp.147, 152

50 Reid (1991:28) presents figures showing the growth indices for different religions in Japan, for each of which 1953 was taken as the base year with an index of 100. Between 1953 and 1988 Christianity had a growth index of 293.1 which was considerably greater than the indices for Shinto (143.7) or Buddhism (195.1)—which probably included at least some of the Buddhist 'new religions' such as the Sōka Gakkai—but the 'other religions'—probably accounting for most of the 'new religions'—had a growth index of 332.7.

51 Dale 1975:144-145; Offner and Van Straelen 1963; Reader 1991a:205

52 Examples are given for Reiyūkai by Hardacre (1984:176-187) and for Mahikari by Davis (1980) and Tebēcis (1982:76-161). Davis describes examples of apparent 'exorcism', but often what is practised is not 'exorcism' but *spirit appeasement*, such as the satisfaction of demonic demands for certain foods or alcohol (Tebēcis 1982:109-114).

53 Aikawa and Leavenworth 1967:23-25

54 Noel Gibson, personal communication. He also quoted a letter to him dated 24th September 1991 from Mrs. Doris Wagner (the wife of Dr. C. Peter Wagner of Fuller Theological Seminary), who wrote, '...I was extremely distressed while I was in Japan to see that there is so little knowledge of deliverance, even among the charismatic brethren...There were several instances when I could have done deliverance, but did not have the proper translator to help me, and I hated to open a can of worms'.

Chapter 14   Communicating the Christian Gospel

1 Boyle 1986:3, 113-114. [His quotation is from Charles H. Kraft *Christianity in Culture* (Maryknoll, New York: Orbis Books, 1979), p.148.]

2 Kitamori's best-known work available in English is his *Theology of the Pain of God* (1965). Several examples of Endō's works could be cited, but the important point to note in this context is that 'his objective is to discover an image of Christ that might be more acceptable to the Japanese' (Ninomiya 1990:227)

3 Boyle 1986:7. Nevertheless, he also notes (p.113) that in Japan 'one is not working in a historical vacuum...With more than a century of Christian work in Japan, the church...has strong, indigenous leadership which must be respected.'

4 Boyle (1986:113) remarks that 'the role of missionaries...should be one

of a catalyst, encouraging and working together with Japanese Christians to win their own people to Christ. It is my prayer that the insights of cultural anthropology and missiology will help to do just that'.

5 It might be helpful to note how I was led to consider these issues. When I was an undergraduate at Cambridge University I was involved with a group of Christians who sought to befriend overseas students in order to have opportunities to share with them about Jesus. With many students I had some idea how I might share Christ with them in a way which would be reasonably sensitive to their own cultures. However, I found myself at a loss to know how to do this with the students from Japan.

One day we invited a missionary with many years' experience of Japan (and who had a position of authority in his mission) to speak to our group and give practical suggestions about how to communicate the gospel to the Japanese. His talk was largely orientated around the 'problems' (such as the Japanese lacking a meaningful concept of 'sin' *etc.*) and he gave relatively little advice on ways to overcome such 'problems'.

When afterwards he learnt that I was studying anthropology, he remarked, 'What we need in Japan is someone like you to come and dig into the culture and help us find how to communicate the gospel in culturally more meaningful ways.' That remark stuck in my mind, even though at the time I was not particularly interested in Japan. Nevertheless, a few years later I ended up doing my anthropological fieldwork in Japan and investigating ordinary people's attitudes towards religion.

6 Boyle 1986:1

7 In some cases they might also need deliverance from demonic holds which draw them back to these cults.

8 Richardson 1981. Richardson is essentially a missionary rather than an anthropologist: at times his knowledge of anthropology seems either simplistic or out of date, especially in the way he appears to think that modern anthropology still follows Tylor's theories of religion. Despite this proviso, I still recommend his very stimulating ideas.

9 Muller 1967: 10-11

10 Boyle 1986:119-120

11 *Ibid.*, p.120.

12 *Ibid.*, p.120. Nevertheless, Boyle also notes that under Christian influence the word *kami* 'is undergoing a gradual shift in meaning somewhat like the word *theos* did in ancient Greece': *cf* Spae 1972:49

13 Anesaki 1930:268, 308-9

14 Anesaki 1930:24

15 Aston 1974:35

16 To some extent these four main categories overlap, because some

people mentioned one answer initially and then gave another as an afterthought.

17 The 'ontological' approach was mentioned by 73% of the 30 women and by 46% of the 24 men questioned on this topic, whereas the argument from experience was mentioned by 29% of the men but only 13% of the women.

18 Spae 1971:31-32

19 Boyle 1986:81-82

20 Kagawa 1934:39

21 Song 1986:54-56

22 *Ibid.*, pp.55-56

23 McElligott 1983:32-33

24 *Ibid.*, p.32

25 *Ibid.*, p.35

26 However, it might be mentioned that a somewhat Puritanical attitude towards current literature and drama is exhibited by many of those belonging to the Mukyōkai ('non-church movement'), influenced by Uchimura Kanzō's criticisms of the 'unscrupulous exaltation of sex, vice and sin' in the literature of his time. In fact, some of those who later became famous Japanese novelists were disciples of Uchimura during their adolescence but later deserted their faith when they began to write (Caldarola 1979:103-4).

27 Germany 1967:162; Takenaka 1991:253-258; Takado 1991:260-269; Warriner 1983:49-50

28 Boyle 1986:79. He also recognizes that these analogies have their shortcomings in so far as 'Jesus conquered through love and suffering and not through physical strength and skill' and 'human rulers who lower themselves to the level of a commoner do so only in a superficial way' whereas Jesus 'came in a thoroughly incarnated form' and 'could return to his "castle" only at the completion of his mission'.

29 Richardson 1981:14-28 discusses this in depth, but omits to mention that the verse in Acts 17:28 is also from Epimenides.

30 Richardson 1981:26

31 Kang and Nelson 1979

32 Boyle 1986:88, 112

33 Boyle 1986:89

34 Richardson 1981:117

35 Boyle :111-112

36 Richardson 1981:26

37 Quoted by Noel Gibson, personal communication.

38 Wimber and Springer 1985

GLOSSARY

anshin: peace of mind

anshinkan: sense of security

'Aoyama': pseudonym used in this book for an estate of owner-occupied homes.

anzen: safety

atoyaku: the year after a main *yakudoshi*

bachi: 'supernatural punishment'

bon: period in mid-August when the ancestors are said to return

bunke: branch lineage

burakumin: an 'outcaste' minority group

butsudan: Buddhist household altar

butsumetsu: a kind of inauspicious day

chimaki: charm thrown from floats in some Shinto festivals

chōnan: eldest son

daian: a kind of auspicious day (= taian)

daijōsai: 'Great Food Offering Ritual' in the course of which a new Emperor communes with the Sun Goddess, Amaterasu Ōmikami.

Edo period: 1603-1868

engi: omen

fuda: talisman, especially one put on a wall

Fudō: god of fire

furusato: one's place of origin, native village

gaki: 'hungry ghosts'

genkan: entranceway to a home

gimu: duty

giri: socially contracted obligation

giri-ninjō: balancing of duties or obligations with 'human feelings'

gomagi: wooden prayer plaques which are later burnt

go-meinichi: the monthly date for worshipping a particular deity

harai: Shinto ritual purification/'exorcism'

haraigushi: Pole used in Shinto *harai* ceremonies

hara-obi: waist-sash

hare: auspicious ritual occasion

hatsu-: 'first-', as in hatsu-miyamairi (first shrine visit for an infant)

hatsumōde: New Year shrine visitation

Hatsu-uma sai: festival on the 'first day of the horse' after Setsubun

higan: equinox (Spring or Autumn)—a time for grave visits

hi no tama: a 'fireball', sometimes equated with ghosts or spirits

hitaki: a Shinto rite performed in November. (At '*Nissen*' the *shu-uma sai* has become merged with the *hitaki* rite.)

hōji: periodic memorial rite

honke: main lineage

honyaku: main *yakudoshi* year

hotoke: ancestors or buddhas

hōza: 'counselling session' in some 'new religions'

ihai: memorial tablets

Inari: the fox god

jichikai: neighbourhood association

jichinsai: rite to appease god of locality before commencing construction of a new building

jinja: a Shinto shrine

Jizō: Bodhisattva regarded as in particular a children's deity

Jizō bon: festival for Jizō, on 24th August

jō: (ritual) purity

jōbutsu: attainment of Buddhahood

kadomatsu: New Year pine decorations on gatepost

kaimyō: posthumous name

kakochō: 'book of the past'; death register

kami: gods, Shinto deities

kamidana: Shinto god-shelf

kanji: Chinese characters

kanpō: East Asian herbal medicine

kasō: direction-lore

ke: 'normal' state (in ritual terms)

kegare: ritually polluted state

kimon: 'devil door'

kinen: a commemoration

kitōshi: shaman, faith-healer

kō: pilgrimage association

ko-shōgatsu: 'little New Year' (15th January)

Kokkuri-san: Japanese equivalent of Ouija boards

koyomi: almanac

ku: nine, associated with *kurushimi* (= suffering)

maeyaku: year before one's main *yakudoshi*

maitsuki meinichi: monthly death day

mamori: safety charm
manju: bean-jam cake
matsuri: Shinto festival
Meiji period: 1868-1912
meinichi: (monthly or annual) death day
miko: female assistant at a Shinto shrine
mikoshi: portable shrine used in festivals
mikuji: type of divination at Shinto shrines
mochi: rice-cake
muenbotoke: 'unattached spirits'
nenki: occasion for periodic memorial rites
'*Nissen*': pseudonym for an industrial company described in this book.
pachinko: pin-ball parlour
rei: (1) bow; worship
      (2) thanks
      (3) spirit, soul (*cf.* reikon)
reikon: soul, spirit, ghost
sakaki: Shinto sacred plant
sake: rice-wine
'Sakurano': pseudonym used in this book for an estate of company hous-
    ing.
-san: suffix meaning 'Mr.', 'Mrs.' or 'Miss'
segaki: rite to feed hungry spirits
seimeihandan: name divination
seishin: mind; spirit; will
senzo: ancestor
Setsubun: last day of winter by old lunar calendar
shataku: company housing
shi: (1) death
      (2) the number four
shikimi: plant used in Buddhist rites
shintai: 'body of the *kami*' in a Shinto shrine
shinza: 'god-seat' resembling a bed which is a feature of the *daijōsai* rite.
shōtsuki meinichi: annual death day
shu-uma sai: 'last day of horse': autumn parallel to *hatsu-uma sai*
Sōka Gakkai: a Buddhist 'new religion'
taian: an auspicious day
taisha: a large shrine
tama: ball; sphere; spirit (*cf.* tamashii)
tamashii: spirit; soul
tanabata: 'festival of the celestial lovers' (7th August)
ta no kami: god of the rice field

tobari: cloth used in the *Nissen* end-of-year 'great purification' ceremony, as a 'soft landing place' for the *kami*.

tokonoma: formal alcove in a Japanese-style formal room

tomobiki: a day which is 'unlucky for funerals'

torii: entrance portal to a Shinto shrine

ujigami: tutelary deity

yakubarai: 'exorcism'; ritual purification

yakudoshi: 'calamitous year' when one is thought to be particularly prone to illness or misfortune

yakuyoke: a charm against misfortune

yama no kami: god of the mountain

yashiro: a small Shinto shrine; the dwelling-place of a deity

yōshi: adopted son-in-law

zushi: a 'quasi-butsudan'

BIBLIOGRAPHY

Agency for Cultural Affairs (1972) *Japanese Religion* (Tokyo: Kōdansha)

Aikawa, Takaaki and Leavenworth, Lynn (1967) *The Mind of Japan: A Christian Perspective* (Valley Forge: The Judson Press)

Aikman, David (1991) *Foreword* to Otis (1991)

Anesaki, Masaharu (1930) *History of Japanese Religion* (London: Kegan Paul, Trench, Trubner and Co.)

Asahi Shinbun (1981) Report and comments on a nationwide religious survey (*Asahi* newspaper, 5th May 1981, pp.10-11)

Aston, W.G. (1974) *Shinto (The Way of the Gods)* (New York: Krishna Press)

Bardwell Smith (1988) *Buddhism and Abortion in Contemporary Japan: Mizuko Kuyō and the Confrontation with death* (*Japanese Journal of Religious Studies*, Vol. 15, No.1)

Basabe, Fernando M. (1968) *Religious Attitudes of Japanese Men* (Tokyo: Sophia University)

Beardsley, R.K., Hall, J.W. and Ward, R.E. (1959) *Village Japan* (Chicago: University of Chicago Press)

Beardsworth, Timothy (1977) *A Sense of Presence* (Oxford: Religious Experience Research Unit).

Befu, Harumi (1971) *Japan: An Anthropological Introduction* (San Francisco and London: Chandler Publishing Company)

Befu, Harumi (1974) *Gift-giving in a modernizing Japan* in Lebra, Takie S. and Lebra, William P. (eds.) *Japanese Culture and Behaviour* (Honolulu: The University Press of Hawaii)

Befu, Harumi (1980) *A Critique of the Group Model of Japanese Society* (*Social Analysis*, 5/6)

Ben-Ari, Eyal (1990) *Ritual Strikes, Ceremonial Slowdowns: Some Thoughts on the Management of Conflict in Large Japanese Enterprises* in S.N. Eisenstadt and E. Ben-Ari (eds.) *Japanese Models of Conflict Resolution* (London and New York: Kegan Paul International)

Ben-Ari, Eyal (1991) *Posing, posturing and photographic presences: a rite of passage in a Japanese commuter village* (*Man*, n.s. Vol.26, No.1)

Ben-Dasan, Isaiah (1972) *The Japanese and the Jews* (New York: Weatherhill)

Benedict, Ruth (1946) *The Chrysanthemum and the sword* (Boston: Houghton Mifflin)

Berentsen, J.M. (1985a) *Grave and Gospel* (Leiden: E.J. Brill)

Berentsen, J.M. (1985b) *Ancestor Worship in Missiological Perspective* in Bong Rin Ro (ed.) *Christian Alternatives to Ancestor Practices* (Taichung: Asia Theological Association)

Blacker, Carmen (1975) *The Catalpa Bow* (London: Allen and Unwin)

Blacker, Carmen (1981) *Japan* in M. Loewe and C. Blacker (eds.) *Divination and Oracles* (London: Allen and Unwin)

Blacker, Carmen (1990) *The Shinza or God-seat in the Daijōsai—Throne, Bed, or Incubation Couch?* (*Japanese Journal of Religious Studies*, Vol.17, Nos.2-3)

Blue, Ken (1987) *Authority to Heal* (Downers Grove: InterVarsity Press)

Bowen, Elinore S. (1954) *Return to Laughter* (London: Gollancz)

Bownas, Geoffrey (1963) *Japanese Rainmaking and Other Folk Practices* (London: Allen and Unwin)

Boyle, Timothy Dale (1986) *Communicating the Gospel in Japanese Cultural Terms: Practical Experiments at the Shintoku Kyodan Church* (Doctor of Ministry thesis, Fuller Theological Seminary, Pasadena, California)

Bunce, William K. (1955) *Religions in Japan* (Rutland, Vermont and Tokyo, Japan: Tuttle)

Burridge, Kenelm (1969) *New Heaven, New Earth* (Oxford: Basil Blackwell)

Burton-Lewis (1990) *Statistics Never Lie—Not Much Anyway* (*Japan Christian Quarterly*, Vol.56, No.1)

Buruma, Ian (1984) *A Japanese Mirror* (London: Jonathan Cape)

Caldarola, Carlo (1979) *Christianity: The Japanese Way* (Leiden: E.J. Brill)

Cary, Otis (1909) *A History of Christianity in Japan: Roman Catholic, Greek Orthodox and Protestant Missions* (Rutland and Tokyo: Tuttle)

Clark, Rodney (1979) *The Japanese Company* (New Haven and London: Yale University Press)

Cole, Robert E. (1971) *Japanese Blue Collar: The Changing Tradition* (Berkeley: University of California Press)

Coleman, William L. (1984) *Today's Handbook of Bible Times & Customs* (Minneapolis: Bethany House Publishers)

Colligan, James P. (ed.) (1980) *The Image of Christianity in Japan* (Tokyo: Sophia University)

Cook, Derek and Lilian (1992) *How to make your church more man-*

friendly (Seminar at 'New Wine '92': Cassette available through International Christian Communications, Eastbourne)

Cooper, Michael (1983) *Christianity* in *Kōdansha Encyclopedia of Japan*, Vol.1, pp.306-310 (Tokyo and New York: Kōdansha)

Corwin, Charles (1967) *Biblical Encounter with Japanese Culture* (Tokyo: Christian Literature Crusade)

Crump, Thomas (1989) *The Death of an Emperor: Japan at the Crossroads* (London: Constable)

Crump, Thomas (1991) *The Making of an Emperor* (*Anthropology Today*, Vol.7, No.2)

Crump, Thomas (1992) *The Japanese Numbers game* (London and New York: Routledge)

Dale, Kenneth J. (1975) *Circle of Harmony: A Case Study in Popular Japanese Buddhism* (South Pasadena: William Carey Library)

Davis, Winston (1980) *Dojo: Magic and Exorcism in Modern Japan* (Stanford: Stanford U.P.)

Davis, Winston (1992) *Japanese Religion and Society* (New York: State University of New York Press)

Dawson, John (1989) *Taking Our Cities for God* (Milton Keynes: Word Publishing)

De Vos, George (1974) *The Relation of Guilt towards Parents to Achievement and Arranged Marriage among the Japanese* in Lebra, T.S. and Lebra, W.P. (eds.) *Japanese Culture and Behaviour* (Honolulu: The University Press of Hawaii).

De Vos, George and Wagatsuma, Horoshi (1966) *Japan's Invisible Race* (Berkeley, Los Angeles and London: University of California Press)

Devereux, Paul (1982) *Earth Lights* (Wellingborough: Turnstone)

Devereux, Paul (1989) *Earth Lights Revelation* (London: Blandford)

Devereux, Paul (1990) *Places of Power* (London: Blandford)

Dore, Ronald P. (1958) *City Life in Japan* (Berkeley: University of California Press)

Dore, Ronald P. (1973) *British Factory, Japanese Factory* (Berkeley: University of California Press)

Dore, Ronald P. (1978) *Shinohata: A portrait of a Japanese village* (London: Allen Lane)

Douglas, Mary (1966) *Purity and Danger* (London: Routledge and Kegan Paul)

Earhart, H.B. (1974) *Religion in the Japanese Experience: Sources and Interpretations* (Encino and Belmont, California: Dickenson)

Earhart, H.B. (1984) *Religions of Japan* (San Francisco: Harper & Row)

Ehara, Jun (1978) *Christian Influence on the Japanese tea Ceremony* in

Pascania, Japanese section (Honolulu: Hawaii District of the United Methodist Church)

Elison, George (1988) *Deus Destroyed: The Image of Christianity in Early Modern Japan* (Cambridge, Massachusetts: Harvard University Press, Council on East Asian Studies)

Embree, J.F. (1946) *A Japanese Village, Suye Mura* (London: Kegan Paul)

Evans-Pritchard, E.E. (1951) *Social Anthropology* (London: Cohen and West)

Evans-Pritchard, E.E. (1962) *Essays in Social Anthropology* (London: Faber and Faber)

Evans-Pritchard, E.E. (1965) *Theories of Primitive Religion* (Oxford: Clarendon Press)

Fisher, Galen M. (1922) *The Missionary Significance of the Last Ten Years: A Survey* (*International Review of Missions*, Vol.11)

Francis, Carolyn B. and Nakajima, John M. (1991) *Christians in Japan* (New York: Friendship Press)

Fukutake, Tadashi (1967) *Japanese Rural Society* (London: Oxford University Press)

Fujita, Tomio (1983) *Sacred, The* in *Kōdansha Encyclopedia of Japan*, Vol.6, pp.361-362 (Tokyo and New York: Kōdansha)

Gardner, Rex (1986) *Healing Miracles: A Doctor Investigates* (London: Darton, Longman and Todd)

Geertz, Clifford (1973) *The Interpretation of Cultures: selected essays* (New York: Basic Books)

Germany, Charles H. (1967) Contributions to Charles H. Germany (ed.) *The Response of the Church in Changing Japan* (New York: Friendship Press)

Gill, Rob (1990) *The Japan Church Growth Institute* (*The Japan Christian Quarterly*, Vol.56, No.1)

Goode, William J. (1963) *World Revolution and Family Patterns* (New York: The Free Press, and London: Collier-Macmillan)

Graburn, N. (1983) *To pray, pay and play: the cultural structure of Japanese domestic tourism* (Centre des Hautes Etudes Touristiques, Série B, No.26)

Grey, Margot (1985) *Return from Death* (London: Routledge and Kegan Paul)

Haak, Ronald (1973) *Nishijin Weavers: The Functions of Tradition in Modern Japanese Society* (PhD. thesis submitted to the Department of Anthropology, University of Illinois at Urbana-Champaign).

Hardacre, Helen (1984) *Lay Buddhism in Contemporary Japan: Reiyukai Kyodan* (Princeton: Princeton U.P.)

Hashimoto, Tatsumi (1962) *Ancestor Worship and Japanese Daily Life*, translated by Percy T. Luke (Tokyo: Word of Life Press)

Hay, David (1987) [revised edition]*Exploring Inner Space* (London and Oxford: Mowbray)

Hayashi, Minoru (1988) *Learning from the Japanese New Religions* (Fuller Theological Seminary, School of World Mission and Institute of Church Growth, Doctor of Missiology thesis)

Hendry, Joy (1981) *Marriage in Changing Japan* (London: Croom Helm)

Hendry, Joy (1984) *Shoes: The Early Learning of an Important Distinction in Japanese Society* in Gordon Daniels (ed.) *Europe Interprets Japan* (Tenterden: Paul Norbury)

Hendry, Joy (1986) *Becoming Japanese* (Manchester: Manchester U.P.)

Hendry, Joy (1987) *Understanding Japanese Society* (London: Croom Helm)

Hendry, Joy (1989) *To wrap or not to wrap: Politeness and Penetration in Ethnographic Inquiry* (*Man*, n.s., Vol.24, No.4)

Hepburn, J.C. (1867) *A Japanese and English Dictionary* (Shanghai: American Presbyterian Press)

Herbert, Jean (1967) *Shinto at the fountain-head of Japan* (London: Allen and Unwin)

Holtom, D.C. (1938) *The National Faith of Japan* (London: Kegan Paul, Trench, Trubner and Co.)

Holtom, D.C. (1940) *The Meaning of Kami* (*Monumenta Nipponica*, 3, pp.1-27; 392-413; and (1941) 4, pp.351-394)

Hori, Ichiro (1968) *Folk Religion in Japan: Continuity and Change* (Chicago: Chicago U.P.)

Hori, Ichiro (1975) *Shamanism in Japan* (*Japanese Journal of Religious Studies*, Vol.2, No.4)

Hoshino, Eiki (1983) *Kegare* in *Kōdansha Encyclopedia of Japan*, Vol.4, p.186 (Tokyo and New York: Kōdansha)

Hoshino, Eiki and Takeda, Dōshō (1987) *Indebtedness and Comfort: The Undercurrents of Mizuko Kuyō in Contemporary Japan* (*Japanese Journal of Religious Studies*, Vol.14, No.4)

Howes, John F. (1965) *Japanese Christians and American missionaries* in Marius B. Jansen (ed.) *Changing Japanese Attitudes Toward Modernization* (Princeton: Princeton U.P.)

Huddle, Benjamin P. (1958) *History of the Lutheran Church in Japan* (New York: Board of Foreign Missions, The United Lutheran Church in America)

Iglehart, Charles W. (1932) *The Churches in 1931* (*The Japan Christian Yearbook*, 1932)

Iglehart, Charles W. (1959) *A Century of Protestant Christianity in Japan* (Tokyo and Rutland: Tuttle)

Ikado, Fujio (1968) *Trend and problems of new religions: Religion in Urban Society* in K. Morioka and W.H. Newell (eds.) *The Sociology of Japanese Religion* (Leiden: E.J. Brill)

Itō, Mikiharu (1983) *Festivals: Matsuri* in *Kōdansha Encyclopedia of Japan*, Vol.1, pp.22-23 (Tokyo and New York: Kōdansha)

Iwata, Keiji (1979) *Kami no jinruigaku* (Tokyo: Kōdansha)

Jaeckel, Theodore (1955) *Japan's Spiritual Situation* (*Japan Christian Quarterly*, Vol.XXI, No.3)

Janeira, Armando Martins (1970) *Japanese and Western Literature: A Comparative Study* (Rutland and Tokyo: Tuttle)

Joya, Mock (1958) *Mock Joya's Things Japanese* (Tokyo: Tokyo News Service)

Kabira, Chosei (1983) *Why Don't More Japanese Become Christian?* in Carl C. Beck (ed.) *All things to All Men: Interaction of Biblical Faith and the Surrounding Cultures*: Major Papers presented at the Twenty-Fourth Hayama Men's Missionary Seminar, Amagi Sansō, 5th-7th January 1983 (Tokyo: publisher unstated)

Kagawa, Toyohiko (1934) *Christ and Japan* (New York: Friendship Press)

Kamata, Satoshi (1982) *Japan in the Passing Lane* (New York: Pantheon)

Kang, C.H. and Nelson, Ethyl R. (1979) *The Discovery of Genesis in the Chinese Characters* (St. Louis: Concordia)

Kasahara, Yomishi (1974) *Fear of Eye-to-eye Confrontation among Neurotic Patients in Japan* in T.S. Lebra and W.P. Lebra (eds.) *Japanese Culture and Behavior* (Honolulu: The University Press of Hawaii)

Keene, Donald (1971) *Appreciations of Japanese Culture* (Tokyo, New York and San Francisco: Kōdansha International Ltd.)

Kenkyusha's New Japanese-English Dictionary (1954) (Tokyo: Kenkyusha)

Kimura, Masanori (1983) *Nikki Bungaku* in *Kōdansha Encyclopedia of Japan*, Vol.6, p.2 (Tokyo and New York: Kōdansha)

Kinoshita, Ritsuko (1983) *Okoku no tsumatachi* (Tokyo: Komichi Shobō)

Kitamori, Kazoh (1965) *Theology of the Pain of God* (Richmond, Virginia: John Knox Press; London: SCM Press, 1966)

Kitagawa, Joseph M. (1966) *Religion in Japanese History* (New York and London: Columbia U.P.)

Kobatake, Susumu (1982) *Kirisutokyō Keichōgaku Jiten, Kon & Sō* [Christian Dictionary of Congratulations and Condolences, Marriage and Funeral] (Tokyo: Inochi no Kotoba Sha [Word of Life Press])

Koyama, Kosuke (1982) *Three Mile An Hour God* (Maryknoll, New York: Orbis Books)

Koyama, Kosuke (1984) *Mount Fuji and Mount Sinai* (London: SCM Press)

Laures, Johannes (1954) *The Catholic Church in Japan: A Short History* (Rutland and Tokyo: Tuttle)

Laymen's Foreign Mission Inquiry—Commission of Appraisal [Chaired by W.E. Hocking] (1932) *Re-thinking Missions* (New York and London: Harper and Brothers)

Lean, Garth (1985) *Frank Buchman: A Life* (London: Collins)

Lebra, Takie Sugiyama (1976) *Japanese Patterns of Behavior* (Honolulu: The University Press of Hawaii)

Lee, Robert (1967) *Stranger in the Land: A Study of the Church in Japan* (London: Lutterworth Press)

Lent, John A. (1989) *Japanese Comics* in Richard G. Powers and Hidetoshi Kato (eds.) *Handbook of Japanese Popular Culture* (New York: Greenwood Press)

Lewis, David C. (1986a) *Religious Rites in a Japanese Factory* (*Japanese Journal of Religious Studies*, Vol. 13, No. 4)

Lewis, David C. (1986b) *'Years of Calamity: Yakudoshi Observances in a City'* in Joy Hendry and Jonathan Webber (eds.) *Interpreting Japanese Society* (Oxford: Journal of the Anthropological Society of Oxford Occasional Papers Series, No. 5)

Lewis, David C. (1986c) *Fortune-telling in Contemporary Japan* (*Proceedings of the British Association for Japanese Studies*, 1986 Conference Volume)

Lewis, David C. (1986d) *Safety First: The Search for Security in Contemporary Japan* (*Values*, Vol. 1, No. 2)

Lewis, David C. (1986e) *Signs and Wonders in Sheffield* in Wimber and Springer *Power Healing* (London: Hodder & Stoughton and also New York: Harper and Row, 1987)

Lewis, David C. (1987) *All in Good Faith* (*Nursing Times and Nursing Mirror*, 18th-24th March 1987)

Lewis, David C. (1989) *Healing: Fiction, Fantasy or Fact?* (London: Hodder and Stoughton)

Lewis, David C. (1990) Contributions to *What is the New Age?* by Michael Cole, Jim Graham, Tony Higton and David Lewis (London: Hodder and Stoughton)

Lo, Jeannie (1990) *Office Ladies, Factory Women: Life and Work at a Japanese Company* (London: M.E. Sharpe)

Lock, Margaret (1980) *East Asian Medicine in Urban Japan* (Berkeley: University of California Press)

Lock, Margaret (1984) *Licorice in Leviathan: The Medicalization of Care for the Japanese Elderly* (*Culture, Medicine and Psychiatry*, Vol. 8, No.2)

Lowell, Percival (1894) *Occult Japan or The Way of the Gods* (Boston: Houghton Mifflin)

Marwin, John J. (1976) *Biblical Encounter with Ancestor Veneration in Contemporary Japan* (Dissertation presented at Fuller Theological Seminary, Pasadena, California)

Marwin, John Jennings (1983) *The Oriental Missionary Society Holiness Church in Japan, 1901-1983* (Dissertation presented to the Faculty of the School of World Mission and Institute of Church Growth, Fuller Theological Seminary, Pasadena, California).

Matsudaira, Narimitsu (1963) *The Concept of Tamashii in Japan* in Richard M. Dorson (ed.) *Studies in Japanese Folklore* (Bloomington: Indiana U.P.)

Matusek, Paul (1986) *Corporate Zen: Zen-meditation in Japanese Companies* in Erich Pauer (ed.) *Silkworms, Oil and Chips: Proceedings of the Economics and Economic History Section of the Fourth International Conference on Japanese Studies* (Bonn: Bonner Zeitschrift für Japanologie, Vol.8)

McAll, Kenneth (1982) *Healing the Family Tree* (London: Sheldon Press)

McElligott (1983) *Using Japanese Literature in Preaching* in Carl C. Beck (ed.) *All things to All Men: Interaction of Biblical Faith and the Surrounding Cultures*: Major Papers presented at the Twenty-Fourth Hayama Men's Missionary Seminar, Amagi Sansō, 5th-7th January 1983 (Tokyo: publisher unstated)

McFarland, H.N. (1967) *The Rush Hour of the Gods* (New York: Macmillan)

McGavran, Donald (1985) *Honoring Ancestors in Japan* in Bong Rin Ro (ed.) *Christian Alternatives to Ancestor Practices* (Taichung: Asia Theological Association)

McKean, Margaret A. (1981) *Environmental Protest and Citizen Politics in Japan* (Berkeley: University of California Press)

MacLeod, Ian (1982) *The Dynamics of Shame and Guilt: A Sociological Study* in Carl C. Beck (ed.) *Can the Gospel Thrive in Japanese Soil? Guilt, Shame and Grace in a Unique Culture*: Major Papers and Critiques presented at the Twenty-Third Hayama Men's Missionary Seminar, Amagi Sansō, 5th-7th January 1982 (Tokyo: publisher unstated)

Mitsumori, Haruo (1992) *Church Growth Statistics* (*Church Growth Digest*, section on *The Church in Japan*, Autumn 1992, p.10)

Miura, Ayako (1968) *Shiokari tōge* (Tokyo: Shinchō Bunko)

Miura, Ayako (1970) *The Wind is Howling* (London: Hodder & Stoughton)

[No date is given for the English edition but the book was first published in Japanese in 1970.]

Miyata, Noboru (1990) *The Popular Beliefs of Contemporary Japan* in Adriana Boscaro, Franco Gatti and Massimo Raveri (eds.) *Rethinking Japan*, Vol. II (Folkstone: The Japan Library)

Moeran, Brian (1984) *Individual, Group and Seishin—Japan's internal cultural debate* (*Man*, n.s., Vol. 19, No. 2)

Mogami, Takayoshi (1963) *The Double-Grave System* in Richard M. Dorson (ed.) *Studies in Japanese Folklore* (Bloomington: Indiana U.P.)

Moody, Raymond (1976) *Life After Life* (London: Bantam Books)

Morioka, Kiyomi (1975) *Religion in Changing Japanese Society* (Tokyo: University of Tokyo Press)

Mouer, Ross and Sugimoto, Yoshiro (1980) *Competing Models for Understanding Japanese Society: Some Reflections on New Directions* (*Social Analysis* 5/6)

Mouer, Ross and Sugimoto, Yoshiro (1986) *Images of Japanese Society* (London and New York: Kegan Paul International)

Muller, George A. (1967) *The Catechetical Problem in Japan (1549-1965)* (Tokyo: Oriens Institute for Religious Research)

Mullins, Mark (1990a) *Japanese pentacostalism and the world of the dead: A study of cultural adaptation in Iesu no Mitama Kyōkai* (*Japanese Journal of Religious Studies*, Vol.17, No.4)

Mullins, Mark (1990b) *The Sociology of Church Growth: An Introduction to the Literature* (*Japan Christian Quarterly*, Vol.56, No.1)

Mullins, Mark (1990c) *The Transplantation of Religion in Comparative Sociological Perspective* (*Japanese Religions*, Vol.16, No.2)

Mullins, Mark (1992) *The Empire Strikes Back: Korean Pentecostal Mission to Japan* (*Japanese Religions*, Vol.17, No.2)

Nakahara, Hideomi and Fuke, Takashi *Making Baloney of Blood Typing* (*The Japan Times Weekly*, International Edition, 2nd. March 1985, p.11)

Nakamaki, Hirochika (1983) *The 'Separate' Coexistence of Kami and Hotoke—A Look at Yorishiro* (*Japanese Journal of Religious Studies*, March 1983, Vol.10, No.1)

Nakamaki, Hirochika (1990) *Religious Civilization in Modern Japan: As Revealed through a Focus on Mt. Kōya* (Osaka: National Museum of Ethnology, Senri Ethnological Studies, 29)

Nakamura, Mitsuo (1969) *Contemporary Japanese Fiction, 1926-1968* (Tokyo: Kokusai Bunka Shinkokai)

Nakane, Chie (1967) *Kinship and Economic Organization in rural Japan* (London: Athlone Press)

Nakane, Chie (1970) *Japanese Society* (London: Weidenfeld and Nicolson)

Namihira, Emiko (1974) *Nihon Minkan-shinkō to sono kōzō* [A Study of the structure of Japanese Folk Belief] (*Minzokugaku Kenkyū*, Vol.38, Nos.3-4)

Namihira, Emiko (1976) *Tsūkagirei ni okeru 'hare' to 'kegare' no kannen no bunseki* [An analysis of 'hare' and 'kegare' in Japanese Rites of Passage] (*Minzokugaku Kenkyū*, Vol.40, No.4)

Nihon Minzoku Jiten (1971) [Japan Folklore Dictionary] (Tokyo: Seibundō)

Ninomiya, Cindy (1990) *Endō Shūsaku: Bridging the Gap between Christianity and Japanese Culture* (*Japan Christian Quarterly*, Vol.54, No.4)

Nishikawa, Shigenori (1990) *The Daijōsai, the Constitution, and Christian Faith* (*Japan Christian Quarterly*, Vol.56, No.3)

Noda, Kesaya (1983) *A Pilgrimage in Shikoku* in *Essays on Japanology 1978-1982/Watashitachi no Nihongaku* (Kyoto: International Cultural Association of Kyoto)

Norbeck, Edward (1952) *Pollution and Taboo in Contemporary Japan* (*Southwestern Journal of Anthropology*, Vol.8)

Norbeck, Edward (1953) *Age-grading in Japan* (*American Anthropologist*, Vol.55)

Norbeck, Edward (1954) *Takashima: A Japanese Fishing Community* (Salt Lake City: University of Utah Press)

Norbeck, Edward (1955) *Yakudoshi: A Japanese Complex of Supernaturalistic Beliefs* (*Southwestern Journal of Anthropology*, Vol.11)

Norbeck, Edward (1970) *Religion and Society in Modern Japan* (Houston: Rice University Studies Vol.56, No.1)

Offner, Clark (1982) *The Place of Guilt, Shame and Grace in other Japanese Religions: A Comparative Study* in Carl C. Beck (ed.) *Can the Gospel Thrive in Japanese Soil? Guilt, Shame and Grace in a Unique Culture*: Major Papers and Critiques presented at the Twenty-Third Hayama Men's Missionary Seminar, Amagi Sansō, 5th-7th January 1982 (Tokyo: publisher unstated)

Offner, G.B. and Van Straelen, H. (1963) *Modern Japanese Religions, with special emphasis upon their doctrines of healing* (New York: Twayne)

Ohnuki-Tierney, Emiko (1984) *Illness and Culture in Contemporary Japan* (Cambridge: Cambridge U.P.)

Ogata, Mamoru (1990a) *Kichō hōkoku: Nihon no kyōkai no genjō to sekai no kyōkai to no hikaku* [Keynote report: A Comparison between the present state of the Church in Japan and the Church in the World] in *Kyōkai seichō shinpojium* [Church Growth Symposium] Vol. 1, 1990 (Tokyo: Shinsei Undō).

Ogata, Mamoru (1990b) *Kichō hōkoku* [Keynote address] in *Kyōkai seichō shinpojium* [Church Growth Symposium] Vol. 2, 1990 (Tokyo: Shinsei Undō).

Ono, Sokyo (1962) *Shinto, The Kami Way* (Rutland and Tokyo: Tuttle)

Ooms, Herman (1967) *The Religion of the Household: A Case Study of Ancestor Worship in Japan* (*Contemporary Religions in Japan*, Vol. 8)

Ooms, Herman (1976) *A Structural Analysis of Japanese Ancestral Rites and Beliefs* in W.H. Newell (ed.) *Ancestors* (The Hague: Mouton)

Ōshima, Kōichi (1990) *Problems of the Daijōsai: Grounds for Christian opposition* (*Japan Christian Quarterly*, Vol.56, No.4)

Otis, George (1991) *The Last of the Giants* (Tarrytown, New York: Fleming H. Revell Company/Chosen Books)

Oto, Tokihiko (1963) *Folklore in Japanese Life and Customs* (Tokyo: Kokusai Bunka Shinkokai)

Philippi, Donald L. (1959) *Norito* (Tokyo: The Institute for Japanese Culture and Classics, Kokugakuin University)

Picken, Stuart D.B. (1980) *Shinto: Japan's Spiritual Roots* (Tokyo: Kōdansha International)

Picone, Mary (1986) *Buddhist Popular Manuals and the Contemporary Commercialization of Religion in Japan* in Joy Hendry and Jonathan Webber (eds.) *Interpreting Japanese Society* (Oxford: Journal of the Anthropological Society of Oxford Occasional Papers Series, No.5)

Pieters, Albertus (1912) *Mission Problems in Japan, Theoretical and Practical* (New York: The Board of Publication, Reformed Church in America)

Plath, David (1964) *Where the Family of God is the Family: The Role of the Dead in Japanese Households* (*American Anthropologist*, Vol.66)

Plath, David (1974) *Christmas: A Modern Japanese Festival* in Earhart, H.B. (ed.) *Religion in the Japanese Experience: Sources and Interpretations* (Encino and Belmont, California: Dickenson)

Platt, Jennifer (1976) *Realities of Social Research* (Brighton: Sussex U.P.)

Reader, Ian (1991a) *Religion in Contemporary Japan* (Honolulu: University of Hawaii Press, and London: Macmillan)

Reader, Ian (1991b) *Letters to the Gods: The Form and Meaning of Ema* (*Japanese Journal of Religious Studies*, Vol.18, No.2)

Reid, David (1989) *Japanese Christians and the ancestors* (*Japanese Journal of Religious Studies*, Vol.16, No.4)

Reid, David (1991) *New Wine: The cultural shaping of Japanese Christianity* (Berkeley: Asian Humanities Press)

Richardson, Don (1981) *Eternity in their Hearts* (Ventura, California: Regal Books)

Ring, Kenneth (1980) *Life at Death* (New York: Coward, McCann and Geoghegan)

Rohlen, Thomas P. (1974) *For Harmony and Strength: Japanese white-collar organisation in anthropological Perspective* (Berkeley, Los Angeles, London: University of California Press)

Rose, Seraphim (1980) *The Soul after Death* (Platina, California: Saint Herman of Alaska Brotherhood)

Russell, Wilmot P.M. (1935) *A Glimpse of Japan* (*The National Review*, February 1935: 'Published by the Proprietors, 18 York Buildings, Adelphi, London')

Saeki, Yoichiro (1967) *The Christian Movement in Japan Today* in Charles H. Germany (ed.) *The Response of the Church in Changing Japan* (New York: Friendship Press)

Saso, Michael R. (1972) *Taoism and the Rite of Cosmic Renewal* (Washington State U.P.)

Schmidt, W. (1931) *The Origin and Growth of Religion* (London: Methuen)

Shillony, Ben-Ami (1991) *The Jews and the Japanese* (Rutland and Tokyo: Tuttle)

Singer, Kurt (1973) *Mirror, Sword and Jewel* (London: Croom Helm)

Smith, Robert J. (1956) *Kurusu: A Japanese Agricultural Community* in J.B. Cornell and R.J. Smith *Two Japanese Villages* (New York: Greenwood Press)

Smith, Robert J. (1974) *Ancestor Worship in Contemporary Japan* (Stanford: Stanford U.P.)

Smith, Robert J. (1978) *Kurusu: The price of progress in a Japanese Village* (Folkstone, Kent: Dawson Publishers)

Smith, Thomas C. (1959) *The Agrarian Origins of Modern Japan* (Stanford: Stanford U.P.)

Song, C.S. (1986) *Theology from the Womb of Asia* (Maryknoll: Orbis)

Sofue, Takao (1983) *Changes in Japanese Culture and Personality after World War II* (Paper presented at the symposium on *Japanese Culture and Mental Health* at the East-West Center, Honolulu, August 15th-19th, 1983)

Southwold, Martin (1983) *Buddhism in Life* (Manchester: Manchester U.P.)

Spae, J.J. (1971) *Japanese Religiosity* (Tokyo: Oriens Institute for Religious Research)

Spae, J.J. (1972) *Shinto Man* (Tokyo: Oriens Institute for Religious Research)

Stoetzel, Jean (1955) *Without the Chrysanthemum and the Sword* (London: Heinemann)

Subritzky, Bill (1986) *Demons Defeated* (Chichester: Sovereign World Ltd.)

Sytsma, Richard (1982) Critique of Offner *The Place of Guilt, Shame and*

Grace in other Japanese Religions: A Comparative Study in Carl C. Beck (ed.) *Can the Gospel Thrive in Japanese Soil? Guilt, Shame and Grace in a Unique Culture*: Major Papers and Critiques presented at the Twenty-Third Hayama Men's Missionary Seminar, Amagi Sansō, 5th-7th January 1982 (Tokyo: publisher unstated)

Takado, Kaname (1991) *Japanese Christian Writers* in K. Yoshinobu and D.L. Swain (eds.) *Christianity in Japan* (Tokyo: Kyo Bun Kwan)

Takasugi, Ryuji (1978) *Akachan no nazukejiten* (Tokyo: Seitōsha)

Takenaka, Masao (1991) *Christian Art and Artists* in K. Yoshinobu and D.L. Swain (eds.) *Christianity in Japan* (Tokyo: Kyo Bun Kwan)

Tamaru, Noriyoshi (1979) *The Problem of Secularization: A Preliminary Analysis* (*Japanese Journal of Religious Studies*, Vol.6, Nos.1-2)

Tebēcis, Andris K. (1982) *Mahikari: Thank God for the Answers at Last* (Tokyo: L.H. Yōkō Shuppan)

Thomsen, H. (1963) *The New Religions of Japan* (Rutland and Tokyo: Tuttle)

Trudgill, Peter (1983) *Sociolinguistics* (Harmondsworth: Penguin Books; revised edition; first published 1974).

Tsurumi, Kazuko (1970) *Social Change and the Individual: Japan Before and After Defeat in World War II* (Princeton: Princeton U.P.)

Tucker, Henry St.George (1938) *The History of the Episcopal Church in Japan* (New York and London: Charles Scribner's Sons)

Ueda, Keiko (1974) *Sixteen Ways to avoid saying 'No' in Japan* in John C. Condon and Mitsuko Saito (eds.) *Intercultural Encounters with Japan: Communication-Contact and Conflict* (Tokyo: The Simul Press)

Ueda, Makoto (1983) *Bashō* in *Kōdansha Encyclopedia of Japan*, Vol.1, pp.144-145 (Tokyo and New York: Kōdansha)

Van Der Geest, Sjaak (1990) *Anthropologists and Missionaries: Brothers under the skin* (*Man*, n.s. Vol.25, No.4)

Vickery, Kenneth (1986) *Choose Health, Choose Life* (Eastbourne: Kingsway)

Van Hecken, Joseph L. (1963) *The Catholic Church in Japan* (Tokyo: Herder Agency, Enderle Bookstore)

Wagatsuma, Takashi (1983) *Family Planning* in *Kōdansha Encyclopedia of Japan*, Vol.2, pp.246-247 (Tokyo and New York: Kōdansha)

Wagner, C. Peter (ed.) (1991) *Territorial Spirits* (Chichester: Sovereign World Ltd.)

Warriner, Austin (1983) *Adventuring in Acculturation: Brainstorming Session* in Carl C. Beck (ed.) *All things to All Men: Interaction of Biblical Faith and the Surrounding Cultures*: Major Papers presented at the Twenty-Fourth Hayama Men's Missionary Seminar, Amagi Sansō, 5th-7th January 1983 (Tokyo: publisher unstated)

Watanabe, Osamu (1989) *The sociology of Jishuku and Kichō: the death of the Shōwa Tennō as a reflection of the structure of contemporary Japanese society* (*Japan Forum*, Vol.1, No.2).

Wheelwright, Carolyn (1983) *Kakemono* in *Kōdansha Encyclopedia of Japan*, Vol.4, p116 (Tokyo and New York: Kōdansha)

White, J.W. (1970) *The Sokagakkai and Mass Society* (Stanford: Stanford U.P.)

Wimber, John with Springer, Kevin (1985) *Power Evangelism: Signs and Wonders Today* (London: Hodder & Stoughton)

Wimber, John with Springer, Kevin (1986) *Power Healing* (London: Hodder and Stoughton)

Yamaguchi, Yoshie (1985) *Blood Type Revealing in Japan* (*The Japan Times Weekly*, International Edition, 12th January 1985, p.11).

Yamamori, Tetsunao (1974) *Church Growth in Japan* (South Pasadena: William Carey Library)

Yanagita, Kunio (1970) *About Our Ancestors* (Tokyo: Japan Society for the Promotion of Science)

Yuasa, Nobuyuki (1983) *Issa* in *Kōdansha Encyclopedia of Japan*, Vol.3, p.348 (Tokyo and New York: Kōdansha)

INDEX